Rules for the Transfer of Movables

A Candidate for European
Harmonisation or National Reforms?

edited by
Wolfgang Faber / Brigitta Lurger

Schriften zur Europäischen Rechtswissenschaft /
European Legal Studies / Etudes juridiques européennes
Band 6 / Volume 6 / Volume 6

European Legal Studies Institute, Osnabrück
Molengraaff Institute for Private Law, Utrecht
Amsterdam Institute for Private Law
Institute of European and Comparative Law, Oxford
Institut für Zivilrecht, Ausländisches und Internationales Privatrecht, Graz

sellier.
european law
publishers

Schriften zur Europäischen Rechtswissenschaft /
European Legal Studies / Etudes juridiques européennes

herausgegeben

im European Legal Studies Institute, Osnabrück
von Christian von Bar

im Molengraaff Institute for Private Law, Utrecht
von Ewoud Hondius

im Amsterdam Institute for Private Law
von Martijn W. Hesselink

im Institute of European and Comparative Law, Oxford
von Stefan Vogenauer

im Institut für Zivilrecht, Ausländisches und Internationales Privatrecht, Graz
von Brigitta Lurger

This book has been published with the financial support of:
Universität Graz; Evers-Marcic-Stiftung an der Rechtswissentschaftlichen
Fakultät Salzburg; Stiftungs- und Förderungsgesellschaft der Paris-Lodron-
Universität Salzburg.

ISBN 978-3-86653-060-7

The Deutsche Nationalbibliothek lists this publication in the Deutsche Nationalbibliografie; detailed bibliographic data are available in the Internet at http://dnb.d-nb.de.

© 2008 by sellier. european law publishers GmbH, Munich.

All rights reserved. No part of this publication may be reproduced, translated, stored in a retrieval system or transmitted, in any form or by any means, electronic, mechanical, photocopying, recording or otherwise, without prior permission of the publisher.

Design: Sandra Sellier, Munich. Production: Karina Hack, Munich. Printing and binding: AZ Druck und Datentechnik GmbH, Kempten. Printed on acid-free, non-ageing paper. Printed in Germany.

Preface

Comparative research in the area of property law is gaining importance. This volume contains the written versions of the contributions to the international conference 'Rules on the Transfer of Movables – A Candidate for European Harmonisation or National Reforms?', held in Salzburg on 15 and 16 February 2007, dealing with key issues in the field of transfer of corporeal movable property. The conference, financed by the EU's 6th Framework Program for Research and Technological Development, the Faculty of Law of the University of Salzburg and DLA Piper Weiss-Tessbach, as well as this volume form part of the activities of the working group 'Transfer of Movables', one of the sub-groups of the 'Study Group on a European Civil Code'.

The publication of this book would not have been possible without financial support by the University of Graz, the Salzburg Law Faculty's 'Evers-Marcic-Stiftung' and the 'Stiftungs- und Förderungsgesellschaft der Paris-Lodron-Universität Salzburg'. The editors wish to thank these institutions for their support. We also express our gratitude to our assistant Ernest Weiker for all his help in linguistic and editorial aspects, and our secretaries Monika Lammer and Eva Reintsch for formatting the manuscripts.

August 2007 *Wolfgang Faber*
Salzburg and Graz *Brigitta Lurger*

Contents

Preface   V

Introduction to the Project 'Transfer of Movables': Organisational Framework, Basic Issues and Goals
Brigitta Lurger

A. The working group 'Transfer of Movables' as part of the Study Group on a European Civil Code (SGECC)	1
B. The working group since 2005: The FWF-project and the Commission's Network of Excellence project 'Common Principles of European Contract Law' (CoPECL)	2
C. Issues covered and methods employed by working group	6
D. Goals of working group	7

Consensual versus Delivery Systems in European Private Law – Consensus about Tradition?
Vincent Sagaert

A. Introduction: An antagonism within the transfer of property rights?	9
B. A *ius commune* in historical perspective?	10
C. Consensual systems of transfer	14
D. Delivery ('tradition') systems of transfer	29
E. Arguments in favour of a functional approach	35
F. Conclusion	45

Private Autonomy in Property Law: Can the Parties 'Design' their Transfer?
Kai Kullerkupp

A. Introduction	47
B. Private autonomy and its peculiarities in property law	48
C. Elements of ownership transfer and potential limitations to 'design freedom' latent therein	50

D. Aspects of transfer parties might wish to modify to suit their interests	52
E. Conclusions	57

An Abstract or a Causal System
Steven Bartels

A. Introduction	59
B. General description of the abstract and causal system	60
C. A closer analysis	63
D. The midway solution of Lars van Vliet: The *animus* theory	66
E. Conclusions	67

How Swedish Lawyers Think about 'Ownership' and 'Transfer of Ownership' – Are We Just Peculiar or Actually Ahead?
Claes Martinson

A. To own or not to own? – That is not the question!	69
B. Go straight to the problem! Ownership is a detour	72
C. Be open to deal with all problems, but only solve the ones which need to be solved!	75
D. Form the questions functionally! Ownership is not a real concern	78
E. The terminology should not be decisive! Ownership is not a magic word	81
F. Use ownership relationally!	84
G. Let the functional interests decide what constructions should be supported!	86
H. Keep problems apart – even if they seem to be assembled!	90
I. The same solution may be used for different problems – but on its own merits!	91
J. Understanding the Swedish approach	93

Scepticism about the Functional Approach from a Unitary Perspective
Wolfgang Faber

A. Introduction	97
B. Some clarifications as to the unitary approach	99
C. Interdependencies between various aspects and relations	111
D. Legal certainty and predictability of judicial decisions	116
E. Scepticism related to 'exporting' the functional approach to a European level or other national systems	117
F. Final remark	121

The Relationship between Transfer Rules and Rules on Creditors' Avoidance of Debtor's Transactions
Caroline Cauffman

A.	Introduction	123
B.	Attachment	123
C.	Pauline action	125
D.	Rights of priority	130
E.	Validity requirements	131
F.	Right of retention	132
G.	Right of quasi-revendication of the unpaid seller and the right of stoppage in transit	134
H.	Simulation	136
I.	Contractual protection	138
J.	Reservation of title	138
K.	Conclusion	139

How to Draft New Rules on the Bona Fide Acquisition of Movables for Europe? Some Remarks on Method and Content
Arthur F. Salomons

A.	Introduction: Subject and purpose of this contribution	141
B.	Representation of the dissension within Europe: The continuum	141
C.	Three possible approaches	144
D.	Socio-political aspects	148
E.	Protecting the interests of trade and the rise of e-commerce	150
F.	Implications of the rise of e-commerce for *bona fide* acquisition protection	151
G.	Conclusion	154

Good Faith Acquisition – Why at all?
José Caramelo-Gomes

A.	Introduction	155
B.	Portuguese law – general rules	156
C.	Portuguese law – exceptions	157
D.	Portuguese commercial law	158
E.	Conclusion	158

Fiduciary Transfer and Ownership
Selma de Groot

A. Should the European debate with regard to the transfer of movables include fiduciary transfers?	161
B. A civil law dilemma	161
C. England & Wales: Division of ownership?	164
D. Germany: Division in time	167
E. France: Division of patrimony	169
F. The Netherlands: Prohibition and alternatives	171
G. Conclusion	172

Obligatory and Proprietary Rights: Where to Draw the Dividing Line – If at all?
Eleanor Cashin Ritaine

A. The *summa divisio* between obligatory and proprietary rights	180
B. Consequences and limits of this *summa divisio*	190

The German Property Law and its Principles – Some Lessons for a European Property Law
Jens Thomas Füller

A. Introduction	197
B. The so-called *Trennungs- und Abstraktionsprinzip* (principles of separation and abstraction)	199
C. *Numerus clausus*	206
D. Publicity	210
E. Some recommendations	214

Intellectual Property Rights: 'Property' or 'Right'? The Application of the Transfer Rules to Intellectual Property
Mary-Rose McGuire

A. Introduction: Three questions	217
B. The distinction between '*property*' and '*right*' in the context of intellectual property rights	218
C. The relevance of IP-rights for European private law	228
D. Criteria for the categorisation of IP-rights	233
E. Conclusions	236

Unification in the Field of Property Law from the Perspective of European Law
José Caramelo-Gomes

A. European integration and private law, background	239
B. The European Court of Justice and property law	243
C. Roadmap to a European private law	248

Transfer of Ownership in Recent Reform Projects: Estonia
Kai Kullerkupp

A. Introduction and background	249
B. The Property Law Act of 1993: From causal to abstract transfer system	250
C. Main characteristics of the new system	251
D. Conclusions	253

Protection and Transfer of Possession
Luboš Tichý

A. Definition of the problem	255
B. Essence of possession	256
C. Legal regulation of possession and its development	256
D. Development of the legal protection of possession	257
E. Transfer of possession	261
F. Critical comments, conclusions and resolution	261

List of Contributors　267

Introduction to the Project 'Transfer of Movables': Organisational Framework, Basic Issues and Goals

*Brigitta Lurger**

Our Conference 'Rules on the Transfer of Movables – A Candidate for European Harmonisation or National Reforms?' pursues several goals: It is a general conference open to everybody – academic or practitioner – who is interested in the development of property law. But it is also a Conference with special guests and speakers: We are particularly happy to be able to welcome to this Conference the reporters of our working group 'Transfer of Movables'. Their information is vital to our project and they took enormous efforts to answer our sometimes picky and complicated questions in extensive reports. Many of them will also contribute to this Conference as speakers. We are also very happy and honoured to welcome here the members of the *'Ius Commune* Group' on property law. In this research group renowned experts of property law of several European countries co-operate to publish a European 'Case Book' on the whole of property law. This conference, therefore, aims at bringing together the different views and experiences of lawyers dealing with issues of property law in their academic or practical work, and to initiate a general discussion on persistent problems and recent developments in this area of law. And the conference shall also provide a forum for discussions and exchange among the members and exponents of European research groups who concentrate their activities on comparative research in European property law, especially the Ius Commune Case Book Group and the working group on 'Transfer of Movables' as part of the Study Group on a European Civil Code.

A. The working group 'Transfer of Movables' as part of the Study Group on a European Civil Code (SGECC)

The first initiative to establish a new working group on the 'transfer of ownership in movables' within the network of working groups within the 'Study Group on a European Civil Code' (SGECC)[1] was taken by Prof Michael Rainer, Salzburg, and Prof Willibald Posch, Graz, in 2001. Until 2004, to-

---

* Dr iur, LL M (Harvard), Professor of Private Law, University of Graz.
[1] See http://www.sgecc.net.

gether with Wolfgang Faber, Salzburg, and Prof Brigitta Lurger, Salzburg, the first comparative studies and draft proposals on the transfer of ownership in movables on the basis of a contract or obligation and on good faith acquisition of movables were elaborated.

The main fields covered by the work of the SGECC are part of the law of obligations: general rules for obligations and for contract law, specific types of contracts, tort law, unjust enrichment, and benevolent intervention. However, also some issues of property law were identified as closely related to the law of obligations or contracts (sales, leases). In their study of 2004 on the interaction between contract law, tort and property law, commissioned by the European Commission, von Bar and Drobnig argued that the Internal Market needs a uniform regime of security rights and probably, not necessarily, also a uniform regime for the transfer of ownership in movables.[2] The 2004 Contract Law Communication of the Commission concluded from this study that the Common Frame of Reference and the optional instrument should cover retention of title clauses, the transfer of title of goods, security rights in movables and other related property law issues.[3]

As for all working groups of the SGECC, the goal of our working group on the 'Transfer of Movables' is the publication of a proposal of black letter rules together with comments and comparative notes (Sellier European Law Publishers). In addition to that, we plan the publication of all our country reports in several volumes.

B. The working group since 2005: The FWF-project and the Commission's Network of Excellence project 'Common Principles of European Contract Law' (CoPECL)

Since 2005 (until 2009) our research project is financially supported by the Austrian *Forschungsförderungsfonds*, the 'FWF', and the European Commission's Network of Excellence Project 'Common Principles of European Contract Law' (CoPECL)[4] on the basis of the 6th Framework Program for Research and Technological Development.[5] Our main financial investments are assistants, country reports, this conference, and travel expenses.

---

[2] Christian von Bar and Ulrich Drobnig, *The Interaction of Contract Law and Tort and Property Law in Europe, Part II: Property Law and Contract Law* (München: Sellier 2004), 468 *et seq*.

[3] Commission Communication 11 October 2004, COM(2004) 651 final, 11, 20.

[4] See http://www.copecl.org.

[5] Under the Sixth Framework Programme for Research and Technological Development (Decision No 1513/2002/EC, OJ L 232, 29.8.2002, 1), the 'Network of Excellence',

Our working group has two centres: a bigger one in Graz – headed by Brigitta Lurger, and a smaller one in Salzburg – headed by Wolfgang Faber. We currently employ four research assistants in Graz (Rui Cascao, Anastasios Moraitis, Ernest Weiker, Alessio Greco) and two research assistants in Salzburg (Martine Costa, Ferenc Szilagyi). 'Advisors' to our working group are Prof Matthias Storme (Belgium), Prof Michael Bridge (Great Britain), Prof Torgny Håstad (Sweden), and Prof Anna Veneziano (Italy).

Thus, our working group is part of the SGECC, the SGECC is the biggest academic group within the CoPECL Project (other groups: Acquis Group, Insurance Law Group et al), and the CoPECL Project forms part of the Commission's Network Project on European Contract Law which comprises apart from the academic CoPECL network of excellence also a 'network of stakeholders' (interest groups) and a 'network of national experts' (representatives of the ministries of justice of the Member States).

The Network Project as a whole is a fascinating, but at the same time also a disputed and obscure project.[6] On the one hand, the broad coverage of private law by an official EU project is new and impressive (law of obligations, parts of property law (chattels); only the procedural law, the law of succession and family law are completely excluded). A lot of pioneer work in comparative law is accomplished by numerous researchers within the project stemming from all jurisdictions of the present EU. There is no doubt that the comparative studies and extensively commented rule proposals published by the numerous participants of the project will constitute an important (historically probably unprecedented) contribution to the discipline of comparative private law in Europe and will have a great impact on the further development of academic research and teaching.

On the other hand, the concrete goals and desired outcomes of the EC Network Project are uncertain and disputed among EU officials as well as among politicians, researchers and practitioners. According to its communication of 11 October 2004,[7] the Commission envisages the 'Common Frame of Reference' (CFR) as a 'tool box', to consist of fundamental principles of contract law, of definitions of legal terms, and of coherent model rules of contract law. Although this tool box should have a non-binding character, some discussion has taken place suggesting that the CFR may lead to the

---

Common Principles of European Contract Law (CoPECL) was established: members of the network are, among other smaller groups, the Study Group on a European Civil Code, the Acquis Group, and the Insurance Law Group.

[6] See the contributions to the ZEuP-Symposium 2006 in Graz in ZEuP (*Zeitschrift für Europäisches Privatrecht*) 2007, pp 109-303, among others, by Reiner Schulze (p 130), Norbert Reich (p 161), Gerhard Wagner (p 180), Dieter Martiny (p 212), Jürgen Basedow (p 280).

[7] Commission Communication 11 October 2004, COM(2004) 651 final, p 2.

conclusion of an inter-institutional contract, which then obliges the EU institutions to adhere to its definitions and rules. The CFR is supposed to be used mainly for two purposes: to improve the existing acquis and to form the basis for elaborating additional legal instruments in the field of contract law. The Commission stated that one of these additional legal instruments could be a so-called 'optional instrument', which horizontally covers wide areas of general and specific contract law and related areas of private law. As to the nature of the optional instrument, the Commission favours[8] the legal form of a regulation that will establish a 28th legal order, which can be chosen by the parties. The optional code will contain both non-mandatory and mandatory provisions, particularly those protecting consumers. These will – following the preference of the Commission – exclude the application of any national mandatory provisions on the basis of Articles 5 and 7 of the Rome I Convention.[9]

The Commission reacted to critique expressed within the Commission as well as critique from outside, by practitioners, interest groups, academics and others, by reaffirming its position[10] that no 'European Civil Code' should be drafted and by officially removing the optional code from the agenda of the Network Project.[11] Contrary to its initial plans, it currently concentrates its activities merely on the revision of the so-called 'Consumer Acquis',[12] ie on the amendment of only eight EC directives. This 'Acquis Review' has no connection to roughly 90 per cent of the rules of the CFR which are currently drafted by the academic groups in the CoPECL Project. It is hard to imagine that the Commission would invest large sums of money in producing a CFR of thousands of pages, with no intention of ever using the roughly 90 per cent of it, which does not deal with consumer protection.[13] What it

---

[8] Commission Communication 11 October 2004, COM (2004) 651 final, Annex II.
[9] 'Rome I would not then apply to matters regulated by the optional instrument.' Commission Communication 11 October 2004, COM(2004) 651 final, Annex II.
[10] Commission Communication 11 October 2004, COM(2004) 651 final, p 8.
[11] See, for instance, the Commission declarations on the second workshop of the stakeholder network on 31 May 2005.
[12] See the Report of the Commission – First Annual Progress Report on European Contract Law and the Acquis Review, 23 September 2005, COM(2005) 456 final, and the Commission's Green Paper on the Review of the Consumer Acquis 8 February 2007, COM(2007) 744 final.
[13] This judgment is shared by the European Union Committee of the House of Lords, 12th Report of Session 2004-05, *European Contract Law – the way forward?*, 5 April 2005, HL Paper 95, p 23: 'We doubt whether it is correct to describe the CFR as envisaged in the Communication as a thesaurus. It would be more than a book of synonyms or a book of specialized vocabulary. We hope the Government has not underestimated what the

really intends to do or will do with the results of CoPECL Project remains unclear. The European Parliament, on the other hand, still strongly supports a horizontal harmonisation or unification of contract law (and related areas of law).[14]

In the general discussion about the Network Project, the democratic legitimacy of a further harmonisation of contract law (and other fields of private law) on the basis of the CFR is put into question.[15] Even though the Commission established two additional networks of 'stakeholders' (interest groups) and of national experts (representatives of the ministries of justice of the Member States), which are supposed to comment on the draft CFR as the researchers present it to them, piece by piece,[16] the involvement of the *demos*, the people outside the EU bureaucracy and the academic circles involved, is perceived as unsatisfactory.[17] In addition, no clear competence of the EC for the harmonisation of contract law seems to exist.[18] At the same time, no scenario of a Europeanisation of contract law can be envisaged which will *not* result in a reduction of national sovereignty. Alternative models of rule-making – like soft law, an 'optional instrument', the 'open

---

CFR might contain or involve. As we explain below, the CFR would be likely to have the potential to become an 'optional instrument' and/or part of a European civil code.'

[14] EP resolution on European contract law and the revision of the *acquis*: the way forward, 23 March 2006, available on the EP homepage: www.europarl.europa.eu/sides/getDoc.do?pubRef=//EP//NONSGML+TA+P6-TA-2006-0109+0+DOC+PDF+V0//EN&language=EN, 30.10.2006, reprinted in ZEuP 2006, 908.

[15] Study Group on Social Justice in European Private Law, 'Social Justice in European Contract Law: a Manifesto' (2004) *European Law Journal* (ELJ), 653-674.

[16] See Hugh Beale, 'The European Commission's Common Frame of Reference Project: a progress report', (2006) 2 *European Review of Contract Law* (ERCL), 303.

[17] Gerhard Wagner, 'Die soziale Frage und der Gemeinsame Referenzrahmen' (2007) *Zeitschrift für Europäisches Privatrecht* ZEuP 180, 189 *et seq*.

[18] Stephen Weatherill, 'Recent developments in the law governing the free movement of goods in the EC's internal market', (2006) 2 ECRL, 90, 100 *et seq*, with further references; Norbert Reich, 'A European Contract Law, or an EU Contract Law Regulation for Consumers?', (2005) 28 *Journal of Consumer Policy* (J Cons Pol), 383; Eve Truilhé-Marengo, 'Towards a European Law of Contracts', (2004) 10 *European Law Journal* (ELJ), 463, 476 et seq; Norbert Reich, 'Der Common Frame of Reference und Sonderprivatrechte im "Europäischen Vertragsrecht"', (2007) ZEuP 161, 170; Brigitta Lurger, 'The Common Frame of Reference / Optional Code and the Various Understandings of Social Justice in Europe', in: Thomas Wilhelmsson (ed), *Private Law and the Cultures of Europe* (The Hague/London/New York: Kluwer Law International 2007) 167, 174 *et seq*.

method of co-ordination' or even the delegation of powers to private institutions[19] – are discussed, but they do not really solve the competence problem.

Thus, whether we need a European contract law or even more – a European tort law or European provisions on the transfer of movables – remains an unanswered question. It is certainly a political question, not a mere technical or academic question, but an answer on the political level is missing.

C. Issues covered and methods employed by working group

In 2005 the official title of our working group and of Book VIII of CFR was changed to '*Acquisition and Loss of Ownership in Movables*'. This title reflects the areas covered by Book VIII (which is drafted by our group) better than the abbreviation 'transfer of movables'. Book VIII contains the following chapters: 1: scope and general provisions; 2: transfer based on a contract or other obligation (bulk transfer, documents of title, registered movables); 3: good faith acquisition; 4: acquisition by continuous possession; 5: production, combination and commingling; 6: protection of ownership and possession; 7: consequences of restitution of the movable (owner-possessor-relationship).

The first topics of the conference reflect our primary concern with the 'transfer rules' where the transfer is based on a contract or other obligation: consensual (romanistic countries) or delivery system (*eg* Germany, Austria, Greece), abstract (Germany, Greece) or causal transfer, functional (Scandinavian) or unitary approach. In our rule proposal we opted for a causal delivery system and we mainly followed the unitary approach. The issue of good faith acquisition is also closely related to the transfer of goods in ordinary commerce. This issue was, therefore, dealt with in the first stage of our research work (2001-2004).

In the second stage of our work (2005 onwards), we now deal with (a) remaining other forms of acquisition of ownership, like acquisition by continuous possession (= acquisitive prescription), and acquisition by production, combination and commingling, and with (b) the controversial line that can or cannot be drawn between obligatory and proprietary rights – namely with the legal position of a 'possessor' (protection of ownership and possession, owner-possessor relationship).

The methods we employ in our work are strongly influenced by two factors: the example of the SGECC and the restricted time frame imposed by the SGECC and the Commission in the CoPECL Project. The most impor-

---

[19] Hans-Wolfgang Micklitz, '(Selbst-)Reflektionen über die wissenschaftlichen Ansätze zur Vorbereitung einer europäischen Vertragsrechtskodifikation', (2007) *Zeitschrift für Gemeinschaftsprivatrecht* (GPR) 2, 6 *et seq.*

tant basis of our work is certainly constituted by the country reports: namely, the detailed information we received by our reporters on their national legal systems. The next crucial step is the evaluation of this information: How do we reach the conclusion that exactly the rules we propose are the most appropriate for a future European legal system or a national reform of property law rules? Where possible, we are certainly looking for common solutions, in accordance with the famous 'functional method' developed by Zweigert and Kötz.[20] However, the number of 'functionally' similar solutions is considerably smaller in the area of property law than it is in the area of contract law. Thus, we are very often confronted with 'real' differences in the solution of legal or social questions, not only with differences in black letter rules. And we are very well aware of the fact that the choice between different solutions (and rules) is not a neutral academic endeavour, but most often implies political choices. As a consequence, the final decisions will have to be taken by political actors, especially parliaments, and not by academic groups. What we intend to do, is, at best, to prepare those decisions by providing a comprehensive set of comparative information and a comprehensive set of arguments for evaluation.

The choice of a particular rule or a system of rules influences the relations, expectations and interests of the parties who own movables or attempt to acquire movables on the various markets. The impact of particular rules on societal relations between people is, therefore, at the centre of our deliberations. We, thus, try to rationalise and justify our choices by examining them on different levels: the impact of a rule on the interests of the parties directly involved in a transaction (or other fact pattern), the impact on other persons indirectly concerned (creditors, other market participants, heirs *etc*), the impact on the whole market or on society (economic efficiency, expectations of people, transparency, notions of justice). Arguments on the different levels are often interrelated: *eg* the balancing of conflicting fundamentals rights affects the party interests and, at the same time, also the whole market system and societal concepts of justice.

D. Goals of working group

We do not take a stand on the question of whether the unification of parts of property law is possible and desirable in the near future. The same questions of EU competences, of democratic legitimacy, and the like, arise with respect to the unification or harmonisation of property law as well as with respect to the further harmonisation of contract law (see point B. above). It

---

[20] Konrad Zweigert and Hein Kötz, *Einführung in die Rechtsvergleichung* (Tübingen: Mohr-Siebeck, 3rd ed 1996) p 31 *et seq*.

is, therefore, our goal to make a proposal of transfer of property rules that is as attractive and convincing for the responsible political actors, on EU and national levels, as possible, whenever they may decide to undertake a reform or harmonisation in this area of law.

In the absence of any EU measures in the field of transfer of ownership in movables in the foreseeable future, our results may still be of interest to national governments and legislators who plan a reform of the respective rules in their national codifications or statutes. This may be the case in some of the new Eastern and South Eastern European Member states, but also in some of the older Member States who want to modernise their civil codes or statutes, which partly date back to the early 19th century.

Besides the uncertain future of our proposals on the EU and national legislative levels, there may be some less uncertain impact of our work on two other levels: academic research and legal education. Our working group hopes to extend the pool of academic knowledge in the field of European property law. Not many comparative studies in this area of law have been published so far. And none seems to be so comprehensive as to cover the systems of all present Member States and the whole range of questions covered by our project. Our publications could provide a useful basis for future comparative research of various kinds of the European and international academic community in this area. And they could be a small contribution to a more international legal education in the field of private law in Europe.

Consensual versus Delivery Systems in European Private Law – Consensus about Tradition?

Vincent Sagaert[*]

A. Introduction: An antagonism within the transfer of property rights?

1. If there is one legal field in which it is frequently argued that European private law systems are characterised by absolute divergence, it is the field of the transfer of goods. Nevertheless, the European institutions have undertaken to investigate whether a harmonisation is possible, given the fact that market economies are dependent upon changes of distribution to facilitate the optimal use of goods by citizens and market participants.

One of the most prominent issues arising, when dealing with transfer issues with respect to movables,[1] is the question about the moment of the transfer of property rights. If the agreement between the parties coincides with the delivery of the goods and the payment of the price, this issue will not arise. Frequently, these moments do not coincide, and the relevant factor for the transfer of property rights must be ascertained.

2. As a matter of principle, three approaches are feasible: the transfer could be effected at the moment of the (1) consensus between parties, (2) delivery of the good to the transferee or (3) fulfillment of the exchange obligation by the transferee (*eg* payment of the purchase price).

The third moment is often chosen by contractual arrangement between the parties, but no European legal system adheres to this moment as a matter

---

[*] Professor of Private Law at the University of Leuven, Professor of Property Law at the University of Antwerp and Catholic University of Brussels, Attorney at the Brussels Bar.
[1] We will only deal with corporeal movables which are subject to the general regime. This contribution, hence, does not imply claims, registered movables (aircrafts, seaships, *etc*) or intellectual property rights, as the transfer of these movables can be made subject to specific rules.

of law. A proposal to introduce this moment into French law has not been approved by the French legislator.[2]

3. Traditionally, the distinction between the first two moments characterises the two main transfer systems within the European legal systems:
- The consensual systems, which do not require delivery in order to effect the transfer of property rights. The founding father of this opinion is often considered to be Grotius. Most often, French-inspired legal systems are said to adhere to this consensual system, such as France itself, Belgium, Italy, Luxemburg, *etc*. The English Sale of Goods Act 1979 also adheres to this starting point.
- The delivery (or *traditio*) systems, in which property rights only pass at the moment of delivery. The Germanic legal family is presented to adhere to this system, with German, Austrian and Swiss law as main legal systems. However, Dutch law has acceded to this group since the introduction of the new Civil Code in 1992.

4. However, the distinction between those two contrasting systems must first be explained in a historical perspective in order to sharpen the contrast between the two systems, and one must first analyse how the distinction has come into existence (cf *infra*, n 5-10). Afterwards, we will deal with the current scope of both systems and investigate the various mitigations which are to be made on the basic principle in each of these systems (cf *infra*, n 11-41). In doing so, it will not be possible to investigate – within the framework of this contribution – all (European) legal systems. We will mainly deal with French, English and Belgian law as examples of consensual systems, and with German and Dutch law as examples of delivery systems.

The results of this analysis will be further developed in section E (cf *infra*, n 42-59), dealing with the possibility of elaborating a functional unified system of transfer between the European private law systems.

B. A *ius commune* in historical perspective?

I. Convergence in Roman law

5. First of all, the historical development of the dichotomy between the several transfer systems must be analysed. This historical development

---

[2] See on this proposal: Gauthier Blanluet, 'Le moment du transfert de la propriété', in: Yves Lequette, *Le Code civil: 1804-2004; Un passé, un present, un avenir* (Paris: Dalloz 2004), p 412, n 5.

should enable one to clarify the exact meaning and scope of the so-called contrast between consensual and delivery systems.

6. Roman law gradually developed into a delivery system in the period of codification by *Justinianus*. Originally, there were several possible forms of transferring property rights, some of which required delivery (*traditio*) but others which did not (*in iure cessio* and *mancipatio*). The *in iure cessio*, however, disappeared because it was not used in legal practice and Justinianus abolished the *mancipatio* in 531.[3]

7. The only remaining manner in which to transfer property rights by way of contract was by delivery. It was argued that the delivery requirement was grounded in natural law: it would, according to this view, be implicit in natural law that the party autonomy is realised by the transfer of possession of the asset.[4] Therefore, Roman law emphasized that it was not possible to transfer property rights by mere agreement. Only the transfer of possession or *usucapio* (acquisitive prescription) could transfer property rights.[5] Delivery, in Roman law, necessarily implied an agreement: the unilateral control assumed by the acquirer would amount to theft in Roman law.[6]

Hence, if the same good was sold to two different persons, the first one to whom the control over the asset was transferred would prevail. The other one would merely have a personal claim against the transferor.[7] It will become clear that this rule still survives, both in consensual and tradition systems, as a rule of European property law (even if the former require the good faith of the second acquirer in order to protect him).

2. Divergence in the pre-codification era: The growth of consensualism in French-based systems

8. Since Roman law provided for a convergence towards a delivery system, all European systems adhered to this system in the following centuries. This was also the case for French law: before the Napoleonic Code, French law required delivery for the transfer of movable (and immovable) property in both '*les pays de droit coutumiers*' (north of France) and '*les pays de droits écrits*' (south of France).

---

[3] C 7, 31, 1, 5.
[4] Inst 2, 1, 40.
[5] '*Traditionibus et usucapionibus dominia rerum, non nudis pactis transferuntur*' (C 2, 3, 20).
[6] D 41, 2, 5.
[7] C 4, 39, 6.

Over the decades, this delivery requirement gradually eroded in legal practice as, in many instances, a genuine transfer of direct possession was no longer needed. Often, a simple declaration that possession had been transferred replaced the actual transfer. This was called '*une clause de dessaisine-saisine*', *eg* a clause in which parties contractually agreed that possession had been passed. In this way, a *tradition feinte* (fictitious transfer) was developed. The practical result of the fictitious *traditio* was that property rights (especially in land) passed in accordance with party autonomy when the contract of sale was concluded. The same practices were transposed to the transfer of movables. The transfer of property rights was disconnected from the transfer of possession.

9. With the introduction of the Civil Code, a clause creating a fictitious transfer was presumed, by the legislator, to exist. It was presumed that parties implicitly included a clause in their contracts that ownership passed immediately.[8] From a theoretical point of view, this conception was possible because of the influence exercised by the *ius cogens*. Contrary to Roman law, the school of *ius cogens* in the 18-19th century adhered to a more 'abstract' notion of ownership. Ownership was no longer equated with possession, an abstract concept of ownership came into force.[9] It became possible to reflect upon the acquisition of ownership without any physical change in the object of the transfer.

More important than the conceptual and theoretical foundations of the development, was the evolution of legal practice. The *tradition feinte*, which had been initiated in the pre-codification era, was generalised in legal practice at the end of the 18th century. The consensual systems were the legal recognition of the *tradition feinte* in legal practice. The development demonstrates that the so-called breach with the past with regard to the system of

---

[8] In French law: Claude Witz, 'Analyse critique des règles régissant le transfert de propriété en droit français à la lumière du droit allemand', in: Michael Martinek (ed), *Festschrift für Günther Jahr zum siebzigsten Geburtstag: Vestigia Iuris* (Tübingen: Mohr 1993), p 535. In Belgian law: Albert Kluyskens, *Beginselen Burgerlijk Recht*, V (Ghent Standaard Uitgeverij 1951), n 102; see also Caroline Lebon, 'Non nudis pactis dominia rerum transferuntur? Kritische bemerkingen omtrent de consensualiteit van de overdracht van eigendom en de vestiging van beperkt zakelijke rechten', *Tijdschrift Privaatrecht* (TPR) 2004, pp 425-426. Pothier – an author whose writings largely influenced the draftsmen of the Civil Code – still pleaded for a *traditio* system (Robert Joseph Pothier, 'Traité du domaine de propriété', in: Robert Joseph Pothier and Jean-Baptiste Louis Philippe, *Oeuvres de Pothier*, VIII (Paris: Letellier 1807), p 186 *et seq*).

[9] See also on this development Jacques Ghestin and Bernard Desche, 'La Vente', in: *Traité des contrats*, I (Paris: LGDJ 1990), n 525.

transfer was rather an expression of continuity.[10] This also emerges from the preparatory works to the French Civil Code, during which Portalis stated that 'with regard to other contracts (*eg* sales agreement), we merely have reconfirmed the general rules. In this field of law, we will never exceed the principles which have been transmitted to us by antiquity.'[11]

The natural way in which things have been developed is confirmed by the views of leading legal scholars and case law. Some legal scholars[12] and case law (even the French supreme Court)[13] suggested, at the beginning of the 19th century, that the transfer was effected at the moment of delivery. This clearly illustrates that the introduction of consensualism was not perceived as a revolution in the beginning of the 19th century.

10. It emerges from the foregoing that the consensual systems have developed as an exception to the general delivery requirement for practical reasons. There is, given this historical genesis, large support for the view that the French Civil Code has not abolished the delivery requirement, but has given this requirement a 'symbolic'/'fictitious' content: a transfer is not effected by virtue of party autonomy, but by virtue of a fictitious transfer.[14] The immediate transfer was dogmatically justified by Portalis during the preparatory works to the Civil Code, by stating that a contract for the transfer of ownership contains a certain fictitious *traditio* which effects the transfer of rights.[15] In other words: the French Civil Code did not introduce a

---

[10] Gabriel Baudry-Lacantinerie, *Traité théorique et pratique de droit civil*, XII (Paris: Sirey, 2nd ed 1906), n 366; Jean-Pascal Chazal and Serge Vicente, 'Le transfert de propriété par l'effet des obligations dans le Code civil', *Revue trimestrielle de droit civil* (Rev trim dr Civ) 2000, p 481, n 7.

[11] Cf Alain Fenet, *Recueil complet des travaux préparatoires du Code civil* (Parijs, 1827) XIII, p 215: «Quant aux autres contrats (dont le contrat de vente), nous nous sommes réduites à retracer les règles communes. Sur cette matière, nous n'irons jamais au-delà des principes qui nous ont été transmis par l'antiquité.»

[12] Cf Charles Bonaventure Marie Toullier, *Le droit civil français*, Vol III (Brussels: Wahlen et comp 1833), n 11.

[13] Cf Req 12 April 1831, Dalloz 1832, I, p 54: 'La délivrance, que le vendeur est dans l'obligation de faire, n'est que le transport de la chose vendue en la jouissance et possession de l'acheteur.'

[14] Claude Bufnoir, *Propriété et contrat. Théorie des modes d'acquisition des droits réels et des sources des obligations* (Paris: LGDJ 1924), p 45; Witz (*supra* footnote 8), p 536.

[15] Jean Guillaume Locré, *Législation civile, commerciale et criminelle, ou commentaire et complément des code Français*, (Brussels: Uitgever 1836), p 71. However, other scholars allege that Portalis did not intend to say that a transfer of possession is still needed, but only that a transfer of direct possession was not needed under the system of the Civil

consensual system, but a fictitious delivery system. This view is, in French and Belgian law, supported by the wordings of art 938 Civil Code, which reads as follows: 'A gift, *if duly accepted, will be effected by the mere consensus of the parties. Ownership of the goods donated will pass to the beneficiary without another traditio being needed*'[16] (emphasis added). The word 'another' implies that there is already a *traditio* in the consensual gift, which is deemed to be executed tacitly.[17] The original draft of this provision even mentioned 'without another traditio than the consensus between the parties being needed', but an amendment has been made in the final version.

C. Consensual systems of transfer

I. General principle

11. The consensual nature of a transfer system means that the obligatory agreement not only gives rise to the existence of rights and obligations, but also triggers the proprietary effects of the agreement. In other words, the obligation to transfer property rights, in general terms, terminates as from the moment it comes into existence, as this transfer is effected automatically by the agreement. Consensual systems of transfer do – according to the main view in current scholarship – not distinguish the obligatory agreement and the real agreement (no *Trennungsprinzip*). There are – in the French-inspired consensual systems – no formal requirements. The signing of written documents is not necessary for the passing of ownership, but merely (in non-commercial cases) for proving the transfer of ownership.[18]

The consequence of the consensual nature of a transfer system is that, in case the obligatory agreement is declared void or is being rescinded, the property rights which were transferred are deemed never to have passed. In other words, the transferor is deemed never to have lost his property rights. As the transfer is implied in the agreement, the validity of the transfer is dependent upon the validity of the agreement. A consensual system can, for this reason, never be an abstract system of transfer.

12. The main legal system, which is the 'mother law' of the consensual systems, is French law. As it has been described before, French law has grad-

---

Code (in this sense: Lars van Vliet, *Transfer of movables in German, French, English and Dutch law* (Deventer: Ars Aequi Libri 2000), p 80).

[16] Art 938: '*La donation dûment acceptée sera parfaite par le seul consentement des parties; et la propriété des objets donnés sera transférée au donataire, sans qu'il soit besoin d'autre tradition*'.

[17] Bufnoir (*supra* footnote 14), p 45 *et seq*.

[18] Art 1341 French and Belgian Civil Code.

ually and naturally developed away from a delivery system in which the *traditio* has been factually eroded (cf *supra*, n 5-10). In this sense, delivery is still part of the French legal system, but is deemed to be effected by mere consensus.[19] It has a purely theoretical foundation. The so-called pure consensual systems are, in fact, rather fictitious delivery systems.

The Civil Codes of Belgium and Luxemburg incorporated the French Civil Code in 1804 and did not amend the provisions on the immediate transfer of property rights. Italian law has also adhered to the system on the basis of art 1376 Civil Code. In this way, Belgian, French and Italian law make a total departure from the basic principles of Roman law in which the agreement in itself was insufficient to effect a transfer of ownership. English law takes a less obvious position.

The English Sale of Goods Act also confirms the immediate passing of ownership: as between the parties, the property right in specific goods passes when it is intended to pass (Section 17). The primary default rule for determining the intention of the parties is as follows: 'Where there is an unconditional contract for the sale of specific goods in a deliverable state the property in the goods passes to the buyer when the contract is made, and it is immaterial whether the time of payment or the time of delivery, or both, be postponed' (Section 18).[20] The Sale of Goods Act 1979 creates a genuine consensual system. We will demonstrate *infra* that English law is even more liberal than French law: even in the case of unascertained goods, delivery is not a requirement for the transfer of title to the goods (cf *infra*, n 25).

13. The immediate transfer of property rights in the French Civil Code is based on the general rule that property rights pass by virtue of the obligation. Art 711 CC makes a list of the derivative ways of the acquisition of property rights: '*Ownership of property is acquired and transmitted by succession, by gift inter vivos or will, and by the effect of obligations*'. Art 1138 CC concretises this last source in providing that 'an obligation of delivering a thing is complete by the sole consent of the contracting parties. The conclusion of a lawful agreement is not only the source of contractual rights and obligations, but has also proprietary effects. It makes the creditor the owner and places the thing at his risk from the time when it should have been delivered, although the handing over has not been made, unless the debtor has been given notice to deliver; in which case, the thing remains at the risk of the latter'.

14. The general rule of art 1138 CC is repeated, in art 1583 CC for sales agreements, and in art 938 CC for gifts:

---

[19] Bufnoir (*supra* footnote 14), pp 44-45.
[20] See on these provisions: Anthony Gordon Guest, *Benjamin's sale of goods* (London: Sweet & Maxwell, 7th ed 2006), n 5-016 *et seq*.

- art 1583 CC provides that 'it[21] is complete between the parties, and ownership is acquired by virtue of law by the buyer with respect to the seller, as soon as the thing and the price have been agreed upon, although the thing has not yet been delivered or the price paid'.[22] As a consequence, the transfer of ownership belongs to the essential features of a sales agreement.[23]
- art 938 CC provides that 'a gift, if duly accepted, will be performed by the mere consensus of the parties. Ownership of the things donated will pass to the donee without *another* traditio being needed'.[24]

15. The consensual nature of the transfer system has important effects as to the parties' position in respect of the obligation.

If the goods are subject to loss or deterioration due to *vis maior* after the agreement has been concluded but before the delivery of the goods has been effected, the creditor of the obligation will have to pay the price notwithstanding the impossibility for the transferor to comply with his obligation to deliver the goods. However, the risk for accidental loss or deterioration of the goods returns after serving notice to the transferor because he is in default in respect of the delivery of the goods (cf *infra*, n 47 *et seq*).

The consensual transfer entails that, from the moment of the agreement, all fruits belong to the transferee. His ownership includes the right to the fruits (*ius fruendi*). This rule is, with regard to sales agreements, expressly provided by art 1614 French Civil Code: 'The good must be delivered in the condition in which it is at the time of the sale. From that day, all the fruits belong to the purchaser'. The solution is, of course, different if the transfer of ownership has been delayed. This provides a counter-balance to the (sometimes inequitable) rule with regard to the passing of risk: the transferee, on the one hand, immediately bears the risk of the loss or deterioration of his good but, on the other hand, is entitled to reap the fruits.

16. The notion of 'real agreement' in civil law consensual systems is usually used in a context different to the one of the transfer of property rights. It is used in the sense of agreements, which only come into existence after deliv-

---

[21] Meaning: a sale.

[22] The original French text providing as follows: '*Elle est parfaite entre les parties, et la propriété est acquise de droit à l'acheteur à l'égard du vendeur, dès qu'on est convenu de la chose et du prix, quoique la chose n'ait pas encore été livrée ni le prix payé*'.

[23] Henri De Page and Anne Meinertzhagen-Limpens, *Traité élémentaire de droit civil belge*, Vol IV (Brussels: Bruylant, 4th, ed 1997), n 21.

[24] The original French text providing as follows: '*La donation dûment acceptée sera parfaite par le seul consentement des parties; et la propriété des objets donnés sera transférée au donataire, sans qu'il soit besoin d'autre tradition*'.

ery, but which do not necessarily have proprietary effects. For instance, a loan agreement only comes into existence at the moment the object of the loan is handed over to the debtor, not by the mere agreement between the parties. Another example: a custody agreement only comes into existence at the moment the custodian is given the physical control over the object of custody. The consensus between the parties does not give rise to a custody contract, but only to a promise to give a good into custody. This agreement is binding upon parties as an agreement *sui generis*, but does not have any proprietary effect: the custodian does not become owner or possessor, but merely detentor of the asset which is given into custody.

However, the concept of real agreement in the sense of a 'property transfer agreement' is increasingly used in consensual systems. As will be analysed under 2, the number of exceptions to the immediate transfer of property rights is still increasing. In many of these exceptional circumstances, the transfer of property rights is postponed until a new agreement between parties, automatically triggering the transfer of property rights, is created.

2. Refinements to the immediate transfer of property rights

17. The principle of the immediate transfer of ownership provides, at first glance, an easy and straightforward rule. However, the legislator and legal practice have been obliged to refine the immediate transfer of ownership. First of all, both the interests of third parties and of the transferor can be jeopardized by the immediate transfer of property rights. Moreover, the nature of the goods can conflict with this immediate transfer. Finally, certain basic principles of property law sometimes exclude the immediate transfer of property rights (*eg* principle of specificity).

For these reasons, the immediate transfer is, in these systems, subject to many exceptions. These exceptions turn an apparently clear and simple rule into a complicated and highly technical system.[25]

18. Four categories of exceptions can be distinguished.
- exceptions with regard to the opposability of the transfer to some third parties;
- exceptions relating to the nature of the transferred assets;
- exceptions relating to the nature of the agreement;
- exceptions relating to the nature of the parties involved.

---

[25] Ghestin and Desche (*supra* footnote 9), n 542: 'Le système apparemment simple du transfert de propriété solo consensu débouche sur un système extrêmement complexe qui est en définitive beaucoup plus complexe que celui fondé sur l'inscription au livre foncier pour les immeubles et la tradition pour les meubles.'

(a) Exceptions with regard to the third party effect of the transfer

19. The consensual transfer of property rights seems to be contradictory to the very nature of property rights. The agreement is only enforceable between parties,[26] while property rights have, by their nature, *erga omnes* effect. The third party effects of property rights require measures in order to make third parties aware of the existence or transfer of these property rights; in other words: publicity is required in order to protect the interests of third parties, even in 'consensual' systems.[27]

The principle of the immediate transfer of property rights does, therefore, not concern the effects of the transfer as against all third parties. In order to protect some third parties, legislators in 'consensual' systems require the fulfillment of formal requirements. As long as these requirements have not been fulfilled, the property rights of the transferee cannot have effect as against a third party in good faith with competing rights.[28] The transfer has effect as against other third parties – those who are in bad faith or do not have a competing right.

20. With regard to corporeal movables, this additional formality required by the law is the delivery to the transferee. Art 1141 CC expresses this third party protection by providing that 'if the asset which a person has obliged to give to two different persons, is a corporeal movable asset, the one who has first been given possession will prevail and will be considered as owner, even if his title is more recent, at the requirement that his possession is in good faith'. In other words: if A sells a good to B and afterwards A sells *and delivers* the same good to C, C will be considered to be the owner subject to the condition that he is in good faith, *ie* that he did not know and should not have known about any previous transfer of the same good.

This is an exception to the principle of consensualism: if we applied the basic principle which has been set out above, A would have nothing left at

---

[26] Art 1165 French and Belgian Civil Code: 'Agreements produce effect only between the contracting parties; they do not harm a third party, and they benefit him only in the case provided for in Article 1121.'

[27] Michel Waelbroeck, *Le transfert de la propriété dans la vente d'objets mobiliers corporels en droit comparé* (Brussels: Bruylant 1961), n 11.

[28] The transfer of property rights would have immediate effects in relation to general creditors or holders of personal rights (such as lessees), as they do not have a competing right: Blanluet (*supra* footnote 2), p 421, n 17; François Terré and Philippe Simler, *Les biens* (Paris: Dalloz, 5th edition 1998), n 392.

the moment he sells to C, and would thus not be able to grant any property right to C. This exception is justified by the possession of movables in good faith. It is an application of the general rule of art 2279 of the French/Belgian Civil Code, which provides that, with regard to movables, possession is equivalent to a title.

21. It emerges from legal literature that the opposability requirements have a wider scope due to the critical observations about the general starting point of 'consensualism'. Legal scholars observe indeed that it is unreasonable that a legal system, which adheres to legal certainty as an important value, accepts the transfer on the basis of mere expressions of intention, without providing, by any means, that third parties are to be informed. Third parties can be surprised by a transfer of which they could not have any knowledge. They can rely, in good faith, on appearances that do not correspond with the legal reality.[29]

22. Especially in Belgian law, this provision is considered as the expression of the general principle that, as long as the *traditio* has not been effected, the ownership of the transferee is not effective as against third parties in good faith with a competing right, *ie* ownership is relative.[30] The rule of art 1141 CC is, under certain circumstances and in some legal systems, extended to the conflict between a transferee and the insolvency administrator of the transferor. As will be considered below (cf *infra*, n 51-53), the position of the transferee, in the case of the insolvency of the transferor, is indeed much more complicated than under a system providing for the immediate transfer of property rights than under a delivery system.

(b) Exceptions relating to the nature of the transferred goods

23. With regard to *generic goods*, which are determined on the basis of their weight, number or measure and not on the basis of their individual characteristics, the principle of consensualism cannot be maintained in the civil law systems. It is a common principle of property law that property rights can only have as their object identified or identifiable goods. Property rights can never concern an abstract value. This is the so-called principle of specificity. This principle is expressed in art 1585 of the French/Belgian Civil Code: 'Where goods are not sold in bulk but by weight, number or measure,

---

[29] Waelbroeck (*supra* footnote 27), p 27, n 11.
[30] This view is, however, debatable: Third parties without a competing right and third parties who are not in good faith are not entitled to claim the non-opposability of the transfer until the taking over of possession.

a sale is not complete, in that the things sold are at the risk of the seller until they have been weighed, counted or measured; but the buyer may claim either the delivery or damages, if there is occasion, in case of non-performance of the undertaking'.[31]

The Belgian Supreme Court ruled, pursuant to this provision, that 'a vindication claim can only be accepted if and to the extent to which it concerns specific goods and cannot be exercised on the amount of the due sum'.[32] Indeed, individualisation does not have retroactive effect back to the moment of the agreement between the parties.[33] By consequence, if A sells generic goods to B, ownership and risk will only pass after the individualisation of the sold goods. Moreover, the non-individualised goods can be seized by the creditors of the transferor as long as individualisation has not taken place.[34]

What does individualisation exactly mean? It seems to emerge from art 1585 CC that the weighing, numbering or measuring of the sold goods is not sufficient to transfer ownership. This is the generally defended viewpoint.[35] The French Cour de cassation has ruled, in application of art 1585 CC that 'lorsque la vente a pour objet une certaine quantité de marchandises à prendre dans un lieu désigné, qui en renferme une quantité qui n'a pas encore été mesurée, c'est seulement l'opération de mesurage qui individualise la chose et entraîne en consequence la translation de propriété.'[36] Traditionally, most legal scholars take as a starting point that the individualisation must be effected in a consensual

---

[31] This provision only provides for, according to a strict interpretation, the passing of the risk. However, this can be explained by the fact that the draftsmen of the Civil Code were inspired by Pothier, who made the transfer dependent upon the transfer of property rights (Gabriel Baudry-Lacantinerie, *Traité théorique et pratique*, Vol XIX (Paris: Sirey 1907), n 145).

[32] Cass 9 May 1947, *Arresten van het Hof van Cassatie* (Arr Cass) 1947, p 148, *Pasicrisie* 1947, I, p 193, *Tijdschrift voor Belgisch handelsrecht* (TBH) 1948, p 208 and *Revue de la banque* 1948, p 282.

[33] Cf Cass fr 31 October 1955, *Bulletin civil* (Bull Civ), III, n 302; Witz (*supra* footnote 8), p 539. Contra: Charles Lyon-Caen and Louis Renault, *Traité du droit commercial*, Vol III (Paris: LGDJ, 3rd ed 1906), n 131.

[34] Cass fr 21 October 1955, Bull civ, III, p 254.

[35] Cf Ghestin and Desche (*supra* footnote 9), n 546. However, an (older) judgment of the Belgian *Cour de cassation/Hof van Cassatie* ruled in another way (Cass 3 January 1952, *Pasicrisie* 1952, I, p 225), but this judgment was severely cricitised by legal scholars (Jean Limpens, *La vente en droit belge* (Brussels: Bruylant 1960), n 1083; see Waelbroeck (*supra* footnote 27), p 24, n 10 and the references he cites).

[36] Cass fr 30 June 1925, Dalloz 1927, I, p 29.

way, in the presence of both parties or their representatives.[37] A unilateral individualisation would trigger the risk that the transferor fraudulently specifies the goods. In this manner, the individualisation would be a contractual operation, *eg* a real agreement.[38] However, legal scholars have, more recently, accepted the validity and effectiveness of unilateral individualisation.[39] It would, according to this opinion, be sufficient that individualisation is the expression of the irrevocable intention of the transferor to deliver specified goods in accordance with the agreement. From the moment at which the transferor cannot revoke the way in which he accomplished the individualisation in order to designate other goods as the object of the contract, individualisation must be deemed to have been accomplished. In this sense, individualisation would be a legal fact, not a legal act (such as a contract).[40] The fact that the transferee did not participate in that process is irrelevant if the transferor did not act in a fraudulent way.[41]

In conclusion, the transfer of generic goods requires a dualistic approach, as the immediate transfer of property rights is excluded. However, it is doubtful, on the basis of the described development, that individualisation can be considered as a separate (real) agreement.

24. The same line of reasoning applies to the contractual transfer of *future goods*. It is, in principle, valid to enter into an agreement transferring property rights in future goods. This emerges, in Belgian and French law, from art

---

[37] In France: cf Cass fr 11 August 1874, Dalloz 1876, I, p 476; Cass fr 31 December 1894, Dalloz 1895, I, p 409. For Belgian law: See the references in Georges van Hecke, 'Le transfert de propriété des choses de genre', *Journal des tribunaux* (Journ trib) 1947, p 49.

[38] François Gore, *Le transfert de la propriété dans les ventes de choses de genre* (Paris: Dalloz 1954), (175) p 176; Witz (*supra* footnote 8), p 540.

[39] In France: Gore (*supra* footnote 38), p 177; In Belgium: Limpens (*supra* footnote 35), n 1093-1103; Waelbroeck (*supra* footnote 27), p 24, n 10.

[40] However, Cloquet defends the contrary opinion: '*L'individualisation suppose non seulement l'identité du bien, mais en outre la volonté de le confier au futur failli comme corps certain à restituer*' (André Cloquet, *Faillite et banqueroute* (Brussels: Larcier, 3rd ed 1985), p 489, n 1648).

[41] In French law: Gore (*supra* footnote 38), p 177; Ghestin and Desche (*supra* footnote 9), n 546; Witz (*supra* footnote 8), p 541. In Belgian law: De Page and Meinertzhagen-Limpens (*supra* footnote 23), n 21B; Waelbroeck (*supra* footnote 27), p 24, n 10.

1130 CC[42] and, in English law, from Section 5 of the Sale of Goods Act 1979:[43]

With regard to future goods, the principle of the transfer *solo consensu* cannot, however, have any effect. The transfer of future goods only operates after the coming into existence of the transferred good.[44] This also means that, if the transferor goes bankrupt after the transfer agreement but before the coming into existence of the future good, the transfer will be frustrated by the insolvency situation. It remains, however, a debated question whether the creation of the future good is sufficient, or whether delivery of the good, which has come into existence, is necessary. The French Supreme Court takes a midway position: it situates the transfer of property at the moment the good, which has come into existence, was capable of being delivered by the seller.[45]

25. The exceptions, with regard to the nature of the transferred goods, do not apply in the same way in common law. The starting point is the same: where there is a contract for the sale of unascertained goods, no property in the goods is transferred to the buyer unless and until the goods are ascertained (Section 16 Sale of Goods Act). As this rule was considered to be too severe for sales *ex* bulk, it has been amended in 1995. The current sections 20A and 20B give to buyers, under certain conditions, a proprietary interest in the goods that form part of a bulk.[46] This section applies to a contract for the sale of a specified quantity of unascertained goods if (a) the goods, or some of them, form part of a bulk which is identified either in the contract or by subsequent agreement between the parties; and (b) the buyer has paid the price for some or all of the goods which are the subject of the contract

---

[42] Free translation: 'Future goods may be the object of an obligation. One may not, however, renounce a succession which is not open, or make any stipulation with respect to such succession, even with the consent of him whose succession is concerned.'

[43] (1) The goods which form the subject of a contract of sale may be either existing goods, owned or possessed by the seller, or goods to be manufactured or acquired by him after the making of the contract of sale, in this Act called future goods. (2) There may be a contract for the sale of goods the acquisition of which by the seller depends on a contingency which may or may not happen. (3) Where by a contract of sale the seller purports to effect a present sale of future goods, the contract operates as an agreement to sell the goods.

[44] Ghestin and Desche (*supra* footnote 9), n 550; Gore (*supra* footnote 38), n 4; Jacques Hansenne, *Les biens*, Vol I (Liège: Éd Collection Scientifique de la Faculté de Droit de Liège 1996), n 210.

[45] Cass fr 1 August 1950, Bull civ, I, n 184, Sirey 1950, I, p 100.

[46] See on this amendment: Guest (*supra* footnote 20), pp 233-235; Van Vliet (*supra* footnote 15), pp 93-105.

and which form part of the bulk. If those conditions are met, the buyer becomes co-owner of the bulk. He will become individual owner after the appropriation of the goods.

The regime of the sales *ex* bulk differs from the civil law approach and illustrates the more liberal approach of common law towards the specificity principle in property law. It entails that common law should be precluded from the exception to consensualism with regard to the nature of the object. However, the Sale of Goods Act 1979 takes the following into account: where a buyer has paid the price for only some of the goods due to him out of a bulk, any delivery to the buyer out of the bulk shall, for the purposes of this section, be ascribed in the first place to the goods in respect of which payment has been made (Section 20A (5)).

(c) Exceptions relating to the nature of the agreement

26. In exceptional cases, the nature of the agreement requires dispossession in order to be able to transfer property rights. A prominent example in civil law consensual systems is the gift from hand to hand (*don manuel/handgift*). Normally, art 931 French/Belgian Civil Code requires that a gift must be effected by notarial deed. However, case law has accepted for decades that a gift of corporeal movables can be effected by the mere handing over of the good. It is a *consuetudo contra legem*, which is justified in the following way: At first, delivery serves to make the disposer aware of the seriousness of his act. It replaces the formal requirements that have to be fulfilled for the validity of other types of gifts. Whoever hands over a good is more strongly confronted with the consequences of his act than the one who promises to make a gift in the future. Secondly, it serves to clarify to society who the present owner of the good is. This second justification, however, could apply to all agreements transferring property rights, not only to gifts.

Delivery implies an immediate and irrevocable loss of the possession of and control over the object of the gift by the disposer and an immediate acquisition of the exclusive possession of and control over it by the beneficiary. If the disposer retains, in some way, the right to remain in or right to recover possession of the object of the gift, there is no delivery and no gift from hand to hand.

(d) Exceptions relating to the nature of the parties involved?

27. It is debated whether the principle of consensual transfer is also subject to an exception relating to the nature of the parties involved. The debate is mainly dealing with the transfer in *commercial* sales. Especially in legal science, the opinion that, in commercial sales, the transfer of property and risk takes place at the moment of delivery is increasingly advocated.[47] In French law, the legislator confirmed, during the parliamentary works of the Commercial Code, that 'sales and purchase agreements have at their object movable assets which are acquired through delivery'.[48] However, he meanwhile stated that, in this respect, he followed the view of the draftsmen of the Civil Code, as the text of the Civil Code (art 1138) does not seem to take into account delivery.[49] Both statements seem to be contradicting.

Most French scholars adopt the view that the statement made during the parliamentary works of the Commercial Code was merely intended to deal with generic goods, and that it did not apply this principle to other commercial sales agreements.[50] However, there is a tendency in French law according to which the agreement of the parties to postpone the transfer is accepted readily and implicitly to the extent that parties to the sale are merchants.[51] Most of the Belgian scholars have adopted the view that the transfer of property in a commercial sale is – by operation of law – subject to delivery[52], but case law remains reluctant to accept such exception. For agreements with regard to generic goods, this would mean that the individualisation of the sold goods would not be sufficient to pass ownership in a commercial sale, and delivery would be an additional requirement.

Statute in consensual legal systems themselves reinforce this development in according the seller (without retention of title) the legal possibility to vindicate the sold assets until the moment they have entered into the possession of the purchaser if the latter has been declared bankrupt (Art L 624-13, para 1 French *Code de commerce*, cf *infra* n 57).

28. This rule is based on trade customs and the common intention of the parties.[53] Case law remains more reserved.[54] The rule is, in any case, one of

---

[47] De Page and Meinertzhagen-Limpens (*supra* footnote 23), n 23, 1, p 48 and n 27 A, p 56; Jean van Ryn and Jacques Heenen, *Principes de droit commercial*, Vol III (Brussels: Bruylant,1981), n 674, pp 521-523.

[48] Jean Guillaume Locré, *Législation de la France*, Vol XVII (Paris: Treuttel & Würtz 1829-1830), p 43: 'Les achats et ventes ont pour objet des valeurs mobilières dont la propriété s'acquiert par la tradition.'

[49] Locré (*supra* footnote 48), pp 43-44.

[50] Lyon-Caen and Renault (*supra* footnote 33), p 87, n 97.

[51] Chazal and Vicente (*supra* footnote 10), p 505, n 53. See François Gore, 'Le moment de transfert de propriété dans les ventes à livrer', Rev Trim dr civ 1947, p 168, n 18.

[52] Van Ryn and Heenen (*supra* footnote 47), n 674; see also De Page and Meinertzhagen-Limpens (*supra* footnote 23), n 21B; Louis Fredericq, *Traité de droit commercial belge*, Vol III (Gand: Fecheyr, 2nd edition, 1968), n 1422.

[53] De Page and Meinertzhagen-Limpens (*supra* footnote 23), n 27 A, p.56.

supplementary law, which implies that parties can agree that transfer of property takes place at another moment.

3. Legal practice in consensual systems: Is the consensus a fictitious ground for transfer?

29. It emerged from the preceding section that a large number of exceptions tend to weaken the scope of the immediate transfer of property rights. Legal practice even strengthens this development. In practice, the seller of a good wants a safeguard for the payment of the purchase price. It has, hence, become legal practice in some domains of trade to contractually postpone the moment of transfer, until the moment the seller has obtained economic certainty that he will receive payment.[55] Ownership is retained by the seller as a security device.

The role of ownership as security device is becoming increasingly important in consensual systems. In the beginning of the 20th century, French-inspired legal systems were hostile towards security ownership, because it creates a security device without any publicity requirements. Therefore, old case law declared that a retention of title agreement was valid between parties, but ineffective as a security device.[56] Nowadays, the validity and effectiveness of a retention of title agreement is recognised in all European

---

[54] See Cass 24 April 1987, *Pasicrisie* 1987, Vol I, 994, n 498, *Rechtskundig Weekblad* (RW) 1987-88, p 806, note Francine Wachsstock that accepts that ownership had already been transferred before delivery.

[55] See the determining arguments of van Ryn and Heenen (*supra* footnote 47), n 674; see also De Page and Meinertzhagen-Limpens (*supra* footnote 23), n 21B.

[56] For French law: see Cass Fr.28 March and 22 October 1934, Dalloz 1934, Vol I, p 151, note Pierre Vendamme and Sirey 1935, I, p 337, note Paul Esmein: 'Attendu que les choses mobilières vendues à un commerçant tombé en faillite par la suite, ne peuvent, quand elles ont été effectivement livrées à l'acheteur et sont devenues ainsi un élément de sa solvabilité apparente, être revendiquées par le vendeur à l'encontre de la masse des créanciers, ni par la voie de l'action résolutoire, ni sur le fondement d'une clause du contrat qui aurait pu suspendre le transfert de propriété sur la tête dudit acheteur jusqu'à paiement complet du prix.' For Belgian law: see Cass 9 February 1933, *Pasicrisie* 1933, I, p 103: 'Les parties ne peuvent, par la clause de réserve de propriété, rétablir le droit de propriété (...). Lorsque le vendeur se trouve en concours avec les créanciers de l'acheteur et que la chose vendue est en possession de celui-ci, le vendeur d'objets mobiliers non payés n'est donc jamais fondé, pour revendiquer en dehors du cas prévu par la loi, à se prévaloir de la clause de réserve de propriété.'

legal systems. This is also the case for the consensual systems of transfer.[57] French law introduced retention of title in the Act of 12 May 1980,[58] Belgian law in art 101 of the Bankruptcy Act of 8 August 1997. Whereas the provisions were originally inserted into the Bankruptcy Codes, French law has recently sealed retention of title in civil law: art 2367 CC, inserted in the Decree of 23 March 2006 with regard to the reform of the law regulating securities, provides that 'the ownership of a good may be retained as security by virtue of a retention of title clause, which postpones the proprietary effect of a contract until payment in full of the obligation which compensates for it.'

Ownership is thereby often used as security instrument (finance leasing, retention of title, *etc*).[59]

30. In legal practice, a retention of title clause is most frequently inserted in commercial sales agreements. In agreements transferring property rights, asset-based financing prevails, meaning that the payment of the purchase price is often secured by maintaining a property right in the sold good. The seller can retain a real security right, but he can also retain ownership. The retention of ownership gives him the strongest security he can get through asset-based financing, both on the level of the powers he can exercise over the good as well as on the level of the exercise of his security right. Ownership is, in other words, used as the queen of security rights.[60] This has as result that ownership, in legal practice, is most frequently not transferred immediately, but the transfer only takes place upon payment of the purchase price.[61]

This analysis demonstrates that the gap between legal theory and legal practice is growing. In other words, legal practice further diminishes the starting point of 'consensual' systems or, to put it in a positive way, dimin-

---

[57] For a general overview: Eva-Maria Kieninger (ed), *Security rights in movable property in European Private Law* (Cambridge: Cambridge University Press 2004).

[58] See Françoise Perochon, *La réserve de propriété dans la vente des meubles corporels* (Paris: Litec 1988), p 332.

[59] Cf Chazal and Vicente (*supra* footnote 10), p 479, n 5. For an excellent overview: Pierre Crocq, *Propriété et garantie* (Paris: LGDJ 1995).

[60] This expression is derived from Jean Stoufflet, 'L'usage de la propriété à des fins de garantie', in: André Bruyneel and Anne M Stranart (ed), *Les sûretés* (Brussels: Feduci 1983), (319) p 320, n 2.

[61] In the same sense: Blanluet (*supra* footnote 2), p 416, n 10; Pascale Bloch, 'L'obligation de transférer la propriété dans la vente', Rev trim dr civ 1988, 673, n 1: 'L'observation de la pratique contractuelle contemporaine révèle d'ailleurs le déclin du transfert de propriété immédiate.'; Chazal and Vicente (*supra* footnote 10), p 477, n 1; Witz (*supra* footnote 8), p 538.

ishes the gap between the unitarian approach of 'consensual systems' and the dualistic approach taken by delivery systems.[62]

4. Critical analysis of 'consensual' transfer systems

31. At first glance, consensual systems have the advantage of simplicity. However, a further analysis undermines this argument. The consensual system was developed at the beginning of the 19th century and corresponded to party autonomy, being emphasized after the French Revolution, and to commercial practice, which contractually determined the transfer at the moment of the consensus. However, the development of commercial trade has resulted in other valuable interests, *eg* the security of trade and protection of third parties. Therefore, the civil law legislator and case law in these systems has been obliged to introduce several exceptions to the principle of immediate transfer of ownership.

32. As a consequence, the immediate transfer of property rights does not have any absolute effects anymore. The position of the buyers, even in consensual systems of transfer, greatly improves after the goods have been delivered to him. Before delivery, the proprietary position of the buyer only has limited effects. We have dealt with the contractual possibilities of protecting the position of the seller (title retention: cf *supra*, n 30). But consensual systems have also developed legal remedies in order to protect the seller in case of the insolvency of the buyer, such as the unpaid seller's lien, the quasi-vincation and the stoppage *in transitu* (cf *infra*, n 57). These devices demonstrate that the seller is entitled to proprietary protection although property rights have already passed. In other words: they demonstrate that the legal systems are not able to adhere to the consensual system in an absolute way.

Analysing the foregoing developments, it can be concluded that the principle of immediate transfer in consensual systems is decreasing.[63] In the same way as delivery was losing importance at the end of the 18th century, it is gaining importance in legal practice and in legal theory at the beginning of the 21st century. The dematerialisation at the end of the 18th century is confronted with a rematerialisation at the beginning of the 21st century.[64] The pendulum is in motion again ...

---

[62] Bloch (*supra* footnote 61), p 675, n 5.
[63] Philippe Malaurie and Laurent Aynès, *Les biens* (Paris: Cujas 1990), n 402; Witz (*supra* footnote 8), p 538. With regard to immovables: Corinne Saint-Alary-Houin, 'Réflexions sur le transfert différé de la propriété immobilière', in: *Mélanges offerts à Pierre Raynaud* (Paris: Dalloz 1985), pp 734-735.
[64] Blanluet (*supra* footnote 2), p 411, n 3.

33. The number and scope of legal exceptions to the consensual nature and the instalment of a different legal practice is such that legal scholars dare to ask the question whether the general principle of immediate transfer of ownership can be maintained.[65]

This has resulted in severe criticism of the consensual system by legal scholars.[66] For instance, the Belgian leading 20th century scholar De Page has written in severe terms: '*On renoncera à l'effet translatif des contrat, qui n'est qu'un non-sens, un nid à difficultés, et que la plupart des législations contemporaines eurent la sagesse de ne pas emprunter au Code civil français.*'[67] The provisions of the French Civil Code have been severely criticised, as they have been described as superfluous,[68] vicious[69] and contradicting.[70] Moreover, it emerges from the drafting history of these texts that it is highly doubtful whether the draftsmen of the Civil Code have aimed to introduce, with regard to movables, the principle of the transfer of property *solo consensu*.[71] Comparative law has confirmed the scepticism of legal scholars as most of the European legal systems and modern civil codes adhere to the delivery approach.[72]

---

[65] Blanluet (*supra* footnote 2), p 411, n 4.

[66] For example in France: Chazal and Vicente (*supra* footnote 10), pp 477-506; Marcel Planiol and Georges Ripert, *Traité pratique de droit civil français*, Vol III (Paris: LGDJ, 2nd ed 1952), n 625.

[67] Henri De Page, *Traité élémentaire de droit civil belge*, Vol V (Brussels: Bruylant 1953), n 95.

[68] Planiol and Ripert (*supra* footnote 66), n 618.

[69] Victor Marcadé, *Explication théorique et pratique du Code Napoléon*, Vol III (Paris: Cotillon, 5th ed 1859), n 480.

[70] Chazal and Vicente (*supra* footnote 10), pp 481-487.

[71] Chazal and Vicente (*supra* footnote 10), p 500, n 42: 'Il est donc abusive d'y voir la consécration du principe du transfert solo consensus de la propriété des biens, y compris des meubles! A vrai dire, personne n'a jamais envisagé d'instaurer un tel principe dans le code: ou bien le système de la transcription a prévalu, et la question ne se pose même pas tant il est évident que la propriété est transférée erga omnes ou ne l'est pas; ou bien c'est le système initialement proposé par Portalis et la commission qui l'a emporté, et il faut en revenir à la solution de l'Ancien droit, sauf à ériger la clause de dessaisine-saisine en loi supplétive.'

[72] Philippe Malaurie and Laurent Aynès, *Cours de droit civil / Les contrats spéciaux: civils et commerciaux* (Paris: Cujas, 10th ed 1996), n 252.

D. Delivery ('tradition') systems of transfer

I. Basic principles

34. Other legal systems adhere to the delivery principle. As we have seen, these legal systems still apply the Roman law system to which the consensual system has made an exception. In delivery systems, property rights do not pass at the moment parties agree upon the transfer. The transfer requires *traditio*, eg transfer of possession of the transferred property right, or its object.[73] This delivery constitutes a separate agreement in order to transfer the property rights.[74] The obligatory agreement obliging the transferor to transfer property rights is thus distinguished from the real agreement which effects the transfer of property rights.[75] Both agreements are subject to different validity requirements: while the obligatory agreement is subject to the general validity requirements of legal acts (capacity, intention, lawful object and lawful consideration), the real agreement is, moreover, subject to the requirement that the transferor must have the power to dispose of the property rights which are the object of the real agreement.[76]

It is possible to make the connection between the characterisation as a delivery system on the one hand, and the characterisation as a causal/abstract system on the other hand.[77] All abstract systems of transfer are delivery systems (such as German law), as the *Abstraktionsprinzip* can not apply in a purely consensual system of transfer. The proprietary effects can not be 'abstract' from the obligatory effects if the same event (*consensus*) has triggered both the personal and proprietary effects. However, causal systems can be consensual or delivery systems. The fact that the consensus and the transfer of property rights do not coincide in time, does not mean that they

---

[73] In German language, it is called '*Übertragung*' or '*Veräußerung*'.

[74] *Motive zu dem Entwurfe eines bürgerlichen Gesetzbuches für das Deutsche Reich* (Amtliche Ausgabe), Vol III (Berlin: Guttentag 1888), pp. 333-334: 'Das franz. Recht, und die demselben folgenden Kodifikationen weichen von dem gemeinen Rechte und den Gesetzgebungen, welche dem gemeinen Rechte sich anschließen, darin ab, daß der einfache formlose Vertrag zu der Übertragung genügen soll, während das gemeine Recht das Traditionserfordernis aufstellt.'

[75] The real agreement is to be defined as an agreement between the parties about the passing of ownership. For a more extensive description: cf Stefan Habermeier, 'Das Trennungsdenken. Ein Beitrag zur europäischen Privatrechtstheorie', Archiv für die civilistische Praxis (AcP) 195 (1995), pp 283-294.

[76] For German law: Manfred Wolf, *Sachenrecht* (München: C H Beck, 23rd ed 2007), p 241, n 531.

[77] We refer, for the latter distinction, to the contribution of our dear colleague Steven Bartels at p 59 of this volume.

are independent from each other. Examples of causal delivery systems are Dutch and Swiss civil law.

35. Delivery systems thus make the distinction (*Trennung*) between the obligatory agreement, which gives rise to all personal rights and obligations, and the real agreement, which triggers the proprietary effects of the agreement. Hence, they adopt a dualistic approach, two legal acts are required in order to transfer ownership. The second act, the real agreement, is mostly implicit: it must be clear from the circumstances that the transferor and transferee had a common intention to transfer property rights.[78] The real agreement normally transfers property rights, except if the transferred goods have not yet been specified – or are not specifiable according to objective criteria – at the moment of the real agreement.[79] This latter exception is similar to the requirement of specificity which applies in consensual systems (cf *supra*, n 23-25).

36. A major debate has been going on in German law on the question whether the obligatory agreement and real agreement can be entered into simultaneously. Frequently, the distinction between the obligatory agreement and the real agreement does not have any factual consequences. In a simple case in which somebody sells the newspaper or a crate of water bottles, parties already agree in their initial agreement about the passing of ownership. This has been a ground for criticism of the dualistic approach.[80] Legal scholars, however, reply to this criticism by arguing that the coincidence of the obligatory agreement and the delivery does not permit them to be identified from a conceptual viewpoint.[81]

---

[78] Fritz Baur and Rolf Stürner, *Sachenrecht* (München: C H Beck, 17th ed 1999), p 570, n 7; Van Vliet (*supra* footnote 15), p 31.

[79] BGH 13 January 1992, *Neue Juristische Wochenschrift* (NJW) 1992, p 1161; Wolf (*supra* note 76), p 241, n 529.

[80] The observation that the German approach is too formalistic has, amongst others, been made by Otto von Gierke, *Der Entwurf eines bürgerlichen Gesetzbuchs und das deutsche Recht* (Leipzig: Duncker & Humblot 1889), p 336.

[81] In German law: Hans Christoph Grigoleit, 'Abstraktion und Willensmängel – Die Anfechtbarkeit des Verfügungsgeschäfts', *Archiv für die civilistische Praxis* (AcP) 1999, (379) p 380. In Dutch law: Willem Hendrik Maria Reehuis and Antonius Hendrikus Theodorus Heisterkamp, *Goederenrecht* (Pitlo-Serie) (Deventer: Kluwer, 12th ed 2006), n 112.

2. General overview of delivery in the national legal systems

37. *German* law is generally considered as the main legal system adhering to this system: The German Civil Code provides that 'in order to transfer ownership of a movable it is required that the owner should transfer possession to the acquirer and that both should agree on the passing of ownership' (§ 929, para 1 BGB). This is the so-called *Trennungsprinzip* of German law. It can be read in the *Motive* to the German BGB that the draftsmen of the BGB were of the opinion, contrary to the draftsmen of the French Civil Code, that the common (in the sense of general) law requires delivery in order to transfer property rights: '*Das franz. Recht, und die demselben folgenden Kodifikationen weichen von dem gemeinen Rechte und den Gesetzgebungen, welche dem gemeinen Rechte sich anschließen, darin ab, daß der einfache formlose Vertrag zu der Übertragung genügen soll, während das gemeine Recht das Traditionserfordernis aufstellt.*'[82] This separate agreement is the so-called real agreement.

Dutch law has been subject to a remarkable development, departing from the French (consensual) system and ending in a German-inspired system. Until 1992, the Dutch Civil Code was strongly inspired by the French *Code civil*, which resulted in the adoption of a consensually-orientated system under the regime of the old Civil Code (1838). The applicable rules, however, largely changed with the introduction of the new Civil Code in 1992. Art 3:84 Dutch Civil Code provides that the transfer of a good requires delivery on the basis of a valid legal ground for the transfer.

In *Austrian* law, the causal system also goes along with a delivery requirement. § 425 ABGB expresses that such delivery constitutes a separate agreement. According to this provision, 'mere agreement does not grant ownership. Ownership and other property rights can, except from the statutorily provided cases, only be acquired by tradition and taking possession.'[83] It is, however, disputed whether the real agreement is concluded upon delivery or when the parties agree on the underlying contract (which seems to be the prevailing view today).[84]

Swiss law has also developed a delivery requirement in order to transfer property rights: art 714 Swiss Civil Code expresses that 'the entering into possession is necessary in order to transfer movable ownership'.[85]

---

[82] Motive (*supra* footnote 74), pp 333-334.

[83] § 425 ABGB: 'Der bloße Titel gibt noch kein Eigenthum. Das Eigenthum und alle dingliche Rechte überhaupt können, außer den in dem Gesetze bestimmten Fällen, nur durch die rechtliche Übergabe und Übernahme erworben werden.'

[84] For an analysis: Thomas Klicka in Michael Schwimann (ed), *ABGB Praxiskommentar*, Vol II (Wien: LexisNexis, 3rd ed 2005), § 425 no 2.

[85] «La mise en possession est nécessaire pour le transfert de la propriété mobilière.»

Other legal systems which organise the transfer on the basis of a delivery system are Greek,[86] Spanish[87] and Scottish law.

3. Refinements to the delivery requirement

38. In the same way that consensual systems sometimes require delivery for some aspects of the transfer, delivery systems do not apply all effects of the delivery requirement in a persistent way. Most delivery systems recognise forms of fictitious delivery in many circumstances.[88] In other words, delivery is often effected without any physical change in the situation of the good. This is the expression of the so-called *traditio ficta*.[89] The *traditio ficta* is a mutual agreement to transfer possession to the acquirer without the asset being subject to any change in its physical condition.

39. Four forms of the fictitious transfer of possession are distinguished in delivery systems:

a. *Traditio brevi manu:* the detentor gets possession of the good over which he already has physical control.[90] For instance, the thief of a car gives his car into the custody of a friend, and subsequently sells the car to that same friend. Or: a leased car is sold to the lessee. The latter, who already had the physical control of the car, will become possessor by the mere sales agreement without any physical change in the situation being necessary. If the seller was the owner, the detentor will become the owner. If not, rules of third party protection will come into play.

b. *Constitutum possessorium:* this is the inverse of the *traditio brevi manu*. Someone is possessor, but he transfers the possession to a third party, reserving, however, the physical control over the good. This is often also denominated as 'constructive delivery'.[91] A frequent example for the purposes of

---

[86] Art 1034 Greek Civil Code is almost identical to § 949 BGB.

[87] Art 1473 Spanish Civil Code.

[88] Comp Ernst von Caemmerer, 'Rechtsvergleichung und Reform der Fahrnisübereignung', *Rabels Zeitschrift* (RabelsZ) 1938-39, p 696. Comp Ulrich Drobnig, 'Transfer of property', in: Arthur Hartkamp, Martijn Hesselink and Ewoud Hondius (ed), *Towards a European Civil Code* (Deventer: Kluwer Law International, 3rd ed 2004), 731-732.

[89] This is, in German and Austrian law, the so-called '*Besitzkonstitut*'.

[90] Baur and Stürner (*supra* footnote 78), p 759, n 20. § 929, para 2 recognises the *traditio brevi manu* in German law: 'Ist der Erwerber im Besitz der Sache, so genügt die Einigung über den Übergang des Eigentums.'

[91] This possibility is, in German law, sealed in § 930 BGB: 'Ist der Eigentümer im Besitz der Sache, so kann die Übergabe dadurch ersetzt werden, dass zwischen ihm und dem

estate planning is the following: A is possessor of a movable object, and makes a gift of this object in favour of a third party, reserving, however, the usufruct of this good. A was possessor, but becomes the mere detentor of the good, possession (and, if A was the owner, also ownership) has passed to the beneficiary.

c. The third exception is the so-called *traditio longa manu*: this is the fictitious delivery applying in case the goods are in the custody of a third person. For instance: The owner of a car (A) gives detention of the car to B, who is obliged to make restitution. During this detention, however, A passes possession of the car to C. C will acquire the property rights by the mere sales agreement, without any change in the physical control of the asset.

Formally, two different systems are in use:[92] In German law, the seller must assign the restitution claim against B to C. This follows from § 931 BGB, which provides that 'if a third party is in possession of a good, delivery can be replaced by the fact that the owner assigns to the acquirer the restitutionary claim on the good.'[93] According to the German *Bundesgerichtshof*, the claim, which is the object of the assignment, is the obligatory claim to restitution, arising out of the legal relationship between the transferor and the person who is in the physical control of the good. Dutch law takes a different approach: the transferor and acquirer must agree that the detention of B, which was effected for the account of A before the transfer, will be henceforth exercised for the account of the buyer (C).[94] Both solutions coincide, as the latter agreement would, in German law, be regarded as an implied assignment of the claim for restitution.[95] Indeed, the assignment of a claim is, according to German law, an agreement which can be entered into impliedly. Notification of the debtor is not a validity requirement. In German law, the assignment can impliedly coincide with the agreement.[96]

Erwerber ein Rechtsverhältnis vereinbart wird, vermöge dessen der Erwerber den mittelbaren Besitz erlangt.'

[92] See Drobnig (*supra* footnote 88), p 731.
[93] 'Ist ein Dritter im Besitz der Sache, so kann die Übergabe dadurch ersetzt werden, dass der Eigentümer dem Erwerber den Anspruch auf Herausgabe der Sache abtritt.'
[94] 'Voor de overdracht van het bezit is een tweezijdige verklaring zonder feitelijke handeling voldoende: [...] wanneer een derde voor de vervreemder de zaak hield, en haar na de overdracht voor de ontvanger houdt. In dit geval gaat het bezit niet over voordat de derde de overdracht heeft erkend, dan wel de vervreemder of de verkrijger de overdracht aan hem heeft medegedeeld.'
[95] Drobnig (*supra* footnote 88), p 732.
[96] Baur and Stürner (*supra* footnote 78), p 586, n 38.

d. Finally, the *traditio sine manu* can be effected if a contract to transfer property rights is entered into between two people living together. This form has, however, been generalised in some tradition systems.[97]

40. As has emerged from this enumeration, the delivery requirement has been eroded to a certain extent. However, it must be said that these concealed forms of transfer of possession (and ownership) are often incomplete. The protection awarded to the fictitious possessor is not as strong as the protection awarded to the 'physical' possessor. For instance, the purchaser, who has received possession through constructive delivery, will not be protected against the vindication of the actual owner of the good.[98] Nor will he be entitled to vindicate his goods against another acquirer to whom the same goods have been sold and delivered, subject to the condition that the latter was in good faith. The position of the transferee is fairly similar to the position he would have had in a consensual system: he is the owner, although his ownership will not have full effect in relation to third parties.[99]

4. Analysis of the delivery systems

41. The underlying idea of the approach is that – in the field of property law and transfer of property rights – the principle of publicity should prevail over the principle of party autonomy. Third parties should be made aware of the change in the proprietary status of a good because they can be subject to the effects of the transfer.[100] Hence, delivery is required in order to transfer property rights in movables. As property rights are effective against everyone, their transfer should be made visible for everyone.

The exceptions made to the delivery systems are less complicated and less infringing on the basic principles of the system than was the case for the exceptions to consensual systems. They tend to give a legal rather than physical content to the delivery requirement.

---

[97] Comp also Dutch law, art 3:95 Dutch Civil Code: 'Buiten de in de artikelen 89-94 geregelde gevallen en behoudens het in de artikelen 96 en 98 bepaalde, worden goederen geleverd door een daartoe bestemde akte.'

[98] In German law: § 933 BGB: 'Gehört eine nach § 930 veräußerte Sache nicht dem Veräußerer, so wird der Erwerber Eigentümer, wenn ihm die Sache von dem Veräußerer übergeben wird, es sei denn, dass er zu dieser Zeit nicht in gutem Glauben ist.' In French law: art 717 *Code Civil*: 'Lorsque celui qui aliène une chose la retient à un titre spécial, le transfert de la propriété n'est pas opposable aux tiers, s'il a eu pour but de les léser ou d'éluder les règles concernant le gage mobilier.'

[99] Comp Drobnig (*supra* footnote 88), p 732.

[100] Stefan Habermeier (*supra* footnote 75), p 284.

E. Arguments in favour of a functional approach

42. Two main systems of the transfer of movables can be recognised in European legal systems: the so-called consensual systems and the delivery systems. It emerges from the foregoing analysis that the category of delivery systems does not coincide with the Germanic legal family, while the consensual systems (if any) do not coincide with the Romanistic legal family. On the basis of a purely quantitative analysis, it should be concluded that more legal systems adhere to the delivery model than to the consensual model. Moreover, most modern civil codes have orientated towards a delivery requirement. The English Sale of Goods Act 1979 is a major exception to this development.

The necessity for this distinction between the obligatory level and the proprietary level is, in German law, often presented as a general principle underlying all European private law systems.[101] Even if this view is rather exaggerated, most legal scholars, who have investigated the issue of a harmonised transfer system, plead for the introduction of the delivery system.[102] We will, in the following analysis, plead for a functional, result-based approach, which gets rid of the distinctions between delivery and consensus.

43. It has emerged in the foregoing analysis that the consensual ('unitarian') approach has been developed as an exception to the delivery ('dualistic') approach, inspired more by legal practice than by philosophical arguments.

However, the immediate transfer of property rights in consensual systems has itself been made subject, over decades, to numerous exceptions, and these exceptions are becoming more and more important. Moreover, the transfer of ownership does not mean that the transferor loses all proprietary protection and that the ownership of the transferee is effective against the whole world. The transferor continues, even after the transfer, to have some proprietary remedies (lien, right of retention), while the ownership of the transferee is only 'perfected' from the moment he has received possession. Moreover, the distance to the delivery systems is small from a conceptual point of view, as consensual systems have developed out of fictitious delivery systems.

---

[101] Stefan Habermeier (*supra* footnote 75), p 283: 'einer universal geltenden, namentlich die europäischen Privatrechtsordnungen prägenden Notwendigkeit, bei allen auf Übertragung von subjektiven Rechten gerichteten Transaktionen zwei unterschiedliche rechtliche Momente sowohl in den Rechtsfolgen als auch tatbestandlich auseindanderzuhalten: die dingliche und die obligatorische Seite eines jedenfalls wirtschaftlich, in vielen Fällen auch tätsachlich einheitlichen Vorgangs.'

[102] Recently: Drobnig (*supra* footnote 88), p 733.

The delivery systems, in their turn, give an interpretation to the delivery requirement which weakens the requirement of delivery in order to fulfil the agreement. In the end, there does not seem to be a great difference between a consensual system providing protection for third parties on the one hand, and delivery systems recognising fictitious tradition on the other hand. This results in the conclusion that the distinction between consensual systems and tradition systems is less substantial than the distinction between causal and abstract systems, and has faded over the decades.[103] In other words: in the same way as consensual systems have made the delivery requirement symbolic, delivery systems have accepted the symbolic nature of delivery requirements under certain circumstances.

44. These developments are caused by the fact that publicity (for movables: delivery) is becoming of increasing importance in consensual systems, and that this requirement is relativised in delivery systems. An exception to this analysis is to be made for the English Sale of Goods Act 1979, which takes the immediate transfer of property rights as a starting point. In that respect, the Sale of Goods Act is going into the opposite direction of the main stream development in European private law.

The opposite developments result in the fact that the distinction between both of the systems is getting narrower from two sides. In the so-called consensual systems, the 'real agreement' has, from a conceptual point of view, never been abolished by the legislator of 1804, but the legislator has implied this agreement in the consensus between the parties. On a more practical level, the exceptions to the immediate transfer of ownership are increasing (cf *supra*, n 17 *et seq*).

45. The consequence is that the distinction between consensual and delivery systems is more a matter of concept than of result. With regard to the personal rights and obligations of parties, it does not make any difference. With regard to the third party effects, the differences are largely mitigated by the exceptions which are made in both systems.

The functional approach of the drawing of the first dividing line between the transfer systems demonstrates that the glass is either half-full or half-empty. The legal systems take a starting point, but both legal exceptions and possibilities of contractual derogations enable parties to go all the way along the dividing line, so as to be able to arrive at the other side of the line. The consensual systems are subject to such a number of exceptions that the transfer of property rights and risk is, in legal practice, most frequently delayed until the moment of delivery.

---

[103] Von Caemmerer (*supra* footnote 88), p 683 *et seq*.

46. The conclusion must be that this so-called 'holy' dichotomy of the European legal systems is not only invincible from a political perspective, but moreover do not serve any specific purpose. A result-based, functional approach is the only manner in which progress can be made in the field of a harmonisation of the transfer rules. It is preferable, in this field, to analyse the importance that the distinction has with regard specific issues, and to make a choice between these specific issues, rather than to stick with holy principles. Some of the most important specific issues, for which the distinction can have any importance, are set out in the analysis below. This analysis will confirm the development which has emerged from the foregoing analysis, *eg* that the difference between consensual systems and delivery systems is much smaller than is often presented.

1. Transfer of risk

47. A first important issue is the question of who has to bear the risk of the loss or deterioration of the good due to *vis maior* if this loss or deterioration occurs after the sales agreement, but before the delivery has taken place. In commercial practice, the location of ownership is frequently of less importance than the location of the risk. In many legal systems, the transfer of risk goes – as a matter of principle – along with the transfer of property rights (*'res perit domino'*).

Taking a closer look, it becomes clear that the location of risk is not a proprietary issue, but an issue of obligation. It determines, indeed, the question whether a party is discharged from its obligation to deliver the goods or to pay the transfer price, but does not determine the proprietary status of the good. This also emerges from the analysis of the rules on the transfer of risk in the various legal systems.

48. In consensual systems, the buyer is obliged to comply with the obligation to pay the price from the moment he has become the owner of the good, even if the good has not yet been delivered. The rule *'res perit domino'* coincides, in these systems, with the rule *'res perit creditori'*.[104] The creditor of

---

[104] For French law: 'L'obligation de livrer la chose est parfaite par le seul consentement des parties contractantes. Elle rend le créancier propriétaire et met la chose à ses risques dès l'instant où elle a dû être livrée, encore que la tradition n'en ait point été faite, à moins que le débiteur ne soit en demeure de la livrer; auquel cas la chose reste aux risques de ce dernier.' (art 1138 CC). In English law: Section 20 (1) Sale of Goods Act 1979: 'Unless otherwise agreed, the goods remain at the seller's risk until the property in them is transferred to the buyer, but when the property in them is transferred to the buyer the goods are at the buyer's risk whether delivery has been made or not.'

the good which must be delivered, is meanwhile the owner of the good. However, this rule is subject to a number of exceptions. If the buyer has given notice to the seller with regard to his obligation to deliver, and the asset perishes or deteriorates afterwards, the seller will normally not be entitled to the sales price, except if he can prove that the good would also have perished or deteriorated if he had delivered it in accordance with his contractual obligations.[105] In other words: after giving notice, the risk returns to the transferor. The fact that the transferor bears the risk after he has been given notice of his obligation to deliver, proves that the issue of risk is dependent not upon the legal transfer but upon the factual delivery.[106] The transferor is, in this case, not in default to comply with his obligation to transfer the goods, but has not fulfilled his obligation to make factual delivery. In other words: a purely personal obligation has not been complied with. The question of who has the burden of accidental deterioration or loss is, in fact, an issue arising on the level of the law of obligations and not on the law of property.

The analysis that the transfer of risk does not necessarily have to coincide with the transfer of goods, is confirmed by the fact that parties are free to contractually disconnect the transfer of risk from the transfer of ownership.[107] Parties can thus stipulate that the risk passes at a different moment than ownership does. It is a debated question whether they can stipulate that the risk passes at a moment at which ownership cannot pass, for instance: can parties agree that risk passes before the individualisation of the generic goods, which are sold, has taken place? Some scholars have denied such a possibility, but the majority opinion tends to accept it.[108]

If the transfer has been delayed due to the nature of the goods, the risk will only pass at the moment the transfer is effected. In case of generic

---

[105] For French law: 'L'obligation de livrer la chose est parfaite par le seul consentement des parties contractantes. Elle rend le créancier propriétaire et met la chose à ses risques dès l'instant où elle a dû être livrée, encore que la tradition n'en ait point été faite, à moins que le débiteur ne soit en demeure de la livrer; auquel cas la chose reste aux risques de ce dernier.' (art 1138 CC). See also Waelbroeck (*supra* footnote 27), p 51, n 41. Comp the English Sale of Goods Act 1979: 'But where delivery has been delayed through the fault of either buyer or seller the goods are at the risk of the party at fault as regards any loss which might not have occurred but for such fault.' (section 20 (2)).

[106] Blanluet (*supra* footnote 2), p 425, n 19.

[107] The French Commercial Code expressly recognises this possibility, and legal scholars have accepted the existence of this possibility in other consensual systems (Waelbroeck (*supra* footnote 27), p 53, n 43).

[108] Jacques Heenen, 'Le transfert des risques et le transfert de la propriété dans les ventes de choses de genre', *Revue de droit internacional et de droit comparé* (RDIDC) 1954, p 116; Waelbroeck (*supra* footnote 27), p 53, n 43.

goods, the risk is, by operation of law, transferred at the moment of individualisation. A seller will normally never be discharged of his obligation to deliver amount X of generic goods, even if the goods which he had in mind have perished due to *vis maior*.[109] This is, however, not the proof that risk and ownership are interconnected, but is an application of the old Roman law rule '*genera non pereunt*'. This rule is expressly repeated in art 1585 of the Civil Code, which is located in the chapter on the contractual rights and obligations of parties to a sales agreement.[110] In case of a transfer of future goods, the transferee will bear the risk of the loss of the goods from the moment of their coming into existence.[111]

49. It follows from the foregoing that the disconnection between the transfer of the risk and the transfer of property is already part of the current transfer systems.[112] As the transfer of risk is to be ascertained at a different level to the transfer of property rights, this aspect is not essential in the debate on the transfer system. Or even stronger: whatever transfer system may be chosen, harmonisation will still require a separate debate on the 'obligation issue' of risk.

2. Third party effects

50. We can refer to the analysis *supra*, in which it has become clear that consensual systems do not transfer property rights by mere consent in relation to all third parties. Indeed, art 1141 French Civil Code provides for a protective rule if the same good has been transferred to two transferees in

---

[109] By contrast, this is the case for specific goods: art 1302 CC provides that 'where a good certain and determined which was the object of an obligation perishes, may no longer be the subject matter of legal transactions between private individuals, or is lost in such a way that its existence is absolutely unknown, the obligation is extinguished if the good has perished or has been lost without the fault of the debtor, and before he was under notice of default.
Even where the debtor is under notice of default, if he has not assumed fortuitous events, the obligation is extinguished in the case where the thing would also have perished in the hands of the creditor if it had been delivered to him'.

[110] 'Where goods are not sold in bulk but by weight, number or measure, a sale is not complete, in that the goods sold are at the risk of the seller until they have been weighed, counted or measured; but the buyer may claim either delivery or damages, if there is occasion, in case of non-performance of the undertaking'.

[111] Waelbroeck (*supra* footnote 27), p 51, n 41.

[112] François Laurent, *Principes de droit civil*, Vol XVI (Brussels: Bruylant-Cristophe & Cie 1893-1903), n 208-209; Waelbroeck (*supra* footnote 27), p 51, n 41.

good faith. Not the first transferee, but the first one to have received *bona fide* possession of the good, is protected in the conflict between two transferees. This rule is analogous to the rule applying in delivery systems, with the exception of the requirement of good faith.[113]

Art 1141 CC literally only applies to the competition between two persons to whom the same person has sold the same good. However, the rule is – as it will be seen below – being interpreted in a very extensive manner. For instance: this rule is, by an important group of Belgian legal scholars, applied to the situation in which the transferor becomes insolvent. The competing creditors of the insolvent transferor are then equated to the competing transferee. Both have crystallised ('realised') their rights, the creditors due to the insolvency situation which has come into existence, the transferee due to the sales agreement. Even individual creditors seizing the goods would be protected in the same manner (cf *infra*, n 52).

3. Risk of insolvency

(a) Insolvency of the transferor

51. In delivery systems, the transferee of the good is – as a matter of principle – not protected against the insolvency of the transferor. If X sells a good to Y, but becomes insolvent before he can transfer the property rights to Y (real agreement), the latter will not be protected. Indeed, he has lost, due to his insolvency, the power to dispose of the goods.[114] Hence, the asset still belongs to the insolvency estate, in such way that the transferee can not exercise property rights. Nor is he entitled to claim property rights on (the part of) the purchase price which he may already have paid. He is confined to a claim for damages as an unprotected insolvency creditor.

52. According to the general principles, the starting point in *consensual* systems of transfer should be the opposite, *eg* that the transferee is entitled to claim property rights in the insolvency proceeding, and is thus protected. As the goods have left the insolvency estate at the moment of the consent, the transferee would not be subject to any risk. He will be entitled to claim property rights in the goods and will not be subject to the rule of the equali-

---

[113] Von Caemmerer (*supra* footnote 88), pp 687-688.
[114] Stefan Habermeier (supra footnote 75), p 290.

ty of creditors (*paritas creditorum*). This is the normal application of the transfer *solo consensu*.[115]

According to a more modern opinion in Belgian case law, the transfer of possession does not only solve the priority conflict between competing transferees of the same good, but can also be applied as between the creditors of the transferor and the transferee if an insolvency proceeding is opened against the transferor or he is the object of seizure measures. If, for instance, A sells his car to B and becomes insolvent before delivery, it is argued that B would not be entitled to vindicate the car. The general creditors of the insolvent seller should, according to this opinion, be protected in the same way as a competing transferee. According to this view, the goods are part of the insolvency estate, on the basis of an analogous application of artt 1141 and 2279 CC: as the creditors had the legitimate expectation that the goods in possession of their debtor would belong to the insolvency estate, the purchaser would not be protected if he had already paid the purchase price.[116] This more recent view acknowledges that the general rule that ownership has passed immediately is applied again if the sale was entered into in the normal course of business. In other words: the transferee could claim proprietary restitution according to this more modern view if the sale occurs in the normal course of business of the transferor. This development demonstrates, to some extent, a direction towards a delivery system.[117]

However, this extension of possessory protection is not the leading opinion in French law. In French law, a more restricted view is taken. The buyer will be entitled to vindicate the goods even if the delivery has not been effected at the moment the seller is declared bankrupt.[118] From the viewpoint of legal practice, however, the difference between French and Belgian law is not that large. First of all, commercial sales agreements often have generic goods as object. Moreover, the buyer will, in practice, only be able to

---

[115] In Belgian law: Court of Appeal Ghent 1 September 1986, *Tijdschrift voor Gentse rechtspraak* (TGR) 1986, 63; De Page and Meinertzhagen-Limpens (*supra* footnote 23), n 676.

[116] Court of Appeal Brussels 7 June 1979, *Bulletin der Belastingen* (Bull Bel) 1981, p 1612; Eric Dirix, 'Lopende overeenkomsten en faillissement', RW 2003-04, p 208, n 20. *Revue pratique de droit belge* (Rev prat dr B), v *Saisie-Exécution*, n 803.

[117] However, it comes into conflict with another development, eg the fact that the theory of reputed ownership is in decline. A creditor can, in none of the countries, rely in a general way on the fact that the assets, which are found in the factual possession of their debtor, belong to the latter. The emphasis on possession and the broad interpretation of the legal provisions stressing the importance of possession, does not seem in line with the general development in patrimonial law.

[118] Lyon-Caen and Renault (*supra* footnote 33), n 96.

claim proprietary restitution of the goods if he has paid the full purchase price: as long as he has not paid the full price, the insolvency administrator will be entitled to exercise his right of retention on the goods. In other words: the protection offered to the unprotected creditors of the insolvency is not materially different, all the more because other remedies (paulian action) are open to the insolvency administrator if the purchase price were to be far below the value of the sold assets.

53. The foregoing analysis demonstrates that consensual and delivery systems adopt a different solution in case the transferor becomes insolvent. However, the analysis has meanwhile showed that the immediate transfer of ownership does not necessarily mean that the transferee is protected against the insolvency of the transferor. It is not a holy principle which can not be deviated from, as the developments in Belgian law have proved. Therefore, the protection against the insolvency of the transferor should not be predetermined by the nature of the transfer system. Here again, a result-based approach could prevail.

(b) Insolvency of the transferee

54. As long as the assets have not yet been delivered to the transferee, the nature of the transfer system will determine the proprietary position of the transferor.

55. In a *delivery* system, the property right will not have passed, so that the transferor is well-protected. He can claim ownership of the goods, so that he has absolute protection. The goods are not part of the insolvency estate.

56. In a *consensual* system, ownership has already been transferred, even if delivery has not been effected. According to a normal application of this starting point, the seller should not have any proprietary protection left. However, this starting point is substantially mitigated in most legal systems. The transferor is entitled, in most consensual legal systems, to exercise a right of retention on the goods as long as the delivery has not taken place, *eg* to withdraw the good as long as the insolvency administrator of the transferee has not been put into possession and has not paid the purchase price. This right of retention is, in civil law systems, an application of the more general Roman law principle '*exceptio non adimpleti contractu*'.[119] The Sale of Goods Act 1979 provides a specific rule on the seller's lien.[120]

---

[119] This right is the expression of a generally recognised principle but is, with regard to sales, expressly sealed in art 1612 Civil Code: 'The seller is not obliged to deliver the

57. But there is more. By way of an exceptional protective measure, the unpaid seller is, in consensual systems, entitled to vindicate – in other words: claim property rights – the goods after the sales agreement has been entered into:

- If the sale has been entered into without any delay with regard to the payment of the price, the seller can – in French and Belgian law – claim restitution of the sold goods as long as they are in the possession of the purchaser, subject to the condition that the restitutionary claim is brought within eight days after delivery and the goods are in the same condition as their condition at the moment of the sales agreement.[121] This remedy is called the 'quasi-revindication'. It is not a real 'vindication', as the seller is no longer the owner, but the concept of 'quasi-revindication' expresses, once more, an infringing exception to the general rule of consensualism.
- The seller can claim restitution of the goods of which he has been dispossessed as long as they have not been in the possession of the purchaser.[122]

---

goods if the buyer does not pay the price of it unless the seller has granted him time for the payment'. Art 1613 CC adds a complementary protection in case of the buyer's insolvency: 'Nor is he obliged to deliver, even if he has allowed time for the payment, where, since the sale, the buyer [is under a judicial arrangement] or insolvent, so that the seller is in imminent danger of losing the price; unless the buyer gives him security to pay at the time-limit'.

[120] Section 41: 'Subject to this Act, the unpaid seller of goods who is in possession of them is entitled to retain possession of them until payment or tender of the price in the following cases: (a) where the goods have been sold without any stipulation as to credit; (b) where the goods have been sold on credit but the term of credit has expired; (c) where the buyer becomes insolvent.' As the common law does not acknowledge the more general rule of *exceptio non adimpleti contractus*, it had to construct the right of retention as a specific type of security right.

[121] In French law, this is art 2332, 4 Civil Code: 'Si la vente a été faite sans terme, le vendeur peut même revendiquer ces effets tant qu'ils sont en la possession de l'acheteur, et en empêcher la revente, pourvu que la revendication soit faite dans la huitaine de la livraison et que les effets se trouvent dans le même état dans lequel cette livraison a été faite.' An analogous provision can be found in Belgian law: art 20, 5 Belgian Mortgage Act (16 December 1851, inserted into the Civil Code).

[122] L 624-13 French Commercial Code: 'Peuvent être revendiquées les marchandises expédiées au débiteur tant que la tradition n'en a point été effectuée dans ses magasins ou dans ceux du commissionnaire chargé de les vendre pour son compte. Néanmoins, la revendication n'est pas recevable si, avant leur arrivée, les marchandises ont été revendues sans fraude, sur factures ou titres de transport réguliers.' Art 104 Belgian Bankruptcy Act of 8 August 1997 is analogous: 'Peuvent aussi être revendiquées les marchandises expédiées au failli, tant que la tradition n'en a point été effectuée dans ses

The English Sale of Goods Act 1979 provides, in a similar way, that 'when the buyer of goods becomes insolvent the unpaid seller who has parted with the possession of the goods has the right of stopping them in transit, that is to say, he may resume possession of the goods as long as they are in course of transit, and may retain them until payment or tender of the price' (Section 44). These provisions entitle the seller to vindicate the goods if they are *in transitu*, eg during the physical transport from the seller to the buyer. This is the so-called 'stoppage *in transitu*'. This 'stoppage *in transitu*' contradicts the immediate transfer of property rights, and tends, in effect, more to a *Trennungsprinzip* than to the delivery systems.[123]

- Even if the quasi-vindication or stoppage *in transitu* can not be exercised anymore, the unpaid seller can – in most consensual legal systems – exercise a statutory lien. This grants to him a legal, non-consensual right to be paid in priority to other creditors out of the foreclosure price of the sold goods.[124]

58. These possibilities of vindicating the goods, as long as they have not yet been put into the possession of the buyer (or have been put into the possession of the buyer a short while ago; cf '*quasi-revindication*'), are a reminder about the delivery requirement in the old law. They demonstrate, once again, that consensual systems are not capable of applying the starting

---

magasins, ou dans ceux du commissionnaire chargé de les vendre pour le compte du failli. Néanmoins, la revendication n'est pas recevable si, avant leur arrivée, les marchandises ont été vendues sans fraude, sur connaissements, ou sur factures et lettres de voiture signées par l'expéditeur. Le revendiquant doit respecter les droits du créancier gagiste saisi par un connaissement ou une lettre de voiture.'

[123] Pierre Crocq, « Propriété-garantie. Réserve de propriété », Rev trim dr Civ. 1996, pp 677-678.

[124] Art 2332 of the French Code Civil provides: 'Debts which have priority over particular movables are: [...]

4° The price of unpaid movable goods, where they are still in the possession of the debtor, whether he has bought on credit or not;

Where the sale was not made on credit, the seller may even claim back those goods as long as they are in the possession of the buyer, and prevent a re-sale, provided the claim is made within eight days after the delivery, and the goods are in the same condition in which the delivery was made;

However, the seller's prior charge may only be enforced after that of the unpaid lessor of the house or of the farm, unless it is proved that the unpaid lessor knew that the furniture and other articles garnishing his house or his farm did not belong to the tenant;

No change is made in the statutes and customs of commerce relating to claims for recovery; [...].'

point in a severe manner. As a result, the protection of the unpaid seller in consensual and delivery systems does not differ as much as it could when emerging from a superficial analysis.

4. Moment to determine the power to dispose of the goods

59. A major distinction underlying the consensual and delivery system seems to be the moment at which the power to dispose must be ascertained. In both systems, a transferor can merely transfer the rights which he holds himself (*'nemo plus iuris potest transferre quam ipse habet'*). However, this control must be effected, in consensual systems, at the moment of the consensus, while the delivery system takes as the control point the moment of the delivery.

Taking a closer look, however, this distinction is not an essential characteristic of the transfer system, but is a consequence of it: it is not the underlying basis of the distinction between consensual and delivery systems, but is rather the effect of the choice between a consensual or a delivery system. If we get rid of the distinction, this difference will automatically disappear. It would be possible to determine the moment of the power to dispose of the transferor 'at random'.

F. Conclusion

60. The distinction between consensual and delivery systems has given rise to abundant studies of legal scholars. Legal theoreticians analysed the sharp contrast between the protection of party autonomy and third party protection, individual intention of the parties against collective rights of society, even liberal approach *versus* social approach. The distinction was canonised in philosophical and legal theoretical concepts.

This contribution aims at placing these differences into their actual dimension. It has been analysed that the differences are not as large as they appear at first glance. The concepts and systems risk blindfolding the rather minor nature of the real differences in the results between consensual and delivery systems. Moreover, the different systems do not differ that much from a legal-historical perspective: historically speaking, consensual systems are delivery systems in which the delivery requirement has been made more symbolic. Finally, there is the risk of blocking, from the very beginning, all attempts of harmonisation for political reasons.

It is necessary to use a functional approach in order to avoid the 'holy *war of the classical dogmas*'. For the comprehension of the actual object of the debate, the results of each approach must be investigated. On the basis of the difference in result, it must be ascertained whether harmonisation of the transfer systems is useful and feasible. This contribution aims at providing a first step forwards for that approach. It analyses that some aspects of the transfer system are common to all systems, *eg* the contractual freedom to determine the moment of transfer, third party effectiveness only from the moment of delivery, proprietary protection of the seller if the buyer becomes insolvent before delivery has been effected, *etc*. In further analyzing these aspects, it has become clear that the differences are far from being unbridgeable.

Private Autonomy in Property Law: Can the Parties 'Design' their Transfer?

Kai Kullerkupp

A. Introduction

As the title suggests, the goal of this paper is to explore, to what extent parties are really restricted in 'tailoring' their transfer as a result of imperative norms of property law. To tackle this goal, I will firstly look at the potential sources of limitations of party autonomy in property law and the somewhat awkward position of the freedom of contract in the law of property.

The starting point thus is: whether, to what extent and in what ways the transfer parties can modify the legal prerequisites and actual legal consequences of the transfer both *inter partes* and with effect to third persons. These are questions, which – by and large – can be answered within the framework of a concrete legal order.[1] Each legal system containing a regime for the transfer of ownership is usually characterised by some degree of flexibility. It is also common knowledge that no transfer system can subsist without exceptions for certain more specific cases or even just in the interest of functionality of the system that would otherwise be hazarded by very strict and rigid rules. Often, there are certain modifications to the main rule, provided for by the very legal order itself. One might ask whether such exceptions and 'detours' do not actually create a situation where the parties are, as a matter of fact, able to freely 'design' or modify the individual aspects of their transfer, relying on the options provided for by the legal order. To attempt to answer that question, I will, later on, propose a list of those aspects in which the parties might wish to specifically 'design' their transfer by choosing the conditions upon which ownership will pass.

---

[1] This paper mainly concentrates on the situation under Estonian law which mostly follows the German model in considerable detail.

B. Private autonomy and its peculiarities in property law

The importance of private autonomy as a cornerstone of private law can hardly be overestimated. It reflects the ability of individuals to 'design' their legal relations as they themselves see fit, within the framework set by the legal order. The most eminent tool to determine the contents and other details of legal relationships is undoubtedly the principle of freedom of contract.

When distinguishing between the law of obligations and property law (rights *in rem*), we refer to the division of subjective rights into absolute and relative rights. While absolute rights[2] involve an entitlement, valid and enforceable against every other person, relative rights only do so with respect to a certain person with whom the entitled person is linked through a concrete legal relationship. This distinction is best illustrated by the general principles of property law which largely underline the specific features of property rights as compared to obligations. These principles[3] are mainly concerned with the position of third persons in property law relationships. Whereas in contract law the parties may largely dispose over their contractual relations and 'customise' the contents and details thereof, a third person normally cannot be made subject to a contract and bound thereby without being a party to the contract. On the other hand, property law relations are characterised by creating legal consequences that are enforceable against all third persons, in addition to the parties to a property law relationship. One can, therefore, claim that freedom of contract generally exists in legal relations where the parties determine their own rights and obligations, leaving the legal position of third persons untouched. Insofar as the position of third persons is concerned, the freedom of contract must be restricted or even excluded.

Traditionally, the freedom of contract is understood to include the freedom of determination,[4] freedom of choice regarding the contract partner, freedom as regards the content of the contract, freedom of form, and the freedom to step out of the contractual relationship.[5] The same elements can be considered from the point of view of property law, including the transfer of movable ownership. For example, one may observe that the freedom of

---

[2] Including rights *in rem*, such as movable ownership.
[3] Including the *numerus clausus* of property rights, publicity, priority as well as the protection of legal (economic) exchange, especially the protection of good faith.
[4] Including decision-making on whether to undertake a transaction in the first place as well as choosing a contracting party.
[5] Such exoneration from contractual duties can be justified in specific situations such as a mutual agreement of the parties, or, where the other party has breached the contract so that the relationship has become detrimental for the retreating contract party.

determination is generally granted.⁶ However, questions regarding the freedom of content and freedom of form prove to be somewhat more complicated at a closer look. In property law, the freedom of content is largely restricted by the principles of *numerus clausus* and 'fixation of types', whereas modifications are only allowed within the boundaries set by law. As a rule, the main essence of rights *in rem* cannot be validly changed. Regarding the transfer of movable ownership, the issue boils down to whether and to what extent the parties can modify the legal consequences of ownership transfer – including the questions whether ownership can pass in 'stages' and whether certain 'elements' of ownership can be excluded from the transfer where the parties so agree. Regarding the freedom of form, a quick conclusion would be that it is granted as far as the transfer of movables is concerned. However, additional requirements such as delivery of possession (*traditio*) may, in effect, come close to form requirements for the transfer transaction.⁷

In addition to these traditional elements of the freedom of contract, the freedom of the parties to 'design' their transfer depends on which requirements a transfer must meet in order to bring about the desired legal consequence – the passing of ownership from the transferor to the transferee. Because of the rather specific colouring of the issues of freedom of contract in the context of ownership transfer, I find that, for the purposes of this paper, there is no real value in distinguishing between aspects of freedom of contract (mentioned above) and the so-called direct legal prerequisites of transfer. They are both an outflow of certain fundamental principles governing property law, limiting the relevance of private autonomy in property law. As a result, both equally affect the ability of the parties to 'tailor' their transfer.

A central postulate of a transfer by way of transaction is that the passing of ownership, as a concretely determined legal consequence, presumes the existence of a corresponding intention and expression thereof by both parties to the transfer. At the most general level, the norms governing the making and interpretation of declarations of intention should guarantee that nobody loses his ownership against his will or, *vice versa*, finds himself as the owner of an asset that previously belonged to someone else. Yet, as in the context of proprietary relations, the interests of general legal commerce and third persons have to be considered, above all with a view to securing clarity as to whom the goods belong to, legal orders have often imposed further requirements in addition to the intention to transfer ownership. There may

---

⁶ Restrictions might arise in cases of pre-emption rights and expropriation.
⁷ In fact, some systems actually do regard *traditio* as a form of a disposition (Titel and Modus): compare Helmut Koziol and Rudolf Welser, *Grundriss des bürgerlichen Rechts*, Vol I: *Allgemeiner Teil, Sachenrecht, Familienrecht* (Wien: Manz, 13th edition 2006), p 240.

be specific standards regarding the content, form or other characteristics of transfer transactions, as compared to other types of transactions. Moreover, transfer systems often require specific conduct (such as delivery of possession) in addition to an agreement of the parties regarding the transfer of ownership. Such additional requirements may limit the possibilities of determining the actual circumstances of ownership being transferred in a way the parties might desire.

The main issues, therefore, are: what requirements does a legal order impose on the expression of intention to transfer and acquire ownership, and secondly, to what extent is there a requirement to carry out additional acts, where the 'mere' intention of the parties, manifesting itself in an agreement, is not sufficient to transfer ownership. At this point, one might set up a thesis that the freedom to 'design' a transfer extends as far as the parties can effect the desired legal consequences merely by way of agreement (consent) – as opposed to the necessity of undertaking further acts requiring a certain factual conduct. In other words, the possibilities of the legal 'tailoring' of a transfer are dependent on whether a transfer is treated according to the rules and principles governing transactions (contracts) in its entirety, or whether parts of it (*eg* delivery) are evaluated according to some other criteria.

C. Elements of ownership transfer and potential limitations to 'design freedom' latent therein

When speaking about the requirements for the expression of intention to transfer and acquire ownership, the central focus shifts to the following question: are transactions containing a transfer/acquisition held to differ in any way from other transactions concluded in civil commerce, and what are their specific characteristics. One of the main issues is, in what form and with how much 'concreteness' the intention to transfer/acquire should be expressed. Depending on whether the intention to transfer/acquire ownership is deemed as manifest by concluding an 'underlying' contract that brings forth an obligation to transfer ownership, or whether the intention to transfer/acquire must be ascertained separately from the underlying obligation, the content of the intention expected from the parties is slightly different. Other questions concern the accepted modes or forms of expressing one's intention,[8] the minimum content of the intention being declared and the methods of interpretation of the declarations; furthermore – also whether the provisions governing the validity of transactions are applicable to the intention to transfer/acquire ownership; the possibility of inserting conditions, and making a transfer transaction by way of representation. The

---

[8] For example, implicit declarations of intention are recognised as well as explicit ones.

'transaction side' of the ownership transfer also includes the aspect of power to dispose which can generally be held as a prerequisite for a valid transfer.

It is hardly plausible that a requirement of a separate real agreement would actually limit the transfer options, since the systems making use of this concept do not impose too severe requirements on the content of the intention expressed to constitute this real agreement. Implicit conduct is usually considered sufficient, nor is there a requirement that the transfer parties should be aware that they are concluding a separate real agreement.

A typical 'additional' requirement to complement the agreement of the parties concerning the transfer of ownership is to be seen in the delivery rule. Other factual acts as prerequisites for ownership transfer are conceivable, as a retrospect at the formal transfer modes of movable ownership in Roman law[9] confirms. In some systems, registration might be required for certain types of movable assets. However, on a general scale, *traditio* remains the most commonplace act required to bring about the legal consequences of transfer.

Generally, possession is understood as the actual power over a thing. Accordingly, delivery of possession or *traditio* is seen as a factual act rather than a transaction. The main question here is, how consistently the requirement of performing such factual acts is implemented and whether the transfer parties are granted a possibility of abstaining from delivering the (direct) possession to the transferee, not jeopardising the passing of ownership. However, even where a transfer system looks upon the requirement of *traditio* as imperative, the various forms, *ie* equivalents of *traditio* may still, in effect, lead to the result that, at least in external appearance, *traditio* is rendered facultative – meaning that the parties still have a choice whether the movable will in fact be handed over to the transferee or not. Many legal orders recognise a number of delivery equivalents, not all of which entail an actual possibility for the acquirer of having a physical impact on the movable. Similarly, there are several ways of delivering possession that may not consist in handing over the movable to the transferee, but rather in the creation of a legal position that, under certain circumstances and by undertaking further acts, enables the transferee to obtain direct influence over the movable. A key concept here is indirect possession that can be created for the transferee on the basis of an agreement between the preceding possessor and the transferee as the new possessor.

Because the so-called 'main form' of *traditio* – the factual (direct) delivery – lacks the quality of a transaction, the possibilities of legal 'tailoring', offered by the various provisions governing the making of transactions,[10] are

---

[9] *Mancipatio* and *in iure cessio*.

[10] Such as: the making and interpretation of declarations of intention, the exercise by way of representation and the inserting of conditions.

generally inapplicable. However, insofar as the acquisition of a position of indirect possession is considered sufficient for the purposes of ownership transfer, the possibilities to 'design' the transfer are available thanks to the agreement-based nature of indirect possession.

D. Aspects of transfer parties might wish to modify to suit their interests

To the extent that the transfer of ownership is based on an agreement between the parties, qualitative requirements on the content of such agreement are generally rather minimal. A coincident wish of the parties that ownership in a specifically determined (or determinable) asset should be transferred from one certain person to another certain person, is expected. In most legal orders, there should further be a consensus that ownership is transferred with a view to performing a certain obligation. Insofar as the agreement on transfer is subject to the general rules applicable to transactions, it is rather difficult to think of aspects, which the parties might wish to devise differently from the statutory regime. Perhaps, the requirement of sufficient determination of the asset(s) being transferred might be perceived as a restriction, especially in case of generic goods.

The 'urge to design' is, therefore, more conceivable in respect of those aspects where additional acts (*traditio*) are required to effect the passing of ownership; and, to some extent, with regard to the legal consequences of transfer. The following aspects could be the points the transfer parties might desire to regulate according to their ideas:
- Determining the exact moment in time ownership passes;
- Determining the factual circumstances under which ownership passes;
- Preventing ownership from being passed to third persons;
- Simplification of transfers by involving third persons in the transfer process;
- Tailoring the legal consequences of transfer.

I. Determining the exact moment in time ownership passes

As a general rule, movable ownership will pass at the moment at which all legal requirements prescribed by the legal order are fulfilled. Various interests may bring about the wish of the transfer parties that the passing of ownership should take place at the moment determined by themselves: ranging from a transfer at the very moment parties have agreed upon the transferring of ownership of an item from transferor to transferee, to a postponed passing of ownership at a later moment in time.

In this context, the legal prerequisites of transfer and, in particular, their imperative or dispositive character, most poignantly come into the picture. However, a 'freedom to design the transfer' by party autonomy cannot be interpreted to mean that the parties should be entirely free to decide what conditions (if any) are to be fulfilled in order to bring about the desired legal consequence (passing of ownership). Such an approach would contradict the fundamental legal logic according to which legal consequences follow a certain set of facts having occurred. For example, since a transfer of ownership can take place with regard to an existing and individualised asset, the transfer parties cannot agree that ownership shall pass before the transferor has acquired full ownership of the asset[11] or the assets have been sufficiently individualised. Thus, there can be no freedom to waive any of the requirements prescribed by law, and the passing of ownership is inconceivable until all legal prerequisites have been fulfilled. A more suitable approach would be to look for flexibility within the transfer system, such as possibilities to replace a transfer prerequisite, normally required, by some alternative. This is an example found in the Draft Articles on the Transfer of Movable Property of the Study Group on a European Civil Code:[12] whereas delivery of possession is treated as the default rule, parties are allowed to agree upon a different time at which ownership should pass.

There are not many arguments against the postponement of the legal effects of a transfer, which is effected, above all, by inserting a suspensive or a resolutive condition. A resolutive condition may also cause ownership to 'fall back' to the transferor automatically upon occurrence of a certain circumstance (provided that other requirements – such as delivery – are met as well). A different matter would be the wish to consider ownership as having passed retroactively. A transfer of ownership with retroactive effect would amount to the same as a possibility to waive any of the conditions of transfer prescribed by law and, therefore, should not be tolerated.

2. Determining the factual circumstances under which ownership passes

This aspect is closely related to what was discussed above: although the parties clearly cannot be entitled to waive any of the legal prerequisites of transfer by agreement, there may be (and usually are) certain leeways in the very provisions requiring delivery. More specifically, the issue here can be

---

[11] Both where the transferor is the first to acquire the asset from a third person and where the asset has not yet been produced.
[12] Available at the website: http://www.sgecc.net, draft articles as of June 2005. Art 2:104 – 2:106.

rephrased as follows: what are the options of the parties to refrain from delivering (direct) possession to the transferee until an undefined moment following the actual transfer. The key is the definition of delivery within a given transfer system: what is to be understood as 'factual power' over an asset and to what extent is a physical proximity to the asset required.[13]

Rather typical are the various delivery equivalents accepted by legal systems, as a result of which there is no necessity to hand over direct possession of the asset to the transferee even where the system is delivery-based.[14] As a general rule, these delivery equivalents involve the creation of indirect possession for the transferee. Indirect possession is always a position based on the agreement of the parties rather than factual circumstances. Therefore, where the parties have the choice of replacing direct delivery by creating indirect possession for the transferee, the parties are not bound by requirements for a specific conduct that might contravene their immediate interests. In certain situations, possession is also recognised as such where there is no manifest physical proximity and actual power of a possessor (transferor) over the asset, yet the possessor (transferor) is in the position to exercise actual power. To deliver that type of possession, an agreement between the current possessor and the acquirer of possession is sufficient if the acquirer is in the position (able) to exercise actual control over the thing.[15]

The 'design freedom' is further influenced by any additional requirements laid upon agreements on which indirect possession can be based.[16] Indirect possession guarantees 'freedom of design' insofar as it is regarded, from the point of view of legal consequences, as equal to direct possession.[17]

---

[13] It is assumed here that, to transfer ownership, the transferor must himself be in a position to exercise actual control over the movable (either direct or indirect possession). The author is of the opinion that lost movables could generally be treated and transferred according to the rules on *longa manu traditio* by analogy.

[14] The perhaps most widespread examples are *brevi manu traditio*, *longa manu traditio*, *constitutum possessorium* and the assignment of a claim to recover the movable from a third person.

[15] The so-called *longa manu traditio*, based upon § 36 (2) PropLA under Estonian law, pursuant to which an agreement between the current possessor and the acquirer of possession is sufficient in order to gain possession if the acquirer is in the position (able) to exercise actual control over the thing.

[16] *Eg*, whether conclusive declarations of intention are considered sufficient and whether a certain type of legal relationship between the direct and indirect possessor is required.

[17] For example, pursuant to §§ 92-94 Property Law Act, indirect possession is equivalent to direct possession as a prerequisite for acquisition. Differences arise in case of good-faith acquisition which is only finalised after the acquirer in good faith obtains direct possession of the movable (§ 95 PropLA).

3. Preventing ownership from being passed to third persons

This aspect relates to the right to dispose, which is one of the component parts of the right of ownership.[18] Again, contractual restrictions on the right to dispose are, in effect, attempts to modify the legal prerequisites of an ownership transfer. Contractual stipulations restricting the freedom of an owner to dispose of an asset are, therefore, not to have an effect as against third persons. Although such contractual stipulations may, as such, be valid *inter partes*, they are not capable of bringing forth the intended legal consequence – to affect the property law situation by determining how and on what conditions ownership passes.[19]

One reason for contractually restricting the right of an owner to transfer ownership may be the wish to reserve, for the other contracting party, the possibility of obtaining the thing at a later time. This objective is similarly achieved by a right of pre-emption which, in many legal orders, is considered to be a specific stipulation of a sales contract not affecting the legal position of third persons.[20]

4. Simplification of the transfers by involving third persons

The involvement of third persons, such as representatives, intermediaries or 'interim' acquirers in the transfer process deserves a separate insight as it has connections both with the contractual and with the factual aspect of the transfer. The more specific issues, however, relate to the non-contractual elements of transfer – *ie* primarily the delivery of possession.

In the case of representatives, it must be kept in mind that acting through a representative is only possible where a transaction (as opposed to a factual act) is concerned.[21] Thus, a representative may conclude an agreement on

---

[18] § 68 (1) Property Law Act.

[19] In Estonian law, this principle is expressed in § 76 General Part of the Civil Code, pursuant to which an agreement, restricting the right of a person to dispose of an object, will not render the disposition void and only claims arising out of the violation of the obligation to refrain from disposing of the object can be filed against a transferor having transferred ownership in violation of a contractual restriction.

[20] Pursuant to Estonian law, a third-party effect is only attributable to rights of preemption concerning immovables and visible in the land register (§ 256 *et seq* Property Law Act), as well as certain pre-emption rights based directly on the law (§ 244 (6) Law of Obligations Act).

[21] This follows from § 115 of the General Part of the Civil Code, pursuant to which a transaction may be entered into through a representative, whereas a transaction entered into by a representative is valid with regard to the principal if the representative en-

the basis of which ownership is to pass to the principal, as well as a real agreement, yet the delivery to a representative will not as such qualify as delivery to the intended transferee. To help out, the same concepts as outlined under 2. above, may be applied. Above all, delivery equivalents may be used in the relationship between the representative and the principal, as a result of which the principal (who is also the intended transferee) would acquire indirect possession of the asset at the moment the representative takes direct possession. In this context, the construction of an 'anticipated *constitutum possessorium*' is known.[22]

The question on chain transfers where, after a number of subsequent sales agreements regarding the same object, the object is handed over directly from the transferor to the last transferee, is mainly concerned with the delivery requirement as well. Again, this is, above all, a matter of interpretation of what constitutes delivery. For example, the fact that the last transferee receives the movable on the instruction of the 'interim' acquirer, can be held sufficient so that ownership can be deemed to have passed to the 'interim' transferee for a logical second.

5. Tailoring the legal consequences of transfer

According to the understanding prevalent in continental Europe, ownership passes from transferor to the transferee as a whole, *ie* all elements of the right of ownership are transferred at once. Thus, the transferee becomes fully entitled *vis-à-vis* the asset at the very moment the entitlement of the transferor ends. There may be situations where the parties wish to modify such clear-cut allocation of legal positions arising from the right of ownership. They may prefer to have ownership pass in stages rather than 'as a bundle', or altogether exclude some of the legal consequences of the ownership transfer from taking effect with respect to the transferee. One example is the fiduciary transfer of ownership where, in addition to a regular ownership transfer, an agreement is concluded pursuant to which the transferee is to exercise his ownership in the interests of the transferor. The transfer parties

---

tered into the transaction on behalf of the principal and if the representative had the right of representation when entering into the transaction.

[22] According to this construction, the intention of the representative and the principal is interpreted to the effect that they have implicitly concluded an in-advance agreement as a result of which the principal acquires indirect possession of the movable as soon as the representative has taken over the direct possession thereof. Already at the this stage where the authorisation (mandate) is agreed upon, the principal and the representative assume that the representative is going to take possession of the movable in the interest of and for the principal.

may further be interested in excluding third persons from having access to the asset *eg* in the course of compulsory execution proceedings. These questions deal with the essence of ownership, in other words – the options of the parties to alter the scope of entitlements belonging to an owner. As and insofar these issues clearly influence the positions of third persons, no such freedom should be recognised.

E. Conclusions

Insofar as the transfer can be effected on the basis of the will/intent of the parties and, to the extent this will/intent is treated the same as transactions (contracts) in general, the parties enjoy an extensive freedom to 'design' their transfer.

Additional requirements, such as delivery of possession, are generally not covered by the rules concerning transactions. In this aspect, an expanded 'design freedom' is granted to the extent that indirect possession is recognised and equated with direct possession.

Restrictions might, above all, arise in what is considered to constitute the legal essence, or content, of the right of ownership. Such restrictions are justified by the protection of the position of third persons that might be affected by changes in the property law situation. Therefore, in those cases, the freedom to design a transfer is not called for.

An Abstract or a Causal System

*Steven Bartels**

A. Introduction

Although it might not be completely customary to do so, I would like to start this paper with some underlying assumptions and my conclusions. The central question in this paper is which system for the transfer of movables should be adopted in a possible future codification of property law in Europe. More specifically, the focus will be on the question whether an abstract or a causal system is to be preferred.[1]

To begin with, I must state that I am not an advocate of such a codification. There is no demand (let alone a necessity) for a European rule that imposes on all jurisdictions/countries a unified system for the transfer of movables. And what is even more important: a uniform rule in a codification, applicable everywhere, will not lead to uniformity. In addition, I think that in making a choice between a causal and an abstract system for the transfer, the law which is applicable to the transfer of immovables must be taken into account. In many countries, no distinction is made between movables and immovables as regards the basic requirements for a transfer. I am not advocating that it should always be the case that no distinction is to be drawn between movables and immovables when it comes to the transfer requirements, only that I would like to make such a distinction explicitly.

If any kind of codification took place, I would be in favour of a 'result-based' approach. With that I mean that it is not so important how the system – *in abstracto* – might be qualified, but that I prefer to highlight what in some important situations is the outcome of a possible conflict of interests. For example, can a seller who has sold under the influence of fraud successfully claim from the buyer the goods sold in the case of the bankruptcy of the latter? In answering this question, one should also pay attention to the circumstances under which fraud may be relied upon in such a case. Obviously, this approach will not provide a general solution, since not all situations can

---

* Professor of civil law at Utrecht University; Professor of civil law at Radboud University Nijmegen as of February 2008.
[1] At p 9 of this volume, Vincent Sagaert deals with the question whether a consensual or a delivery system should be adopted.

be anticipated or dealt with. However, it is the only way to strive for any kind of uniform or harmonised results. Only dogmatic uniformity, leading to different results in similar cases, is not worth striving for. Nevertheless, it will be useful to indicate what the starting point will be.

B. General description of the abstract and causal system

I presume that the basic characteristics of both systems have been frequently described and debated in the past[2] in many countries (at least in civil law systems). I will therefore confine myself to brief descriptions.

In an abstract system of transfer – such as in Germany, Greece, Scotland, South Africa and Estonia – the transferee remains the owner of the goods delivered to him even if the legal basis for the transfer – often an obligation to transfer ownership resulting from a contract – is not valid, either *ab initio*, or when the legal basis appears to become invalid subsequently, for example due to the avoidance of the contract. In such a situation, the transferor will have delivered the goods without being obliged to do so and normally he will only have a personal right to have the goods returned to him. Until the goods are retransferred, he will not become the owner of the goods; therefore, when the transferee becomes bankrupt he will not have a right *in rem* and he will have to be satisfied out of the insolvency estate, together with the other creditors of the transferee.

In a causal system, on the other hand, the invalidity of the obligation to transfer affects the validity of the transfer itself. In a consensual system, this result is almost self-evident.[3] Also, in a causal tradition system ownership reverts to the seller with retroactive effect at the moment the obligation ceases to exist. This is, for example, the case when a sales contract, being the legal basis for the delivery, appears to be void or is avoided.[4] Consequently, the seller is entitled to claim the goods when the buyer becomes bankrupt because the goods do not belong to the insolvency estate.

---

[2] See, for example, Ulrich Drobnig, 'Transfer of Property', in: *Towards a European Civil Code* (Nijmegen: Kluwer Law International, 3rd ed 2004), pp 736-740; Lars P W van Vliet, *Transfer of movables* (Nijmegen: Ars Aequi Libri 2000); Eva-Maria Kieninger (ed), *Security Rights in Movable Property in European Private Law* (Cambridge: Cambridge University Press 2004), see especially cases 1 and 2.

[3] Cf van Vliet (*supra* note 2), p 24.

[4] Termination on the ground of breach of contract does not revest ownership in the seller in the traditional systems of Austria, Spain and the Netherlands. In the Netherlands, this was different before the introduction of the present Civil Code (*Burgerlijk Wetboek*) in 1992. Up until 1992, termination did have retroactive effect, and therefore had immediate effect on the ownership of the buyer.

This can be highlighted by means of an example.[5] Let us assume that A sold and delivered a painting to B. A inherited the painting and knows nothing about art. B is an art collector. It turns out that it is quite a valuable painting. B paid approximately 1/10 of the actual value. A claims that B knew that the painting was far more valuable than the purchase price at the time he bought the painting. He claims that he entered into the contract under the influence of fraud or mistake. Let us assume that his claim is successful. The contract is avoided; in a causal system, the ownership of the painting returns to A with retroactive effect. From a juristic point of view, B has never become the owner. In an abstract system, the transfer of ownership remains valid.

The German legal system is the traditional example of an abstract system of transfer of ownership. The *Abstraktionsprinzip* was introduced in Germany by Savigny and is – as far as I am aware – not really contested in the literature at the moment.[6] As has been stated, the principle of abstraction means that the validity of the real agreement (transfer) is independent from the validity of the contract of sale or other obligation to transfer ownership. Due to this principle, the avoidance of the contract alone has no effect on the real agreement.[7] The main – or perhaps nowadays only – argument in favour of the abstract system is the protection of trade practices. The abstract system is praised because of the clarity and certainty it creates for third parties. When an object is delivered by A to B, B is the owner thereof. Whatever may have occurred in the relationship between A and B is irrelevant as far as third parties are concerned. This is very important for third parties, such as the creditors of the transferee and the successors of B, as they have acquired a right in the object (ownership or a limited real right) from B. The general idea is that abstraction from the underlying *causa traditionis* – the legal basis for the transfer – is necessary for the fair protection of third parties.

In a causal system, the requirement that a transfer needs a valid legal basis is based on the idea that the transferor should not be divested of ownership of his property when there is no good reason for doing so. And the transferee should not obtain property without a legal justification. The choice of a causal system is, to an important extent, inspired by the desire to protect the transferor against the transferee and third parties in bad faith. A conflict of

---

[5] The example is – expressly – comparable with Case 2 of the already mentioned Trento exercise on Security Rights in Movable Property.
[6] See for a very thorough and comparative study on this topic Astrid Stadler, *Gestaltungsfreiheit und Verkehrsschutz durch Abstraktion* (Tübingen: Mohr-Siebeck 1996), pp 800 *et seqq*.
[7] Eva-Maria Kieninger in her German report on case 1 in *idem* (*supra* note 2), pp 171-174; van Vliet (*supra* note 2), pp 32-34.

interests between the original owner and the third-party acquirer in good faith is, in principle, decided in favour of the former. Shortcomings in the relations between A and B have far-reaching effects for third parties (C). The disadvantage of the causal system is hereby identified: it offers less legal certainty than an abstract system, which is considered to be undesirable from a market-economy perspective.[8] On the other hand, in a purely abstract system the interests of the original owner are undermined even in favour of persons who do not deserve protection such as third parties in bad faith.

The preceding may be true for the most pure forms of abstract and causal systems, but, in practice, these systems have sharpened their provisions to meet everyday practices. That is what happened everywhere and the reality is that the practical consequences of both systems often do not differ as much as one would perhaps expect on the basis of these opposite starting points. Almost all countries with a causal system also have far-reaching provisions protecting third parties in good faith. Because of this, the result is often that a problem in the relationship between A and B has no legal effects for C. Also, abstract systems have been mitigated here and there, for example in Germany in the case of fraud or duress by the transferee. If a contract has been made under the influence of such a defect, the real agreement (the transfer) will, as a rule, be voidable on the same ground.[9]

This does not imply that it is of no relevance at all which system will be chosen. Especially with regard to the position of creditors the difference is prominent. In a causal system, the avoidance of the *causa traditionis* leads to the result that the transferor (A) always remains the owner (provided that the thing is identifiable), so that creditors of the transferee (B) cannot have recourse to the object in question. A can claim the thing back even when B has become bankrupt. In an abstract system, A is only one of the creditors of the insolvency estate. It is considered to be one of the disadvantages of the abstract system that the position of the transferor/seller is weak in a situation where goods are delivered without a valid legal basis.[10]

---

[8] The causal system is, of course, not only dangerous for third-party acquirers of movable property. When A sells his house to B, normally the purchase price is financed by means of a bank loan. The bank (C) will want to have a security right in the form of a mortgage on the house. In a causal system, the invalidity of the contract of sale invalidates the mortgage. Without protection, the bank has no security to fall back on for the purpose of the clearance of the debt.

[9] Cf van Vliet (*supra* note 2), pp 35-36.

[10] Stadler (*supra* note 6), p 447, correctly puts this in perspective by pointing out that the buyer who has paid in advance is also subject to a risk of insolvency if the seller becomes bankrupt. In a sense, the seller and the buyer in an abstract system run a comparable risk of bankruptcy.

Imagine that in a future not too far from now a European Civil Code is being drafted, including the rules on the transfer of movables; which of these two systems (or: starting points) should then prevail?[11] I have great difficulty in answering this question with conviction. First, because such a codification is not attractive as far as I am concerned. Second, because a choice between abstract and causal cannot be made without looking at the nuances that must be and will be included. It is, for example, unthinkable that a causal system without third-party protection will be opted for. So the real questions will be the following: if we prefer a causal system, how far-reaching should third-party protection be? Or, when an abstract system is preferred, what adjustments are to be made so that third parties in bad faith are not protected? Via these kinds of adjustments the (practical) results of both systems can be brought very close to each other. The choice between causal and abstract is therefore – in many respects - rather a choice of one starting point over the other instead of a matter of principle.

C. A closer analysis

The basic idea set out in the previous section is that the actual meaning of a choice of a certain system for transferring movables depends on many other provisions than just an article on the requirements for such a transfer. These 'other provisions' are therefore of great importance, not only from the perspective of desirability but also from the perspective of unification/harmonisation.

In this section, I will first examine the definition of 'legal basis for transfer' and the flexibility that might be included in that definition. Then I will analyse in which situations ownership might automatically revert to the transferor in a causal system. Also of importance is under which conditions nullity and avoidability may be relied upon or reliance may be placed on a provision protecting third parties acting in good faith. This brings us to the next point to be addressed: which techniques are available to adjust the causal system to the needs of practice as optimally as possible.

I will make it easy for myself by taking a Dutch example to clarify that one causal system can differ from the other just by using another definition of *'causa traditionis'*. In the Netherlands, it was for a long time the dominant idea that *causa* meant: the obligatory juristic fact that obliges property to be

---

[11] Drobnig has a (light) preference for the abstract system: 'Serious consideration should be given to adopting the idea of the validity of proprietary dispositions from defect of the underlying contractual relationship between transferor and transferee, unless the parties otherwise agree or a defect affects also the proprietary disposition.' See Drobnig (*supra* note 2), p 739.

transferred. This definition is also to be found in the comments on the Civil Code of 1992. At the end of the sixties and the beginning of the seventies a change occurred. Especially the later Procurator-General of the Dutch Supreme Court Arthur Hartkamp defended a more flexible approach. He suggested the following definition of 'legal basis for transfer': the legal relationship that justifies the transfer in social life on economic or other grounds. Nowadays, almost all books on property law use this definition. It is perhaps not immediately clear what the purport of the change of definition is. In almost all situations the difference is to be neglected from a practical point of view, since the justification of the transfer will practically always be formed by an obligation to transfer, like in the case of a contract of sale. There is nevertheless a fundamental difference. Under the 'old' definition a preceding *obligation* to transfer was indispensable. With the 'new' definition, the essential question is whether or not there is a *justification* for a specific transfer. It is not necessary to find an obligation to transfer. There are cases – although not many – in which an obligation to transfer is lacking but the law nevertheless acknowledges a transfer. Time and space unfortunately preclude me from delving into Dutch law in too much detail here. I merely want to emphasise that according to Hartkamp under the new approach, the automatic link between the validity of the obligation to transfer and the validity of the transfer itself is being abandoned. This implies that although a valid sales contract may exist – taking into account all the relevant circumstances of the case – this does not justify a (complete) transfer of ownership. The reverse is also conceivable: a void contract but nevertheless a legal relationship that justifies a transfer. The first possibility has twice been acknowledged by the Dutch Supreme Court (in 1970 and in 2000).[12] The second is perhaps to be found in article 6:211 paragraph 2 of the Dutch Civil Code (dealing with a very specific case of the *condictio indebiti*). I hasten to add two aspects. First, these exceptions to the normal scheme where the validity of the transfer depends completely on the validity of the obligation to transfer are rare. Second, although legal scholars almost unanimously use Hartkamp's definition of 'legal basis', the majority do not support the abandoning of the link between the validity of the obligation and the validity of the transfer. Article 6:211 CC, which declares a transfer valid even though the underlying contract is void (under very specific circumstances), is generally qualified as providing an exception to the causal system. The two mentioned decisions of the Supreme Court were critically received.

Also, apart from the filling in of the notion of 'legal basis for transfer', causal systems can differ substantially. It is, for example, of importance which grounds for avoidance are to be acknowledged, for which period of

---

[12] HR 6.3.1970, Nederlandse Jurisprudentie 1970, 433 (*Van Wessem/Traffic*); HR 17.11.2000, Nederlandse Jurisprudentie 2001, 580 (*Breezand/Veere*).

time a certain ground for avoidance may be relied upon and whether or not the parties can deviate from this contractually. The more often obligations can be avoided with retroactive effect and the easier it is to fulfil the requirements of the various grounds for avoidance, the more impact a choice for a causal system will have. Furthermore, it is important to look at the effects of a termination of a contract due to breach of contract. Does this automatically revest ownership in the seller? In some systems it does, in others it does not.[13] Dutch law, for example, was altered in 1992. It abolished the retroactive effect of termination and from that time onwards the termination of a contract on the ground of a breach has not been accorded real effect. Ownership remains with the transferee after the termination, and the transferee will have to retransfer the thing to the transferor. When he is not able to do so (for example, because he has transferred the thing to a third-party in the meantime) he will have to pay damages. In the case of the insolvency of the transferee, the transferor only has a personal claim against the insolvency estate; he cannot revindicate the thing. In many ways, this is a result that is comparable with the results of an abstract system.

In examining the attractiveness of a possible causal system of transfer for a future European Civil Code it is of great importance to pay attention to the various techniques available to adjust the causal system to the needs of practice and the elaboration of these techniques. Besides the already mentioned provisions protecting third parties in good faith and the restrictions with respect to relying upon a ground for avoidance, some systems give their courts the possibility of refusing to give effect to an avoidance, for example by removing the retroactive (and/or real) effect. Comparative studies show that there are considerable differences between the provisions granting protection to transferees in good faith in the various countries with a causal system of transfer.[14]

The above sets out that in a causal system there is a very strict interaction between the law of obligations and property law. The practical impact of choosing a causal system is, to a large extent, linked with contract law provisions, since the validity of a transfer in many cases directly depends on the validity of the contract that creates the obligation to transfer. It is obvious that a possible causal system must be accompanied by a strong system of third-party protection. With regard to the position of third-party acquirers there should be a fair balance between the interests of the original owner and those of third parties. It is not difficult to say this, but realising this in a

---

[13] See, for a comparative overview of choices made in countries of the EU, Kieninger (*supra* note 2), pp 227-229 and p 244.

[14] See, for example, Drobnig (*supra* note 2), pp 738-739 and Arthur Salomons in this volume.

way that is acceptable and comparable for all Member States is somewhat more difficult.

Comparable observations can be made when the abstract system is to be the dogmatic scheme for answering questions relating to the transfer of movables in a future European Civil Code. It is unthinkable to my mind that no alterations will be made to the purely abstract approach. And then the question immediately arises what alterations these should be.

D. The midway solution of Lars van Vliet: The *animus* theory

In the past, several authors have expressed their preference when it comes to the central question of this paper. I have already mentioned Drobnig, who declared himself to be a supporter of the abstract system. His final remarks in a comparative overview of transfer systems are:

> 'In the light of the preceding considerations it does not yet seem to be possible to submit a definitive proposal for a rule to be adopted by a future European Civil Code. In the light of the presently existing national provisions and rules, the present author has a preference for the solution sketched sub 1) [i.e. insulating the validity of proprietary dispositions from defects of the underlying contractual relationship between transferor and transferee, unless the parties otherwise agree or a defect also affects the proprietary disposition, add. SB] since it most effectively protects the first transferee and successive transferors and transferees.'[15]

Another author who has asked himself which system should prevail is Lars van Vliet. He is not enticed by the abstract theory:

> 'The principle of abstraction makes an artificial segregation between two legal acts which economically and in the mind of parties are part of one and the same transaction. (…) When a party in reality did not consent to the contract in question, he certainly did not want the transfer of ownership based on it.'[16]

However, he stresses that we are not forced to choose between the two extremes of causal and abstract. He suggests – without specifically declaring himself to be a supporter thereof – a midway solution, which he calls *the animus theory*:

> 'In such a theory all defects of will are treated equally. Avoidance of the contract for a defect of will nullifies the transfer as well. To use the German terminology, as

---

[15] Drobnig (*supra* note 2), p 739.
[16] van Vliet (*supra* note 2), p 205.

regards defects of will there should always be *Fehleridentität*, identity of defect. In the *animus* theory ownership passes only if there is a genuine will to make the transfer. A valid contract is not needed however. Where for example the contract is void for illegality ownership nonetheless passes to the acquirer because there is a true will to make the transfer.'[17]

Van Vliet realises that 'it is very unlikely that such a theory has ever been current', but states that it might be an acceptable compromise for future law to bridge the gap between causal and abstract systems. Thus, he puts forward yet another flavour of midway solutions between the extremes of causal and abstract systems. To my mind, this idea leans more towards the causal system than the abstract.

E. Conclusions

It is certainly not unimportant to choose dogmatic starting points when developing a 'European system of transfer of movables'. That will be helpful, perhaps even indispensable, in answering many concrete problems. On the other hand, when it comes to the realisation of harmonisation or even unification, such a dogmatic choice on its own will not lead to the desired result. Many nuances will have to be taken into account. With respect to the choice between the causal and the abstract system of transfer, there will always be a midway solution. One should not approach this topic as a choice between two extremes.

---

[17] van Vliet (*supra* note 2), p 205.

How Swedish Lawyers Think about 'Ownership' and 'Transfer of Ownership' – Are We Just Peculiar or Actually Ahead?

*Claes Martinson**

Internationalisation has increased the exchange of influences also in the area of private law. A phenomenon that has the potential of leading to such influences, or at least to some questioning of one's own ways, is the Swedish (Nordic) approach to 'ownership' and 'transfer of ownership'. It could be held that the Swedish approach is ahead since the Swedish (Nordic) lawyers have since long abandoned argumentation that we still seem to recognise in other legal traditions. However, it might well be that we are just peculiar, or just exaggerating the differences in our approach. This article is an attempt to explain the Swedish approach by showing how Swedish lawyers deal with some specific questions of law. The chosen problems are meant to be particularly illustrative for the differences between the Swedish (Nordic) and some other approaches. To conclude, the article ends up in eight requests that not only clarifies the Swedish lines of thinking, but also should be generally useful in legal argumentation concerning ownership.

A. To own or not to own? – That is not the question!

It can be a pedagogically challenging task to explain to non-Scandinavian lawyers how Swedish law deals with the Transfer of Ownership. The concept – 'Transfer of Ownership' – plays such a central role in many other traditions of legal thinking, that explaining the Swedish (Nordic)[1] tradition

---

* Claes Martinson is Jur Dr at the Dep of law, School of Business, Economics and Law, Göteborg University, www.law.gu.se. I would like to thank Jens Andreasson for his constant help as a research and discussion partner and also Dr Wolfgang Faber, Universität Salzburg, for his help with identifying suitable examples and discussions. I would also like to thank my colleague Professor Christina Ramberg for comments on a draft version, and Ernest Weiker, LL B, Universität Graz, for helpful comments on the English language.
[1] In my experience the approach is common to all Scandinavian or Nordic countries (Sweden, Finland, Denmark and Norway). Since I, in this article, have mainly had Swedish sources in my mind, I have chosen to just point out Sweden in my text. It should be noted that many lawyers from the other Nordic countries have influenced

is, in some cases, probably a bit like trying to explain how football can be played without a football field. Namely, the fact is that Swedish lawyers do not use the concept 'Transfer of ownership', and also that we might even use the concept 'ownership' differently to many other lawyers.[2]

One strategy of explanation could be to point out historical facts, and try to convince the audience that their tradition, at some time in history, also has been to cope without the transfer of ownership concept. Using the same simile as above, it would show that football was, once upon a time, not played in a field, but was rather a game that took place in the streets and on the squares of the villages and cities.[3] However, this would not provide a comprehensible or correct picture of the Swedish way of thinking either. Taking history into the picture would rather show that the Swedish thinking actually has, to some extent, been using a transfer of ownership concept. What has happened is that the Swedish lawyers have successively abandoned the concept. In fact, the last shakes in the emancipation procedure could be said to have ended as late as the 1970-ies.[4] It could also be added

---

Swedish thinking and thereby contributed to the Swedish part of what is a rather Nordic tradition.

[2] Rodhe stated, with reference to the different conflicts that may arise in the relationship between transferor and acquirer, their respective creditors and others, that: '*the prevailing opinion not only implies that each of the questions at hand are discussed separately, without connection to a certain time of transfer of ownership, but also that one refrains from using the traditional ownership terminology*'. (I am responsible for this translation and all other translations of sources in this article.) Knut Rodhe, *Handbok i sakrätt* (Stockholm: Norstedt & Söners 1986) at 175-6. See also Henrik Hessler, *Allmän sakrätt* (Stockholm: Norstedt & Söners 1973) at 17-19, 64-68. Torgny Håstad, *Sakrätt avseende lös egendom* (Stockholm: Norstedts Juridik, 6:th ed 1996) at 25. Compare Östen Undén, *Svensk sakrätt I* (Lund: Gleerup, 8:th ed 1973) at 57 (note the 1:st ed is from 1927). Axel Adlercreutz, *Finansieringsformers rättsliga reglering* (Lund: Studentlitteratur, 3:rd ed 2001) at 20-21.

[3] See any encyclopedia, or use www.wikipedia.org.

[4] In his standard work from 1973, Henrik Hessler describes the situation of the time and the dominating approach: '*One did earlier – and sometimes does so even today – ask the question: When is the ownership of ie a movable transferred from the seller to the buyer? And when one had decided that this should be at the conclusion of the contract, or at the delivery, it was argued that, since the ownership was transferred at the decided moment, it follows that the buyer could from this moment: demand performance, be given priority before the creditors, be given priority in cases of double sales, etc – There is, however, obviously nothing that in itself 'passes' from the seller to the buyer. What has to be done is to decide the moments for the different legal consequences to occur. If one finds that it is in accordance to the law that priority over the seller's creditors is achieved at the moment of delivery, you could express it as if the ownership in this aspect passes at this moment in time. But, such a statement is then obviously*

that today the concept still pops up sometimes, although usually just as an odd manner of speech concerning a certain aspect.[5]

I will leave the historical explanations and the descriptions of the legal system *etc*, and instead try to describe how the Swedish tradition works. The most direct approach is to try to answer the question: How do Swedish lawyers think? – If they do not use the transfer of ownership concept, what do they use instead? And how do they arrive at a solution at all?

One could say that this perspective is also a legal realist's approach – and that it makes some sense using a realist approach, since the Swedish tradition concerning 'ownership' has, for more than a hundred years, been influenced by the Scandinavian legal realist thinking. Since it is an important starting point for the legal realist that law is a social construct that does not exist in any other way than through the human mind, it is consistent to describe law as a generalisation of the thoughts and behaviour of the lawyer rather than as a description of a system.[6]

---

rather uninteresting.' See Hessler (n 2) at 18. From the same epoch you can also find that the concept 'transfer of ownership' was being used in the argumentation, even though it was used more relationally than conceptually, Gösta Walin, *Separationsrätt* (Stockholm: Norstedt & Söners 1975) at 20. See also section 5 below.

[5] Compare Torgny Håstad, *Den nya köprätten* (Uppsala: Iustus, 4th ed 1998) at 145 and the latest edition from 2003 where the remark is left out. There are, however, also examples of attempts to sharp argumentation, but those attempts are more or less immediately rooted out as the weed they are generally seen to be. As Jens Andreasson shows in his article from 2005 the concept very surprisingly popped up very late in the legislating process of the new Swedish Companies Act (2005:551). Andreassson makes the assumption that this was a result of the influence of the wording of the EC-directive. The wording was soon altered back to what had been suggested and considered by the different instances in the earlier part of the legislating process. Jens Andreasson 'Inlösen, äganderättsövergång och legal transplants', *Svensk Juristtidning* (SvJT) 2005 at 522.

[6] It should be noted that it is indeed a generalisation that I will make, and that there probably are some Swedish lawyers who would not at all agree with the descriptions I will give. It should also be noted that there are not so many Swedish lawyers (academics or other) that would call themselves legal realists or would agree with the opinion that it is important to analyse law from the starting point that law does not exist in itself. However, the functional approach to ownership is a common and strong tradition, although it might be that it is not anymore evident to everybody that this functionalistic tradition was substantiated by the first Scandinavian legal realists. – Concerning the Scandinavian Legal Realistic School see *eg* (in the English language) – Axel Hägerström, *Inquiries into the Nature of Law and Morals* (Stockholm: Almquist & Wiksell 1953); Vilhelm Lundstedt, *Law and Justice* (Uppsala/Stockholm: Almquist & Wiksell 1952); Alf Ross, *Towards a realistic jurisprudence: a criticism of the dualism in law* (Copenhagen: Munksgaard 1946); Karl Olivecrona, *Law as fact* (London: Stevens & Sons, 2nd ed 1971).

To give a description of how the Swedish lawyer thinks, I will use some examples that I think are particularly illustrative for different approaches. Some are examples where the first part of the analysis by a non-Scandinavian lawyer might be to decide who owns, and others are examples of where the concept of ownership can play a role in a non-Scandinavian system. There are also a few examples just as to give a broad picture and to indicate to what extent the differences in approaches might be of significance.

I do like to point out that the intention is to describe the Swedish approach as a ground for reflection. The aim is not to prove in what ways the Swedish approach is different compared to every other approach, that is another and much more extensive task. There are of course many variations in different legal traditions. Some approaches are closer to the Swedish than others and some lawyers might conclude they share the main starting point, and maybe more. I do, however, have good reason to believe that the Swedish approach in many cases is as different as I have depicted in this introduction.[7] In particular, I think that the differences between the Swedish approach and the various unitary approaches are evident. My intention is to try to explain to lawyers with such a tradition how a different approach such as the Swedish is used.

B. Go straight to the problem! Ownership is a detour

Mr Bond sells his used car to Mrs Copeland who pays but leaves the car with Mr Bond until she will get her son to fetch it two weeks later. Should Mr Bond be entitled to use the car until delivery?

To solve this problem in the Swedish lawyer's way of thinking you must not, and I repeat *must not*, at any stage, ask yourself who owns the car! What we need to decide is if the seller should be able to use the car. We do not even need to consider other actions, such as if the seller should be allowed to pawn the car for a week's credit, or if he should be entitled to rent it to someone or, for that sake, repaint it. Since we do not need answers to those other questions, the Swedish lawyer would instead ask a more direct and,

---

[7] I base this assumption *inter alia* on the exchange I have had with the ECC project (Study Group on a European Civil Code http://www.sgecc.net), and on my experiences as a teacher in international environments where the approach has met rather strong reactions from more than 20 different nationalities (one of these environments being the, all European, Salzburg Summer School). The contributions in this book 'Rules for the Transfer of Movables – A Candidate for European Harmonization or National Reforms?' are also a clear indicator.

regarding relevant aspects here, more finite question: – What are the interests of the parties in this particular type of situation?[8]

One such interest that the Swedish lawyer would come up with would then be the increase of risk of damage done to the car when it is used, as compared to when it is parked. Another interest is the wear and tear the car suffers during usage. A third, and contradictory interest, would be that it is inefficient that a car is parked when someone who has it in possession needs to use it *etc.*

Closely connected to the assumptions concerning interests would also be arguments and assumptions concerning the consequences of a decision in the one way or the other. The possibilities and the normalities would be considered. It could be argued: that the buyer can protect himself through a contract clause, that the buyer has some protection by the rule that the seller bears the risk until delivery, that it is normal that a car is insured and the buyer will, therefore, at least have some possibilities to get economic compensation, regardless of which party bears the risk and regardless of the seller's economic strength, *etc.* On the other hand, if the seller may use the car he might be more careless since his risk of suffering damage is lower. Even if he is obliged to deliver the car in a way that it is not considered to be faulty according to the sale of goods principles, it might be that the risk for small deviations is higher.

The arguments and considerations can be multiplied and are not limited to interests and consequences, even if those two are often emphasised in Swedish argumentation. One other aspect that would be taken into consideration in the particular case would be the fact that the wording of the Mrs Copeland problem implies, although not decisively, that the car was left at the seller's place because the buyer wanted her son to pick it up later. This could be used as an argument for interpreting what the parties agreed upon concerning usage. Compared to the situation where it is the seller who takes the initiative concerning the delivery date, it is easier to imply a term of non-usage if it is the buyer who wants the deferred delivery. For some lawyers such an analysis of implied terms would be the first part to start with.

What is important is, however, that the Swedish lawyer does not at all ask who owns the car. The concept is simply not used in an analysis like this.

---

[8] There are no provisions in Swedish law concerning the right to use problem and the question does not seem to be dealt with much. It is also an interesting observation that the matter is not discussed in connection with the Sale of goods act's provisions concerning yields. Although it could be held that the use of goods would be a kind of yield, the two questions are not treated as the same problem. This is in line with the Swedish approach, although it should be mentioned that it would not be considered very spectacular if the provisions concerning yields were put forward *as an argument* in respect of the question of the right to use.

This is true if we speak about the legislator, as well as if we speak about the academic lawyer, the advocate or the judge.

To have an argumentation or analysis like this we do of course have to assume that there are no particular normative arguments, such as an applicable statute, to this problem. Once norms have been established in one way or the other (through legislation, precedence, conduct or in the academic doctrinal writing), norms are of course used and normally given decisive weight. But, the important thing to bear in mind is that the concept of ownership will not occur at any level of legal reasoning concerning a problem like this.

There are several reasons for the Swedish lawyers not to use the concept of ownership. Some of them are historical and it is, as mentioned, a tradition that has developed throughout the 20:th century. The material reason that the example of Mrs Copeland aims to illustrate is, however, that a decision on ownership is simply not needed. It is seen as a detour. A decision on who owns is extra and unnecessary work. For the Swedish lawyer, a decision on ownership is of no importance for the actual problem. Whether Mr Bond or Mrs Copeland – whether the seller or the buyer, or both – call themselves the owner, simply does not matter.

The said does not mean that the concept of ownership is unimportant. Also in the Swedish approach, this concept does, of course, generally simplify comunication. There is, in the Swedish lawyer's mind, however no need to use the concept of ownership for this type of problem. If the problem with the seller's usage of a sold car was a common problem that often had to be referred to, it is actually more probable that a special concept would evolve, rather than the probability of the concept ownership being used. This is of course only an assumption, but I use it to illustrate to what extent the Swedish tradition avoids applying the solution to a problem found in one case to solve the problem that another case gives rise to.

An effect of the said characteristic is that the question whether the seller prevails concerning the right to use the car, is not in its own decisive for other questions, such as if he, the seller, can rent the car to another or pawn it for a weeks' credit. Those other questions have to be decided on their own merits, although some of the same arguments might be valid again. But, on the other hand, it should be noted that a solution of one problem does not exist independently from its surroundings. A normative solution of the 'right to use' problem might influence other solutions. It would, for example, be rather peculiar if the seller was not permitted the personal use, but allowed to rent it to someone else. One could say that the argumentation in these situations takes shortcuts. The main reason for having the same solution is, however, that the interests and arguments are more or less the same.

Having said this, there is an evident risk of misinterpreting the Swedish lawyer as more casuistic and less foreseeable than others. That is, however, not a good way of describing the differences. The amount of normative arguments does create a system. Other lawyers would recognise many of the solutions as well as the reasoning. What they will not find are just the unitary starting points that the Swedish lawyers see as detours, or worse.

C. Be open to deal with all problems, but only solve the ones which need to be solved!

> *The car dealer Mr Ball manages to buy a used car from Mr Allen by telling Mr Allen that the car was stolen from Mr Ball a year earlier. This is, however, a complete lie. The market value of the car is 15 000 Euros/Dollars, but Mr Ball convinces Mr Allen to sell it for 2 000 Euros/Dollars. – Mr Ball then sells the car to Mrs Collins who pays in advance. After receiving the money, Mr Ball has the idea of selling the car to Mrs Douglas who pays and now has the car in her garage. – Right before the delivery, but after the agreement between Mr Ball and Mrs Douglas, Mrs Douglas sells the car to Mr Elton, who is a collector and is delighted already by seeing a photo of the car. Who would (formally) be allowed to sue whom to get the car? – Does it matter if Mr Allen does not want to have anything at all to do with this sad story anymore?*

A Swedish lawyer would not have much trouble to answer this question. In the initial phase the answer namely needs no specific analysis concerning the material solutions or which one of the mentioned persons should win. The answer is more or less that anyone could sue anyone.

The Swedish lawyer would, in the mess of transactions and claims, see each relationship as a problem of its own. With such an approach we do not need to start with the question 'who owns', and we do not need to decide on all of the relationships. It is only the immediate relationship that has to be dealt with, and the immediate one is the problem that one of the parties wants to have decided, by suing another.

Since it is just the immediate relationships that have to be decided, it *would* matter if Mr Allen did not want to have anything to do with the car. It would matter in the way that he would not sue and that he would not care. Nor will the court have to deal with his relationships with the others.

If Mr Allen wanted to have his car back, we would only have to deal with the case he chooses. Mr Allen has, in this situation, some alternatives but he would probably be advised to sue Mrs Douglas. It is she who now has the car in her possession, and it is therefore only she that can give Mr Allen what he primarily wants – the car. We will decide that case with effect for these two parties and would not involve other relationships if the parties do not put them forward.

In the same way that it matters what Mr Allen wants, it would also matter what initiatives the other parties take. It might, for example, be that Mrs

Collins is interested in claiming priority over Mrs Douglas, because she acquired the car before Mrs Douglas did. The problem with priority to the car could therefore be tried not only in one, but in several different processes, depending on what actions the involved parties take.

It should be noted that each case concerning priority to the car, would only lead to a decision about the priority between the two parties at hand. One such decision will not affect the priority in a case between two other parties. To underline that this is just a priority limited to the relationship between two parties, the Swedish judge would by tradition use the term 'better right', rather than to award a party 'ownership'. The 'better right' terminology is used to make it easier to keep the course in the analysis. If a judge used the term 'ownership' it would however not matter. The judgment would still be limited to the question of priority between the two parties.

The Swedish lawyer's way of thinking about the right to sue is, in other words, not to decide the problem as one problem. It is not considered to be a question of ownership. Or to put it differently – it is considered that ownership is a relational matter. What the Swedish lawyer does is, therefore, to keep his mind open for all the different interests that all the parties might have. The Swedish lawyer is prepared to deal with each of the problems that the situation creates. He or she does not exclude anyone by defining the problems from a certain angle. The way to simplify this is to let the parties' initiatives decide what is necessary to solve the problem.

> The complexity of interests and also different norms that needs to be considered can be illustrated by a simple description of the position Mr Allen has in the example. As said, Mr Allen would probably be advised to sue Mrs Douglas. The case against Mrs Douglas would concern the Swedish principles of good faith acquisition. Mr Allen would try to present evidence that Mrs Douglas did not have enough reasons to be in good faith about Mr Ball's competence to sell the car. If Mr Allen wins, the judgment would state that he is given priority over Mrs Douglas concerning the car.
>
> Since there are few facts in the example, supporting that Mrs Douglas was in bad faith, Mr Allen would probably use a secondary claim. He would claim the right to obtain the car by paying Mrs Douglas whatever she paid for the car or, as a maximum, the market value. To protect herself from this claim, and also from the eventuality that she will be proven to be in bad faith, Mrs Douglas could put up the defence that Mr Ball actually had the competence to sell the car. That would be to argue that Mr Allen did not lose the car due to fraud. In principle, this line of defence and the question of Mr Ball defrauding Mr Allen could be decided in the case between Mr Allen and Mrs Douglas. It would not be necessary for Mr Allen to first sue Mr Ball and win against him before he can sue Mrs Douglas. However, if Mr Allen chooses to have the question of the fraud by Mr Ball tried only in the case against Mrs Douglas, the decision only concerns Mr Allen and Mrs Douglas. The possible cases between Mr Allen and Mr Ball are still open.

With this line of handling the rather complex situation, it might be that there will never have to be a case between Mr Allen and Mr Ball. There could be a variety of reasons for those parties not to sue each other, and in this way we do not have to deal with their possible claims.

It might, however, be that Mr Allen has good reasons for suing Mr Ball, and to choose to do it after he has won the car back from Mrs Douglas. Mr Allen would, for example, probably like to be compensated for his costs, either the only costs of the proceedings or also the costs of having to use his secondary right to buy the car back. It might also be that Mr Ball is of the opinion that he bought the car fair and square. If Mr Ball wins the case against Mr Allen after Mr Allen having won his case against Mrs Douglas, he, Mr Ball, can claim the car by referring to the valid contract. As the winner, Mr Ball might have the car and he might have to deliver the car to Mrs Douglas once again, if Mrs Douglas claims the car on the basis of her contract with Mr Ball.

If all of the named cases are sorted out in court, it could, in retrospect, be concluded that the crucial question was whether Mr Ball acquired the car by fraud. It could then be held that it would have been better if Mr Allen had been obliged to have his case against Mr Ball tried before he went on to sue Mrs Douglas. This might well be, but we did not know in advance what problems we would have to deal with. Mr Allen based his choice of strategy upon what he believed to be best, considering the evidence at hand, the parties' different circumstances, the costs and the possibilities for the different counterparts not to bother with the problem. It should be noted that there is also a possibility for Mr Allen, and also for the court, to decide that the different cases should be tried at the same time before the same judge.

To underline to what extent the relationships are kept apart it should be added that if Mr Allen chooses to sue Mr Ball first, and wins that case, the decision is not formally decisive when Mr Allen, as a second measure, sues Mrs Douglas. It might, although it is highly unlikely, be that the judge in the second case comes to the conclusion that Mr Ball did acquire the car rightfully. This could, for example, happen if there is new evidence that makes it clear that Mr Ball did not do anything wrong. The verdict between Mr Allen and Mr Ball would still be effective as between them, but the question is open in the case between Mr Allen and Mrs Douglas since the decision in one case is not formally decisive for the other.

Compared to other ways of dealing with the example it might seem that the Swedish approach is complicated. It might seem easier to use an ownership concept and to start with a preliminary decision of who owns. However, the Swedish way is actually rather practical as it is close to the basis of the problem: different parties want different things at different times and they should all have the possibility to argue their case independently. It is therefore not really complicated. Having said this, it should be mentioned that the problems we deal with here are not easy, irrespective of what approach that is used. You do probably need to be a property lawyer to have the more immediate understanding of how the relationships will be sorted.

The description of the Swedish lawyer's line of thinking is in itself an explanation of one the reasons behind how we deal with the question of who shall be able to sue. To 'be open to deal with all problems, but only solve the ones which need to be solved' is a positively loaded description. A reason for dealing with the example in the way we do is, in other words, that we find it efficient.

It should, however, be underlined that it is important that every party has a chance to argue the case from their position. To have a method that is open to consider and to weigh all different interests is seen as beneficial. A method where the concept of ownership would be used in an initial phase would be seen as highly unsuitable. Some Swedish lawyers would say that it is to begin at the wrong end, so as to begin with the conclusion rather than with the analysis. Others would emphasise that such a method would give unfounded, coincidental and unconscious precedence to some interests before others. A decision on ownership might limit the perspective, even if it were just used to obtain a preliminary decision to decide who shall be able to sue. The risk would be that the interests and considerations behind the solution of the problem seen from that limited perspective would be too decisive for other problems where the interests are rather different. This would, in the Swedish opinion, lead to solutions that would run a higher risk of being unfunctional and out of touch with reality.

This article does not have the aim of criticising the use of an ownership concept in other legal traditions. In order to underline why the Swedish lawyer thinks as he or she does, I will, however, point at a line of argumentation that illustrates the Swedish preferences. The Swedish lawyer does not think that the concept of ownership facilitates the determination of issues, such as in the example concerning the right of action. On the contrary, the Swedish belief is that if you start with the concept of ownership you would need a lot of exemptions to get a method that works and creates suitable solutions. You would also need more abstract considerations to identify the exceptions that have to be provided for. The ownership concept is therefore seen as a tool that is too general and, as such, a tool that often causes more damage than it is of use.

D. Form the questions functionally! Ownership is not a real concern

> *Askan AB sells a machine to BGI Big General Importers who pays the full price, 9000 Euros. BGI sells the machine to CISA for 10 000 Euros. CISA pays 60 % of their price upon signing the contract. The Machine shall be delivered directly from Askan to CISA. a) What happens if BGI goes bankrupt*

before delivery? b) Does it matter if BGI entered into the contract with CISA before BGI bought the machine?

The Swedish lawyer would, in this example, see a question of priority in bankruptcy. Shall CISA get the machine if they pay the remaining 40 % or shall they be treated as a creditor without priority?

This question is not solved directly in the Swedish regulations. The main normative argument to use would be the tradition principle and the requirement of delivery (traditio). This principle is not laid down by statute but has been elaborated during the last century through court decisions, legal doctrine and various regulations that all take this principle as a starting point. Since the circumstances regarding the delivery of goods can have multiple variations, a lot of argumentation about what shall be decisive has resulted. The main arguments that have been stressed are factual. A central concern in deciding the question would therefore be whether a solution that gives the buyer priority would be a safe general solution considering the risk of defrauding the creditors. It would also be of interest to what extent a solution gives the seller possibilities to take risks that might eventually make the situation worse for every creditor. (This is seen as important since it is assumed that a person in an economically stressful situation typically has a high preference towards even extreme risks.)[9] Another concern would be whether such a solution creates any problems in identifying what goods are the object of the contract. This is of course a practical aspect but there is also a normative aspect in the form of the speciality principle (priority is only given to specified objects – a claim for just any property is placed on the same level as the claims for money in bankruptcy, and only awarded a dividend of the estate).

The considerations regarding the example would, in other words, be rather functional aspects. There are no concerns about 'ownership'. A Swedish lawyer would not even see why ownership could be a relevant question. What has to be decided is whether the buyer shall be given priority in bankruptcy. If he gets it, he might call himself the 'owner' but that is just a description and any word to describe his priority will do. Since the Swedish lawyer does not think about ownership in this situation, he or she would most likely not use the word ownership, but rather 'priority', 'right to separate' or 'protection from creditors'.

The material solution to the problem would probably be that the buyer would be given priority. Even if the machine is not delivered, it is out of the

---

[9] This argument is often not used explicitly, but rather forms the core of other arguments that are used by tradition, rather than being thought through to the full extent. At least this is my own way of describing it, see Claes Martinson, *Kreditsäkerhet i fakturafordringar* (Uppsala: Iustus 2002) at 306-17.

physical reach of the seller BGI, and the possessor of the machine, Askan, knows that they shall deliver the goods to CISA. Askan holds the machine in CISA's interest. Under these circumstances, it is clarified that there was an actual transaction and not an attempt to defraud the creditors. It can also be concluded that BGI has limited possibilities to sell the machine once again. And, it is evident which object is contested. Since the machine is in possession of the third party, Askan, we will have no problems identifying it.

So far, I have described how Swedish lawyers address the example and, especially, question a). From what has been said, it could however also be understood that the Swedish lawyer would not have any problem considering the question whether the seller, BGI, 'owns' the machine when he sells it. The circumstances in the b)-question would only make a difference in that the buyer, CISA, might not get priority. If BGI buys the machine after they entered into the contract with CISA, there is a risk that BGI might go bankrupt before they conclude the contract with Askan. If this happens, CISA will not have a claim for a specific object, and they will, according to the speciality principle, not be awarded priority in bankruptcy. Instead of getting the machine, they will have a claim for money in bankruptcy: the 60 %, which were paid, and the damages they can claim on the basis of the failure to deliver.

From some of the other cultural perspectives on this example, it is probably strange that BGI can sell a machine, which they do not 'own'. As said, that is not a concern of the Swedish lawyer. The aspect that the Swedish lawyer would find relevant rather is – whether there are any sufficient interests to prevent such behaviour? There would then be assumptions made about whether these situations are common, whether they, more often than others, lead to failures to deliver, whether economically distressed persons, more often than others, would act in this way (thus making it worse for themselves and for their creditors), whether the trust in the market is affected by the possible problems this conduct leads to, and so on. – The sale of goods not yet acquired is not considered problematic. We do allow such conduct and see no functional reason not to do so.

The conclusion that can be drawn from the BGI example is as indicated in the heading: Swedish lawyers do focus on the functional aspects and they form the questions accordingly. The question of ownership is not seen as a real question since it is not a question that deals with concerns of reality. It is rather seen as a question that conceals the real problems and makes it more difficult to solve them. However, this view is of course based on the Swedish context. If a certain culture of legal reasoning has developed techniques of using the ownership concept and of considering them functional and practical, the efficiency in these aspects can of course be high. Since there are well-functioning legal traditions in many countries with unititular ownership approaches, there is no reason to believe otherwise. The Swedish tradition is however constituted by what has been described: to avoid the concept of ownership. In the Swedish experience it is not useful.

E. The terminology should not be decisive! Ownership is not a magic word

> Some of the company Big W's customers bought their goods on credit, paying part of the total price in monthly instalments. Some customers can not pay. Can Big W retrieve the goods if the contract states: 1) 'Retention of title'; 2) 'Retention of ownership'; 3) 'Ownership is granted to the buyer only when the full amount is paid'; 4) 'Big W has a security right in the goods for its claim for payment'; 5) 'Yo-yo-clause applicable, according to the parties' understanding of this clause'.

Presented with this problem, the Swedish lawyer would recognize the article in the Sale of Goods Act providing: 'If the goods have come into the possession of the buyer, the seller may only rescind the contract if he has reserved himself a right to do so.' The rationale behind this provision is that it shall be clarified to the buyer that this rather harsh remedy might be used. Since the reservations most often are made in writing, it might also be that they contribute to clearer evidence when bankruptcies are solved. Therefore the provision could be said to be in the interest of the buyer's creditors. If a reservation is not made, the seller has to restrict himself to the remedies for overdue payment: interest and debt collecting fees.

The question would then be if Big W, the seller in the example, has fulfilled the requirement to reserve. There would be no problem with deciding the alternatives 1, 2 and 3. In all those cases, Big W will be given the right to retrieve the goods. The alternatives 4 and 5 might cause a bit of discussion about what the parties actually intended. They might also cause hesitation concerning the ways in which they should be given partially different effects to the other three. It would, however, not be very problematic for the Swedish lawyer to reach the decision that Big W should receive the goods back also in these cases. In the alternative number 5, the decision would be made after a thorough investigation of the evidence supporting that the parties intended that the 'Yo-yo-clause' should have that effect.[10] A specific word does not have to be spoken, written or otherwise communicated, it is enough that the parties have agreed and that their intentions can be proved.

---

[10] Since 'Yo-yo' provides certain associations, implying the goods going back and forth, it can be underlined that the word need not give such associations. It could have been a 'Banana-clause' or a 'No bullshit-clause'. The word in itself does not matter, as will be outlined in the following.

A case like this case was actually decided by the Swedish Supreme Court in 1975.[11] It is the last case in the emancipation away from the conceptual reasoning connected to ownership. The parties had a written contract, which had the following wording (in full):

> 'I Mats Berg have on the 8 of July 1972 sold 1 Volvo for 6500 kr, which shall be paid to me the 18 of July by Lasse Taikumer. If payment is not effected before the 18 of July, the car shall fall back to me with an interest of 1000 kr. In original condition, affirmed: Lasse Taikumer.'

The buyer, Lasse Taikumer, shortly thereafter, sold the car to Krister Hellberg, for 4250 kr, and did not pay Mats Berg. Since Mats Berg, after Lasse Taikumer had shown his character so explicitly, now probably saw poor chances of getting paid, he sued Krister Hellberg to get the car or the sum of money equivalent to its value. Krister Hellberg contested and argued that his seller, Lasse Taikumer, 'had the ownership of the car' and, as the second reason, that he had acquired in good faith.

All but one of the judges in all the three court instances decided in favour of the original seller Mats Berg. They did, for reasons that are of no interest here, not think that Krister Hellberg had been in good faith, and they held that the reservation that Mats Berg had stipulated was effective.

> Two of the judges in the district court (first instance) wrote: 'This provision, which evidently had the purpose of protecting Berg in case of non-payment, must have the same effect towards a third party as a common reservation of ownership.'
>
> The judges in the Supreme Court wrote: 'As the courts have found the reservation that Berg stipulated, concerning right to take the car back in case payment was not effected in due time, must be seen as having the same effect as a reservation of ownership'.

An interesting observation is that one judge in the district court, who held against his colleagues, was of the opinion that the term ownership was of importance.

> He did, in other words, decide in favour of the second buyer, Krister Hellberg, and wrote: '… it is not clear that Berg had the intention of selling the car under the reservation that the ownership should stay with him until payment was effected. Considering this and the content of the written contract, I find that Taikumer has become the owner of the car. Taikumer hereby had the right to sell the car to Hellberg.'

---

[11] NJA 1975, p 222.

The words that this judge used clearly seems to be based on another view of 'ownership' and 'transfer of ownership' than the other judges expressed. As said, this case was, however, one of the last steps in the emancipation away from the conceptual approach. The case shows that the Swedish judges used the functional approach and did not consider questions such as 'where the ownership was situated' or whether the second seller 'was the owner when he sold'. It should be noted that the case was decided after a period where the academic doctrinal writings had condemned conceptual logic in legal reasoning.[12] Concerning the 'retention of title'-clause it was shown that a differentiation between clauses using ownership and clauses using other words to express the seller's wish to retrieve the goods, would have no functional use.

What the example and the case also shows is that there is a preference of avoiding a 'Harry Potter'-logic concerning the law.[13] It would, to a Swedish lawyer, seem silly to have a requirement to use a certain term, almost seeming like a requirement to pronounce a magic formula.[14] Having said this, it is, however, very common among sellers to still use terms like 'reservation of ownership'. It is a simple and easy way of describing what you want. The more common variations that are used are: 'right to take back' and 'right to rescind'. Taking this custom to use certain concepts into consideration, it could be held that it is more 'silly' not to require them than to bother with the question. It would of course not be hard for a Swedish lawyer to follow a requirement to use a certain word.

> There are, however, also a few other implications that could be thought of if you seek to explain the Swedish preference of not requiring a certain wording. One aspect concerns the fact that contracts often are written by persons other than lawyers. There is, in Sweden, a common ambition to make legal matters comprehensible for the ones with no legal knowledge. It has also been a conscious choice of style by the Swedish legislator to avoid formality requirements. There are, for example, only very few requirements for contracts to be in writing and those, which are dictated, are rather simple.[15]

---

[12] The Supreme Court even refers to Henrik Hessler, 'Om äganderrättsförbehåll och återtagandeförbehåll i 1966 års lag om vad som är fast egendom' in: *Nordisk Gjenklang – Festskrift til Carl Jacob Arnholm* (Oslo: Tanum 1969). Hessler refers to Arnholm, Ross and Schmidt.

[13] As is known to the many readers of J K Rowlings famous novel suite, the novel character Harry Potter and his friends at the Hogwarts school of magic have to practise how to pronounce the magic formulas correctly to get the wanted effects.

[14] Hessler (n 12) actually uses the simile with 'magic', pp 470, 472.

[15] One example that in an international comparison often stands out is the sale of land. The decisive requirements are only to use a written contract signed by both parties that

A requirement of using a certain word would also, in some aspects, restrain the development of new legal constructs. If the requirements were connected to certain terminology, it would be harder to create and acknowledge new trades and customs. If, for example, a new trade concerning credit was invented that aimed at giving the seller the right to just prevent the buyer from using the sold object until it was paid for (because this, under the circumstances, was more suitable for both parties than taking the sold object back), a requirement of using certain terminology to protect the seller would have a restraining effect. It would probably not hinder the development of the mentioned kind of security construct, because the market actors could use the required term together with a more elaborated description of the innovation. Even so, the requirement could cause hesitation and legal uncertainty and such a requirement, therefore, at least to some extent, reflects the level of openness the legal culture has towards market constructivism and innovations.

In the same way, it could be argued that a formal requirement might make it harder to take all relevant circumstances of a case into such consideration, which the Swedish climate of reasoning acknowledges sympathy towards. Since we do not today know every possible situation that reality can bring, we do like to leave openings for the yet unknown. A formal requirement concerning the exact wording does, in a way, affect this culture of thinking although it probably just makes a slight difference and certainly much depends on how different lawyers view legal theoretical matters.

F. Use ownership relationally!

> *The Mumba company has a two meter high sculpture in their Swedish office. They just bought it from the artist Karin A. Before they have paid for the sculpture, it falls over and destroys a laptop belonging to Ms Tina, who is visiting the office. Who is responsible for the damage?*

To solve this case, the Swedish lawyer would start by deciding upon the legal ground for responsibility. Since there, in this case, is no explicit indication of any negligent act the solution would be that no one is responsible. It seems to be a pure accident and, therefore, Ms Tina has to rely on her own insurance, if she has one. However, to get a closer illustration of the Swedish approach, we could add negligence to the example. A sculpture of that size should not just fall over, and if it does someone might have caused the fall.

---

expresses the intention to sell and the price. See Jordabalk (1970:994) Chapter 4, article 1. To protect the acquisition from some kinds of third parties, the buyer must also register his acquisition and, to facilitate this procedure, it is helpful if the signing of the contract is witnessed by two other parties.

It could be that the sculpture was designed in a way that made it unstable. It could also be that the janitor who placed the sculpture at the chosen spot in the office did not mount it as would have been necessary to minimize the risk of a fall. The janitor might, on the other hand, have been unable to do more than he did because it was not his decision to place the sculpture on the chosen spot. Another possibility is that someone caused the fall by leaning on the sculpture ... etc. Depending on what happened and who was involved, the legal responsibility would be placed on those who were negligent, or if they are employees doing their work, on their employers. Of the parties mentioned in the example, it could therefore be either Mumba, as the employer of a negligent janitor, or it could be the artist Karin A, or it could be both.

The Swedish basic line of thinking would, in other words, be to decide upon what caused the damage and whether there is a legal ground for responsibility that should be used. Negligence would then be the main legal ground. In some specific situations we also use a stricter liability, such as product liability for personal injuries.

Interestingly, there are however cases where 'owners' are subject to strict liability. There are statutory provisions making owners of animals strictly liable. In one of the articles from 1736 that is still in force 'the owner' is liable for half of the damage that an animal causes to another animal.[16] In a more modern update of this legislation from 1943 'the owner' is strictly liable for damage that his dog causes generally.[17]

Since the dog liability regulation states that any person who has received the dog for maintenance or use is liable in addition to the owner, and also that the owner may, in his turn, bring a claim against any person who might have caused the damage by, for example, provoking the dog or failing to supervise it; the liability can in many cases be handled without making the decision on ownership a crucial one. When the damage is caused without any human negligence involved, the Swedish lawyers do, however, have to decide who owns. In those dog-cases, where there are doubts concerning ownership, the Swedish lawyer will, however, most probably take a rather functional approach. If a dog is sold and paid for but left with the seller, the Swedish lawyer would not primarily think of ownership as such to decide where to place the responsibility for damage caused by the dog. An argument that would be given more relevance to is that the seller, in this case, has better possibilities to prevent the dog from doing damage than the

---

[16] (Byggningabalk), 22:7.
[17] The act on the supervision of dogs and cats (Lag 1943:459 om tillsyn över hundar och katter), §6.

buyer.[18] Another argument of interest would be whether it is typically more likely that the seller has insurance to cover the damage, rather than if the buyer has such insurance. In other words, the statutory provision 'ownership' would be decided by functional considerations and aspects. It would not be decided on as a separate entity and it would not be linked to other problems like the seller's right to rescind the contract or the buyer's protection from the seller's creditors.

This description shows that the Swedish lawyer sees the concept of ownership as a relational concept. The word 'ownership' has no specific meaning until it is put in relation to a certain aspect.

G. Let the functional interests decide what constructions should be supported!

Trackrace AB has a right to buy 10 horses that they have trained for a year. The horses are in Trackrace's stables. When the horse owner, Mr Goop, goes bankrupt Trackrace wants to use the contract clause and buy the horses. Will they be allowed to?

The common way for a Swedish lawyer to handle this example would be to start with a classification of the contractual clause as some kind of preemption right. This classification would then lead on to a doctrinal discussion about whether these kinds of rights should be given priority before the

---

[18] It might be that the decision is to share the liability between the seller and the buyer since the regulation opens up for a shared liability solution between an owner and certain kinds of possessors. The mentioned functional arguments can be used to reach this solution, and the line of thinking might be that the risk is even more limited if both parties have an interest in avoiding damage from occuring. The question of doubt concerning who should be considered the owner, such as when the dog is sold, is not mentioned in any of the preparatory works concerning the statute, (the statute has been amended four times in different aspects). Nor do there seem to be any cases in the higher court instances. The legislator's motive behind the choice of making the owner liable is rather functional, although it is partly explained by the choices made by the legislators of 1734. The legislators of 1943 actually considered the alternative imposing liability on the possessor of the dog, but chose, in the last round of the legislating procedure, the solution to make both the possessor and the owner liable. It was said to be unreasonable that the aggrieved party could not get compensation if the possessor was insolvent, considering the fact that the owner could insure his interests, and also that dog owners should be aware of the importance of supervising dogs. See Proposition 1943:191, Riksdagsskrivelse 1943:348 and Första lagutskottets utlåtande 1943 nr 48, pp 16-18.

creditors in a bankruptcy.[19] The main concern in that doctrinal discussion has been to uphold the Swedish principle of tradition, with its requirement of 'delivery' (traditio), also mentioned above (section 4). This principle is used in a way that the buyer is protected from the seller's creditors if the goods have come into the buyer's possession or, at least, have come out of the seller's possession.

For a case like the Trackrace example, where the goods are in the possession of the buyer at the time of bankruptcy, it has been argued that the tradition requirement should be seen as fulfilled. The right to use the pre-emption clause should, in other words, be given priority over the creditors if the (future) buyer already has the goods in his possession. This solution is supported by a functional argumentation. Behind the tradition principle we find several lines of argumentation. The arguments that has been seen as most important in the Swedish discourse, concern the prevention of the defrauding of creditors, see above.[20] With a tradition requirement, there is some kind of factual indication of a transfer that can be observed. The requirement, therefore, narrows the possibilities for the parties of giving the buyer priority by simply claiming that they had a contract. Applied to the Trackrace example and the pre-emption right, it can be argued that the possibilities to defraud are narrowed by the fact that the buyer has possession.

> To avoid the risk that a foreign reader has a problem of understanding how the Swedish lawyer sees these arguments as functional and, therefore, has a hard time understanding the main theme, being the way in which we think, it can be noted that the assumptions about the factual effects concerning risk are actually mere assumptions. There is little evidence to support these assumptions, and it is interesting that there are rather different assumptions made in countries that, concerning the risk of fraud, could be assumed to be rather similar to Sweden. Interestingly, the tradition requirement has recently also been abolished for consumer sales. The reason that the assumptions in different countries are different can probably, to a large extent, be explained by the fact that the assumptions have been made by lawyers who actually have rather poor methods of studying a society. The core of the assumptions also concerns old and since long disappeared societies. Furthermore, the factual observations are to some extent based on cases where the most fraudulent of characters have been involved. It is easy to criticise assumptions made from such a material, but it is at the same time important that lawyers can decide normatively also when mere assumptions are what we have. The theme shall, however, not be developed in this article.

---

[19] Torgny Håstad (n 2) at 442-446.
[20] Section 4.

The Swedish lawyers would also be concerned about whether a priority for pre-emption rights would cause any other risk of damage to the creditors. Since a pre-emption clause is often constructed in a way that the buyer only uses it if it secures him a good price, it is typically a disadvantage for the creditors if the pre-emption clause is used. The creditors typically get a higher dividend if the bankruptcy administrator sells the goods in the open market. However, this concern regarding the creditors would be met by the argument there are possibilities of using recovery claims (actio Pauliana) in respect of agreements that are not commercial. If the price to be paid using the pre-emption clause is too low, the pre-emption clause would, in many cases, allow recovery and the buyer could not benefit from it. Since this, more or less, makes it possible to disqualify only the pre-emption rights that affect the creditor's interests negatively, the pre-emption right would probably be accepted.[21]

What the description concerning pre-emption rights shows is that Swedish lawyers do not decide upon what 'kinds of rights' should be allowed, acknowledged or supported. There is, accordingly, no *numerus clausus* principle or any such limitations connected to the 'kinds of rights' involved. The Swedish lawyers rather try to decide whether a party construction is too detrimental to the different kinds of interests involved. Amongst these interests are of course the interests of third parties and it is, therefore, generally not possible for the parties to award themselves priority over third parties, or to put them under an obligation. In practice, this approach might lead to rather small differences compared to a *numerus clausus* principle, but the difference as to the starting points is important.[22]

---

[21] Since an administrator in bankruptcy often wants to sell off the property of the estate with as little trouble as possible in finding buyers, it could be argued that it does not make any practical difference if a pre-emption clause is given priority to in bankruptcy. The administrator will sell the goods to the holder of the pre-emption right if the price is on a commercial level, regardless of priority. There could, however, be circumstances where the question of priority will be of importance, even though the pre-emption price is commercial. It might, for example, be that the pre-emption clause gives the buyer a good price to motivate him to increase the value of the goods. In the horse example, Trackrace could have been given the pre-emption clause to motivate them to do a good training job for a low fee. There might also be someone who wants to pay the same price for the goods but also likes to buy the whole estate and, therefore, is a buyer preferred by the creditors.

[22] This theme can be elaborated and there are short descriptions in Swedish law where the Swedish principles are described as kindred to *numerus clausus*, Torgny Håstad (n 2) at 130. The question is not much discussed from the perspective of a general principle. Stefan Lindskog has, however, made a remark that reflects what would probably not be an uncommon opinion from a Swedish perspective: 'The thought behind the principle

It should be clarified that the ordinary legal analysis would draw conclusions based rather heavily on comparisons with the common categorisation of rights that also the Swedish lawyer uses: ownership, security rights, rights to use and obligatory rights. If the situation could be fitted into one of the two first mentioned categories and the usual requirements for priority are fulfilled, it is seen as a strong argument to accept and give priority to. What is important for the theme in this article is, however, that the 'kinds of rights' concept is not conclusive. The decisive considerations have to do with functional matters. Even if a party construction such as the pre-emption clause is accepted through an analysis that basically relies on a comparison to an ordinary sales situation (ownership right), the aim is to test whether the differences can be accepted on the basis of functional aspects. The functional considerations that have been used to develop the principles to regulate the ordinary sales situations are also applied to the unusual (new) construction. This is shown by the description above, where some of the arguments behind the tradition requirement (traditio) are used for considering the consequences of accepting a priority for pre-emption.

Thinking of the reasons for Swedish lawyers to approach new constructions in the described way, it may seem that the 'freedom of contract' principle and the ideologies behind that idea are a possible explanation. By keeping the door open to new initiatives, we promote efficient solutions, at least according to the basic market economic theory. It can, however, be discussed to what extent this is a reason which Swedish lawyers would use to justify the approach. Maybe it is a more valid assumption to say that they simply appreciate the conception of dynamics, although it is, in practice, probably just a matter of a rather slight agility. It should also be pointed out that the chosen way is inherited. The advantages and disadvantages are not something that is much discussed. It has always been the Swedish legislator's policy only to regulate questions that have been seen to be of central importance, very practical or of a certain political interest. With such a policy, there is no tradition of thinking of the legal system as a systematic whole and it is easy to see the needs of creating new solutions for the new problems that occur.

---

of numerus clausus is probably that two parties should not be able to regulate the extent of the protection of third parties to the latters' detriment. Irrespective hereof, the principle of numerus clausus, in my view, means a directly detrimental limitation to the formation of law in a dynamic society.' See Stefan Lindskog, *Kvittning* (Stockholm: Norstedts Juridik, 2nd ed 1993), at 35.

H. Keep problems apart – even if they seem to be assembled!

The company Selleria AB in the north of Sweden sells paper to the company Buyman Printing AB in the south. According to the standard clause, all goods shall be transported by an independent transporting company. After the goods have been picked up, the seller shall not have the right to change the destination during the transport, nor shall he have the right to dispose of the goods or sell them to another. The buyer shall pay half of the price before the pick-up and the rest one month after delivery. – After a turbulent month in the paper industry, both Selleria and Buyman go bankrupt. At this moment, one truck from the transport company is on its way to Buyman with a load of 20 tons of paper. How should the situation be solved?

When the Swedish lawyer starts to solve this problem he or she will regard it as two questions concerning priority over creditors. One question is whether Selleria should be able to stop the transport because of the anticipated non-payment from Buyman. The other question is whether Buyman should be given priority to the goods over the creditors in Selleria's bankruptcy. It might be seen as remarkable but the Swedish lawyer would, in this case, probably end up with the conclusion that both parties are protected. Selleria is protected against Buyman's creditors because they should be given the right to stop the delivery (right of stoppage in transit). Buyman is protected against Selleria's creditors because the tradition requirement (traditio) should be seen as fulfilled. The goods are namely out of the control of Selleria. They can not order the driver back, or sell it and redirect the delivery. The fact that Selleria can stop the delivery because of anticipated non-payment would not be seen as sufficient in order to be able to say that the tradition requirement is not fulfilled. At least it is not seen as problematic that the conclusion might be that both parties are protected.[23] It is not seen as necessary to coordinate the solutions concerning protection in such a way that one party looses his protection when the other party gets his.

The conclusion that both parties should be protected does, however, not solve the problem. We do need to decide on who should get the goods and the money already paid. What the conclusion gives us are normative arguments to be used in arriving at a solution. One way to argue would, therefore, be that the seller's estate should have the right to stop the goods since they are not going to be fully paid. Unless the buyer's estate pays the rest of the claim the buyer's basic claim is to recover the money already paid. Since this is a claim for money, and not specific property, the buyer's estate will

---

[23] Svante O Johansson, *Stoppningsrätt under godstransport* (Stockholm: Norstedts Juridik 2001) at 232-3.

only get a dividend out of the seller's estate.²⁴ The buyer's claim to get the goods is a claim for property, but the claim is conditional on payment and should not be dealt with differently just because the seller goes bankrupt. If the buyer's estate pays the rest of the claim they will, however, get the goods since the seller's estate in that case has no right to stop the delivery (retain his performance).

What this argumentation suggests is that a Swedish lawyer would approach the complex of problems from separate starting points. The problems are defined by the interests of the different parties and the problems are kept apart. To decide on the solutions, the same norms and the same considerations are used as if the problems had not been assembled. It is not seen to be of primary importance to coordinate the solutions. To the Swedish experience it is seldom necessary to coordinate them.

I. The same solution may be used for different problems – but on its own merits!

> *A steel company sells some steel plates to a ship wharf. They do not use a retention of title clause and the wharf goes bankrupt just a day after the delivery. a) Can the wharf get the steel plates back? b) Does it matter if the minister of industries has promised, on the national television, that the government has the intention to support Swedish wharfs – and that the wharf influenced the seller's decision by referring to an agreement, in principle between the governmental working group on these issues and the wharf?*

Question a) of this example would be easy to decide. The Swedish lawyer would, as mentioned in section 5 above, use the Sale of Goods Act and the requirement on the seller to reserve himself a right to rescind in case of non-payment. Since the seller has not reserved himself this right he cannot get the plates back. It could also be added that a reservation clause would not have been acknowledged since the goods, in this case, were steel plates that the wharf was supposed to assemble into the ships they were building.²⁵

Against this background it might seem that it would be easy to decide the b)-question in the same way. However, the fact that the seller seems to have relied on the public promise from the minister could be seen as a ground for

---

[24] It might, in this case, be that the seller's estate likes to claim compensation for the costs and the loss of profit. In that case, this amount should be deducted before the dividend is calculated.

[25] The Swedish policy towards reservation of title is rather strict compared to other systems. It may, according to doctrine and practice, not be used for goods that the buyer is supposed to consume, mix, assemble or dispose of, see SOU 1988:63 p 37 *etc.*

deciding that the contract should be void. The contract and the delivery were made under wrongful assumptions concerning the preconditions. Since the estate would not have got the goods if this had not been the case, the same argument could be used to give the seller priority. It would, however, also be of importance what general consequences a decision in either way would have. A problem with priority would be to, in practice, draw the line between these cases and other cases where the contract is void for different reasons. There might, for example, be many cases where the seller claims that the buyer said he would pay but actually never intended to do so.

In 1985 the Supreme Court decided a case somewhat similar to the b)-example. The Supreme Court judges saw the contract as void and gave the seller priority, referring mainly to what was said to be the predominant doctrinal position that goods under void contracts should be given back also in case of bankruptcy; at least as long as the goods were still individualised and not mixed with other goods. The judges did, however, at the same time point out that there had been doubts in the doctrinal statements concerning to what extent such a principle should be used. These doubts concerned:

> '... contracts becoming void because of future conditions and some other situations in which it does not appear to be natural that a party should be given priority to the detriment of the counterpart's other creditors'.[26]

This remark is of interest in that the judges limit the scope of the principle that they reinforce by using it. It is also interesting that they, in very general words, refer to the need for a balance of interests in these situations.

The judgment and the argumentation suggests that the Swedish lawyer might sometimes use a solution that is rather close to a logic based on the conceptions of ownership. To use a principle that gives priority, primarily based on the judgment concerning whether the contract is void, is namely not a very functional approach. The questions concerning which contracts should be void are questions that concern the two parties to the contract and they do not specifically consider the interests of the creditors. However, it is not an all-in-all correct conclusion to view the solution as a principle that gives priority to the return of the performances of all void contracts, regardless of the circumstances. The remarks made above concerning the judgment and the extent of the principle shows an ambition not to use solutions that are so far-reaching that the consequences can not be overviewed. The principle could, therefore, be claimed to be a solution that is based also on considerations of the creditors' interests. It is mainly the same solution as for the contractual relationship, but it is used only in so far as it shows to be a reasonable balance, also considering the creditors' interests.

---

[26] NJA 1985 p 178.

J. Understanding the Swedish approach

The purpose of this article is to present a picture of how Swedish lawyers think. More exactly, it is to show how we work without using the concept 'transfer of ownership' and how we use the concept of 'ownership'. I have done this by using eight examples and outlining eight recommendations:
- Go straight to the problem! Ownership is a detour
- Be open to deal with all problems, but only solve the ones which need to be solved!
- Form the questions functionally! Ownership is not a real concern
- The terminology should not be decisive! Ownership is not a magic word
- Use ownership relationally!
- Let the functional interests decide what constructions should be supported!
- Keep problems apart – even if they seem to be assembled!
- The same solution may be used for different problems – but on its own merits!

Through these examples and the descriptions of how we handle them I hope that I have managed to show that the Swedish approach is not unintelligible. Actually, I even hope to have shown that the Swedish lawyers have a rather comprehensible and direct way of analysing and dealing with the problems. According to the Swedish tradition, the question of 'ownership' is simply an irrelevant question. It is considered a detour in the analysis. To think as a Swedish lawyer you, therefore, very seldom ask who owns. The relevant questions are instead more direct: who should be responsible, who should bear the risk, who should be given priority? *etc* To answer these questions, it is not seen as necessary to decide who owns. The questions are, instead, dealt with by using normative arguments (norms), and these norms do not concern ownership. Behind the norms are, instead, mostly considerations that rely on assumptions of functionality. The same preference for functional considerations are relevant also when deciding the so-called hard cases.

The type of argumentation that the Swedish lawyer uses is, in comparison with other legal traditions, not very different in essence. There are of course differences concerning the assumptions and the opinions of what is functional, as well as what is relevant to consider, but in general a foreign lawyer would recognize the arguments and the way of deciding between them. The remarkable difference between the Swedish tradition and some others is that the Swedish lawyers do not use the concept of ownership and do not have to bother with the consequential conceptions that follow from that concept.

In the few cases where the Swedish lawyer uses the concept of ownership it is used in a relational way. Ownership is seen as a description, which is used in order to define certain aspects of a relationship between two parties.

Ownership is therefore interesting only in respect of the questions: with regard to whom, what and why?[27] Usually, we find it easier not to use the concept.[28]

As said, the ambition has been to explain how Swedish lawyers think and describe how we work. However, even after reading the whole article there are probably some readers who still think: So what? Why is it of any importance for a foreign lawyer to understand how Swedish lawyers think?

Well, I hope that my text has at least taken the reader to a point at which he or she can be convinced that the Swedish approach is interesting simply because it is different. An approach that is different to others could, sometimes, be significant for the approach of one's own legal system. It can initiate thoughts on the advantages and disadvantages of one's own system. Another reason to know how Swedish lawyers think is to be able to more explicitly learn about the advantages of the Swedish system. However, the advantages have not been an explicit theme in this article. To get to know more of that part requires further reading in addition to the first step, that this article can hopefully serve as.[29]

I can of course not give an answer to whether it was worth reading this article and if it would be of any use to read more about this theme. Something I can do is, however, to point out that the process of emancipation away from the conceptual, substantial or unititular thinking has been conducted in a way that it has become a part of the Swedish tradition to regard such analysis as an unfit method and rather useless. This is of course also true as long as the dominant surrounding thoughts are based on another kind of logic, as has been the case in Sweden.

---

[27] Compare the description of 'property' that is used in anthropology where 'property' is not seen as things, but as a network of social relations that governs the conduct of people with respect to the use and disposition of things. And note that they speak of differences between societal systems. Some place greater weight on relationships with things rather than on the social networks within which they are held. See, *eg*, C M Hann (ed), *Property Relations* (Cambridge: Cambridge University Press 1998) at 4 and 8.

[28] It is interesting that some anthropological schools have similar approaches for analytical reasons. One idea in anthropology is not to use the concept 'property', since the use of the concept easily amounts to an over-simplification of a very complex reality and also since it is too heavily populated with common sense meanings. See, *eg*, *Property in Question* (Oxford: Berg 2004), edited by Katherine Verdery and Caroline Humphrey.

[29] The ECC study project and the Salzburg group are working on the theme. A part of my own contribution to this work can be read in the publication by Claes Martinson (with the participation of Jens Andreasson), *'Transfer of Title Concerning Movables Part III – National Report: Sweden* (Frankfurt a M: Lang 2006) = Johannes Michael Rainer (ed), *Salzburger Studien zum Europäischen Privatrecht*, Vol XX.

To claim that the functional approach would predominantly have advantages also if it were used in other surroundings, or used to direct such surroundings towards the functional approach, would of course be to put my chin out. It would also be rather unscientific since there is no research to support the proposition. Maybe it is even a bit silly since legal cultures should not be compared in terms of advantages. However, let me still do just that in order to try to get your attention. Let me suggest that we, the Nordic legal traditions, have something good to share with you – a relatively new and modern approach to 'ownership' and the 'transfer of ownership'.

Scepticism about the Functional Approach from a Unitary Perspective

*Wolfgang Faber**

A. Introduction

Scepticism is probably the usual reaction of lawyers from continental European legal systems when being confronted with the Scandinavian 'functional approach'[1] for the transfer of movable property. Splitting up the right of 'ownership' into its different aspects and applying different rules to the 'transfer' of each of these aspects may even be considered impossible by continental lawyers, as they, from their traditional background, are used to understanding 'ownership' as forming an integrated whole, both in general and, in particular, when it comes to a transfer (unitary transfer concept).[2]

---

* Assistant professor at the Department of Private Law, University of Salzburg; co-leader of the working group on 'Transfer of Movables' within the Study Group on a European Civil Code. – I would like to thank Dr Claes Martinson, University of Gothenburg, for commenting on draft versions, numerous discussions and constant help in understanding the Scandinavian way of thinking and Jens Andreasson, LLM, University of Gothenburg, for helping me to find my first steps through Swedish literature. I do, however, bear full responsibility for all remaining mistakes in understanding. I also thank my colleague Ernest Weiker, LLB, University of Graz, for linguistic support.

[1] As explained by Claes Martinson, 'How Swedish Lawyers Think about 'Ownership' and 'Transfer of Ownership'', at p 69 in this volume. In English language, see also Claes Martinson, *Transfer of Title Concerning Movables Part III – National Report: Sweden* (Frankfurt am Main: Peter Lang 2006); Torgny Håstad, 'Property Rights regarding Movables', in: Michael Bogdan (ed), *Swedish Law in the New Millennium* (Stockholm: Norstedts Juridik 2000), 411. Cf also Alf Ross, 'Tû-Tû', (1956-1957) 70 *Harvard Law Review* 812, reflecting the philosophical viewpoint of Scandinavian Legal Realism.

[2] A different terminology is used by Michael Rainer (in collaboration with Jakob F Stagl) and Ulrich Drobnig in Christian von Bar and Ulrich Drobnig (eds), *The Interaction of Contract Law and Tort and Property Law in Europe – A Comparative Study* (München: Sellier. European Law Publishers 2004), at 325 *et seq* (n 481 *et seq*), where the term 'unitary approach' is used for the French model of a transfer of ownership *solo consensu* as opposed to a 'split approach' applied, for instance, in German law, where tradition is required in addition to the consent of the parties. The basic distinction between a

The functional approach may be suspected of being potentially contradictory and, if some of those aspects remain unregulated and/or too much freedom is left for a free weighing of interests, of bearing a considerable risk that judicial decisions become unforeseeable.[3]

The task of this paper is, on the one hand, to reflect such scepticism. On the other hand, I would be the wrong person to write this article in terms of fundamental opposition, as I do in fact believe that a 'functional' way of thinking can have a positive impact in several respects.[4] However, there do remain some problematic aspects on different levels also from my point of view. These aspects do not only relate to the view continental lawyers have on the Scandinavian 'functional' approach, but also to the Scandinavians' view on the (continental) 'unitary' approach. The second task of this paper is, therefore, to make a contribution to mutual understanding between continental and Scandinavian lawyers. I should also clarify that my perspective, partly, is future-orientated, having in mind ongoing discussions in projects like the Study Group on a European Civil Code, which may serve as a basis when deciding whether property law harmonization shall take place on a European level[5] and, if so, in which direction it should go.[6]

It is of course not possible to deal with these issues exhaustively in an article like this; some selection must be made. In doing so, I will partly lay my

---

'functional' and a 'unitary' approach in the purpose of this paper and Claes Martinson's contribution to this volume (n 1 above) is not reflected in that study.

[3] It should be clarified that most continental lawyers know very little or even nothing about the Scandinavian functional approach. There is also hardly any debate in literature, at least in the German speaking countries. The 'unitary perspective' reflected in this article, therefore, is mainly based on discussions with continental academics, students and, partly, practitioners, as well as on experience in international projects. I do, however, believe that what I refer to as a 'unitary perspective' is more or less representative, in particular, for the German legal family and similar systems.

[4] For instance, we try to apply this approach as a working method when developing our draft proposals for the Study Group on a European Civil Code. To a certain extent, it may also be helpful for developing well-balanced solutions for non-regulated or not clearly regulated issues within a 'unitary' system (see, for instance, n 43 below).

[5] This paper will not deal with the question of whether European harmonization of property law is desirable or in which form it should be achieved, if at all. I just take that as a current development on an academic level, the outcome of which is completely open.

[6] For the sake of academic fairness, it should be noted that Claes Martinson does not take this perspective in his article (n 1 above; he only aims at presenting the Swedish lawyer's way of thinking *de lege lata*) and that my contribution, insofar as I express scepticism as to the functional approach's suitability for a European integration process, goes one step further than his article.

emphasis on issues which occur in Claes Martinson's contribution to this volume.[7] This may also help to understand to what extent the approaches actually differ or where similarities can be observed. Furthermore, I will only touch a very limited number of legal systems: I will basically refer to Swedish law as a representative for the Scandinavian functional approach and to German and Austrian law as examples for unitary systems.[8]

B. Some clarifications as to the unitary approach

My first remarks do not address the functional approach directly. However, both from reading Scandinavian (Swedish) literature[9] and from my experience of being involved in European projects, I have the clear impression that Scandinavian lawyers tend to see the traditional 'continental' unitary approach in a very negative way.[10] There is nothing to be said against this in an academic debate as long as the reasons for this reaction are based on correct assumptions and material arguments. But, partly, it seems that Scandinavian functional approach proponents *overestimate* what they consider the disadvantageous effects of the unitary approach by *linking many more consequences to the 'transfer of ownership'* than contemporary unitary systems, like the German or Austrian one, actually do.

My first 'scepticism', if I may stick to the terminology of the title to this contribution, therefore relates to these starting points of the functional *versus* unitary debate. Hence, I will start with some clarifications as to what a unitary approach implies and what it does not imply.[11] I should stress that I

---

[7] See n 1 above. In order to avoid unnecessary repetitions, I will, in part, simply refer to this article and the cases discussed there. It may, therefore, be necessary to read parts of Martinson's article in order to understand the context.

[8] There is no scientific reason for this choice; the explanation simply is that I know these systems best. I am fully aware of the fact that '*the* unitary approach' does not exist, nor does '*the* functional approach': taking into account, for instance, French law or Finnish law would require certain changes. I also leave aside English law which, on the one hand, applies a relational approach in property law, but, in principle, lets all aspects of 'ownership' pass at one moment in time as under a unitary system.

[9] See the references given below, B.2.

[10] Typical reactions are, for instance, that linking practical consequences to a 'transfer of ownership' concept would be 'hocus-pocus law', a 'step backwards for 100 years' (in case people want to be very polite: for 50 years) or that someone adhering to such an approach is 'not discussing real questions'. – I wish to clarify, however, that this observation in no way relates to Claes Martinson's contribution to this volume (n 1 above).

[11] I will do so by referring to today's German and Austrian law, which is of course a simplification, as pointed out above. However, it should be emphasized that the proposals

do not at all aim at blaming anyone for misunderstanding: my observation also implies that we continental lawyers should probably increase our efforts in communicating the practical consequences of our approaches. A general problem in this context seems to be that we normally try to restrict ourselves to very basic principles[12] in our first steps of communication. This entails some risk of over-simplifying things – which may immediately be associated with the supposed downsides of a unitary way of thinking (and it is no secret that it is hard to make good progress in a debate when there is complete disagreement right at the beginning). However, when exchanging more information and reaching a higher level of mutual understanding, we may see that there are less negative consequences[13] and, to a certain degree, also some similar approaches to be found.[14]

1. The basic idea of a 'unitary' transfer concept

In the sense of the terminology used here,[15] a 'unitary' system is a system under which the right of 'ownership' is linked to a wide range of 'aspects', such as the power to transfer good title in the asset to another person (the right or ability to dispose); the right to use, modify or destroy the asset; rights to defend the asset against dispossession or other unlawful interference by others, including protection against general creditors in the other party's insolvency or where the asset is seized in execution proceedings against another person.[16] The characteristic element of a 'unitary system' is that it

---

made by the 'Transfer of Movables' working group in the Study Group on a European Civil Code, which are (at least at the current stage) phrased in rather 'unitary' terminology, should be understood in the same light.

[12] Like the basic ideas listed below, 1.

[13] See 2., below.

[14] See 3., below.

[15] See footnote 2 for a different understanding.

[16] For German law, see, for instance, Hans Josef Wieling, *Sachenrecht*, Vol I: *Sachen, Besitz und Rechte an beweglichen Sachen* (Berlin: Springer, 2nd edition 2006), 14 *et seq*, 270 *et seq* (also dealing with the historical development); for Austria: Helmut Koziol and Rudolf Welser, *Grundriss des bürgerlichen Rechts*, Vol I (Wien: Manz, 13th edition 2006), 280 *et seq*; for the Netherlands: Arthur Salomons, *Transfer of Title Concerning Movables Part IV – National Report: The Netherlands* (Frankfurt am Main: Peter Lang 2006), 14 *et seq*, 43. – It may be added that the characteristic idea of transferring all these 'aspects' in one moment in time is often not dealt with explicitly, as it is considered self-evident from the traditional background. For a partial description of the unitary transfer idea, see Andreas von Tuhr, *Der Allgemeine Teil des Deutschen Bürgerlichen Rechts*, Vol II/1 (München and Leipzig: Duncker & Humblot 1914), 59 *et seq*.

defines one particular moment in time when 'ownership' passes from the transferor to the transferee. Upon this passing of ownership, all the 'aspects' linked to ownership also 'pass' from the transferor to the transferee. Accordingly, there is, in principle, one rule (one point in time) decisive for all aspects.

2. What a 'unitary' system does not mean

In Swedish legal literature, the unitary approach of connecting the solutions to more than one problem ('aspects') in one rule for a transfer of 'ownership' has a considerably bad reputation. This is often underlined by examples stating that under a unitary approach, for instance, the 'transfer of ownership' is decisive for the passing of the risk in a sales transaction;[17] that it is the passing of ownership which produces a right to performance; that the passing of ownership necessarily provides the final decision in a double sale case[18] or that the private law rules on ownership are decisive for consequences in tax law.[19] Tying such different 'aspects' to one moment in time under a uniform 'transfer of ownership' concept is associated with a method of jurisprudence deriving its results from legal concepts and notions in a purely formalistic way (*begreppsjurisprudens*, *Begriffsjurisprudenz*),[20] which is, as indicated above, generally seen as a very bad – and even comic – way of reasoning.[21] It should be noted that such statements usually do not relate to any particular contemporary legal system: it is not said that, for instance, the

---

[17] Cf Torgny Håstad, 'Inför en europeisk sakrätt – några principfrågor', (2002-2003) *Juridisk Tidskrift* (JT) 745 at 753; idem, 'General Aspects of Transfer and Creation of Property Rights, including Security Rights', in: Ulrich Drobnig, Henk J Snijders and Erik-Jan Zippro (eds), *Divergences of Property Law, an Obstacle to the Internal Market?* (München: Sellier. European Law Publishers 2006), 37 at 39.

[18] For the last two points see Henrik Hessler, *Almän sakrätt* (Stockholm: Norstedt & Söners 1973), 18.

[19] Håstad (n 17) *loc cit*.

[20] Hessler (n 18), 18 *et seq*; Torgny Håstad, *Sakrätt avseende lös egendom* (Stockholm: Norstedts Juridik, 6th edition 1996), 209 *et seq*. – As there is no suitable expression for this methodological theory in English language, I will stick to the Swedish and German terms in the following.

[21] See the overview provided by Ulf Göranson, *Traditionsprincipen* (Uppsala: Iustus förlag 1985), 419 *et seq*, who, however, proposes a less critical understanding. Göranson suggests using parts of this method and developing a clear content for at least some legal terms (like possession and individualisation), which could also be used for other questions than the buyer's protection against the seller's creditors. He argues that this will make the law clearer and easier to apply.

German, Dutch, Swiss or Austrian law in force today would contain such rules. With some authors, it seems rather clear that what they have in mind when making such critical statements is actually the former Swedish law of the late 19th century, which has been criticised and finally overcome by the functional approach.[22] In this context, the tendency of partly exaggerating the (real or presumptive) negative effects of 'the other' approach appears understandable. However, it may well be that such descriptions also leave their mark on the way of looking at contemporary unitary national legal systems and on Scandinavian reactions where proposals of starting from a unitary approach in a European harmonisation discourse are put forward.[23]

However, such assumptions would misinterpret existing national rules as well as proposals for future developments: The passing of the risk is generally understood as an issue to be solved in contract law (comparable to articles 66 et seq CISG),[24] just as a right to performance is a consequence of concluding a contract of sale,[25] not of a transfer of ownership.[26] Proprietary

---

[22] See, for example, the important Swedish precursor of the contemporary functional approach (and social democrat politician) Östen Undén, *Svensk sakrätt*, Vol I: *Lös egendom* (Lund: Gleerups förlag 1927), 83 et seq (the passage being kept unchanged up to the 10th and last edition, Stockholm: Norstedts Juridik 1976, reprint 1995 by Fritzes förlag, Stockholm, at p 57 et seq), who states that deriving solutions for certain questions of macroeconomic and social importance (such as how the rights of the owner of a forest should be limited) from an '*a priori* principle' of ownership, adhering to the 'holiness of the right of ownership' would be 'non-scientific' ('non-scientific' being a common term in the discourse of legal realism of that time, expressing that it is considered impossible to draw conclusions from value-based concepts and call the result a logic, ie 'scientific', solution; what is proclaimed instead is that values should be used as values, openly, not hidden in concepts).

[23] I actually made the experience in discussions within the Study Group that some of the named examples were associated with the (unitary-based) proposals our working group made there.

[24] For contracts of sale, see §§ 300, 446, 447 BGB; §§ 1048-1051, 1064 ABGB; see also articles 5:101 et seq of the forthcoming Principles of European Sales Law (PESL) elaborated within the Study Group on a European Civil Code (version as at December 2004, quoted from www.sgecc.net).

[25] § 433 BGB; § 1061 ABGB; articles 2:001, 2:101 PESL in the named version.

[26] There are, however, legal systems where the passing of risk is, traditionally, understood to be connected to the passing of ownership; see, for instance, Henri de Page and Anne Meinertzhagen-Limpens, *Traité élémentaire de droit civil belge: Les principaux contrats (première partie)*, Vol 4/1 (Bruxelles: Bruylant, 4th ed 1997), n 25 at p 52 et seq for Belgian law. Cf also Vincent Sagaert's contribution on p 9 of this volume (at n 15 and 47-49) who, however, argues in favor of disconnecting the transfer of risk from the transfer of property.

consequences of a double sale are partly subject to individual regulation.[27] Finally, contemporary tax law regulations in Germany[28] and Austria[29] explicitly provide that ownership in the sense of the private law rules is not necessarily decisive for tax law. This principle is often referred to as the principle of 'economic ownership', the basic idea being that things must be looked upon from a viewpoint of economic reality. One may also add that the former method of *Begriffsjurisprudenz* is generally agreed to have been overcome in the German speaking jurisdictions. In private law methodology, there is consensus, at least in principle, that positive norms are the result of

---

[27] On a general level, the rules converge insofar as the buyer who first obtains possession will get priority over the other buyer, provided he is in good faith. Cf articles 1141, 2279 Code civil; § 430 ABGB (the good faith aspect being implied indirectly; cf below, section 3.(d) with n 48). In German law, there is no explicit regulation, but the result is comparable to a certain extent; see Mary-Rose McGuire, *Transfer of Title Concerning Movables Part II – National Report: Germany* (Frankfurt am Main: Peter Lang 2006), 98.

[28] § 39 of the German *Abgabenordnung* (AO) basically states that, for the purposes of tax law, an asset is to be attributed to its civil law owner, unless another person has factual control over this asset in a way that enables this person to exclude the owner. In fiduciary relationships (*Treuhand*), for instance, the asset is to be attributed to the fiduciary; where ownership has been transferred for security purposes (*Sicherungseigentum*), the asset is to be attributed to the security giver. In case of a sale under retention of title, the rule provides for the attribution to the buyer, in case of theft to the thief. In a transfer situation, the decisive factor may be, according to the individual circumstances of the case, the transfer of possession, the passing of the risk, uses or the responsibility for charges; not necessarily the transfer of the right of ownership. Confer the text of the norm and, for the rest of the issues mentioned, Heinrich W Kruse in: Klaus Tipke and Heinrich W Kruse (eds), *Abgabenordnung* (Köln: Otto Schmidt Verlag, loose-leaf edition from 1961, last update 2006), § 39 n 29, 53 and 55.

[29] Similarly to German law, according to § 21 of the Austrian *Bundesabgabenordnung* (BAO), the principle of 'substance over form' (*wirtschaftliche Betrachtungsweise*) is to be applied unless provided otherwise (which is not the case for our context). § 24 BAO contains a provision corresponding to the German § 39 AO (n 28). Its structure even goes a step further than the German rule in that the principle of 'economic ownership' is not formulated as an exception. Historically, the predecessors of these rules in the Tax Law Acts from 1919 and 1934 (and also doctrinal writings before) intended to overcome the method of *Begriffsjurisprudenz* by explicit regulation. See, for instance, Werner Doralt and Hans Georg Ruppe, *Grundriss des österreichischen Steuerrechts*, Vol II (Wien: Manz & LexisNexis, 5th edition 2006), 214 *et seq*, 223 *et seq* (n 425 *et seq*, 442 *et seq*), or the standard commentary by Gerold Stoll, *Bundesabgabenordnung Kommentar*, Vol I (Wien: Orac 1994), comments on §§ 21 and 24 BAO, in particular at 237-239 and 282 *et seq* on the relation between tax law and civil law and the historical developments.

value judgements made by the legislator, who has to decide which interests involved in typical conflict situations shall be worth of being considered. The courts have to take these value judgements into account and 'think them to the end' when deciding individual cases, also taking into account that there may be different conflicting values involved.[30] It is, however, not considered contradictory to these principles to use a unitary concept for the transfer of ownership.[31]

What may we conclude from these clarifications? The typical contemporary unitary approach does not link *every* aspect one may think of to the 'transfer of ownership'. It connects some, but still a remarkable number, of aspects.[32] For a fruitful international debate, the proponents of the Scandinavian functional approach could focus on this 'nucleus' of the unitary concept and show which concrete results could be improved or, in other words, which *specific* consequences appear inappropriate because – or if – they are connected at one moment in time. There, one may think of providing deviating rules.

3. Other parts of law may partially provide 'functional effects' in a unitary system

There are still further clarifications to be made in order to understand how a unitary system like the German or the Austrian one works in practice. Even if we only take into account the aspects listed under section B.1., it should be stressed that the question 'who owns' does not necessarily decide all cases, or the whole set of problems in one particular case, respectively. Sometimes there are *additional rules* or even something like an *additional 'level' of law* to be applied, practically derogating the property law rules or limiting their effects. One may well describe this as partial functional effects in a unitary environment. I will give some examples, mainly by falling back on some of the cases Claes Martinson discussed in his article in this volume.[33]

---

[30] For the German debate on the methodological development see, for instance, Karl Larenz, *Methodenlehre der Rechtswissenschaft* (Berlin: Springer, 6th edition 1991), 19 *et seq*; Franz Bydlinski, *Juristische Methodenlehre und Rechtsbegriff* (Wien: Springer, 2nd edition 1991), 109 *et seq*.

[31] A certain difference to the Scandinavian legal systems is, of course, that the unitary transfer approach is codified law in the German speaking jurisdictions.

[32] As listed *sub* 1., above.

[33] See n 1, above.

(a) Contract law rules

In the case discussed in chapter B. of Claes Martinson's article, it is asked whether Mr Bond shall be entitled to use the car he sold to Mrs Copeland. As the question is put, it is an issue between the two parties to the contract of sale: May the buyer demand that the seller refrains from using the car between the conclusion of the contract and physical delivery, which is scheduled two weeks later?

It is correct that under the unitary systems applied in Germany or Austria, property law provides that the owner is entitled to use his property.[34] But it is important that here, in the transfer situation, as far as only the seller and the buyer are concerned, there is a *'higher'* or *'more specific' level of contract law* which will be applied in order to solve the case: As under Swedish law, the question of whether the seller may, in relation to the buyer, still use the car will be solved by an *interpretation of the contract,* and it turns out that German or Austrian lawyers would – at least partly – even use the same arguments: The risk of damage done to the car and the wear and tear can serve as strong arguments that the seller will – contractually – not be entitled to use it.[35] Also the question which one of the parties takes the initiative of postponing delivery will be an issue when interpreting the contract (it is easier to imply a term of non-usage if it is the buyer who requests the deferred delivery). There is no closed list of aspects that may be taken into account when interpreting the contract.

In case the interpretation of the contract does not provide a clear outcome, *dispositive norms of contract* law are to be applied. In our case, these rules would provide that the seller in possession was entitled to use the asset in a normal way until the agreed date of delivery.[36] This largely coincides with the property law rule providing that the owner is entitled to use, but it is not a direct consequence of the unitary system.

I should perhaps clarify this result a bit more closely: When interpreting the contract in this case (*ie* the first step in the analysis above), the question will precisely be whether the seller is under a contractual obligation *to refrain from using* the car between the conclusion of the contract and delivery. If the result is that the seller is bound by such obligation, this does not automatically mean that 'the right to use' has already *passed* to the buyer:

---

[34] § 903 BGB; §§ 354, 362 ABGB. Linked with the delivery requirement provided by the German and Austrian transfer rules, this *would* mean that the seller was entitled to the 'right to use' until delivery.

[35] This argument would be even stronger if the car was a new one.

[36] § 1050 ABGB as interpreted by modern practice; cf Martin Binder in Michael Schwimann (ed), *ABGB Praxiskommentar,* Vol IV (Wien: LexisNexis, 3rd edition 2006), § 1050 n 3. For Germany, see § 446 BGB.

depending on the circumstances, the buyer might not be entitled to use the car either. The arguments for this conclusion can be rather similar to those used for the first conclusion. If the buyer had not paid the price yet but the parties had agreed on cash payment at delivery,[37] for instance, the wear and tear and the risk that the car gets damaged would interfere with the seller's interest of securing his claim for the purchase price with the value of the car. The dispositive contract law norms I referred to above (*ie* the second step in the analysis given) will, however, give an answer to both questions: the seller's and the buyer's 'right to use' *inter partes*. There could be a third question, which is, however, not raised in the example, namely who would be entitled to proceed against a third person using the car without permission between the conclusion of the contract and the agreed date of delivery.[38] For this question, which addresses third party effects and is not restricted to the relation between seller and buyer, the *right of ownership* would actually be the starting point.

(b) Insolvency law rules

(i) Right of stoppage in transit

Also insolvency law provisions may act as a more specific level of rules, taking priority before the general transfer rules in property law. I will first demonstrate this for the case discussed by Claes Martinson in chapter H. of his paper, where goods are in transit when both the seller and the buyer go bankrupt, by applying the relevant provisions of Austrian[39] law.

In such a constellation of 'double insolvency', Austrian law protects both the seller and the buyer: The buyer will be protected by the rules on the *transfer of ownership*, as ownership will pass to the buyer when the goods are handed over to the independent carrier (§ 429 ABGB). But, at the same time, a special insolvency law provision will come into play, affording the seller – regardless of him having already lost the right of ownership – a *right*

---

[37] In Martinson's example, the buyer has already paid.

[38] *Eg*, a thief or someone who takes the object in order to go for a ride and then returns it to the seller's place. I will not discuss this constellation in more detail as it has not been referred to in Claes Martinson's contribution. It would take a lot of additional remarks to describe sufficiently how a unitary system would tackle the issue; what is said in the text only marks a starting point.

[39] German law differs for two reasons: First, there is no general rule that ownership passes to the buyer when the goods are handed over to the carrier. Second, the new German Insolvency Act (*Insolvenzordnung*, InsO) abolished the former rule providing a right of stoppage in transit (see n 41, below).

of stoppage in transit as long as the goods have not been physically taken over by the buyer (§ 45 KO).[40] This right provides protection against the buyer's creditors in insolvency.[41] Like in Sweden, the buyer's administrator in bankruptcy can terminate the right of stoppage by paying the full purchase price.[42]

What this example shows is that also a 'unitary' system like the Austrian one can offer a solution protecting both parties. One can say that the insolvency law rules applicable to this case provide some 'functional' effect where this has been considered adequate by the legislator. When using the term 'functional' in this context, I mean that specific conflict situations may be governed by special rules (which do not stick to the general transfer concept). There will, however, still be differences to a functional approach in

---

[40] *Konkursordnung* (KO), the Austrian Bankruptcy Act.

[41] In more detail, exercising the right of stoppage is considered to create an *obligatory right to re-transfer ownership* of the goods to the seller; but this right is of special character insofar as it has the *quality of a right of separation in insolvency* (*Aussonderungsrecht*), which means that the right to claim back the goods is protected vis-à-vis the insolvent buyer and his creditors in bankruptcy. For Austria, cf Peter Schulyok in Andreas Konecny and Günter Schubert, *Kommentar zu den Insolvenzgesetzen* (Wien: Manz 1997, as amended by additional instalment 2002), § 45 KO n 4; Georg Petschek, Otto Reimer and Karl Schiemer, *Das österreichische Insolvenzrecht* (Wien: Manz 1973), 453 *et seq*. In Germany, the same provision was contained in § 44 of the former *Konkursordnung* (Bankruptcy Act), but the rule was not taken over into the new *Insolvenzordnung*, which entered into force in 1999. The reasons were that the right of stoppage has little practical relevance today (because the parties usually stipulate a retention of title clause or issue a letter of credit [*Akkreditiv*]), and that it was said to contradict the system in strengthening the seller's position in case insolvency proceedings are opened; see the (very short) reasoning in the government's proposition: 'Entwurf einer Insolvenzordnung', *Bundestags-Drucksache* (BT-DruckS) 12/2443 of 15 April 1992, at p 121. Today, German law only contains mere obligatory rights (without particular effects in the buyer's insolvency) to stop dispatched goods before they reach the buyer: This is allowed by § 321 (1) BGB (*Unsicherheitseinrede*), cf Hansjörg Otto in *Staudingers Kommentar zum BGB* (Berlin: Sellier – de Gruyter 2004), § 321 n 44. Under § 418 HGB (Commercial Code), the consignor (seller) is entitled to give instructions to the carrier under the contract of carriage before the goods reach their destination; cf Roland Dubischar in *Münchener Kommentar zum Handelsgesetzbuch*, Vol 7a (München: C H Beck & Franz Wahlen 2000), § 418 n 1-5 (similar rules are provided by § 433 Austrian UGB).

[42] Schulyok (n 41 above), § 45 n 17 (referring also to other authors who argue for some limitations of such right).

the Scandinavian sense, at least in what regards justifying and communicating these rules.[43]

(ii) *Avoidance in bankruptcy (actio Pauliana)*

Another well-known insolvency law instrument, which may provide 'functional' effects in a unitary system, is constituted by the rules on avoidance in bankruptcy (*actio Pauliana*). Subject to certain requirements, the creditors – represented by the administrator in bankruptcy – can set aside the debtor's transactions which result in a diminishment of the debtor's estate. The effect of such 'avoidance' is a relative one: the transaction is to be disre-

---

[43] This may be demonstrated when asking whether the seller's right of stoppage also has effect against third parties who already acquired rights in the goods from the buyer (eg, subsequent buyers or pledgees). A lawyer from a unitary system will typically describe the problem as follows: The right of stoppage is not a right *in rem* but only an obligatory right with certain qualifications (cf n 41, above) and 'therefore' the right is not valid against third parties who have acquired new rights in the goods from the owner (the buyer); cf Schulyok (n 41 above), § 45 n 6; most illustrative for the former German law: Ernst Jaeger and Friedrich Lent, *Konkursordnung* (Berlin: De Gruyter 1958), § 44 n 5-7, 29. A Scandinavian lawyer would not use categories like 'rights *in rem*', 'obligatory rights' or certain forms in between these two, but would address the interests of the seller and the third party in a more direct way. The 'unitary lawyer' will also put forward arguments, but the usual way to communicate the analysis – at least for this specific problem – is to use these arguments in order to classify the 'nature' of the seller's right (*in rem* or obligatory character *etc*) and, then, to spell out the solution to the problem by referring to this categorisation. For the problem at stake, the common argument is that the hypothetical alternative solution – namely retroactively vesting ownership back to the seller, unless the sub-purchaser was in good faith (good faith would have to refer to the 'non-revocability' of the transfer in terms of a right of stoppage) – would create unacceptable insecurity in commerce; see Jaeger and Lent, *loc cit*, § 44 n 6, 29. Personally, I do think that for problems like this, a more direct way of reasoning as applied under the functional approach is in fact favourable; at least, one should not confine oneself to arguments like the one reflected above. However, this does not say anything about the outcome of such analysis: the preferred solution may converge with the general transfer rule or constitute an exception, depending on the weight of the arguments. This approach may be taken *de lege ferenda* and could, for the present question, eventually also be argued *de lege lata*, as the right of stoppage in § 45 of the Austrian Bankruptcy Act already establishes an exception to the unitary concept (but does not expressly regulate in which relations this exception is effective).

garded (only) between the third party acquirer and the insolvency creditors.[44]

(c) Civil procedure rules

In chapter C. of his contribution, Claes Martinson discusses a case where a used car is first sold by A to B (the latter defrauded A when concluding the contract) and then twice from B to C (without delivery) and from B to D (with delivery) and, further on, from D to E. The car is still in the possession of D, and the question of who may sue whom to get the car is put forward. The author stresses that, for a Scandinavian lawyer, it is important that deciding one conflict should not impose binding effects on third parties who did not take part in these court proceedings. In the Swedish legal system, this effect is achieved on the level of property law, by the functional approach. This means, for instance, that B could sue A after A won the car back from D and the decision established between A and D is not binding as between A and B. Also, the relation between A and B would not be taken into account when deciding the case between A and D. The question 'who owns' at the different stages would not be an issue.

Conversely, under a unitary property law system like the German or Austrian one, the question who owned the car at the different stages of the transactions would in fact be a main issue. In a lawsuit between A and D, the relation to certain third parties (in our case: B) and the question of whether this third person acquired ownership in the course of the multiple transactions would certainly be taken into account.[45] However, that does *not* mean that this would *produce binding effects* on a person who did not take part in the lawsuit between A and D. This, however, is not achieved by the property law rules but by rules on civil procedure, providing that a judgment

---

[44] See §§ 129-147 German InsO; §§ 27-43 Austrian KO. There are also respective provisions for 'avoidance' outside insolvency proceedings, cf the German *Anfechtungsgesetz* and the Austrian *Anfechtungsordnung*. For a more detailed comparative overview see Caroline Cauffman, 'The Relationship between Transfer Rules and Rules on Creditor's Avoidance of Debtor's Transactions', on p 123 of this volume, *sub* C.

[45] Due to the German 'abstraction principle' (§ 929 BGB), the validity of the contract between A and B will be of less practical importance under German law. For Austrian law and other systems, such as Dutch law, however, this issue will be of central importance. – As to the solution of the case at stake, it may be noted that, different to Swedish law, Austrian law does not provide the original owner A with a right to buy back the object from a good faith acquirer D (the same applies to German law). So, if D wins the case against A, this will practically be the end of the story.

is only binding between the parties to the lawsuit (*materielle Rechtskraft*).[46] This is based on the principle that the binding effect of a judgment presupposes that the respective party had a right to be heard before the court and, therefore, was able to influence the course of the proceedings by providing evidence *etc*. There is even a constitutional background to this rule.[47] Accordingly, the court could decide that A or B is the owner in a lawsuit between these two parties and – theoretically – come to a different conclusion in a trial between A and D, or vice versa.

(d) Further examples and conclusion

One could list further examples where specific rules provide a deviation from the general (unitary) transfer concept. In a double sale, the second buyer who acquired possession, knowing of the first sale to another person, may be forced to transfer the object to the first buyer under tort law principles.[48] Where goods are bought by means of indirect representation (such as under a buying commission), a unitary system may provide for special rules such as a direct acquisition by the principal from the third party[49] and/or establish special priority rights in the goods in order to secure the agent's claims against the principal.[50] One may also think of unpaid sellers' liens, which are usually provided in systems where ownership is transferred upon the conclusion of the contract[51] *etc*.

---

[46] For Germany: § 325 ZPO and Peter Gottwald in *Münchener Kommentar zur Zivilprozessordnung*, Vol I (München: C H Beck, 2nd edition 2000), § 325 n 1, 7-10. For Austria: Walter H Rechberger and Daphne-Ariane Simotta, *Grundriss des österreichischen Zivilprozessrechts – Erkenntnisverfahren* (Wien: Manz, 6th edition 2003), n 694 *et seq* (especially n 699/1) at p 397 *et seq*.

[47] Article 6 of the European Convention for the Protection of Human Rights and Fundamental Freedoms. On the impact of this rule in great detail (but with a somewhat different focus: binding effect of an executory title for proceedings based on the *actio Pauliana*): Gottfried Musger, 'Verfahrensrechtliche Bindungswirkungen und Art 6 MRK', (1991) 113 *Juristische Blätter* 420 and 499.

[48] For Austria see, for instance, Renate Pletzer, *Doppelveräußerung und Forderungseingriff* (Wien: Orac 2000).

[49] For the Netherlands, see article 3:110 NBW and Arthur Salomons (n 16 above), 38, 67.

[50] Like §§ 397, 398 of the German *Handelsgesetzbuch* (HGB) and §§ 397, 398 of the Austrian *Unternehmensgesetzbuch* (UGB).

[51] See sections 38-43 of the English Sale of Goods Act 1979. Cf also the legal lien provided by article 20, 5° para (1) Belgian *loi hypothécaire / hypotheekwet* (Mortgage Act) and the unpaid seller's right to claim back the goods within eight days from delivery provided by para (6) *leg cit*, both under the precondition that the unpaid goods can be

I think that for the further dialogue between lawyers from legal systems following a functional approach on the one hand, and systems following a more unitary approach on the other hand, identifying and enumerating such provisions will be an important step towards mutual understanding. This could make it easier for Scandinavian lawyers to see (modern) unitary concepts in a less negative light. Having reached this level of mutual understanding, it could be that a functional approach proponent gets the impression that the unitary-based systems become enormously complicated because one always has to find one's way through the unitary principle and a jungle of exemptions and different levels of law to be applied. Well, such impression will be correct in the sense that the legal reality in today's unitary systems is more complex and complicated than it may seem at first sight. But it should also be stressed that combining a 'unitary nucleus' with 'functional exemptions and surroundings' is not more complicated than a fully functional (relational) approach.

C. Interdependencies between various aspects and relations

1. Interdependencies between different 'aspects' of ownership

I will now turn to more direct scepticism against the functional approach: It will be a more or less natural reaction that a lawyer with a 'unitary background', being confronted with the Scandinavian functional approach, will tend to think that it is *impossible to split all aspects of 'ownership'*. He or she will assume that there are, necessarily, interdependencies between the various aspects. Against the background of being educated in German or Austrian law, for instance, it would seem a bit strange if the buyer was already protected against the seller's general creditors but the seller could still validly dispose of the goods: the effect would be that the buyer could still lose the asset to third parties who have contractual claims against the seller. We would regard it rather contradictory if the 'right to use' was still with the seller but the buyer was already entitled to a claim under unjustified enrichment in the case of a third person having unlawfully used the asset.[52] It would also seem a bit strange to us if the right to use was still with the seller but the buyer, and not the seller, was entitled to claim for physical recovery in case a third party unlawfully dispossessed the seller.

---

found *in natura* in the possession of the buyer at the moment he gets insolvent. The same rule applies in French law: article 2332, 4° para (1) and (2) Cc.

[52] However, unjustified enrichment usually plays no important role in the Scandinavian legal systems, so this case may, perhaps, not occur.

However, this does not necessarily give rise to fundamental critique against the functional approach, neither from the theoretical point of view nor from its practical handling in the Scandinavian jurisdictions: Results like those given above would be considered strange, considerably strange maybe, but we would, perhaps, go too far in saying that they were absolutely and cogently contradictory on a logical level. And I do not know whether any of the Scandinavian systems would, after all, come to such solutions in a practical case.

In fact I, so far, have not come across any practical case decided by a Scandinavian court where the potential freedom granted by the functional approach actually led to contradictory results (in the sense of a unitary understanding of the transfer of ownership). One aspect is, of course, that my experience is not too advanced. Also, some of the hypothetical problems do not occur because they are tackled from another angle.[53] Another point might be that some questions, which would be an issue for a 'unitary lawyer', simply do not seem to be discussed. For instance, the 'right to dispose' in the sense of a unitary concept (meaning the capability of legally transferring the right of ownership to another person or pawning the asset *etc*) is, on the one hand, recognised and more intensively dealt with where the content of

---

[53] An example may be the first point I raised in this section (the buyer already being protected against seller's creditors but the seller still has power to dispose): Concerning ordinary sales, Swedish law provides a mandatory delivery requirement for the buyer's protection against the seller's creditors; cf Håstad (n 20), 205 *et seq* (in particular 221 *et seq*). The problem we address here is, to a large degree, avoided by applying the tradition principle in a way that requires the seller not to be able to dispose of the goods (however, understood in a rather factual way, see the Swedish Supreme Court in [1975] *Nytt juridiskt arkiv* [NJA], 638 and Håstad, *cit*, at 224 *et seq*, which is not the same as under a unitary understanding). – For consumer sales, the tradition requirement was, however, abolished in 2002 by introducing a new § 49 to the Consumer Sales Act (*konsumentköplagen*). Under this rule, the named constellation (buyer already protected against seller's creditors while seller is still entitled to dispose) can actually occur. In Swedish literature, such a constellation is discussed from the perspective that the buyer's protection should not be achieved too easily where the sale involves generic goods and individualisation of the goods has not taken place by both parties acting together or, at least, by the seller giving notice to the buyer, and that the seller should, in such a case, be free to sell these goods to a third party; cf Torgny Håstad, *Supplement 2004 till Sakrätt avseende lös egendom, sjätte upplagen 1996* (Stockholm: Norstedts juridik 2004), 19 (relating to p 215 *et seq*). The effect of this argumentation actually is that the 'aspects' of 'protection against the seller's creditors and the 'right to dispose' do not conflict with each other. But this is not the argument put forward by Håstad. The concern rather seems to be minimizing the risks of fraud and uncertainties in bankruptcy.

property rights is explained in general.[54] But the issue does not seem to be touched as an 'aspect' of its own in the discussion of transfer situations[55] (I may add that this is something a 'unitary lawyer' will actually miss). Finally, however, it should be noted that also important Swedish authors underline that it 'can be practical and adequate to have, at least to a certain extent, a common starting point for the different legal consequences in the context of a transfer'.[56]

Another issue that could be mentioned here is *acquisitive prescription*: If a legal system provides for a possibility of acquiring ownership by continuous possession over a certain period of time, the central motive usually is to provide legal certainty.[57] If this is the basic decision of a legislator, I think that very much will speak in favour of providing such legal certainty in all relations (so that certainty is really certain), as this motive may operate in various categories of constellations. That would mean to provide the acquirer a safe position against the original owner and his creditors;[58] certainty

---

[54] See, for instance, Hessler (n 18), 20, 27 *et seq* (perhaps most illustrative) and Håstad (n 20), 22 *et seq*.

[55] Cf Håstad, (2002-2003) JT 745 (n 17), at 765, who argues that the question when the 'right to dispose' shall pass does not need to be regulated in a code. In his view, it would be 'natural' that – unless an explicit contractual regulation has been established – in case of specific goods, the right to dispose will pass upon conclusion of the contract, in case of generic goods with (binding) individualisation. There are, however, no arguments given for this solution. I may add that I generally doubt whether lawyers with a functional approach background and those coming from unitary systems actually mean the same when talking about a 'right to dispose' (cf n 53, above).

[56] Quoted from Hessler (n 18), 19. See also chapter I. of Claes Martinson's contribution to this volume (n 1) and of course Göranson (n 21), 419 *et seq*, who, however, goes further than the dominant view.

[57] For German law and the historic development see, for instance, Wieling (n 16), 419 *et seq*.

[58] I should, perhaps, give some reasons for including the aspect of 'protection against creditors' here, as this might create some difficulties from a functional approach perspective, whereas other aspects listed in the text will probably not: Acquisitive prescription, in the sense of continental European legal systems, may take place in different constellations. 1) Where the person who has acquired ownership by acquisitive prescription (in the following: the acquirer) has obtained possession from the real owner, but on an invalid legal basis, the argument of legal certainty will justify awarding protection against the former owner's creditors after the same period of time and under the same preconditions as protection against the former owner himself is granted, so that the owner and his creditors are treated alike. *Before* the period of prescription has ended, accordingly, the creditors can attach their debtor's property as he himself could. *After* the period of prescription has ended, the creditors could still attach the property,

as to the fact that the new position encompasses a right to use the object, including a right to sell it and to convert it into money; certainty for subsequent buyers that they will acquire good title, and so on. This example may show that it can make sense to have the same rules for different aspects of ownership. It will have, however, little relevance, at least for some of the Scandinavian legal systems, as they partly do not have a strong tradition regarding the acquisitive prescription of movable assets: There is no acquisitive prescription of movables in Finland.[59] In Sweden, there are, from 1 July 2003, at least some phenomena in the Act for good faith acquisition, which can be described by 'acquisitive prescription' (*hävd*).[60] Norwegian[61] and Danish[62] law do provide for acquisitive prescription of movables.

2. Must we sometimes take more than one relation into account?

My next point refers to the functional approach's demand to deal with each relationship as a problem of its own: involving relations to other parties (or even asking 'who owns') is not regarded necessary.[63] I would like to draw up the hypothesis that literally obeying such demand, *ie* not involving other relations at all, is not possible in a number of constellations. I try to set forth this hypothesis by coming back to the case discussed in chapter C. of Claes Martinson's article (B fraudulently purchases a car from A and then sells it, first to C and, subsequently, to D who now has it in his possession). There,

---

provided the transaction (which was, in fact, invalid) could be avoided under the rules of the *actio Pauliana*, which should probably prevail based on their specific purposes (this issue, however, will not be a practical problem in many jurisdictions, as the periods for acquisitive prescription, at least in bad faith, where this is possible at all, will usually be longer than the time limits for the *actio Pauliana*). 2) Where the acquirer obtained possession from a non-owner, protection against the creditors of the real owner should be granted in the same way as against the real owner himself. 3) Where possession is obtained from a non-owner and the creditors of this non-owner seek to attach the property, I think there is nothing to be said against protecting the acquirer *at least* after the prescription period has ended, for the sake of legal certainty (under a unitary system, one will, of course, argue that such creditors have no rights at all because their debtor had no rights either).

[59] I rely on a national report written for the 'Transfer of Movables' project by Miki Kuusinen, University of Helsinki (not yet published).

[60] Cf Martinson, *Transfer of Title* (n 1), 94.

[61] Cf Thor Falkanger, *Tingsrett* (Oslo: Universitetsforlaget, 5th edition 1999), 279 *et seq*.

[62] I rely on a national report provided for the 'Transfer of Movables' project by Jan-Ove Færstad, University of Bergen (not published so far).

[63] See chapter C. of Claes Martinson's article in this volume (n 1).

the case is analysed by stating that in the relation A – D, particular norms, namely the Swedish Act on Good Faith Acquisition,[64] must be observed. Based on these rules, the former owner A can make use of a secondary claim and 'buy back' the car from the good faith acquirer D.

But which are the requirements for such a right to buy back? D must have acquired the car based on the rules on good faith acquisition (§ 5 *leg cit*), which requires that B, who transferred the car to D, 'was neither the owner nor entitled to dispose of' the object (§ 2 *leg cit*). As there was a contract of sale between A and B, I assume that B can only be regarded as a 'non-owner' if this contract of sale was void or avoided. This, however, shows that it is sometimes in fact necessary to take another relation (A – B) into account to solve the conflict at stake between two parties (A – D). Otherwise, the relevant norms could not be applied. One may also phrase this result by referring to the different 'aspects' of ownership: The example does not necessarily say that the only way to do it right is to determine whether B was 'owner' and whether D became 'owner' or whether A is still 'owner'. But to get a result for one aspect of ownership (A's right to get the asset back from another person, D) it proves to be necessary to operate with another aspect of ownership as a tool (the entitlement to dispose, which B either had or did not have, depending on A's avoidance).

Well, I do, however, think that a Swedish lawyer would not disagree heavily as to substance. He or she may use different expressions, but we will probably agree that for solving the case between A and D we need to decide whether B acquired the car rightfully or not. So why do I discuss this case at all? I think that it directs us to a problem, which is partly a problem of communication and partly a problem of methodological self-reflection: As a basic principle of the functional approach is to keep problems apart, I think that this principle sometimes is a bit over-emphasized.[65] The example, however, shows that there is *nothing bad in acknowledging that there may be interdependencies* between the different relationships involved in a case and admitting this openly. I do not at all say that this forces the functional approach proponents to throw in the towel. But I want to underline that stressing something like a principle of the strict separation of all relations, in cases where interrelations are hard to deny, is exactly one of the main reasons why continental European lawyers feel sceptic about the functional approach at first sight.

After all, what the functional approach in essence wants to achieve, by pronouncing the principle of keeping apart the different relationships in a case like this, seems to be the following: to avoid that a decision on one relation could have *binding effects* on another relation, *ie* on parties who did

---

[64] *Lag* (1986:796) *om godtrosförvärv av lösöre*, as adapted by *lag* 1998:1574 and 2003:161.
[65] Just as we 'unitary lawyers' sometimes over-emphasize our starting point.

not take part in the court trial. As pointed out above,[66] such a result would not be achieved under unitary systems either, due to procedural law principles. Accordingly, a court may theoretically assess the same question differently in different proceedings between different parties, no matter whether the case between A and D[67] or the case between A and B is decided first.[68]

D. Legal certainty and predictability of judicial decisions

In my experience, a rather widespread scepticism among lawyers from unitary systems, who are getting into contact with the functional approach, is the assumption that deciding each problem separately, based on the individual interests involved, will bear a considerable risk of uncertainty and unpredictability of judicial decisions. Naturally, one will admit, this risk can be mitigated by providing a relatively intensive set of statutory regulations, covering most or all of the practically relevant problems. Then, of course, these rules should go together smoothly (and people may suspect that this would imply that there would not be much substantive difference to a uni-

---

[66] See B.2.(c).

[67] In this case, a lawyer with a 'unitary' background may be puzzled at first sight when Claes Martinson continues his case in chapter C. by stating that B might win the case against A after A won against D, so that B may claim the car (again) from A. This may have the implication of being contradictory because coming to the conclusion that A is entitled to get the car back from D presupposes that the contract A – B was avoided (which will require some declaration by A and further substantive prerequisites); and a contract which has been avoided should not serve as a sufficient legal basis for a second transfer A – B. But again, the described further development of the case does not create problems if we take the procedural perspective and focus on the question of the binding effects of a judicial decision: The solution, which the court arrives at about the validity of the contract A – B, when deciding the case A – D, will have no binding effect on possible subsequent proceedings between A and B (it could, for instance, well be that A managed to persuade the judge of having been defrauded in the first trial, but B, who will of course know the circumstances upon the conclusion of the contract better than D, can provide additional evidence to the contrary in his own proceedings).

[68] A practically relevant example is that A initiates proceedings against B for avoiding the contract but B does not show up before court and *therefore* loses the case. According to the named procedural principles, this decision will not be binding in a later trial between A and D. This will even be so in a system like the Austrian one, where avoidance of a contract can only be effected in a court trial. If D can show that B, in fact, did not defraud A, the court will regard the contract A – B valid (for the purposes of the proceedings between A and D) and D will win.

tary approach left). But the more 'white spots' remain,[69] which have neither been decided by statute, courts nor doctrine, the more insecurity is considered to be left.[70]

This, however, is probably no good point of criticism as to existing legal systems following a functional approach: For parts of the problems, there are positive norms to be observed, and where no statutory regulation exists, the Scandinavian jurisdictions had time enough to establish common grounds for legal practice, and they seem to work perfectly well. After all, there will probably not be significantly less predictability than under unitary systems.

E. Scepticism related to 'exporting' the functional approach to a European level or other national systems

1. Again: Legal certainty

But the aspect of legal certainty pops up immediately when we come to the question of whether the functional approach would be a good article to export to other national jurisdictions or to the drafts prepared for a hypothetical European unification. I should, perhaps, deal with this point on two different levels.

(a) In case only a few issues are regulated

As indicated above, lawyers from unitary systems tend to fear that approaching the transfer of movables with a functional method will leave too many issues unregulated. I also already said that such apprehension is not necessarily justified, as the existing Scandinavian jurisdictions show. The question of whether to follow a functional or a more unitary approach is, above all, a question of whether there shall be a uniform *superstructure* or not; it is not primarily a question of whether there shall be norms or whether there shall be no norms. It *could*, however, be that if the functional approach was fol-

---

[69] Such as a clear answer under which requirements the 'entitlement to dispose' is transferred, as indicated above, C.1. with n 54 and 55.

[70] This reflects that lawyers from unitary systems often regard it as something positive to have a common starting point and to strive for consistency. Obviously, this is exactly what the functionalists see as a downside of a unitary approach and why they find the unitary solutions too remote from reality. I should add that, where sticking to the common starting point would lead to unacceptable results, also 'unitary lawyers' will try to reach another solution and there are often methods to develop such solutions. But the differences are still considerable, of course.

lowed outside of a legal environment with a functional approach tradition, for instance in a European harmonization process, such 'white spots' (in the eyes of the unitary view) would, in fact, be left. Actually, some statements of Scandinavian lawyers could be interpreted in such a direction.[71]

I would not fulfil my task of reflecting the unitary perspective's scepticism about the functional approach without addressing these apprehensions. Maybe the main problem would not be that lawyers from a unitary tradition would consider it impossible to solve cases where explicit rules are not given. This must often be done under unitary systems as well. But I think most people will fear *too much arbitrariness* in case only parts of the issues were regulated: usually, one can find somewhat plausible arguments for supporting totally different solutions. This might make it hard for courts to decide and it would be considered equally hard to foresee the outcome of potential proceedings. Moreover, one would probably feel slightly uncomfortable if the court of last instance was a court that, as a tendency, does not or only seldom overrule its own precedents if they turn out to go the wrong way (like the ECJ, if it was declared competent).

Furthermore, I think that both lawyers and businessmen from countries with a unitary tradition would tend to believe that, also for the *parties to a transaction*, it would be easier to cope with a more unitary approach than with a functional approach with a considerable number of remaining 'white spots'. They will probably regard it advantageous to foresee the results of a transaction, just to know what the risks are in the various possible interrelations, and to have a chance to mitigate these risks by contractual agreements or insurance, where possible, or by undertaking certain acts, like delivery. I believe (but have no evidence for this) that many continental market par-

---

[71] Cf Håstad, (2002-2003) JT 745 (n 17), at 752 *et seq*. In order to avoid taking on a too ambitious workload and dealing with detailed questions of little practical importance, he proposes (with a view to the preparations in the Study Group on a European Civil Code) to limit the draft, in a 'first round', to some main questions of major importance for international trade and finance. If these proposals are well-accepted by the Member States, they should form a stable basis for dealing with the rest of the questions in a 'second round'. As main questions to be dealt with in the first round, he lists: the buyer's protection against the seller's creditors, the seller's protection against the buyer's creditors (effects of conditions and contractual defects on the buyer's creditors), security rights in specific goods and fluctuating assets, the impact of defects in the contract on the acquisition of property rights and security rights, good faith acquisition, the right to vindicate entrusted goods and proprietary protection of rights to use (leasing contracts). – I assume that there would be too many 'white spots' left in the first round for most of the lawyers with a unitary background, such as the owner's right to use, the right to dispose and the aspect of protection against third party interferers. They would, at least, regard it as insufficient to restrict statutory regulations to those 'first round' issues at all.

ticipants will consider a simple system easier to handle in this respect (and that they will regard a more unitary system as a simple system).[72]

(b) General aspects

From a European harmonisation perspective, the issue of legal certainty also involves some general aspects, which may come into play also in case the 'white spots' are rather limited and functionally (relationally) formulated rules cover most of the questions that may arise. They will, in this case, not be of such a major practical importance, but I will shortly reflect them, as I think that lawyers with a unitary background would tend to put forward such issues when being asked to formulate scepticism about the functional approach: If there are different rules for different aspects and one has to decide upon one of those (few) aspects which remained unregulated, it may be more difficult to foresee which of the (different) normative starting points will be considered most relevant by a court. This is a general problem, yet getting an additional facet on a European unification level, where there may be a certain risk that judges from different countries and different traditions could tend to follow the lines they used to follow under their national systems before, unless the intention of the parties or the circumstances, somewhat clearly, point into another direction. Finally, I think that the functional approach 'lives from' disclosing the relevant arguments and legal reasoning in the judgments. Where courts have a tradition of rendering rather short judgments without intensive reasoning, legal certainty will not be served best.

2. Different 'legal cultures'

There is another aspect, actually closely related to issues that have already been touched under the previous sections 1.(a) and (b), which should, however, not only be mentioned in the context of legal certainty: Probably not all Europeans – especially those coming from 'codification countries' – could easily live with a legal tradition like the Scandinavian one, where it is a

---

[72] This, evidently, is a question of perspective: Scandinavian lawyers, against the background of their own tradition, consider their own approach to be much easier to understand for businessmen; cf Håstad, (2002-2003) JT 745 (n 17), at 753. I should also clarify once more that the potential scepticism reflected in this section (a) relates to a hypothetical functional regulation, which only contains some basic issues and leaves the rest open. Håstad rather refers to the general question in which way property law rules should be formulated.

traditional policy that the legislator only regulates questions that are regarded to be of central importance, very practical or of a certain political interest.[73] This is, of course, no real argument against a functional approach on a European level: if the rules are formulated in a rather unitary tradition, the Scandinavians will have the same problems.[74] I just mention it here, because many lawyers from continental European systems would probably feel a bit worried about 'cultural' changes of this kind.

3. Compatibility with other parts of the private law system

My last point is that sometimes also other norms – the legal surroundings of property law, so to speak – may play a certain role in deciding whether a functional or a more unitary approach will be more suitable. This may be relevant when thinking about incorporating a functional approach into national property law reform projects outside of Scandinavia. It should definitely be taken into account when thinking of private law harmonisation on a European level. I will concentrate on this latter development in the following and focus on the Study Group's proposals in particular.

Under many national legal systems, and apparently under the Study Group's draft proposals as well, it is an important starting point for *unjustified enrichment law* that an *asset is simply 'attributed' to a person*.[75] The same can be true for tort law in order to decide whether a specific person has suffered a loss.[76] Such 'attribution' does not consist of one single aspect but may con-

---

[73] Cf the description given in Martinson's article in this volume (n 1), chapter G. *in fine*.
[74] Cf Håstad, (2002-2003) JT 745 (n 17) at 753, who assumes that it should be much easier for lawyers from countries with a dogmatic (unitary) approach to become familiar with the functional approach than the other way round.
[75] For the draft proposals elaborated within the Study Group on a European Civil Code, this becomes most manifest in articles 3:101 (on enrichment), 3:102 (on disadvantage) and 4:101 (on the attribution of the enrichment to another's disadvantage); see www.sgecc.net (version of February 2006). Under article 3:101 (1)(a), a person is enriched by 'an increase in assets...', which is mirrored in article 3:102 (1)(a); article 4:101 (a) provides that an enrichment is attributable to another's disadvantage where 'an asset of that other is transferred to the enriched person by that other'. Articles 3:101 (1)(c), 3:102 (1)(c) and 4:101 (c) contain respective rules for the case a person is enriched by the 'use of another's assets'. From the (provisional and yet unpublished) comments to these provisions it is quite clear that an 'asset' must, in some manner, be recognised as 'belonging' to one party, which implies an element of protected exclusivity.
[76] Cf article 2:206 (on loss upon infringement of property or lawful possession) of the Study Group's draft on non-contractual liability for damage; see www.sgecc.net (un-

sist of several aspects: One may think of the possibility of using the object and of the value of its substance, which again can not be strictly parted from the right to dispose, because it is the market that creates the value and market participants will insist on acquiring good title, *etc*. Where such other parts of private law, as it seems to be the case, for instance, with unjustified enrichment law in the Study Group's drafts, presuppose a general attribution of an asset to a person, a unitary transfer approach in the sense in which it is understood here[77] may provide a suitable interface between property law and the respective other part of law. If, on the other hand, the point of reference was a functional property law regime, this could cause difficulties in identifying the suitable 'links', in particular, in case the single rules were diverging. This shall not mean that I regard unjustified enrichment concepts as incompatible with a functional transfer approach in general. These concepts *can* fit together. But where the unjustified enrichment rules are of a certain shape, the one or the other property law approach may fit in more smoothly. It may be noted, but this is not an argument in any direction, that unjustified enrichment law is not a frequently used concept in the Scandinavian jurisdictions; it is, however, a quite central part of the draft proposals prepared by the Study Group.

There may be further examples to be taken into account, both on a potential national reform level and with the perspective of possible European harmonization. For instance, one would have to consider that the Scandinavian systems do not strictly distinguish between obligations (the right of one person against another person to demand some kind of performance) and rights *in rem* (the right of a person related to a thing).[78] This goes hand in hand with the 'functional' way of thinking, which tries to eliminate concepts as far as possible. In other legal environments, taking such an approach may involve a range of related issues to be taken into account.

F. Final remark

I do not want to conclude this paper with concrete proposals. The reader will have no difficulties guessing that at the present stage of research and understanding, I (still) have a slight preference for a unitary tendency when it comes to the question of European harmonization. But this can only be

---

dated version). However, the draft comments accessible to me leave it open whether this concept comes equally close to a unitary concept of ownership as the unjustified enrichment rules quoted in n 75 above.

[77] See B.1. above.

[78] The distinction is quite well known, but criticised; see, for instance, Hessler (n 18), 1 *et seq*; Håstad (n 20), 15 *et seq*; Undén (n 22, 10th edition), 5 *et seq*.

the end of a process. This process should involve increasing efforts in communicating the solutions of our own systems, not only in what regards the basic starting points, but also as to the details. From the unitary side, this includes identifying issues where we already have some 'functional' effects in our legal systems.[79] It goes without saying that the single 'aspects' of ownership need to be examined thoroughly as to their transfer implications. Evidently, the functional approach's tradition and experience in weighing interests and revealing value-based arguments can be of considerable benefit here. If the same result seems adequate for some of these aspects, I think one may well formulate this in a unitary rule. Where another solution seems preferable, explicit rules may be provided.

---

[79] Chapter B. of this paper may be seen as an attempt in this direction.

The Relationship between Transfer Rules and Rules on Creditors' Avoidance of Debtor's Transactions

Caroline Cauffman*

A. Introduction

The debtor's estate constitutes the fund from which his creditors are to be paid. By transferring assets from his estate, the debtor can diminish his creditor's possibilities to receive payment. In principle, the creditor cannot prevent this: the debtor can freely dispose of his assets. However, in order to protect the creditors, legal systems have recognized certain exceptions to this principle. These exceptions give rise to difficult questions as to the position of the third party to which the debtor has illegally transferred his assets or whom he has otherwise given rights in those assets. In many cases, the third party in good faith will be protected by the rules on good faith acquisition, but this is not always so. A diligent analysis of the various instruments to enable the creditor to avoid his debtor's transfers is necessary.

In legal terminology, the term 'avoidance' is used in different senses. In the Principles of European Contract Law, it is used in the context of defects of consent. 'Avoidance' then means that the contract becomes void *ex tunc*. The CISG uses the term 'avoidance' to indicate that a contract is terminated *ex nunc*. In this contribution, the term 'avoidance' is used in a wider sense. It refers to every way in which a creditor can interfere with the free transfer of the assets of his debtor. Within the limits of this contribution it is not possible to give a complete and broadly comparative overview of all of these means. I will only attempt to give an overview of the most important means to protect a creditor from disadvantageous transfers by his debtor, and I will only focus on Belgium, the Netherlands, Germany and England.

B. Attachment

The most important limitation to the debtor's right to dispose of his assets follows from the creditor's right to take recourse to his debtor's goods by way of attachment or by the opening of a collective procedure. Besides the ex-

---

* Attorney at law, scientific collaborator K U Leuven and University of Antwerp.

ecutive attachment, leading to the forced sale of the confiscated good(s), most legal systems also provide conservative measures preventing a debtor from transferring his assets, defrauding his creditor's rights.

In civil law the most important conservative measure is the conservative attachment (*saisie conservatoire*). Transactions made by the debtor in spite of this measure will not be opposable to the acting creditor, who may act as if those transactions had never occurred.[1] However, as far as these measures concern movable goods, third acquirers of these goods will in general be protected. The fact that the attachment is subject to publication measures does not always deprive the third acquirer of good faith (*eg* in Belgium).[2] Third acquirers in bad faith will have to accept that the acting creditor takes recourse to the concerned goods. Moreover, they can incur delictual liability against the acting creditor and they can also incur penal sanctions.

The common law equivalent to these conservative measures is the freezing injunction (previously known as the Mareva Injuction): an injunction depriving the creditor of the possibility to dispose of his assets. The debtor who disobeys such an injunction, as well as any third party who knowingly contributes to such disobedience may be held to be in contempt of court.[3] *Bona fide* purchasers without notice and for value are protected and will obtain a good title.[4]

---

[1] Belgium: Cour de Cassation (Cass) 11 February 1993, *Arresten van het Hof van Cassatie* (Arr Cass) 1993, 176; Cass 25 October 2001, *Pasicrisie* (Pas) 2001, I, 1706; Ilse Banmeyer, 'L'action paulienne et la tierce complicité' in: Patrick Wéry, *La théorie générale des obligations* (Liège: Formation permanente, CUP 1998), n 11 at p 255-256; Stéphanie Bar and Cédric Alter, 'Les effets du contrat', in: *Pratique du droit* (Waterloo: Kluwer 2006), n 279, p 152; Ludo Cornelis, *Algemene theorie van de verbintenis* (Antwerpen: Intersentia 2000), n 307, p 381; Eric Dirix, 'De vergoedende functie van de actio pauliana', (note under Cass 15 May 1992), *Rechtskundig Weekblad* (RW) 1992-93, n 1 at p 331; Robert Kruithof, Hubert Bocken, Filip De Ly and Bart De Temmerman, 'Overzicht van rechtspraak (1981-1992) Verbintenissen', *Tijdschrift voor Privaatrecht* (TPR) 1994, n 369 at p 693; Sofie Stijns, *Leerboek verbintenissenrecht*, Vol I (Bruges: Die Keure 2005), n 325 at p 232. The Netherlands: art 453a (1) of the Dutch Code of civil procedure (Rv). Germany: Eberhard Schilken in: *Münchener Kommentar zur Zivilprozessordnung*, Vol III (München: C H Beck, 2nd edition 2001), § 803 of the German Act of civil procedure (ZPO), n 38; Peter L Murray and Rolf H Stürner, *German Civil Justice* (Durham: Carolina Academic Press 2004), 436 et seq and 448.
[2] Eric Dirix and Karen Broeckx, *Beslag*, in: *Algemene Praktische Rechtsverzameling* (Antwerpen: Kluwer 2001), n 32, p 21-22.
[3] Civil procedure rules part 25 and the practice direction.
[4] Richard Aird, 'The Scottish Arrestment and the English freezing order', *The International and Comparative Law Quarterly* (ICLQ) 2002, 165.

C. Pauline action

I. Generalities

Another important instrument to protect the creditors against their debtor's acts that diminish their estate is the pauline action, in Germany known as the *Anfechtung*.

Most civil law systems provide a general pauline action and one or more special regimes for the pauline action in the case of insolvency of the debtor. The main, and in some legal systems the only result of the pauline action is that the acting creditor may execute against the good transferred by the contested act as if it had never left his debtor's estate.

The insolvency pauline action differs from the general pauline action because it can only be introduced by the insolvency administrator[5] and the result of the action benefits all of the insolvency creditors.[6] Furthermore, most national laws on insolvency provide extra cases in which a pauline action is possible and/or alleviate the burden of proof for the disadvantaged creditor. Dutch and German Insolvency law provide for an actual return of the good to the insolvency estate.[7]

In England, the pauline action does not exist as such, but sections 238 *et seq* Insolvency Act concerning company insolvency, 339 *et seq* Insolvency Act concerning individual insolvency and 423 *et seq* Insolvency Act con-

---

[5] § 8.1 Principles of European Insolvency Law. Belgium: Cass 11 January 1988, Arr Cass 1987-88, 594, *Journal des Tribunaux* (JT) 1988, 190, Pas 1988, I, 558, RW 1987-88, 1406 and TBH 1989, 971, note. The Netherlands: Art 42 of the Dutch Bankruptcy Act (Fw). Germany: § 143 of the German Insolvency Act (InsO). Concerning the exceptions to this rule (*Eigenverwaltung, vereinfachtes Insolvenzverfahren, Insolvenzplanverfahren*) see Michael Huber, 'Die Geltendmachung der Anfechtung', in: Peter Gottwald, *Insolvenzrechthandbuch* (München: Beck 2001) § 51, n 5-7. Also Scots and Danish law allow a creditor, in some cases, to challenge an act of the debtor after the opening of an insolvency proceeding, but in practice challenge by a creditor is rare, see William W McBride and Axel Flessner, 'Principles of European Insolvency Law and General Commentary', in: William W McBride, Axel Flessner and Sebastianus C J J Kortmann, *Principles of European Insolvency Law* (Nijmegen: Kluwer 2003), 54-55.

[6] Belgium: Cass 11 January 1988, Arr Cass 1987-88, 594, JT 1988, 190, Pas 1988, I, 558, RW 1987-88, 1406 and *Tijdschrift voor Belgisch Handelsrecht* (TBH) 1989, 971, note; Koen Van Raemdock, 'De actio pauliana: vaak een ongeladen wapen tegen de splitsing met een beweerd frauduleus oogmerk', (note under Com Dendermonde 9 December 1997), *Vennootschapsrecht en fiscaliteit* 1998, n 3, p 368. The Netherlands: Art 42 Fw; Trijntje J Mellema-Kranenburg, *De actio pauliana* (Zwolle: Tjeenk Willink 1996), 4-5. Germany: § 129 and 143 InsO.

[7] Cf *infra*, C.3.

cerning both individual and company insolvency take account of similar cases to that resulting in the pauline action: 'transactions entered into at an undervalue', such as gifts and transactions without consideration or for a consideration the value of which, in money or money's worth, is significantly less than the value, in money or in money's worth, of the consideration provided by the debtor. The rules of sections 238 et seq and 339 et seq only apply in the context of formal insolvency procedures, the rules of sections 423 et seq also apply in the absence of formal insolvency procedures and even in the absence of factual insolvency.[8] In the aforementioned cases, the English legal authority has the discretion to make such order as it thinks fit for restoring the position to what it would have been if the debtor had not entered into that transaction (orders requiring any property transferred to be vested in any person, requiring any person to pay any other person money in respect of benefits received from the debtor, …). As these rules do not really correspond with the civil law pauline action, I will not deal with them further in this essay.[9]

2. Prerequisites for the Pauline action

The prerequisites for a (civil law) pauline action are essentially: a juridical act performed by the debtor (1) resulting in a diminution of his creditor's possibilities to receive payment (2). Traditionally, it is further required that the debtor acted fraudulently (3) and, at least in the case of non-gratuitous legal acts, that the third party who contracted with the debtor was aware (or should have been aware) of the fraud (4). Further national prerequisites are mainly further explications of these main prerequisites or concern the question whether the pauline action is to be seen as a purely executive measure or whether it (also) has a conservative function.[10]

---

[8] Robert Stevens and Lionel Smith, 'Actio pauliana in English law', in: Joaquín J Forner Delaygua, La protección del crédito en Europa: La acción pauliana (Barcelona: Bosch 2000), 199-200.

[9] For a more extensive study of these rules, see Stevens and Smith (n 8 above), 195 et seq.

[10] Comp § 8.1 Principles of European Insolvency Law: 'A juridical act unfairly detrimental to the creditors performed by the debtor within a certain period of time before the opening of the proceeding, is subject to reversal. (…)'. § 8.2 provides some examples of acts that are subject to reversal, eg a transaction with the intent of defrauding creditors.

3. Effects of the Pauline action

The main rule is, as I have already indicated, that a successful pauline action results in the fact that the claimant may execute against the good as if it had never left his debtor's estate.[11] He may 'avoid' the contested act. This result is, in several countries such as Belgium and France, achieved by declaring the contested act *non-opposable* to the creditor who has successfully filed a pauline action. This implies that the debtor may act as if the contested act never took place, but the contested act remains valid and continues to exist.

National terminology sometimes causes confusion on this point. This is *eg* the case in the Netherlands where article 3:45 of the civil code (NBW) considers an act to which the conditions for the pauline action apply 'vernietigbaar' (voidable), but, further on, the civil code specifies that a successful pauline action annuls the act *only for the benefit of the claimant and as far as necessary to annihilate the disadvantage it has caused him*. The result is thus the same as that which is, in Belgium and France, indicated by the term 'non-opposability'.

If the sanction of non-opposability is not possible[12] (*eg* because the good has been transferred to a third party) or is not appropriate given the circumstances of the case (because the execution against the transferred good would cause enormous harm to the third party, while the creditor can be

---

[11] Belgium: Cass 11 February 1993, Arr Cass 1993, 176; Cass 25 October 2001, Pas 2001, I, 1706; Banmeyer (n 1 above), n 11, p 255-256; Bar and Alter (n 1 above), n 279, p 152; Cornelis (n 1 above), n 307, p 381; Frédéric Coryn, 'De derde medeplichtigheid van de verkrijger ten bezwarenden titel als voorwaarde voor het welslagen van de pauliaanse vordering', (note under Ghent 12 March 2003), *Tijdschrift voor Belgisch Burgerlijk Recht* (TBBR) 2005, n 3, p 150; Diego Devos, 'La réparation du préjudice du créancier demandeur à l'action paulienne', (note under Cass 15 May 1992), *Revue Critique de Jurisprudence Belge* 1995, n 11, p 325; Eric Dirix (n 1 above), n 1, p 331; Kruithof, Bocken, De Ly and De Temmerman (n 1 above), n 369, p 693; Stijns (n 1 above), n 325, p 232; Stefaan Loosveld, 'L'action paulienne: une institution séculière en pleine vogue', TBBR 2001, n 22, p 165; Koen Van Raemdonck, 'Inbreng in natura in een vennootschap en (deelneming aan) bedrieglijk onvermogen', (note under Rb Mechelen 5 February 1997), RW 1997-98, n 5, p 986. Germany: Michael Huber, *Anfechtungsgesetz (AnfG): Gesetz über die Anfechtung von Rechtshandlungen eines Schuldners ausserhalb des Insolvenzverfahrens*, in: *Beck'sche Kurzkommentare* (München: Beck 2000), Einf n 9, p 10. Comp § 8.1. Principles of European Insolvency Law: '(...) The administrator can recover or seek annulment of any benefit which has been obtained from the debtor'. It follows from the German translation of this article that 'recovery' implies the return of the object of the challenged act to the debtor's estate.

[12] Cass 25 October 2001, Arr Cass 2001, 1706, JT 2003, 858, Pas 2001, 1706 and RW 2002-03, 940, note.

equally satisfied with compensation in money), the court can, in Belgium, decide to grant the creditor who filed a pauline action, compensation by equivalent (in money).[13]

The Dutch view limits the consequences of the pauline action to the non-opposability (although it uses the word 'voidable'), but it recognizes the possibility for the creditor of filing a tort claim in order to obtain damages. By way of compensation in natura, the non-opposability of the contested act can also be achieved in a case based on a tort claim.[14]

This view, which seems to lead to a clearer doctrinal analysis, is followed by a minority of Belgian scholars.[15] This clear distinction does not apply to the Dutch insolvency pauline action. A successful insolvency pauline action implies that the transferred good returns to the insolvency estate; if this is no longer possible, pecuniary compensation is due.[16] If the third party has paid the debtor something in return, the insolvency trustee has to return this or its value as far as the insolvency estate has benefited from it. When the debtor has consumed the received assets before the declaration of insolvency, the creditor can only be treated as a competing creditor.[17]

The German *Anfechtungsgesetz* stipulates in its § 11 (1), concerning the legal consequences of the *Anfechtung*, that what has disappeared from the debtor's estate by the contested act has to be attributed to the claimant as far as this is necessary for his satisfaction. When this is no longer possible, the rules concerning the consequences of an unjustified enrichment, in respect of which the transferee is aware of the defects of his title, apply *mutatis mutandis* to this situation. The beneficiary of a gratuitous performance only has to return the received assets as far as he is enriched by them, but this restriction does not apply when he knows or should in the given circumstances know that the gratuitous performance disadvantages the creditors (§ 11 (2) AnfG). The creditor can also choose to file a delictual action besides or instead of exercising his *Anfechtungsrecht* or subsidiarily to his action based on his *Anfechtungsrecht*.[18] § 143 *Insolvenzordnung* differs from § 11 *Anfechtungsgesetz* and from the main rule concerning the results of the pauline action, in such respect that the assets which have disappeared from the debtor's estate have to return to the insolvency estate.[19]

---

[13] Dirix (n 1 above), n 2, p 331.
[14] Mellema-Kranenburg (n 6 above), 55.
[15] Matthias E Storme, *Zekerheden- en insolventierecht*, 2006, http://www.webh01.ua.ac.be/storme/zekerheden2006Ipdf, 95 *et seq.*
[16] Art 51 (1) Fw.
[17] Art 51 (3) Fw.
[18] Huber (n 11 above), § 11, n 12.
[19] Cf Huber (n 11 above), § 11, n 20.

4. Further acquirers

What happens if the debtor has in the meantime transferred the asset he received from the debtor to a third party?

As the pauline action does not invalidate the debtor's transfer, it does not annihilate the ability of the debtor's counterparty to dispose of the asset, nor does it invalidate the subsequent transferee's title of acquisition.

It seems to be generally accepted that a pauline action against a subsequent transferee is only possible if its prerequisites are fulfilled against every previous transferee in the chain between the fraudulent debtor's counterparty and the subsequent transferee in question.[20] Even if this requirement is fulfilled, third parties in good faith, who received in return for consideration, are protected. Third parties in good faith who received gratuitously are not protected by Belgian and German pauline rules.[21] Dutch law is more refined at this point and protects the third party in good faith who received gratuitously as far as he proves that he is not enriched by the transfer at the moment the good is claimed from him.[22]

How are these pauline rules on third party protection to be combined with the general rules on third party acquisition?

The traditional opinion in Belgian law was that the pauline rules prevailed over the rules on good faith acquisition. This was justified by the fact that article 2279 of the civil code (CC) on third party protection only concerns rights *in rem*, but does not offer protection against obligatory claims such as the pauline action.[23] Modern case law and legal scholars have refined this rule. The general pauline action of article 1167 CC and also the general insolvency pauline action of article 20 of the Belgian Insolvency Act (Faill W) are still considered as *actions in personam* in respect of which article 2279 CC does not offer any protection.[24] But, the special pauline actions provided by the articles 17 and 18 Faill W are, at present, considered as

---

[20] Belgium: Cass 9 February 2006, http://www.juridat.be; Henri De Page, *Traité élémentaire de droit civil belge*, Vol III, *Les obligations (Seconde partie)* (Brussels: Bruylant 1967), n 242, p 250. The Netherlands: Mellema-Kranenburg (n 6 above), n 10, p 9. Germany: Huber (n 11 above), § 15, n 15.

[21] Belgium: Loosveld (n 11 above), n 20, p 164; Stijns (n 1 above), n 327, p 235. Germany: § 15 (2) AnfG; § 145 InsO.

[22] Art 3:45 (5) NBW.

[23] Henri De Page and René Dekkers, *Traité élémentaire de droit civil belge*, Vol V, *Les principaux contrats usuels (Deuxième partie). Les biens (Première partie)* (Brussels: Bruylant 1975), n 1044, p 924.

[24] De Page and Dekkers (n 23 above), n 1044, p 926.

actions *in rem*[25] in respect of which article 2279 CC does offer protection.[26] This results in the fact that the general pauline actions prevail over the rules on good faith acquisition, whereas article 2279 CC prevails over the special pauline actions of articles 17 and 18 Faill W.

Dutch law seems to solve the problem of the conflict between the pauline rules on third party protection and the rules on good faith acquisition on the basis of the rule *specialia generali derogant*: special rules prevail over general rules. The pauline rules are special rules that prevail over the general rules on good faith acquisition.[27] The real *vs* obligatory character of the rules seems to be left out of consideration. Anyhow, as far as movables are concerned, the rules on good faith acquisition do not offer more protection to the good faith transferee than the pauline rules. On the contrary, the third party who received gratuitously and in good faith is not protected by the rules on good faith acquisition, whereas he receives a certain protection under the pauline rules.[28]

In Germany, the rule of § 932 BGB is not applicable in this matter, only the rules on the *Anfechtung* apply.

D. Rights of priority

Rights of priority attribute the creditor a right to be paid by priority from the revenues of a forced sale.[29] They do, in principle, not enable the priority creditor to avoid transfers of the movables on which his right of priority rests. However, there are certain exceptions to this rule. In Belgium, for example, the lessor has a right of prority on the goods the lessee placed in the leased property. In principle, the lessee is entitled to dispose over the

---

[25] Concerning art 17 Faill W: Sven Mosselmans, 'De positie van de onderverkrijger van een lichamelijk roerend goed bij faillissement' (note under Cass 31 January 2002), RW 2002-03, n 2, p 984; Ivan Verougstraete, *Manuel du curateur de faillite* (Brussels: Swinnen 1987) n 324, p 207. *Contra*: Louis Frédericq, *Traité de droit commercial belge*, Vol VII (Ghent: Fecheyr 1949), n 131, p 251. Concerning art 18 Faill W: Mosselmans (above in this note), n 2, p 984.

[26] Mosselmans (n 25 above), n 4, p 984.

[27] Bernardina W M Nieskens-Isphording and Anne E M Van der Putt-Lauwers, *Derdenbescherming*, in: *Monografieën Nieuw BW* (Deventer: Kluwer 1993), 58.

[28] Nieskens-Isphording and Van der Putt-Lauwers (n 27 above), 55.

[29] Art 12 *et seq* of the Belgian Mortgage Act (Hyp W); art 3:277 *et seq* NBW; section 175 Insolvency Act. German law has abolished the system of preferences (*Vorrechte*) with the introduction of the *Insolvenzordnung* in 1998. Cf Stefan Smid, 'Nationale Insolvenzrechte. Deutsches Insolvenzrecht', http://www.europainstitut.hu/pdf/beg17-2/smid.pdf, 23.

goods he brought into the leased property. But, if he removes so many of them as to undermine the lessor's right of priority without the lessor's consent, the lessor has the right to revendicate them within 15 days (40 days for agricultural leases) irrespective of the person in whose hands they are to be found. This person cannot benefit from the protection of article 2279 CC, not even if he possesses the goods in good faith. This right of quasi-revendication of the lessor constitutes an exception to the general rule that movables are not subject to a right to follow (*meubles n'ont pas de suite*).[30]

E. Validity requirements

A contract that is concluded by a debtor with the intention to disadvantage his creditors can, in certain legal systems, be avoided (annulled, *annulé*) because it (has a cause that) is contrary to the public order and good morals.[31] This is the case in Belgium and in the Netherlands. Because of the causal nature of the system of transfer of property in these countries, the annulment of the contract will have the effect that the good is considered never to have left the debtor's estate and the creditor can execute against it. Unlike in the case of the pauline action, the return of the good to the estate of the debtor will benefit all the debtor's creditors and not only the one who has filed the action. Third acquirers in good faith are protected by article 2279 CC.

In Germany, the rules on *Anfechtung* prevail over § 138 BGB in cases in which creditors have been disadvantaged, in the sense that one can only invoke § 138 BGB in cases in which creditors have been disadvantaged if the rules on *Anfechtung* do not apply; this will *eg* be the case when the contracting parties have fraudulently misled a creditor concerning the credit worthiness of the debtor.[32] If § 138 BGB applies, a distinction is to be made between the obligatory contract and the real contract. Because of the *Abstraktionsprinzip* the invalidity of the obligatory contract will not render the real contract invalid, unless the real contract is defective for the same reason. If only the obligatory contract is invalid, the transferee remains the owner of the transferred asset. But, because of the invalidity of the obligatory contract, the transaction has lost its economic justification. The transferee is unjustly enriched. He will have to retransfer the asset to the trans-

---

[30] Dirix and Broeckx (n 2 above), n 32, p 22.
[31] Belgium: Rb Charleroi 2 October 1991, *Jurisprudence de Liège, Mons et Bruxelles* 1992, 1110. See also Antwerp 14 March 1983, RW 1983-84, 172. The Netherlands: Art 3:40 NBW; Mellema-Kranenburg (n 6 above), n 49, p 58. Germany: Rolf Sack in: *Staudingers Kommentar zum BGB* (Berlin: Sellier – de Gruyter 2003), § 138 BGB, n 348 *et seq*.
[32] Rolf Sack (n 31 above), § 138 BGB, n 349.

feror. The real transfer follows the general rules, a real contract and a *traditio*. The underlying cause for the retransfer is the claim *ex* unjustified enrichment.[33] Subsequent acquirers in good faith will be protected by § 932 BGB.

In English law, it seems to be accepted that the intention to defraud one's creditors is a cause of illegality for contracts and trusts. But, it seems also to be accepted that property can pass under an illegal contract, although the Court might not have assisted in the enforcement of the contract if it had been executory. The scope of this last rule and the exceptions to it seem not very clear. *Dicta* in one case suggest that an exception to this rule is made when the turpitude of the plaintiff is very gross.[34] It seems feasible that an exception will also be accepted if the debtor's counterparty, the accomplice in the fraud, is confronted with a disadvantaged debtor.

In any case, if the asset has been subsequently transferred to third parties in good faith and without notice of the seller's defective title, before the contract has been declared void, their title is protected by section 21 Sale of Goods Act 1979.

F. Right of retention

The creditor who seeks protection against the transfer of movables by his debtor should also consider making use of the right of retention (French: *droit de retention*, German: *Zurückbehaltungsrecht*, English: possessory lien), which enables him to withhold a good he received for detention from the debtor. In most legal systems, this right is only conferred by law to the creditor whose claim is connected to his debtor's good or to the creditor's obligation to release the good. However, English common law recognises, in some exceptional cases, a right to retain any good of the debtor as long as he has not paid all his debts (general liens in contrast to particular liens).[35]

The right of retention will not allow the creditor to annul transfers by his debtor, but it will, in general, enable him to refuse delivery of the retained good until the debtor's debt in relation to the retained good is paid.

In Belgium and in the Netherlands, the right of retention can be invoked against third parties that have acquired a right in the good after the creditor's claim arose and the good came into the possession of the creditor. The

---

[33] Mary-Rose McGuire, *Transfer of Title Concerning Movables Part II – National Report: Germany* (Frankfurt am Main: Peter Lang 2006), pp 72 *et seq.*

[34] Law Commission, *Illegal transactions: the effect of illegality on contracts and trust*, http://www.lawcom.gov.uk/docs/cp154.pdf, 38 *et seq.*

[35] Sarah Worthington, *Personal Property Law. Text, Cases and Materials* (Oxford: Hart 2000), 102-103.

creditor can also invoke the right of retention against third parties with an older right if his claim arises from a contract the debtor was capable of concluding with regard to the good, or if he had no reason to doubt the debtor's capacity.[36] As article 2279 CC installs in Belgium a presumption that the possessor of a movable is its owner, the creditor will normally be entitled to believe that the debtor was capable to contract in relation to the movables in his possession.

The German *Zurückbehaltungsrecht* of § 273 BGB can be invoked against every owner of the retained good as far as it concerns the *Zurückbehaltungsrecht*, which is based on a material relation between the creditor's claim and the retained good. The commercial *Zurückbehaltungsrecht* of § 369 HGB can be invoked against further acquirers. The right of retention of § 369 HGB cannot arise in respect of goods owned by a person other than the debtor, not even if the creditor could reasonably believe that he was dealing with the owner.

In England, the lien can in general be invoked against the real owner of the good even if the good subject to the lien has been brought into the possession of the lienor by a third party, of whom the lienor could think that he was its owner[37] or, at least, that he was capable of giving the lienor possession of the good. The effect of resale on the seller's lien is regulated by section 47 Sale of Goods Act, which provides:

(1) Subject to this Act, the unpaid seller's right of lien or retention or stoppage in transit is not affected by any sale or other disposition of the goods which the buyer may have made, unless the seller has assented to it.
(2) Where a document of title to goods has been lawfully transferred to any person as buyer or owner of the goods, and that person transfers the document to a person who takes it in good faith and for valuable consideration, then –
(a) if the last-mentioned transfer was by way of sale the unpaid seller's right of lien or retention or stoppage in transit is defeated; and
(b) if the last-mentioned transfer was made by way of pledge or other disposition for value, the unpaid seller's right of lien or retention or stoppage in transit can only be exercised subject to the rights of the transferee.[38]

---

[36] Belgium: Eric Dirix, 'Retentierecht' in: Eric Dirix, *Voorrechten en hypotheken: commentaar met overzicht van rechtspraak en rechtsleer (Comm Voorr)* (Antwerp: Kluwer rechtswetenschappen 1999), n 39. The Netherlands: art 3:291 NBW.
[37] *Tappenden v Artus* [1964] 2 QB 185.
[38] See also section 10 Factors Act 1889.

G. Right of quasi-revendication of the unpaid seller and the right of stoppage in transit

Both the right of quasi-revendication and the right of stoppage in transit constitute, in a certain way, a prolongation of the right of retention. They become relevant when the unpaid seller has already parted with the goods but wants to regain possession in order to secure payment of the price. They may even be stronger than the right of retention as they result, in certain legal systems, in the fact that not only possession returns to the seller, but also ownership.

1. Stoppage in transit

The right of stoppage in transit enables the seller to resume possession of goods which he has already parted with, but which have not yet reached the buyer. In Belgium and in England, the right of stoppage in transit exists only as such when the buyer becomes insolvent during the transportation of the goods.[39]

In England, the right of stoppage in transit is indeed a prolonged variety of the lien. Once the seller regains possession by means of stoppage in transit he can withhold the goods until payment or tender of the price. However, the mere exercise of the right of stoppage in transit does not in principle rescind the contract.[40] But, where the seller expressly reserves the right of resale in case the buyer should make default, and on the buyer making default re-sells the goods, the original contract of sale is rescinded but without prejudice to any claim the seller may have for damages.[41]

In Belgium, the right of stoppage in transit, dealt with by article 104 Faill W, seems to be conceived as a consequence of the automatic termination of the sale because of the fact that the buyer's non-performance has become certain by his declaration of insolvency.[42]

The consequences of a resale by the buyer on the right of stoppage in transit are, in England, identical to those of the resale on the right of retention.[43] In Belgium they are similar: a resale does not affect the right of stop-

---

[39] Art 104 Faill W; Section 44 Sale of Goods Act 1979 as amended.
[40] Section 48 (1) Sale of Goods Act 1979 as amended.
[41] Section 48 (4) Sale of Goods Act 1979 as amended.
[42] Concerning the similar art 568 old Belgian Insolvency Law: Louis Frédericq, *Handboek van Belgisch Handelsrecht*, Vol IV (Brussels: Bruylant 1981), n 32566, p 451-452.
[43] Section 47 Sale of Goods Act 1979 as amended.

page in transit, unless the goods have – before they have reached the buyer – been resold on bills of lading or invoices signed by the sender.[44]

German law recognizes a limited right of stoppage in transit by § 321 BGB concerning the *Unsicherheitseinrede*, a variety of the right of retention destined for the situation in which it has become clear to the retainer, who is already obliged to perform but does not yet have an actionable claim against his debtor, that his claim is in danger because of his debtor's inability to perform.[45] In this case, the retainer cannot only withhold his performance, but he can also stop the goods that have so far been sent to the debtor, but have not yet reached him.[46]

In the Netherlands, the right of stoppage in transit seems inexistent, but article 7:39 NBW recognizes the right of quasi-revendication (*recht van reclame*). It seems that the seller can invoke his right of retention as long as the good has not actually been delivered, by him or in his name, to the buyer and that, from then on, he can use his right of quasi-revendication.

In fact, also in the other legal systems, the general right of retention seems to allow, in many cases, a stoppage in transit even when this is not explicitly mentioned by law, because it allows the seller to retain the goods as long as they are in his power, which will generally be the case for as long as they have not been (materially) received by or in the name of the buyer.

2. Quasi-revendication

The right of quasi-revendication is the right of a seller who is no longer the owner of a good, to nevertheless revendicate that good because the seller has not paid the price.

In Belgium, the unpaid seller's right of quasi-revendication, will only poorly protect the seller against transfers of the sold good by his buyer. For, one of the conditions for the invocation of the seller's right of quasi-revendication is that the good is still present in the buyer's estate,[47] but it can also be exercised with regard to the sales price, which is substituted for

---

[44] Art 104 Faill W.

[45] Up to 1998, German law had an actual 'right of stoppage in transit' in § 44 KO, see Wolfgang Faber's contribution at pp 97 *et seq* of this volume, footnote 41.

[46] Hansjörg Otto in: *Staudingers Kommentar zum BGB* (Berlin: Sellier – de Gruyter 2003), § 321 BGB, n 44. Comp § 418 (1) and (2) HGB concerning the contract of carriage that attributes the sender of goods the right to dispose of the goods and give instructions to stop the goods in transit or to order delivery at a different destination as long as the goods have not reached their original destination.

[47] Art 20, 5, § 8 Hyp W.

the original good.[48] Moreover, it is presently taught that the quasi-revendication does not result in the return of the ownership to the seller, but only in the return of possession. It enables the seller thus only to regain his right of retention.[49]

In the Netherlands, the seller of a movable that is not subject to registration can, if the price has not been paid, but the good has already been delivered to the buyer, revendicate the good by a written declaration addressed to the buyer, if the conditions for termination of the contract are fulfilled. This declaration terminates (dissolves) the contract and ends the right of the buyer and the subsequent acquirers (article 7:39 NBW). The property returns to the seller by the operation of the seller's declaration.[50] But, unless the good remained in possession of the buyer, the right of revendication ends if the good has been transferred for consideration to a third acquirer that did not need to fear that the right of revendication would be exercised (article 7:42 NBW).

In German law, the right of quasi-revendication seems not to exist, at least to have a very limited scope. The starting point in German law is, as it is also in Belgium and in the Netherlands, that the *Zurückbehaltungsrecht* only exists as long as the good remains in retainer's possession. Once the creditor has released the good, he cannot claim it back on the ground that he could have made use of his *Zurückbehaltungsrecht*. An exception to this rule exists in case the retainer has released the good because of a judgment that did not recognize the right of retention and that is later annihilated or modified.[51]

In England, a right of quasi-revendication seems not to exist.

H. Simulation

When a debtor, in collusion with a third person, simulates the transfer a movable to that person in order to save that movable from the recourse by his creditors, while he agrees with that third person that he in fact remains

---

[48] APR, v *Afbetalingsovereenkomsten*, n 489, p 176; Vincent Sagaert, *Zakelijke subrogatie* (Antwerp: Intersentia 2003), n 631.

[49] Henri De Page and Anne Meinertzhagen-Limpens, *Traité élémentaire de droit civil belge*, Vol IV, *Les principaux contrats (première partie)*, Vol I (Brussels: Bruylant 1997), n 256, p 347-348.

[50] Arthur Salomons, *Transfer of Title Concerning Movables Part IV – National Report: The Netherlands* (Frankfurt am Main: Peter Lang 2006), 54 *et seq*.

[51] § 717 (2) and (3) ZPO; Claudia Bittner in: *Staudingers Kommentar zum BGB* (Berlin: Sellier – de Gruyter 2004), § 273 BGB, n 126. Comp RGZ 139, 17, 21 *et seq* and RGZ 109, 104, 105.

the owner of the movable in question, the creditors can, in civil law countries, apply the doctrine of simulation (Dutch: *veinzing* or *simulatie*, French and English: simulation, German: *Simulation*)[52] in order to avoid the simulated transfer.

In Belgium, France and in the Netherlands, the theory of simulation allows third persons to invoke at their best interest either the underlying actual agreement between the parties, or the ostensible transaction, while the parties to the ostensible transaction, are bound by the underlying actual agreement.[53] In Germany, a simulated transaction is void between the parties as well as in relation to third parties.[54] In England, there is no general theory of simulation.

As a third party in good faith can, in Belgium, rely on the simulated transaction, such a third party to whom the person to which the good was transferred by the simulated transaction, has transferred the object of that transaction by means of a title, which is not void for other reasons, has acquired ownership by means of a valid title. He can oppose his title to another third party, for example a creditor of the original debtor, who chooses to invoke the actual juridical act between his debtor and his counterparty. It is indeed generally accepted that, in case of conflict between two third parties of whom one invokes the actual agreement and the other invokes the ostensible agreement, the one who invokes the ostensible transaction will prevail.[55]

In Germany and in England, the third party in good faith to whom the debtor's counterparty has transferred the good that is the object of the osten-

---

[52] Comp Walter Van Gerven, '*Algemeen Deel*', in: *Beginselen Belgisch Privaatrecht* (Brussels: Story-Scientia 1987), n 104, p 308.

[53] Art 6:103 PECL.

[54] Karl Larenz, *Allgemeiner Teil des deutschen Bürgerlichen Rechts* (München: Beck, 1989), 366 et seq; Claude Witz, *Droit privé allemand*, Vol I, *Actes juridiques, droits subjectifs. BGB, Partie générale. Loi sur les conditions générales d'affaires* (Paris: Litec 1992), 224.

[55] Pierre Van Ommeslaghe, 'La simulation en droit des obligations', in: *Les obligations contractuelles* (Brussels: Edition du Jeune Barreau de Bruxelles 2000), 189 et seq; Pierre Van Ommeslaghe, *Droit des obligations* (Brussels: Presses universitaires de Bruxelles 1989), 155. See also in France: Cour de Cassation (France) 22 February 1983, Bull civ 1983, I, 62 and JCP 1985, II, n 20359, note Jean-Pierre Verschave; Charles Beudant, *Cours de droit civil français*, Vol IX (Paris: Rousseau 1953), 73; Christian Larroumet, *Droit civil*, Vol III (Paris: Economica 1996), 764; Philippe Malaurie and Laurent Aynes, *Cours de droit civil, Les obligations* (Paris: Cujas 1999), 366; Gabriel Marty and Pierre Raynaud, *Droit civil, Les obligations*, Vol I, *Les sources* (Paris: Sirey 1988), 318; Boris Starck, Henri Roland and Laurent Boyer, *Obligations*, Vol II, *Contrat* (Paris: Litec 1995), 418; François Terré, Philipe Simler and Yves Lequette, *Droit civil, Les obligations* (Paris: Dalloz 1996), 432.

sible transaction, will not have acquired on the basis of a valid title, because the ostensible transaction is void and the debtor's counterparty has never acquired ownership and, consequently, he cannot transfer it. However, the third party who has dealt with the debtor's counterparty may acquire ownership on the basis of the rules on good faith acquisition *a non domino*. In the Netherlands, the leading opinion is that an apparent act is not void *per se*.[56] The position of a third party who received a movable from a person who is only its owner on the basis of an apparent contract that is contradicted by an actual transaction, is protected by means of the rules of article 3:86 NBW on good faith acquisition.

I. Contractual protection

Creditor and debtor can further agree on contractual limitations of the debtor's power to dispose of his goods. But, it is a common European legal principle that contracts in principle only bind the contracting parties and cannot give rise to obligations for third parties. However, third parties who knowingly conclude a contract with the debtor by which the debtor breaches his contractual obligations to the creditor can incur liability on the basis of the theory of interference with contracts, la *théorie de la tierce complicité*.

The most important contractual protection of a creditor against further transfers by his debtor is the reservation title (Dutch: *Eigendomsvoorbehoud*, German: *Eigentumsvorbehalt*).

J. Reservation of title

In the case of a reservation of title, the creditor/original owner remains the owner of the good sold, until the price has been fully paid. As his debtor does not become the owner of the good and a person cannot transfer more rights than he himself has, he will not be able to transfer ownership to a third party, without the prior consent of the conditional seller.[57] In Germany, this prior consent is presumed if the conditional seller is a resale busi-

---

[56] Arthur S Hartkamp and Carel Asser, *Verbintenissenrecht*, Vol II, *Algemene leer der overeenkomsten* (Deventer: Tjeenk Willink 2001), 119-120.
[57] Salomons (n 50 above), 96.

ness.⁵⁸ This presumption does not exist in Belgian, in Dutch and in English law.⁵⁹

However, the rules on good faith acquisition will often enable third parties in good faith to acquire ownership of the good (article 2279 CC and the general theory of apparency, article 3:86 NBW, § 932 *et seq* BGB; section 21 Sale of Goods Act 1979,⁶⁰ Factors Act 1889).

K. Conclusion

The various legal systems provide a large number of measures enabling a creditor to avoid transactions concluded by his debtor, defrauding his interests. However, as far as the debtor's transaction concerns movable goods, these measures will often not suffice to annul the rights, at least the property rights, acquired by a third party in good faith.

An important exception to this rule concerns the pauline action whose effects generally prevail over the rights acquired by a third person in good faith who acquired gratuitously. However, in Belgium a further exception to this exception is made for the special insolvency pauline actions, provided for by the articles 17 and 18 Faill W, that do not prevail over the rules of article 2279 CC on good faith acquisition. Further, Belgian law recognizes an exception to the principle that the rules on good faith acquisition prevail over the rules on creditor protection, where it recognizes the right of the lessor to revendicate the goods, which the lessor removed from the rented good and concerning which the lessor has a right of priority.

---

[58] BGH NJW 1991, 228.
[59] This was decided in HR 14-2-1992, NJ 1993, 623 (*Love-Love*) concerning the sale of the hull of a ship which was transferred under reservation of title by a shipbuilder to another shipbuilder, who was to finish the ship and market it. The mere fact that the ship was destined to be resold to a customer did not imply that the second shipbuilder was entitled to dispose of it before completing his performance towards the first shipbuilder.
[60] '21. Sale by person not the owner
1) Subject to this Act where goods are sold by a person who is not their owner and who does not sell them under the authority or with the consent of the owner, the buyer acquires no better title to the goods than the seller had, *unless the owner of the goods is by his conduct precluded from denying the seller's authority to sell.*
2) Nothing in this Act affects
   a) the provisions of the Factors Acts or any enactment enabling the apparent owner of goods to dispose of them as if he were their true owner;
   b) the validity of any contract of sale under any special common law or statutory power of sale or under the order of a court of competent jurisdiction'.

Third parties in bad faith will not be protected. In most cases, the measures taken in order to protect the creditor will enable the creditor to act as if the transaction never took place. Moreover, the third party in bad faith can incur delictual liability.

Finally, I would like to point out that, although there are differences between the national legal systems, the similarities prevail, so that – if the political will would exist – harmonisation or even unification might be easier than one would expect.

How to Draft New Rules on the Bona Fide Acquisition of Movables for Europe? Some Remarks on Method and Content

*Arthur F. Salomons**

A. Introduction: Subject and purpose of this contribution

My topic is the position of the *bona fide* acquirer, that is to say the person who acquires a movable from someone he erroneously considers to be entitled to transfer it to him. This lack of title on the part of the transferor may have been caused by a number of reasons: he had previously stolen or embezzled the thing, he had acquired it under reservation of title, he was declared bankrupt, *etc*. But whatever the cause, we are dealing with someone who is not entitled to transfer the thing, but tries to do so nevertheless.

To what extent the transferee is protected against this lack of title of the transferor differs from country to country. Yet, if we are going to harmonize the law on the transfer of movables, we have to include this element. I will here focus on the question of how we are to proceed: what methods are available, which of these should be preferred and what obstacles may we expect to encounter? Next, I will discuss some aspects of the content of the new rules, building upon the outcome of the method we have chosen: what is the ultimate objective of these rules and how best to achieve that objective, what real-life developments do we have to take into account *etc*?

B. Representation of the dissension within Europe: The continuum

If one compares the rules on our topic within Europe, it becomes apparent that a large measure of dissension exists: almost every country has created its own solution to the problem of *bona fide* acquisition. To demonstrate just how great the dissension is, I refer to the Continuum below in which the

---

* Professor of Private Law, Centre for the Study of European Contract Law of the Amsterdam Institute for Private Law (CSECL), Universiteit van Amsterdam, The Netherlands.

Continuum – Protection of Owner vs Protection of bona fide acquirer

↑ Protection of bona fide acquirer	Germanic law	*Hand wahre Hand*, except for stolen things.
	Italy	Protection of acquirer in good faith, also in respect of stolen or lost things. Exception for things entered in public Registers.
	Austria, Slovenia	Protection of acquirer in good faith and for value in case of public auction, sale by registered commercial seller or in case dispossessed owner voluntarily entrusted the movable in the hands of the transferor. No exception for stolen or lost things. Only Slovenia: former owner has, for 1 year, personal right to buy back object of special importance (e.g. family jewels) for market value.
	Sweden	Until 2003 like Italy. Now owner may (within 6 months) revendicate stolen thing. Owner is entitled to buy back from *bona fide* acquirer against market value or purchase price paid by acquirer.
	Netherlands	Like France, but only revendication of stolen things. Protection of consumer who buys stolen thing in a store. Acquirer must give information about the whereabouts of the alienator.
	France	Acquirer *a non domino* in good faith becomes owner.
	Belgium	Owner can revendicate stolen and lost things within three years. Restitution of purchase price to buyer on market or from trader.
	Switzerland	Like French law, but limitation of revendication of stolen and lost things after five years.
	Germany, Spain, Greece	Like French law, but no protection of acquirer of lost or stolen things. Exceptions for trade. In Spain: restitution of purchase price for buyer at auction.
	Scotland	In principle no protection of acquirer in good faith. Exceptions: protection of acquirer in good faith and for value *eg* against the ending of previous transaction (*ex tunc* and *ex nunc*) and in case of double sale. No protection in case of stolen or lost things, registered things, money, works of art.
	England & Wales	In principle no protection of acquirer in good faith against legal owner. Exceptions, *eg*: acquirer in good faith of negotiable instrument; acquirer in good faith of thing already transferred but still in the hands of transferor; acquirer in good faith of thing already in the hands of his transferor but transferred to him under reservation of title; acquirer *via* mercantile agent.
Protection of owner ↓	Finland	Owner may revendicate even from acquirer in good faith, but only against payment in case the thing was not robbed or stolen.
	Czech Rep.	Like Portugal, but reform is on the way, and exceptions have already been introduced for trade and negotiable instruments.
	Portugal	No protection of acquirer in good faith, other than acquisitive prescription and restitution of purchase price paid to trader.
	Roman Law	*Ubi rem meam invenio, ibi vindico.* No *usucapio* for *res furtivae*

rules on *bona fide* acquisition of a considerable number of European countries have been ranked. The manner in which some of the rules are summarized may not do them full justice, in particular where exceptions of secondary importance have been omitted. I think, however, that this is justified by the fact that the purpose of the Continuum was merely to demonstrate the measure of dissension within Europe: hardly any of the national sets of rules are identical. Furthermore, the Continuum indicates the width of the gap between the different solutions: the national sets of rules are often substantially different from each other, and in some cases they are even diametrically opposed to others.

The two extremes in the Continuum are not current law, however, but they are included nevertheless because of their paradigmatic status: Roman Law and Germanic Law respectively. In Roman Law, the acquirer *a non domino* received no protection whatsoever, normally not even by way of *usucapio* (acquisitive prescription).[1] In early medieval Germanic Law we find the other extreme: the acquirer *a non domino* is protected,[2] unless the movable concerned was stolen.

Nowadays, sets of rules identical to either of these two extremes cannot be found anywhere in Europe. But the gap between the two extremes of modern property law within Europe in this respect – Portugal and Italy – is hardly less impressive: the Portuguese solution approaches Roman Law, the Italian one resembles Germanic Law. The rules of the Czech Republic, Finland, England & Wales, Scotland, Germany, Spain, Greece, Switzerland, France, Belgium, The Netherlands, Sweden, Austria, and Slovenia rank

---

[1] See *eg* Alfred Söllner, 'Der Erwerb vom Nichtberechtigten in romanistischer Sicht', in: *Europäisches Rechtsdenken in Geschichte und Gegenwart. Festschrift für Helmut Coing zum 70. Geburtstag*, Vol I (Munich: C H Beck 1982), 363-381, and Ulrich von Lübtow, 'Hand wahre Hand. Historische Entwicklung, Kritik und Reformvorschläge', in: Ulrich von Lübtow, *Gesammelte Schriften*. Abteilung II: Bürgerliches und Öffentliches Recht (3). Berliner Rechtswissenschaftliche Untersuchungen, Vol VII (Rheinfelden: Schäuble 1990), 1-138 (especially 3-68).

[2] Obviously, this is not the way the outcome of the conflict would be phrased in Germanic law. The central notion in Germanic law is not ownership or possession, but *Gewere*. Our conception of 'Germanic law's protection of the acquirer *a non domino*' is based upon the fact that several Germanic legal sources indicate that someone's *Gewere* could not be challenged successfully when it was received from someone who had obtained the thing by means other than theft. See on *Gewere*: Werner Ogris, 'Gewere' in: Adalbert Erler and Ekkehard Kaufmann (eds), *Handwörterbuch zur Deutschen Rechtsgeschichte* (HRG) (Berlin: Erich Schmidt Verlag 1971), 1658-1667, and on the way our topic was dealt with in Germanic law *eg* Söllner (*supra* footnote 1), Von Lübtow (*supra* footnote 1), Werner Hinz, 'Die Entwicklung des gutgläubiger Fahrniserwerbs in der europäischen Rechtsgeschichte', *Zeitschrift für europäisches Privatrecht* (ZEuP) 3 (1995), 398-422.

somewhere in between, where their order is determined by the measure in which their legal system protects the *bona fide* acquirer to the detriment of the dispossessed owner.

C. Three possible approaches

1. Historical approach?

How are we, in view of this dissension, to proceed in drafting a set of rules regarding *bona fide* acquisition in order to be part of a harmonized European property law? First of all, a historical approach of the kind which Reinhard Zimmermann advocates does not seem to be particularly fruitful here. It may, generally speaking, be true that historical research enables us 'to take stock of our present legal condition. It may help us to map out, and to become aware of, the common ground still existing between our national legal systems as a result of a common tradition, of independent but parallel developments, and of instances of intellectual stimulation or the reception of legal rules or concepts.'[3] But where the history of our topic consists, roughly speaking, of a jumping to and fro between protection of the dispossessed owner and protection of the *bona fide* acquirer, academia will not be able to reconstruct any real tradition or evolution to build upon. In other words: the outcome of historical research would first and foremost be determined by the number of centuries one would go back: if we were to go back twenty centuries, we would hit upon the Roman solution (*nemo dat quod non habet*), ten centuries would yield the Germanic solution (*Hand wahre Hand*), five centuries would bring us back to the Roman law rules, and a journey back in time of three or less centuries would once again result in the Germanic solution, now disguised in adagia like *meubles n'ont pas de suite* and *en fait de meubles possession vaut titre*.[4] In short, historical research will not be able to yield an

---

[3] Reinhard Zimmermann, 'Roman Law and the Harmonisation of Private Law in Europe', in: Arthur Severijn Hartkamp *et al* (eds), *Towards a European Civil Code* (Nijmegen, The Hague, London, Boston: Kluwer, 3rd ed 2004), 21- 42, at 41.

[4] In early modern times, the shift from the Roman Law protection of the owner towards the protection of the *bona fide* acquirer occurred initially in trade centres like Antwerp and Amsterdam (see Hugo de Groot, *Inleidinge tot de Hollandsche Rechts-geleerdheid. Met de te Lund teruggevonden verbeteringen, aanvullingen en opmerkingen van den schrijver en met verwijzingen naar zijn andere geschriften uitgegeven en van aantekeningen voorzien*, Folke Dovring *et al* (eds) (Leiden: Universitaire Pers, 2nd ed 1965), 50-55, especially 53 footnote 1). In 18th century Paris, the same occurred with the adoption of the rule '*en matière de meubles, possession vaut titre de propriété*' by the Paris law court, the Châtelet de Paris, again in view of trade interests: see below.

outcome which the European nations will accept as some sort of logical next step in the development of their law, and so it will not contribute to the removal of dissension on our topic.

Historical research focusing on the *reasons behind* the aforementioned jumping to and fro is all the more valuable, as it adds detail to the 'big picture' which we already have: in each case, external factors (political, educational, economic) were the cause of the change. Obviously, the fall of the Roman Empire and its replacement by Germanic kingdoms[5] is the reason for the replacement of the *nemo dat quod non habet* rule by the *Hand wahre Hand* rule in the Middle Ages.[6] The re-emergence of *nemo dat quod non habet* around 1500 forms part of the Reception of Roman law, a process of the scientification of law on the basis of Roman sources, which started at Italian Universities in the 12th century.[7] Finally, the return to *bona fide* acquisition protection in the 17th and 18th centuries in several European cities (especially in the Low Countries and France) had economic reasons: mercantile interests in the larger trade centers were translated into case law favouring *bona fide* acquirers over dispossessed owners, and this case law was subsequently incorporated into legislation.

2. A law & economics approach?

However, we do not *need* historical research to find out more about the relationship between economics and *bona fide* acquisition protection. An alternative approach to historical research would be a Law & economics analysis of the issue at hand. Usually, it is claimed that the protection of the

---

[5] In his *The fall of Rome and the end of civilization* (Oxford: Oxford University Press 2005), Brian Ward-Perkins forcefully argues that this did not constitute, contrary to current opinion among historians, a peaceful transition but was, just as popular culture has always envisaged it, a violent process with catastrophic consequences for the inhabitants of the former Roman Empire.

[6] See *eg* for the Frankish kingdom Raymond Poincaré, *Du droit de suite dans la propriété mobilière, l'ancien droit et le Code civil* (Paris: Librairie nouvelle de droit et de jurisprudence, 1883) and Walther Merk, 'Die Entwicklung der Fahrnisverfolgung im französischen Recht', *Rheinische Zeitschrift für Zivil- und Prozeßrecht* (RheinZ) 7 (1915), 81-130 and 173-236.

[7] See, in general, Paul Koschaker's well-known *Europa und das römische Recht* (Munich: Biederstein Verlag, 1st ed 1947, Munich/Berlin: C H Beck, 4th ed 1966) and, with regard to the place of our topic within the Reception process, *eg* Robert Feenstra, 'Vindikation von Mobilien und Lösungsrecht in den nördlichen Niederlanden im 17. Jahrhundert. Bemerkungen zu zwei neueren Arbeiten', *Tijdschrift voor Rechtsgeschiedenis* (TvRg) 63 (1995), 355-375.

bona fide acquirer is indispensable for the interests of trade.⁸ This claim has a long history, as becomes apparent from the *oeuvre* of François Bourjon, the *chroniqueur* of the 18th century Parisian case law I have just referred to, and accordingly the spiritual father of art 2279 *Code Civil*, in which the case law regarding our topic was codified in 1804. Bourjon wrote, as early as 1747, that protection of the acquirer is indispensable for '*la sûreté du commerce*', the certainty of trade.⁹ In modern legal publications, this is nothing short of a *topos*: *bona fide* acquisition protection is a prerequisite for a thriving trade sector.

Is that really true, however? A falsification of that claim requires a Law & economics analysis of our topic in its entirety, and indeed there is a great deal of material available, but the greater part of this is written within an Anglo-American context and/or is focused on stolen works of art. In order to harmonize European property law, we need a comprehensive Law & Economics analysis of *bona fide* acquisition within a European context, and this seems to be lacking.¹⁰

3. A theoretical approach?

A third possible approach is rooted in Legal Theory. The approach consists of weighing the legal principles which are at stake in the conflict of interests between the dispossessed owner and the *bona fide* acquirer, in order to establish requirements for the protection of the acquirer. It is this approach that is most commonly followed by legislators and scholars alike.

A very good example is the recent Austrian *Habilitationsschrift* of Ernst Karner, published in 2005, entitled *Gutgläubiger Mobiliarerwerb*.¹¹ This book,

---

[8] The word 'trade' should be understood, here and elsewhere in this contribution, as an equivalent to the German notion of *Verkehr*.

[9] François Bourjon, *Le droit commun de la France et la Coutume de Paris réduits en principes* (Paris: 1747, 2ⁿᵈ ed 1770), 145. See Hans Kiefner, 'Qui possidet dominus esse praesumitur. Untersuchungen zur Geschichte der Eigentumsvermutung zugunsten des Besitzers seit Placentinus', *Zeitschrift der Savigny-Stiftung, Romanistische Abteilung* (ZSSt RA) 79 (1962), 239-306, especially 283-286.

[10] Compare the references made by Barak Medina at the end of his 'Augmenting the Value of Ownership by Protecting it Only Partially: The "Market-overt" Rule Revisited', *The Journal Of Law, Economics, & Organization* (J L Econ & Org), Vol 19, No 2, 343-372. See p 369 (with footnotes 40-41) for the relevance of time and place (and for the role of intuitive perceptions in the creation of rules on *bona fide* acquisition protection).

[11] Ernst Karner, *Gutgläubiger Mobiliarerwerb. Zum Spannungsverhältnis von Bestandschutz und Verkehrsinteressen* (Vienna: Springer 2006).

one of the most thorough and extensive recent analyses of our topic, is – despite a fairly extensive comparative and historical introduction – entirely based on the method of weighing legal principles. Karner has brilliantly succeeded in providing the Austrian rules with a more solid theoretical foundation, also in view of the reform of these rules at the beginning of this year. But his conclusions are restricted to Austrian law: Karner did not try to make statements with 'universal meaning' by presenting some kind of equilibrium of the many principles he distinguishes, to be used when drafting rules for Europe. Nor should he have done so, I think, because research efforts like his do not succeed in escaping the limitations of time and place. This can be inferred from the simple fact that Karner's findings may suit current Austrian law, but similar studies in other countries present different outcomes. And even in a slightly more recent *Dissertation* from Austria itself, by Margareth Prisching,[12] the theoretical analysis of our topic is not entirely congruent with that of Karner.[13] Apparently, it is not at all possible to determine an objective or universal equilibrium of the many relevant principles. And yet, the method itself has not lost its popularity, as a consequence of which discord on our topic is undiminished.

One might suppose that this could be explained by local economic circumstances: in a country where commerce predominates, like The Netherlands, the interests of trade may be expected to weigh more heavily than in an essentially agriculturist country like Portugal. But, at best, this offers only a partial explanation, for when one studies the Continuum, one sees nothing but a patchwork quilt without any clear pattern; there is, in particular, no North-South or East-West divide. This also rules out that cultural differences lie hidden behind the discord.

Apparently, something is wrong with the method of weighing legal principles, but what is so problematic about it? I think that the problem is threefold.

A first problem with the theoretical approach is that the weighing of principles is an intellectual activity, the outcome of which is very often determined more by the rules of logic than by reality itself. For just one example we can, again, turn to Karner's *Habilitationsschrift*, in which we read that *Verkehrsschutz* is an *Optimierungsgebot* which derives its importance from the *Allgemeininteresse* and which must be weighed against the *Eigen-*

---

[12] Margareth Prisching, *Gutgläubiger Erwerb an beweglichen Sachen im Rechtsvergleich. Ein Beitrag zur Diskussion um ein europäisches Zivilgesetzbuch* (Graz: Grazer Universitätsverlag [et al] 2006).

[13] The greater part of Prisching's book is, however, based upon a comparative analysis, and it focusses on the European *ius constituendum*. It culminates in an appealing proposal for European legislation (p 305-309), modestly and pragmatically presented as a 'balancierenden Mittelweg' (p 342).

tumsschutz, taking into account the sub-principles of a lesser abstraction level, such as *Vertrauensschutz*, *Rechtsscheinprinzip* and the *Prinzip der Gefahrenbeherrschung und Risikoverteilung*.[14] Again, this may be the proper way to construct a theoretical foundation under current national law (like that of Austria), but for a successful harmonization effort we would have to keep the palette of principles with which we are to construct our provisions as simple as possible. Better still, we would look for another method, for, in my estimation, consensus will not ensue from the theoretical approach, however brilliantly it is pursued.

A second drawback of that approach is the fact that we are dealing with principles of differing ranking: how, for example, could one weigh the principle of fairness, which operates on a micro level, against the interests of trade, which manifest themselves in their effect on the economy, that is to say: on a macro level? These are questions to which the answers cannot be found in legal science; they are of a political nature and must be addressed not in a study, but in parliament.

In the third place, a complication is the fact that the principle of fairness plays only a minor role here, while the interests of trade, which dominate the issue, do not have a moral dimension. Generally speaking, the protection of the owner against the *bona fide* acquirer or *vice versa* cannot be called 'fair' or 'socially just', nor could the withholding of protection to either of them be called 'unfair' or 'socially unjust'. This gives legislators a freer hand than would have been the case if fairness were at stake more often or the interests of trade had ethical aspects. An exception is the case where the transfer to the *bona fide* acquirer was a gift: in such a case, fairness requires that protection is withheld from the acquirer. The interests of trade would not be at stake in such an outcome, as donations usually take place outside the *quid pro quo* world of trade and business.

D. Socio-political aspects

Let us, before we proceed, come to an interim conclusion. We have established that the issue we are dealing with is, to a large extent, morally indifferent. This fact enables us to allow economic considerations to guide us. But, for this we need to know whether the protection of the *bona fide* acquirer is indeed beneficial to the economy and, if so, what kind of protection would be best. The best method for establishing this is a Law & economics analysis, but a comprehensive European analysis of that kind is lacking. Therefore, we can only postulate that it would be economically sound to protect the *bona fide*

---

[14] Karner (*supra* footnote 11), 424-425.

acquirer, for this is in line with economic analyses which are available.[15] This is what I will do for the remainder of this contribution.

In doing so, I do not question the correctness of the claim by Brigitta Lurger[16] that there are socio-political aspects to our topic as well. An example is the fact that *bona fide* acquisition protection is predominantly concerned with second-hand goods, and that this protection is therefore especially relevant to persons who, in view of their limited financial recourses, are dependent on the purchase of such goods.[17] But I do not think that these aspects ought to be given a great deal of attention in the drafting process: property law is not the proper place for distributive justice.

I merely remark that, in my opinion, the dichotomy between 'individualistic' and 'altruistic' is not very helpful for our topic when connected to the extremes of 'protection of ownership' and 'protection of third parties'. To describe a legal system or a rule as individualistic means that they allow the individual to 'mind his own business', but that description fits the dispossessed owner, granted the right to revendicate his property, just as well as it fits the *bona fide* acquirer, granted the right to keep his acquisition. The notion of 'altruism', which Lurger locates at the opposite end of the spectrum, implies selflessness, and that is misleading here: the protection of the *bona fide* acquirer does not mean that the dispossessed owner has to make a sacrifice in his favour, but only that the owner, instead of the acquirer, is forced to look for redress elsewhere, in the direction of the unauthorized transferor: in the final analysis, rules on *bona fide* acquisition deal with risk apportionment. Besides, no one would describe a rule which forces a *bona fide* acquirer to surrender the acquisition as a rule asking for altruism on his part to the benefit of the dispossessed owner. Similar objections can be raised against an 'autonomy versus solidarity divide'. In any case, even if it were possible and useful to describe an existing legal system or set of rules along the lines of dichotomies like individualistic-altruistic or autonomy-solidarity, they do not seem to be particularly helpful instruments when drafting new rules.

---

[15] See Brigitta Lurger, 'Political Issues in Property Law', in: Martijn Willem Hesselink (ed), *The Politics of a European Civil Code* (The Hague: Kluwer 2006), 33-54, at 46: 'Economic analysis writers generally favour a generous approach to good faith acquisition as the more efficient solution for markets' (Lurger refers, *inter alia*, to the already mentioned research by Barak Medina).

[16] Lurger (*supra* footnote 15), *passim*.

[17] This fact was not lost on the Dutch legislator: it was brought forward as a justification for the rule of art 3:86 § 3 (a) of the Dutch *Burgerlijk Wetboek* protecting consumers who buy a stolen object in a store against revendication by the dispossessed owner; see *Parlementaire Geschiedenis van het Nieuw Burgerlijk Wetboek*, Invoering Boeken 3, 5 en 6, Boek 3, Vermogensrecht in het algemeen, edited by W H M Reehuis and E E Slob (Deventer: Kluwer 1990), 1217.

E. Protecting the interests of trade and the rise of e-commerce

At this point, we can finally turn to the issue of content: what kind of rules are necessary to protect the *bona fide* acquirer if this protection is based upon – and therefore in the service of – the interests of trade? In my opinion, the answers to these questions become clear when we acknowledge that a rapidly increasing proportion of the trade in movables is the result of e-commerce. This phenomenon has implications for private law in general, and certainly for the law on the transfer of movables, including the rules on *bona fide* acquisition, to which I restrict myself.

One may ask whether it is already necessary to take the implications of the emergence of e-commerce into account. Most people seem to think that e-commerce is still only a small niche in the market but, in reality, this is no longer so. This can be illustrated by some figures, taken from my native country as an example, from the year 2005. In that year, Dutch companies realized 10 percent of their turnover through online sales; for manufacturing and trade companies, the figures were even higher: 14 and 12 percent respectively. Even though the pace of the growth of e-commerce seems to be slackening in The Netherlands, the figures are still growing rapidly for larger companies and for trade companies. Be that as it may, within Europe, The Netherlands ranks below average: in 2005, European companies realized 13% of their turnover through online sales. The front runners are Germany, the UK and Ireland. See the following graph.

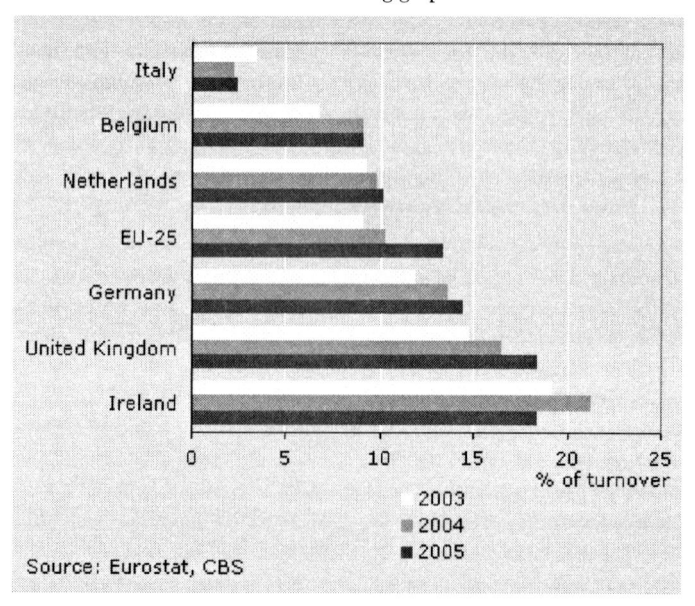

E-commerce in some EU countries 2003-2005[18]

In my opinion, these figures indicate that we cannot afford to ignore e-commerce when we are contemplating harmonizing transfer of movables law: we will have to take into consideration what effects the provisions have on online sales.

However, before we try to assess the relevance of the emergence of e-commerce for the rules on *bona fide* acquisition protection in particular, we should look at the characteristics of e-commerce by comparing an offline sale with an online one.

A standard offline sale is characterized by direct contact between the buyer and seller in a shop, the location not only of the conclusion of the sales agreement but also of the corporeal delivery and the instantaneous payment. The Americans have invented the catchphrase 'cash and carry' for this, traditional, type of trade.

In contrast, an online sale is characterized by indirect contact between buyer and seller. All of their legal acts are performed *via* intermediaries: the sale itself (as well as pre-sales marketing) through an internet provider, the payment through a credit card company, and the delivery through a postal service.

F. Implications of the rise of e-commerce for *bona fide* acquisition protection

It goes without saying that the shift from offline to online trade has implications on a practical level: what is needed for an e-buyer (the buyer in a sales agreement concluded online) to be called 'in good faith'? At what moment should this good faith be measured? What inquiries with regard to the authority of the seller can be expected from an e-buyer? *Etc.*

However, there are also implications on a more abstract level: the theoretical foundation of the protection itself is at stake.[19] For decades, law students have been taught that the acquirer of a movable deserves protection because he should be able to rely upon the actual possession of the transferor: this actual possession legitimizes the transferor as the owner, or – in the words of the National report of Slovenia:[20] the possession of the transferor

---

[18] The graph has been taken from http://www.cbs.nl/en-gb/menu/themas/bedrijven/publicaties/artikelen/archief/2006/2006-2085-wm.htm on the website of CBS (Statistics Netherlands = *Centraal Bureau voor de Statistiek*), with reference to Eurostat.

[19] I have argued this at greater length in my 'Inpassen of aanpassen? Vermogensrecht voor het digitale tijdperk', *Weekblad voor Privaatrecht, Notariaat en Registratie* (WPNR) 6427 (2000), 901-907.

[20] See Claudia Rudolf, Vesna Rijavec and Tomaž Keresteš, *Transfer or movables – Slovenia* [not yet published], 84.

'creates an image of ownership'. This is what the *Rechtsscheinprinzip* purports.[21] How well-established in Europe this theoretical foundation for the *bona fide* acquisition protection may be, can be inferred from the fact that *all* legal systems providing good faith acquisition protection require possession by the non-authorized seller.[22]

This requirement does not accord with the world of e-commerce: good or bad faith on the part of the e-buyer is not based upon the presence or absence of actual possession by the e-seller. In fact, it may well be that the e-seller does not have possession of the movable at the moment of concluding the sales agreement, as is the case when one orders a new computer online: assembly starts only after the order (and payment) is received and the component parts are collected by the manufacturer. But this should not mean that protection is withheld from the e-buyer, because that would be in conflict with the goal of protecting the interests of trade: e-commerce may be a novel way of doing business and not 'business as usual', but it is business none the less, and an increasingly important one too. In sum: withholding protection from the *bona fide* acquirer in the case of an online sale is not in order, but his good faith should not be linked to the possession of his counterpart and, as a consequence, the requirement of possession on the part of the seller can be abandoned.

If this is correct, we need a new object for the requirement of good faith. In my opinion, we should shift the focus from possession to a duty of care. The e-buyer should exercise the observance and attentiveness of a regular market participant, which translates, depending on the circumstances, into a duty to inquire into the authority of the transferor.[23] In the end, the interests of trade are served best, not by protecting possession, but by protecting (and therefore enhancing) diligence. It seems both difficult and unnecessary to substantiate the rule just formulated any further; this should be left to case law.

---

[21] The development of this principle is linked to publications like *Entwerung und Eigentum im deutschen Fahrnisrecht* (Jena: Fischer 1902) and *Das Publizitätsprinzip im deutschen bürgerlichen Recht* (Munich: C H Beck 1909) by Herbert Meyer and 'Publizität und Gewährschaft im deutschen Fahrnisrecht', *Jherings Jahrbücher* (JherJB) 49 (1905), 159-186, by Alfred Schultze.

[22] According to Lurger (*supra* footnote 15) 46.

[23] A similar link between good faith and a duty to inquire is to be found in art 3:11 of the Dutch *Burgerlijk Wetboek*: 'Where good faith of a person is required to produce a juridical effect, such person is not acting in good faith if he knew the facts or the law to which his good faith must relate or if, in the given circumstances, he should know them. Impossibility to inquire does not prevent the person, who had good reasons to be in doubt, from being considered as someone who should know the facts or the law.'

There is no need to abandon the requirement of possession by the transferor altogether, *ie* for traditional offline transactions as well, but in my opinion there is no reason to maintain it either. Besides, for some 'offline transactions' case law has already established that the mere fact that the transferor is in possession is insufficient to establish the good faith of the acquirer. Think, for example, of the abundance of case law on the *bona fide* acquisition of used cars and the duty of the acquirer to examine the car registration papers.[24] In any case, the alternative for possession-based good faith, which I proposed above, would suffice for online and offline sales alike. In the case of an offline sale, the duty to inquire into the authority of the transferor could be regarded as having been met where the *bona fide* acquirer has had eye-to-eye contact with the transferor in possession of the thing: the possession requirement and the duty to inquire coincide here.

In order to make our law 'e-commerce-proof', we should also scrutinize current provisions which grant special protection in the case of acquisition at certain locations, such as markets (France, Belgium),[25] stores (the Netherlands)[26] or auctions (Austria, Germany, Greece, Slovenia).[27] First of all, we

---

[24] For example: the rule that such an enquiry is indispensable for good faith was confirmed by the Dutch *Hoge Raad* in its recent judgement of 7 October 2005, *Nederlandse Jurisprudentie* (NJ) 2006, 351 (Coppes vs Van de Kolk); see Lars van Vliet, 'Feitelijke macht en derdenbescherming', *Nederlands Tijdschrift voor Burgerlijk Recht* (NTBR) (2002), 282-291 in a comparative perspective, and Arthur Salomons, 'De onderzoeksplicht van de verkrijger van een tweedehands auto', *Vermogensrechtelijke annotaties* (VrA) 2006/3, 101-124.

[25] Until 1995, England & Wales belonged to this list too, but on January 3 1995, the 'market overt rule' was abolished by the Sale of Goods (Amendment) Act 1994. The rule provided protection against the seller's defect in title to a good faith purchaser from a market overt, but it also applied to sales in shops in the city of London and, outside London, to sales from any open, public and legally constituted market. See Sandra Frisby and Michael Jones, *National Report for England and Wales on the Transfer of Movable Property* (2007) [not yet published], § 10.1.7. Until 1992, The Netherlands had a rule (art 637 *Burgerlijk Wetboek*) protecting purchasers from a market, similar to art 2280 *Code Civil* in France and Belgium; in the new Dutch *Burgerlijk Wetboek*, enacted in 1992, the rule did not reappear.

[26] As stated in the previous footnote, the Dutch *Burgerlijk Wetboek* no longer provides special protection to the purchaser from a market, as was the case before 1992. Nowadays, special protection is given to – in short – consumers who buy a stolen object in a store: 'the owner of a moveable thing, who has lost its possession through theft, may revendicate it during a period of three years from the day of theft, unless the thing has been acquired by a natural person, not acting in the exercise of a profession or business, from an alienator whose business it is to deal with the public in similar things, otherwise than at a public sale, on business premises destined for that purpose, being an immov-

have to determine why we should grant special protection to the acquirer in certain types of sales; how does that relate to our starting point that the interests of trade should guide us? But on top of that, we have to establish whether the buyer at an online market (such as Marketonline), an online store (such as Amazon) and an online auction (such as eBay) is entitled to similar protection as his offline counterpart.

G. Conclusion

For present purposes it is not necessary to give more examples of the implications of the rise of e-commerce. It suffices to conclude that – in order to protect the interests of trade – provisions on *bona fide* acquisition are needed which, in principle, also apply to online sales. This requires rules which are indifferent to the way in which the transferee acquired the movable concerned: an acquirer should, in principle, be entitled to protection, as long as he
- has acquired the movable for value,
- was unaware of other, earlier proprietary interests and
- acted according to the standard of care and
- has proceeded to acquire visible control over the movable.

Of course, it may, for some cases, be necessary to rule out protection in the public interest, for example with regard to stolen objects, in order to prevent crime (theft and handling). But these are mere exceptions to our starting point that the interests of trade are to be taken as guiding. '*La sûreté du commerce l'exige ainsi.*'[28]

---

able structure or part thereof with the land belonging thereto, and provided that the alienator be in the ordinary exercise of his business'. It is unlikely that an e-buyer will be allowed to invoke this protection; see H A G Fikkers, 'E-commerce en de derdenbescherming van art. 3:86 lid 3 sub a BW', WPNR 2000 (6406), 432-436 and Salomons (*supra* footnote 19), 901-907.

[27] See Karner (*supra* footnote 11), 24, with references.
[28] Bourjon 1770 (*supra* footnote 9), 145.

Good Faith Acquisition – Why at all?

*José Caramelo-Gomes**

A. Introduction

This contribution deals with the good faith (*bona fide*) acquisition of property and, as its title suggests, questions whether there should be any such acquisition within the framework of the Transfer of Moveable's team (TOM) of the Study Group on the European Civil Code (SGECC).

The first issue one must clarify is the concept of good faith (*bona fide*) acquisition of property and for that I appeal to Arthur F Salomons' article[1] in this volume: the '*[acquisition of] a movable from someone he [the buyer] erroneously considers to be entitled to transfer it to him.*'

Arthur Salomons opts, quite naturally, to focus his article solely on the good faith acquisition of movables, as it is delivered within the context of the TOM. My approach to the issue will be broader, as in my view, although included in the same working group, the pertinence of good faith acquisition should be discussed in both movable and immovable things.

The starting point for the discussion is the assumption that 'The approaches to acquisition in good faith adopted by the legal systems of the EU Member States span from total rejection of any such acquisition in Portugal to its general admissibility in Italy ...';[2] Salomons' article retains this same assumption.

Good faith acquisition is, as the team recognises, a 'grave intrusion to the original owner's rights ... justified only because it satisfies two interests: firstly, the interest of the public at large in a steady functioning of commerce. It is common opinion that acquisition in good faith is an expression of distributive justice (*iustitita distributiva*), as the individual freedom of an owner has to yield, under certain circumstances, to the general welfare, the safety of commerce, and the interests of specific purchasers.'[3]

---

* Professor of European Law, Faculty of Law, Universidade Lusíada.
[1] Arthur F Salomons, 'How to draft new rules on the bona fide acquisition of movables for Europe? Some remarks on method and content', in this volume at p 141, *sub* C.1
[2] SGECC-TOM 2006, Activities 2005-2009, http://www.uni-graz.at/bre1www/tom/page 19/page20/page20.html, 2006.
[3] See SGECC-TOM 2006, above.

These statements clearly justify the need for a Portuguese input into the discussion and that, I think, is the reason why the team invited me to deliver this article.

B. Portuguese law – general rules

To discuss the legal framework of good faith acquisition I must, in the first place, clarify some aspects of contractual invalidity in Portuguese law.

There are several degrees of contractual invalidity in Portugal: inexistence, nullity and annullability (as in French legal order *annulabilité*). The first degree, inexistence, refers to situations where it is so obvious that no intention to contract is present, that no legal effects whatsoever can be extracted from the situation; the classical examples of such situations are physical coercion (if someone's harm is pushed during an auction as opposed to moral coercion considered in Portuguese law as an illegal intimidation with or without infliction of physical or psychological harm) and *non-serious* declarations (*eg*, when a law professor gives an example in class). Nullity, on the other hand, occurs when the interests that the law protects when establishing the cause of invalidity are, although protecting one, both or none of the parties, public interests; in such case, the cause for invalidity may be relied upon by any interested third party and may be raised, *ex propriu motu*, by a court of law. The annullability is the third degree of invalidity and, generally speaking, applies to the situations where the interest protected by the law establishing the invalidity is a party's only interest – the classical situation includes the mistake theory in the formation of contracts. The main differences between nullity and annullability are, because of the nature of the underlying interests, the time-driven legalisation that occurs in respect of the latter, the limited legitimacy to argue annullability, the general legitimacy to argue nullity and the powers of the *ex officio* declaration that exist in relation to nullity but not in relation to annullability.

The general solution for the sale of things by someone who is not legally entitled to do so is, according to the article 892 of the Portuguese Civil Code (CC),[4] nullity. This would mean, if no exception is made, that the invalidity of the contract could be relied upon by any interested third party

---

[4] Article 892 CC: The contract by which one sells third party assets is null and void (*ab initio*) if the seller has no legitimacy to contract; the seller may not bring a plaint against the good faith buyer, as the bad faith buyer may not against the good faith seller.

as well as between the parties themselves at all times,[5] and that the nullification would produce retrospective effects.[6]

This is not exactly the case in a sale of things by someone who has no legitimacy to do so. In the first place there is a limitation on the right to claim the nullity: the seller may not bring such claim against the good faith buyer, as article 892 CC clearly shows. In the second place, contrary to the general rule of non-legalisation of null contracts, article 897 CC imposes on the seller a mandatory legalisation; ie, when the buyer is in good faith the seller must convalidate (legalise) the contract by acquiring the asset;[7] the breach of such obligation vests the seller with the duty to additionally compensate the good faith buyer.[8]

Because the sales contract, when the seller lacks the legitimacy to sell, is null the original owner has the power to demand the asset before a court of law; if he has been dispossessed, according to article 1311 CC, he may take direct action within the limits of articles 1314 CC and 336 CC and may bring a negatory action before the court. The good faith buyer in entitled to compensation in any case, even if he has not been evicted.[9]

C. Portuguese law – exceptions

There are a number of exceptional situations where the good faith buyer is protected under Portuguese law. The first relates to assets subject to registration in a national register (immovables, vehicles); in such cases, when the inscription of the acquisition in the national register is still pending, then nullification has no effects on the good faith buyer (doctrine of register acquisition) – Article 291 CC. Another situation where the good faith buyer enjoys legal protection against the original owner is a sham contract: the original owner who simulated a sale cannot argue the nullity against the good faith buyer – articles 240 and 243 CC.

Apart from these two situations, all other exceptions to the general rule depend on acquisitive prescription periods and, eventually, on the way the seller came into possession of the asset.

---

[5] Article 286 CC – Nullity can be relied upon at all times by anyone interested and may be raised by the court of its own motion (*ex proprio motu*).

[6] Article 289 CC – Nullification of the contract produces retrospective effects.

[7] Although there is no obligation of the original owner to agree on this legalisation; the basic principle of the freedom to contract (article 405 CC) applies to him without restrictions.

[8] Article 900 CC.

[9] Manuel Baptista Lopes, *Do contrato de compra e venda no direito civil, comercial e fiscal* (Coimbra: Livraria Almedina 1971), p 543.

The general rules on acquisitive prescription apply to the good faith acquirer, and the particular circumstances of a case may determine the existence of special solutions. This is the case of the reduced period for acquisitive prescription of lost or missing movables, if the finding was announced (one year instead of three or six years, depending on the type of possession of the movable – article 1299 CC) – article 1323 CC.

The Portuguese system of acquisitive prescription establishes different acquisitive prescription periods depending on the nature of the asset and the type of possession. As to movable assets, the acquisitive prescription period is three or six years, depending on whether the possession is good or bad faith possession; entitled possession is presumed to be good faith possession (entitled possession is the one that is grounded on a regular modus of property acquisition, even if invalid for some reason) – articles 1259 CC, 1260 n 2 CC and 1299 CC.

D. Portuguese commercial law

If the seller is a professional trader, article 467 n 2 of the Commercial Code 1888 applies. The contract by means of which one sells another person's assets is permitted, and the seller is obliged to acquire the asset and deliver it to the buyer, otherwise he is liable for damages. Although there is a different degree of validity of contract, the contract now being a valid contract, for the good faith acquirer to keep the asset it is required that legalisation occurs, that property is acquired by acquisitive prescription or that rules on sham contracts or on registration in the ational registry apply.

E. Conclusion

The Portuguese system appears, in my view, to be a logical consequence of the 'consensual approach' to the transfer of property – the first consequence of the sales contract is the property right transfer – article 879 a). *Traditio* is not an immediate effect of the contract and occurs only as a consequence of one of the ways established in article 1263.

Getting back to Salomons' article in this book,[10] and the possible explanation for the different solutions found across Europe, I would stress the hypothesis of the loyalty of the 20th century Portuguese legal doctrine to Roman law, the inherent consideration that the fall of Rome was the end of

---

[10] See Salomons (*supra* note 1).

civilisation and that the best way to scientification of the law is trough Roman sources.

Finally, Good faith acquisition – Why at all?

In spite of all the differences Salomons points out, I consider that it is quite common for European systems to acknowledge some sort of good faith protection in this matter. Its extent may vary, but I think one thing we all agree on is: some protection should be provided. The problem here, I think, is to find the *quantum*.

Fiduciary Transfer and Ownership

Selma de Groot

A. Should the European debate with regard to the transfer of movables include fiduciary transfers?

A fiduciary transfer is a transfer of ownership accompanied by an obligation that limits the rights of the transferee with respect to the transferred property in such a way that the latter is obliged to use the ownership for a specific purpose and then to (re)transfer it to the original owner or a beneficiary.

For this contribution I will examine the effect of the fiduciary transfer on civil property law concepts, with an emphasis on ownership, and link the outcome to the debate on the transfer of movables. I argue that the fiduciary transfer should be part of this debate since it infringes upon, or challenges the object of a transfer of movables: the civil law concept of ownership.

Fiduciary transfers in civil law are generally divided into two types: the *fiducia cum creditore* (security device) and the *fiducia cum amico* (management/administrative device).[1] The former is usually discussed within the debate on trust-like devices, whilst the latter forms part of the discourse on real security rights. Since the two institutions differ in purpose and economic relevance, a separate approach is desirable and justified. But seeing that the structure that underlies both types is similar and might affect the civil concept of ownership, both the management and the security device are considered here.

B. A civil law dilemma

The structure of the *fiducia* results in an unequal distribution of rights: the transferee is the legal owner of the transferred movable(s), while the trans-

---

[1] The terminology refers to the legal structure, which is similar to the Roman structure of fiduciary devices (the transferor is entitled to a personal right, the transferee is the full owner), not to its roots. Michele Graziadei in: Richard Helmholz and Reinhard Zimmermann (eds), *Itinera Fiduciae: Trust and Treuhand in a Historical Perspective* (Berlin: Duncker & Humblot 1998), p 356.

feror is protected by a mere personal claim.[2] Since the fiduciary is characterised as the owner, he is able to transfer the property to third parties, notwithstanding the fiduciary agreement that limits his rights of disposal. Apart from that, his creditors are able to seize his patrimony, including the movables that he 'owns' as a fiduciary. In these two circumstances the transferor's personal claim is considered too feeble to protect his interest in the transferred property.[3] Thus, it is desirable to balance the rights of the transferee with the rights of the transferor,[4] by strengthening the position of the transferor (and his creditors). But when the rights of the parties involved are modified in a way that corresponds with the actual purpose of the transfer, the civil law perception of real rights is put to the test. Before we investigate the effect of the fiduciary transfer on property rights, it is necessary to discover the reason why the transferor parts with his right of ownership in the first place.

Depending on the type of fiduciary agreement, the transferor's motives differ. The development of the *fiducia cum creditore* is closely linked to the rules on real security rights. The transfer of ownership by constructive delivery was (and is) used to evade the stringent rules of pledge, in particular the inconvenient requirement of *traditio*.[5] In a number of civil law systems the *fiducia cum creditore* developed from a conditional sale into a form of debtor-held pledge.[6] Drobnig explains that the resemblance between fiduciary transfer and the right of pledge is not surprising 'since both the economic function and the basic legal structure, namely the grant of a proprietary right in the debtor-held assets, correspond to each other.'[7] This functional similarity enables us to deduce the debtor's interest in the transferred property from the rules of pledge; like the pledgor, the transferor/debtor should be entitled *in rem* to the movable after payment or, in case of default, to the surplus (if there is any) of the execution sale. The equivalence between the transfer of

---

[2] This is the rudimentary structure of a fiduciary transfer, which I take as a starting point.

[3] Stefan Grundmann, 'Trust and *Treuhand* in the 20th Century', in: Helmholz and Zimmerman (*supra* note 1), p 471.

[4] I will define, depending on the type of arrangement, the transferor as debtor or beneficiary, and the transferee as fiduciary or trustee. I do not consider three party structures whereby A transfers property to B for the benefit of C.

[5] The physical delivery of property.

[6] Jan Dalhuisen, 'Conditional Sales and Modern Financial Products', in Arthur Hartkamp, *et al* (eds), *Towards a European Civil Code* (The Hague: Kluwer Law International, 2nd ed 1998), pp 535-538. The author refers to the development of the German *Sicherungsübereignung*, the Dutch *zekerheidsoverdracht* (before 1992) and the English chattel mortgage.

[7] Ulrich Drobnig, 'Present and Future of Real and Personal Security', (2003) 5 *European Review of Private Law* (ERPL), pp 652-653.

ownership and pledge makes it possible to bring the latter under the umbrella of real security rights. This functional approach involves at least one difficulty: in order to subject security transfers to a regime of real security rights, it is necessary to distinguish these transfers from other similar devices, like for example sale and lease-back transactions.

While the *fiducia cum creditore* is in the interest of the fiduciary/creditor, the *fiducia cum amico* is in the interest of the beneficiary. Civil law offers a number of contractual management devices such as agency or mandate, but these are inferior to management devices based on the transfer of movables. Mattei points out that the effectiveness of a management device based on ownership lies in the 'exclusive decision-making power' of the fiduciary. It enables the beneficiary to devote his resources to a different activity, whilst a more competent trustee manages his property. Nevertheless, this 'efficient division of labour' is only possible when a system attributes powers to the beneficiary as well.[8] These powers should reflect that, from an economic perspective, the transferred movables belong to the patrimony of the beneficiary.

Civil property law is ill-equipped to facilitate balanced fiduciary transfers due to its strict order and definition of property rules. The following principles, which underlie property rules, might impede the development of fiduciary transfer into a more balanced legal relationship. To start with, civil law adheres to a comprehensive, undivided concept of ownership; the owner is exclusively entitled to enjoy, manage and dispose of this right for his own benefit.[9] When an owner is deprived of his right, he may compel a forced return (*revindicatio*). Although it is possible that more persons co-own property, split ownership, in the sense that two or more persons have different ownership rights in the same object, is not accepted. The concept of undivided ownership overlaps with the *numerus clausus* (of rights *in rem*) doctrine and the principle of transparency. A right over property (right *in rem*) is either a right of ownership (*dominium*), or a limited right (*ius in re aliena*), such as a right of usufruct, which derives from a right of ownership. The list

---

[8] Ugo Mattei, 'Basic Issues of Private Law Codification in Europe: Trust', (2001) 1 *Global Jurist Frontiers*, pp 5-7.

[9] See the definition of ownership in the German, French and Dutch Civil Codes (in that order):
Art 901 BGB: *Der Eigentümer einer Sache kann, soweit nicht das Gesetz oder Rechte Dritter entgegenstehen, mit der Sache nach Belieben verfahren und andere von jeder Einwirkung ausschließen.* (...)
Art 544 CC: *La propriété est le droit de jouir et disposer des choses de la manière la plus absolue, pourvu qu'on n'en fasse pas un usage prohibé par les lois ou par les règlements.*
Art 5:1(1) BW: *Eigendom is het meest omvattende recht dat een persoon op een zaak kan hebben.*

of proprietary rights is closed; parties cannot adjust or create new types of proprietary entitlements.[10] Since rights *in rem* are absolute and have effect against the world at large, it is deemed necessary that the world knows which rights exist in which objects. Publicity of proprietary entitlements is generally seen as a prerequisite for the enforcement of such rights against third parties. With respect to movables, the methods to comply with this requirement are *traditio*[11] or, alternatively, registration in a public register. It is important to note that both the ways in which proprietary rights are communicated towards third parties and the level of third party protection against 'secret' proprietary rights vary considerably from jurisdiction to jurisdiction.[12]

Confronted with fiduciary transactions, courts and legislators have to find a balance between the demands of the legal trade and the interests of the parties involved in and affected by the transaction.[13] The doctrines that dictate not to split, add or alter proprietary rights in ways not provided by the law, serve as filters for new proprietary rules.[14] In the following, I investigate three possible ways to approach the development of the fiduciary transfer within the boundaries set by civil property law. But before looking into the possibilities in civil law, it might be interesting to see why the fiduciary transfer does *not* pose a dilemma in common law.

C. England & Wales: Division of ownership?

English law distributes proprietary rights to both parties in a fiduciary relationship, whereby each right is suited to the specific position of the party

---

[10] With respect to this principle, see: Sjef van Erp, A Numerus Quasi-Clausus of Property Rights as a Constitutive Element of a Future European Property Law?, 2003 (2) *Electronic Journal of Comparative Law*; Thomas Merill and Henry Smith, 'Optimal Standardization in the Law of Property; The Numerus Clausus Principle', (2000) 110 *Yale Law Journal* (Yale L J); Teun Struycken, *De numerus clausus in het goederenrecht* (Deventer: Kluwer 2007).

[11] *Supra* note 5.

[12] Eva-Maria Kieninger, 'Evaluation: a common core? Convergences, subsisting differences and possible ways for harmonisation', in: Eva-Maria Kieninger and Michele Graziadei, *Security Rights in Movable Property in European Private Law* (Cambridge: Cambridge University Press 2004), p 655-656.

[13] Conflicting interests might arise between the transferor (debtor or beneficiary) and his creditors on the one hand, and the fiduciary and his creditors on the other.

[14] Sjef van Erp, 'European and National Property Law: Osmosis or Growing Antagonism?', in: *Walter van Gerven Lectures*, Vol VI (Groningen: Europa Law Publishing 2006), pp 13-17.

involved. This distribution is often described, by both civil and common lawyers, as a 'division of ownership'.[15] Divided ownership is, as we have seen above, difficult to approximate to within the civil law. Apart from that, it is particularly difficult to understand for the civil lawyer, who seeks to understand English law by defining it with familiar concepts.

English law distinguishes the following property rights in personal property:[16] legal ownership, possession and (a variety of) equitable interests. Like in civil law, proprietary rights are universal and can be asserted against the world at large.[17] Ownership is conventionally described as the residue of legal rights remaining in a person, or in persons concurrently after specific rights over the assets have been granted to others.[18] Common law is not familiar with ownership in the sense of an absolute title, which can be ascribed to the system's protection of property rights. The remedy at common law for such protection is not the *revindicatio*, but damages. The person with the best possessory title is the owner. When two or more people have conflicting rights of possession, the person with the first (earliest) right of possession wins. Thus, with respect to the protection of property, the concept of ownership is redundant and possession essential.[19]

Although ownership under common law is indivisible, this principle is subject to a very significant exception. It is possible that two persons are simultaneously entitled to a different proprietary interest in one asset. This 'division of ownership' occurs when a person holds property as a trustee for the benefit of a beneficiary, but also when a creditor holds property for his own benefit in the case of a mortgage.[20] The existence of two concurrent proprietary interests in the same object is a consequence of the (historic) division between the courts of common law and the courts of Chancery. The Chancellor recognised the existence of common law, but modified shortcomings of the law administered by the common law courts.[21] The most important contribution of the law of equity to property law is, without

---

[15] Michael Bridge, *Personal Property Law* (Oxford: Oxford University Press, 3rd ed 2002), p 31; Roy Goode, *Commercial law* (London: Penguin Books 3rd ed 2004), p 39.

[16] 'Personal property is all the property that is left once land, that is real property (or realty), has been substracted'. See: Frederick Lawson and Bernard Rudden, *The Law of Property* (Oxford: Oxford University Press, 3rd ed 2002), p 1.

[17] Bridge (*supra* note 15), p 12.

[18] Goode (*supra* note 15), p 31; Anthony Honoré, in: Anthony Guest (ed), *Oxford Essays in Jurisprudence* (London: Oxford University Press, 1961), p 126.

[19] Property remedies require that the claimant was in possession, ownership is not relevant, see: William Swadling in: Peter Birks (ed), *English Private Law*, Vol I (Oxford: Oxford University Press 2000), no 4.37-4.40.

[20] Goode (*supra* note 15), p 39.

[21] Lawson and Rudden (*supra* note 16) p 82.

doubt, the trust. The beneficiary of a trust is protected by an equitable right, which refines the transfer of title to the trustee. This right entails, in the first place, that the trust property and the proceeds of authorised investments thereof are held in a separate fund, distinct from the trustee's patrimony, and are therefore protected against claims from the trustee's creditors.[22] When the trustee wrongfully disposes of trust assets, he holds the proceeds on constructive trust for the beneficiary. Moreover, the beneficiary can follow the original assets or trace their proceeds, being in the hands of a third party, and then institute an action.[23] The equitable interest of the beneficiary will be overridden when the third party is a purchaser for value without notice.[24]

The development of the English chattel mortgage is similar to the civil law *fiducia cum creditore*.[25] A mortgage is the conveyance or assignment of property by a mortgagor to a mortgagee as security for the repayment of a debt or the performance of some other obligation.[26] The mortgage has been accepted as a security right for immovable property since the sixteenth century, but it was not until the introduction of the Bills of Sale Acts in 1878 and 1882, which introduced a system of registration, that the mortgage in movables acquired legal status.[27] The legal interest of the mortgagee is protected by an equitable right; the 'equity of redemption'. This right guarantees that the 'mortgagee's interest shall be effective only as a security interest, and that the economic benefits of ownership shall remain in the mortgagor'.[28] It entitles the mortgagor to redeem even after the due date and this right cannot be excluded by contract.[29]

The concept of ownership is different from the civil perception of absolute ownership and, even though the common law regards the list of proprietary interest as closed,[30] it contains the equitable interest, which is unknown

---

[22] David J Hayton, *The Law of Trusts* (London: Sweet & Maxwell, 4th ed 2003), p 169.

[23] Tracing is not a remedy, but a technique to identify the proceeds.

[24] Lawson and Rudden (*supra* note 16) p 176.

[25] See Dalhuisen (*supra* note 6) and for a historic exposé: Harold Hazeltine, 'The *fiducia cum creditore* and the English mortgage', in: Richard Turner (ed), *The Equity Of Redemption* (Cambridge: Cambridge University Press 1931).

[26] *Keith v Burrows* (1876) 1 CPD 722.

[27] Before that time 'the non-possessery chattel mortgage was almost invariably doomed to failure, for the debtor's continuance in possession after granting a security bill of sale was regarded as nearly conclusive evidence to defraud creditors within the Fraudulent Conveyance Act 1571'. Goode (*supra* note 15), p 586.

[28] Lionel Smith in: Birks (*supra* note 19), no 5.06.

[29] Goode (*supra* note 15), p 641.

[30] Thomas W Merill and Henry E Smith, 'Optimal Standardization in the Law of Property; The Numerus Clausus Principle', (2000) 110 *Yale Law Journal* (Yale L J), pp 23-24,

to civil law. The equitable interest is difficult to define in civil law terms. This right, which derives from a supplementary jurisdiction, is not comparable to an existing real right *in rem*, nor can it be described as a right that is split off from the right of ownership. Maybe it is better to put the dogmatic puzzle aside and focus on the ways in which the transferor's position is protected in civil law.

D. Germany: Division in time

The German concept of *Treuhand* developed outside the German Civil Code (BGB) and covers both types of fiduciary relationships (*Sicherungsübereignung* for security transactions and *Verwaltungstreuhand* for management purposes).[31] Fiduciary transfers are regulated by general property and contract law rules and the German fiduciary transfer is, at first glance, not distinguishable from the normal transfer of ownership. The fiduciary (*Treuhänder*) is traditionally characterised as the owner of the property and his right of disposal is, from an internal perspective, limited by the fiduciary agreement. Yet, the right of the transferor is not always a purely contractual one.

Since the fiduciary has, from an external perspective, unrestricted ownership, he is entitled to transfer the property with which he is entrusted. Considering his legal title, the rules on *bona fide* acquisition from a *non dominus* (§§ 932 *et seqq* BGB) are not relevant. An unauthorised transfer might be void due to *Sittenwidrigkeit* (contrary to the *boni mores*, § 138 BGB) in the rare circumstance that the third party acted fraudulently when purchasing the property. Apart from that, the transferor's only option is to claim damages (*Schadenersatz*) as the fiduciary did not act in accordance with his personal obligation.[32] The limit of the transferor's protection is related to § 137 BGB: a stipulated restriction of the power of disposal does not work against

---

Bernard Rudden, 'Economic Theory v Property law', in John Eekelaar and John Bell, *Oxford Essays on Jurisprudence* (Oxford: Oxford University Press, 3rd ed 1987), p 239.

[31] The *Verwaltungstreuhand* is a management device and the *Sicherungstreuhand* is seen as a form of real security. The latter concept covers *Eigentumsvorbehalt*, *Sicherungsübereignung* and *Sicherungsabtretung*. Fritz Baur and Rolf Stürner, *Sachenrecht* (München: C H Beck, 17th ed 1999), no 3 I 34. Harm Peter Westermann, *Sachenrecht* (Heidelberg: C F Müller, 7th ed 1998), no 44 I.

[32] Peter Bülow, *Recht der Kreditsicherheiten. Sachen und Rechte, Personen. Ein Lehrbuch*. (Heidelberg: C F Müller, 3rd ed 1993), no 862-864; Hein Kötz, 'National report for Germany', in: David Hayton, Bas Kortmann and Hendrik Verhagen (eds), *Principles of European Trust Law* (The Hague: Wolters Kluwer Law 1999), p 96.

third parties.³³ The transferor is better protected when the transfer is made by constructive delivery (*Besitzkonstitut*) and the property remains, as a consequence thereof, in his hands. This delivery technique is commonly used when property is transferred by way of security (*Sicherungsübereignung*). When the fiduciary transfers his right of ownership to a third party, the transferor may refuse to release the property; his right of possession is protected through § 404 and § 986 II of the BGB.³⁴ The *Sicherungsübereignung* is sometimes made under the resolutive condition of payment, which results in an automatic retransfer of the property upon compliance with the loan agreement. German law characterises the transferor's expectancy right (*Anwartschaftsrecht*) as a (quasi) proprietary right.³⁵

In the event of execution (*Zwangvollstreckung*) or bankruptcy (*Insolvenz*), the transferor's rights *in personam* tend to change status. In the first place, the transferor may set aside acts of sequestration, seizure or garnishment by creditors of the fiduciary against the property (§ 771 ZPO).³⁶ In the fiduciary's bankruptcy the transferor is entitled to an *Aussonderungsrecht* (§ 47 InsO), which entails that he can claim the property as if he were the owner, provided that the property is clearly recognisable as property belonging to the *Treuhand*.³⁷ On the other hand, the fiduciary who holds the property by way of security is, like a pledgee, entitled to an *Absonderungsrecht*; a right to separate execution (§ 51 InsO). The application of these provisions from the Code of Civil Procedure (ZPO) and the Insolvency Code (InsO) reveals a functional approach to the effects of the *Treuhand*: the formal right of the transferor coincides with his interest.

So, the ownership of the *Treuhänder* can be defined as conditional, or limited in time. Grundmann points out that the *Treuhand* is similar to the trust, but whereas the beneficiaries of the trust are entitled to a right *in rem*, German law offers protection to the transferor in third party relationships if 'specific legislative policies can be found in one field or the other.'³⁸

---

[33] Grundmann (*supra* note 3), p 477.
[34] Marin Josef Schermaier, 'Sicherungsübereignung und Sicherungszession im deutschen Recht', in: *La garanzia nella prospettiva storico-comparatistica* (Turin: Giappichelli 2003), p 308.
[35] Schermaier (*supra* note 34), p 309.
[36] Kötz (*supra* note 32), p 101.
[37] Hans Gerhard Ganter in: *Münchener Kommentar zur Insolvenzordnung*, Vol I (Munich: C H Beck 2001), § 47, no 19, 32, 34
[38] Grundmann (*supra* note 3), pp 477-478.

E. France: Division of patrimony

On 19 February 2007 the French parliament adopted a law which institutes the fiduciary transfer (*fiducie*) in French law.[39] Before that date, the legislator had a reserved attitude towards the *fiducie*; the use of fiduciary devices was limited to a few specific applications in the financial sphere[40] and a similar law proposal was withdrawn from the political agenda in 1994. Specific objections related to the security transfer (*fiducie-sûreté*). This device was considered incompatible with two specific rules on pledge (*gage*); the requirement of *traditio* (art 2067 CC old) and the prohibition to appropriate (forbidden *pacte commissoire* (art 2078 CC old).[41] However, the law applicable to real security rights changed in 2006; the law reform introduced a general non-possessory pledge (2237 CC) and a more liberal regime towards the *pacte commissoire* (2248 CC). The absolute nature of ownership (article 544 CC) and the unity of patrimony (article 2092 CC) are considered the general drawbacks with respect to the acceptance of fiduciary transfers.[42] Raffenne clarifies that absolute ownership is more than a 'conceptual particularity' in French legal thinking as it symbolises the absolute power of Man over things and the breach with the fragmented ownership structures of the feudal past. Absolute ownership is counteracted by surveillance of ownership, another logic underlying French legal knowledge, which influences the theory with respect to the unity of patrimony. The latter theory implies that, in order to prevent opacity and to guarantee the protection of creditors, '(T)he individual must offer himself/herself as a readable unit, controllable by a centralized gaze'.[43]

The recent law overcame the obstacles. First of all, the creation of the *fiducie* does not involve a fragmentation of ownership, but a division of patrimony (2011 CC). On the one hand, the fiduciary holds the property transferred to him in a special fund (*patrimoine d'affectation*), and deals therewith

---

[39] http://www.legifrance.gouv.fr/html/actualite/actualite_legislative/2007-711/ppl_fiducie.htm (this web-page includes the new law, parliamentary history and the complementary reports).
[40] See, for a list of fiduciary transactions: M Xavier de Roux, Rapport n° 3655, I A 3 (*supra* note 39).
[41] Philippe Rémy, 'National Report for France', in: Hayton, Kortmann and Verhagen (eds) (*supra* note 32), pp 131-132.
[42] Rémy (*supra* note 41); the author describes that the motives for the withdrawal of the first law proposal remain vague (as the proposal was never debated in parliament) but are probably related to the fear of tax evasion and fraud.
[43] Coralie Raffenne, 'Why (Still) No Trust in French Law?', in: Andrew Harding and Esin Örücü, *Comparative law in the 21ˢᵗ century* (London: Kluwer Academic Publishers 2002), pp 82-86, 90-93.

for a specific purpose (either management or security). The fiduciary owns two separate patrimonies; personal creditors of the fiduciary are not entitled to seize the *patrimoine d'affectation*, they can claim the personal patrimony of the fiduciary. On the other hand, the private patrimony of the transferor decreases: his personal creditors cannot seize the special purpose fund, except in case of a fraudulent transfer or when the property is encumbered with a prior real security right (2025 CC). However, debts that arise from the *fiducie* can be claimed from the personal patrimony of the transferor when the fiduciary fund appears empty (2025 CC), a rule which aims to prevent '*patrimoines phantômes*'.[44] The new law contains more safeguards against abuse. To begin with, only financial institutions may act as a fiduciary (2015 CC), which subjects the *fiducie* to another level of internal and administrative control. Moreover, the possibility to create a *fiducie* is restricted to companies subject to company taxes (2014 CC). In addition, registration of the *fiducie* in a special public register within a month after creation is obligatory (2019 CC). It is important to mention that registration does not necessarily reverse the presumption of good faith, after all the fiduciary's power of disposal is unrestricted (2023).[45] Finally, the *Loi instuant le Fiducie dans le Droit Français* contains, apart from the new rules in the Civil Code (I), rules to prevent money laundering (II) and tax provisions that guarantee fiscal transparency (III). The French rules with respect to the *fiducie* slightly affect the concept of ownership as they, in the words of de Richemont, constitute a *propriété dégradée*,[46] but the values underlying the unity of patrimony are similarly protected through other means.

Division of patrimony is generally held as a sensible method to create fiduciary transactions in civil law jurisdictions. The Scottish trust[47] is based on a separation of patrimony and so is the *fiducie* in Luxembourg. Moreover, in the Principles of European Trust Law, the separation of patrimony is defined as a main characteristic of the trust.[48] Without breaking the principle of absolute ownership, the transferor is indirectly protected against the claims of third parties. Moreover, the presence of a separate fund facilitates more complicated fiduciary structures whereby both fiduciaries and beneficiaries (or debtors) tend to change.[49]

---

[44] Philippe Dupichot, Opération *fiducie* sur le sol français, (2007) 11 *Semaine Juridique Édition Générale* (JCP G), p 7.

[45] Dupichot (*supra* note 44).

[46] M Henri de Richemont, Rapport no 11, session 2006-2007 (*supra* note 40).

[47] Kenneth Reid, 'Patrimony not equity: the trust in Scotland',(2000) 3 ERPL, p 427-437.

[48] Hayton, Kortmann and Verhagen (eds), *Principles of European Trust Law* (*supra* note 32), p 13.

[49] Reid (*supra* note 47), p 429-430.

F. The Netherlands: Prohibition and alternatives

In 1992, the Dutch regime with regard to fiduciary transfers changed considerably with the introduction of a new civil code (NBW). According to Art 3:84 (3) NBW: 'A judicial act which is intended to transfer property for purposes of security or which does not have the purpose of bringing the property into the patrimony of the acquirer, after transfer, does not constitute a valid title for transfer[50] of that property'.[51] This provision was introduced to ban the fiduciary security and management devices developed by legal practice and accepted by case law.

The first phrase of article 3:84 section 3 is related to the fiduciary security, as it prohibits the transfer of ownership for security purposes. The legislator compensated the prohibition of fiduciary security with the introduction of a general right of non-possessory pledge (article 236 NBW *et seq*). Meijers, the 'founding father' of the (new) civil code, proposed to create a non-possessory security interest, which fitted into the system of the law and disclosed the existence of security rights through a public register. He objected to the presence of two parallel security rights; on the one hand, a non-possessory security transfer, modified (to a certain extent) by the rules of pledge and, on the other hand, the possessory pledge.[52] Eventually, the creation of public registers was abandoned, but the idea of creating a 'tailor-made' security which was compatible with the closed system of real rights survived.[53] A few years after the introduction of the 'fiducia ban', the Supreme Court provided standards according to which article 3:84 section 3 BW had to be interpreted in a case that dealt with the validity of a sale and lease-back agreement.[54] It was decided that a transaction, which is intended to transfer the property without any limitations *in rem*, is not prevented by the provision. However, a transaction is invalid when parties intend to offer the creditor a right to recover the debt from the secured object with an obligation to return the surplus. This is a security right in disguise, and for this type of transaction the civil code offers an alternative in the form of the non-possessory pledge. Although the case related to a sale and lease-back transaction, the Supreme Court did not restrict this criterion to purchase finance transac-

---

[50] To transfer property under Dutch law, a valid title is required (3:84 section 1 BW).
[51] Translation by Peter Haanappel and Ejan Mackaay, in: *Nieuw Nederlands Burgerlijk Wetboek* (Deventer-Boston: Kluwer Law and Taxation Publishers 1990).
[52] Eduard Maurits Meijers, *De algemene begrippen van het burgerlijk recht* (Leiden: Universitaire Pers Leiden 1958), p 285; See also: Johannes Lokin and Corjo Jansen, *Tussen Droom en Daad* (Zwolle: W E J Tjeenk Willink 1995), pp 84-86.
[53] Parlementaire Geschiedenis Boek 3 (Invoering Boek 3,5 en 6), pp 1197 *et seq*.
[54] Sogelease case, HR 19-5-1995, NJ 1996, 119 (annotated by Kleijn).

tions.[55] Consequently, also a transfer that supports a loan is valid, as long as the transferee obtains unrestricted ownership. As a result of the strict dividing line between pledge and ownership, the debtor's future interest is purely *in personam* since a right *in rem* would point towards a forbidden security transfer.

The second phrase of article 3:84 (3) NBW prohibits trust-like devices (*fiducia cum amico*) based on a division of rights *in rem*. A *fiducia cum amico*, which results in a full title transfer to the fiduciary, is not affected by this provision.[56] Although the legislator meant to prohibit the latter fiduciary transfers as well, this idea was abandoned as it was closely related to draft rules with respect to a general management device (*bewind*), which never came into force. *Bewind* is restricted to rules in the law of succession and family law, but it would be a refined substitute for the *fiducia cum amico*. In his draft, Meijers proposed to expand the rules on *bewind*, recognising that this device reflects the interest of the parties involved: the person who administers the property (*bewindvoerder*) has a far-reaching power of disposal whereas the beneficiary remains the owner. *Bewind* is not a real right in the strict sense as it is not vested in the administrator, but can be qualified as a 'proprietary encumbrance' which paralyses the beneficiary's right of disposal.[57]

Meijers fiercely objected to security transfers, but took the demands of legal practice seriously. Therefore, he opted to replace the fiduciary transfers with alternatives: the introduction of a registered pledge and the expansion of the rules on *bewind*. His ideas still resonate in the current law, although they were not completely implemented. The transfer of ownership still exists as a security instrument next to the right of pledge and a commercial variant of *bewind*, the alternative to the *fiducia cum amico*, never came into force.

G. Conclusion

The recognition of fiduciary transfer in civil law jurisdictions, whereby the transferor is entitled to a proprietary interest, seems to entail either the recognition of a hybrid kind of ownership or an additional real right. This brief sketch of the four different systems revealed four different approaches. With respect to the (historic) development, the starting point of each fiduciary transfer is the full transfer to the fiduciary. But indifferent to the accepted fiduciary device (or proposed alternatives), all systems show a tendency to protect the economic position of the transferor as an acknowledg-

---

[55] As was suggested by Advocate-General Hartkamp.
[56] Parlementaire Geschiedenis Boek 3, pp 1200 *et seqq*.
[57] Struycken (*supra* note 10) pp 520-526.

ment of the fact that the transfer of ownership is used for managment and security purposes, when suitable legal substitutes are lacking. The question whether the fiduciary transfer should be part of the European debate with respect to movables depends on the approach taken in this field. When the general rules on transfer and delivery apply to fiduciary transfers, it might be relevant to create additional rules or instruments (such as a separate fund) that modify the effects of the transfer. The other option is to expand the application, or broaden the number of limited rights *in rem*, which removes the fiduciary transaction from the rules of transfer. In both cases, the status of civil law ownership requires reflection. When the effects of the right of ownership are modified towards third parties, this results in the recognition of a less encompassing, or degraded form of ownership. The creation of new limited rights *in rem* does not affect the civil law concept of ownership, but requires a clear identification of the owner; since ownership is a parental right, the owner should be traceable. Maybe it is possible to replace the description of ownership as 'the most comprehensive right a person can have over a movable' with the description of ownership as 'the residue of legal rights remaining in a person after specific rights over the assets have been granted to others.'[58] This definition encompasses both the identification of the owner and the possible modification of ownership.

---

[58] Honoré (*supra* note 19).

Obligatory and Proprietary Rights: Where to Draw the Dividing Line – If at all?

Eleanor Cashin Ritaine*

1. Most European legal systems[1] distinguish between obligatory and proprietary rights.[2] Classic French law,[3] for example, describes two legal techniques about how to use goods. It explains to whom a thing or an interest belongs and the scope of this right. On the one hand, a thing, or some of its benefits, can be reserved for the direct use of one or more persons. On the

---

* Director of the Swiss Institute of Comparative Law, Lausanne, Switzerland.
[1] It has not been possible in the scope of this paper to cite extensively all European jurisdictions. The examples given serve only the purpose of demonstrating the differences and similarities of legal analysis throughout Europe. Many examples have been gleaned in the so-called 'TOM reports' drafted by the Study Group on an European Civil Code (Working Group on the Transfer of Movables) due to be published by Sellier in 2008. Where reference is given to these reports in the following, this refers to provisional versions; changes may still occur in the 2008 final published version, but such changes should not, as a rule, affect the content of these reports, but only their internal organisation. – A general presentation of these issues can also be found at Christian von Bar and Ulrich Drobnig, *The Interaction of Contract Law and Tort and Property Law in Europe, A Comparative Study* (Munich: Sellier 2004), pp 320-323.
[2] Except, for example, Denmark (Bo von Eyben, 'Danish Property Law', in Børge Dahl, Torben Melchior and Ditlev Tamm (ed), *Danish Law in a European Perspective* (Copenhagen: Thomson Publishers Copenhagen, 2nd ed 2002), pp 209-236, (209)) and Norway (Jan-Ove Færstad, TOM Report – Transfer of Movables – A Functional Approach: A National Report for Norway and Denmark 3.1.). – See however Jesper Berning, 'Property Law', in: Hans Gammeltoft-Hansen, Bernhard Gomard and Allan Philip (ed), *Danish Law, a General Survey* (Copenhagen: Gad [in Komm] 1982), pp 177-219 (177): 'The right *in personam* is directed towards the evolution and fulfilment of the contract, whereas the proprietary right concerns the protection reached at a certain stage of fulfilment'.
[3] See also German law: Fritz Baur and Rolf Stürner, *Sachenrecht* (Munich: C H Beck, 17th ed 1999), § 2, n 2-5 and § 3, n 23. – Spanish law: Isabel González Pacanowska and Carlos Diez Soto, TOM Report Spain: Transfer of Ownership in Movables in Spanish Law, Part I, 1.2.

other hand, a person can entitle another person to use the thing. This distinction generates a dual classification[4] between rights *in rem* (*droits réels*) and obligations (*droits personnels*).[5]

2. The sole function of rights *in rem* or proprietary rights (*jus in re*) is to distribute the uses of things between persons.[6] Obligations, on the other hand, have many functions: they can be used to distribute the uses of things between persons[7] but can also entitle to demand a service or a payment from another person. Both rights *in rem* and obligations are subjective rights as they confer a legal power to an individual person.[8]

3. This distinction comes from Roman law,[9] but the concept was developed in the Middle Ages.[10] In Roman law, the distinction between obligatory and proprietary rights appeared in civil procedure where an action *sacramentum in rem* was possible for real rights and an action *sacramentum in personam* for obligations.[11] Formally, at a later stage, in litigation on real rights, the introductory brief (*intentio*) only contained the name of the liti-

---

[4] According to Henri Capitant (Henri Capitant, 'Les notions fondamentales du droit privé d'après le livre de M Demogue', *Revue Trimestrielle de Droit civil* (RTDciv) 1911, pp 729 and 738), this distinction forms the 'backbone of patrimonial law'. Let it nevertheless be stated, that this distinction is not mentioned at all in the French civil code.

[5] This distinction has been largely criticised by Marcel Planiol, *Traité élementaire de droit civil* (Paris: LGDJ, 1st ed 1897, 4th ed 1906), n 2159 *et seqq*, who developed the notion of a universal passiv obligation ('*l'obligation passive universelle*'). – See also Caroline Cauffmann and Vincent Sagaert, TOM Report – Transfer of movables in Belgian Law, Introduction.

[6] France: Christian Atias, *Droit civil, Les biens* (Paris: Litec, 8th ed 2005), p 1, n 2. – Austria: Helmut Koziol and Rudolf Welser, *Bürgerliches Recht*, Vol I (Vienna: Manz, 13th ed 2006), p 238: '*Recht der Güterzuordnung*'.

[7] For example, the contract of lease creates obligations between the lessor and the lessee.

[8] German law: Baur and Stürner (*supra* footnote 3), § 2, n 2.

[9] Jean-Philippe Lévy and André Castaldo, *Histoire du droit civil* (Paris: Dalloz 2002), p 262, n 209 *et seqq* – This distinction was made in the Institutes of Gaius and Justinien because real rights were treated in Book 1 and obligations in Book 3.

[10] Presenting the pan-European influence of Roman law: Gábor Hamza, *Le développement du droit privé européen – Le rôle de la tradition romaniste dans la formation du droit privé moderne* (Budapest: Eötvös Loránd University [Faculty of Law] 2005).

[11] According to Bo von Eyben (*supra* footnote 2), p 209, 'this distinction […] is based on the notion that "personal" and "real" rights are different in kind: the law of obligations deals with claims for performance according to a contract, whereas the law of property deals with rights to dispose of real or movable property, which are legally protected against third parties'.

gant and not of the defendant, as real rights were opposable to all.[12] In the Middle Ages, the glossators rediscovered and developed these concepts. However, 13th century canon lawyers created a third category: the *jus ad rem*: the 'right towards a thing'.[13] This situation appeared when a person had been designated to occupy a function such as to become a bishop or a vassal of a lord, but had not yet entered into possession of this function or territory. The beneficiary was deemed to possess a right *ad rem* which would give him the right to revindicate the position or territory. This concept has disappeared in most European legal systems,[14] yet it would be possible to compare the '*Anwartschaftsrecht*' in German law to this mechanism.[15]

4. The distinction between proprietary rights and obligations has not always been used in every country, nor is today. Typically, the distinction between real rights and contractual rights was only established in Holland by a famous ruling of the Dutch Supreme Court, the *Hoge Raad der Nederlanden* in 1905.[16] Since then, there has been a division between rights *in rem*

---

[12] Lévy and Castaldo (*supra* footnote 9), p 262, n 209.
[13] Lévy and Castaldo (*supra* footnote 9), p 263, n 210.
[14] Spain: González Pacanowska and Diez Soto, TOM Report Spain (*supra* footnote 3), Part I, 1.2.: 'The so-called *ius ad rem*. Some authors have used this expression, to describe those situations in which the creditor enjoys a certain preference against third parties as to the acquisition of a property right (*ius in re*) on a certain thing. It could be the case, for instance, of the preference granted by art. 1.473 CC to the first buyer of a thing, who has not acquired ownership yet, against a second buyer with a more recent title, or the preference against all granted to the titleholder of certain credit rights (e.g., the rights of the creditor arising from a contract subject to a suspensive condition) as a result of their preventive annotation in the Land Register. The practical interest of this dogmatic construction is not very clear, since the cases therein included lack a common nature and efficacy'. See Ruiz Martinez-Cardoz, 'El ius ad rem', *Revista de Derecho Privado* (RDP) 1988, p 3 *et seq;* – compare the Canadian case *Duchesneau v Cook* [1955] S C R 207 commented by D. A. B. Steel, 2 *McGill Law Journal* (McGill LJ) 1955-1956, pp 162-167 discussing whether the seller's right of redemption *pendente conditione* is a right *in re* or *ad rem*.
[15] Germany: Moritz Brinkmann in: Hanns Prütting, Gerhard Wegen, Gerd Weinreich, *BGB Kommentar* (Neuwied: Luchterhand, 2nd ed 2007), § 161, n 12-14; – Baur and Stürner (*supra* footnote 3), § 3, n 44-46; – See also in Swiss Law: Bénédict Foëx, *Le "numerus clausus" des droits réels en matière mobilière* (Lausanne: Payot 1987), pp 234-267, n 553-617.
[16] HR 3-3-1905, W 1905, no 8191 (*Blaauboer-Berlips*): In this case, the *Hoge Raad* ruled that contractual obligations with regard to an immovable do not bind the person to whom the immovable is sold and transferred; after this transfer, the person obliged to transfer is the one who has entered into the contract, not the new landowner.

with absolute effect and personal obligations which only bind the original parties involved.

5. In the Scandinavian countries, this double concept is not used. In Finland,[17] Sweden[18] and in Denmark,[19] the fundamental question behind the concepts of obligations and rights *in rem*, is actually the protection of the right both *inter partes* and *ultra partes*. Danish law is based on a 'relational theory', that lays down that the right of priority may be achieved in relation to one third party, but not in relation to others.[20] Obligations involve *inter partes* relations, ie relations between the contracting parties.[21] Rights *in rem* concern *ultra partes* relations, ie rights of the holder of a right in relation to third parties.[22] As a result, all rights and all transfers of rights involve a contractual (*inter partes*) as well as a proprietary side (*ultra partes*), irrespective of the object and the substance of the right. Of utmost importance in property law is thus the question of the protection[23] of the holder of a right and his/her legal status in relation to *ultra partes* actors such as the transferor's successors, creditors in bankruptcy and execution proceedings.[24]

---

[17] Matias Collan and Juha Koivula, 'Finland', in: Christian von Bar (ed), *Sachenrecht in Europa, Systematische Einführung und Gesetzestexte*, Vol I (Osnabrück: Universitätsverlag Rasch 1999), pp 209-492, (229); Leena Kartio, 'Property Law', in: Juha Pöyhönen (ed), *An Introduction to Finnish Law* (Helsinki: Kauppakaari, 2nd ed 2002), pp 211-244, (212).

[18] Reinhard Herrmann and Dirk Westermann, 'Schweden', in: Christian von Bar (ed), *Sachenrecht in Europa, Systematische Einführung und Gesetzestexte*, Vol I (Osnabrück: Universitätsverlag Rasch 1999), pp 493-606, (502).

[19] Von Eyben (*supra* footnote 2), p 209 citing Frederic Vinding Kruse, *Ejendomsretten*, Volumes I-V (Copenhagen: Gad [i Komm] 1929-33; 3rd ed [Volumes I-III] 1951) translated into English by P.T. Federspiel (Vol. I) and David Philip (Vol. II), *The Right of Property*, Vol I-II (Oxford: Oxford University Press 1939-53) and into German by Knud Larsen, *Das Eigentumsrecht*, Vol I-III (Berlin: de Gruyter 1931-36). Tanya-Caroline Hitchcock and Malene Stein Poulsen, 'Dänemark', in: Christian von Bar (ed), *Sachenrecht in Europa, Systematische Einführung und Gesetzestexte*, Vol I (Osnabrück: Universitätsverlag Rasch 1999), pp 8-91, (18).

[20] Von Eyben (*supra* footnote 2), pp 209-236 (210).

[21] Or between parties linked in tort.

[22] See Berning (*supra* footnote 2), pp 177-219 (177).

[23] This protection is twofold: 'dynamic protection' in respect to the transfer of ownership, solving conflicting rights over a movable, and 'static protection': protection against interference of third parties. See Færstad (*supra* footnote 2), 3.1.

[24] See Miki Kuusinen, TOM Report, National Report Finland, Regarding the transfer of Corporeal Movables in Finnish Law, 1.1.1.

6. Most legal systems also acknowledge other rights such as personality rights and intellectual rights that do not fit into the traditional distinction between proprietary and obligatory rights.[25] They generally neither apply to a thing (*in rem*), nor have a passive subject (*in personam*). Intellectual rights (*droits intellectuels*),[26] on the one hand, arise neither on a thing nor against a person. They have an immaterial scope relating to the intellectual work of their bearer. These rights entitle their bearer to practise his/her creative activity and make a living out of it. They have as object either an intellectual creation[27] or a clientele (*ie* goodwill).[28] An example of such rights is the right of a composer on his/her work.[29] These rights generate a form of property (*propriété intellectuelle*).[30] Nevertheless, even if the immaterial right relates to a corporeal movable thing, ownership of the corporeal movable thing should not be confused with the intellectual property right on the

---

[25] France: These concepts fall under the qualification of 'new goods' as described by Jean-Louis Bergel, 'Rapport general – Les nouveaux biens' –, in: *La propriété, Travaux de l'association Henri Capitant des Amis de la Culture Juridique Française*, Vol LIII (Paris: Société de Législation Comparée 2006), pp 203-223. – Germany: Baur and Stürner (*supra* footnote 3), § 60, n 1 *et seqq*.

[26] France: Cass crim, 22 sep 2004: D 2005, p 411, note Bertrand de Lamy and p 961, note Jacques Raynard; AJ Pénal 2005, p 22, note Jocelyne Leblois-Happe, Thierry Revet, RTDciv 2005, Chr p 164.

[27] France: See also the possibility to own information: Pierre Catala, 'La «propriété» de l'information', in: *Mélanges offerts à Pierre Raynaud* (Paris: Dalloz-Sirey 1985), p 97. Jean-Christophe Galloux, 'Ébauche d'une définition juridique de l'information', Dalloz 1994, chron p 229. Nathalie Mallet-Poujol, '*Appropriation de l'information: l'éternelle chimère*', Dalloz 1997, chron p 330. Jérôme Passa, 'La propriété de l'information, un malentendu?', *Droit et patrimoine* (Dr et patrimoine) 3/2001, p 64. – Marie-Anne Frison-Roche, 'Le droit d'accès à l'information ou le nouvel équilibre de la propriété', in: *Le droit privé français à la fin du XXe siècle: Etudes offertes à Pierre Catala* (Paris: Litec 2001), p 759.

[28] France: Atias (*supra* footnote 6), p 367, n 637 *et seqq*. – François Terre and Philippe Simler, *Les biens* (Paris: Dalloz, 7th ed 2006), p 63, n 55 *et seqq* for further references.

[29] France: For the ownership of a software program: Paris, 18 oct. 1996: Gaz Pal 1998, 1, somm p 91, note Isabelle Matthyssens.

[30] France: Michel Vivant, 'L'irrésistible ascension des propriétés intellectuelles`, in: *Mélanges Christian Mouly* (Paris: Litec 1998), p 441. – Michel Vivant, 'L'immatériel, nouvelle frontière pour un nouveau millénaire', *Juris-Classeur Périodique* (JCP) éd G 2000, I, 194. – Frédéric Zenati, 'L'immatériel et les choses', in: *Le droit et l'immatériel, Archives de philosophie du droit*, Vol XLIII (Paris: Dalloz 1999), p 79. – Adde critisising, Daniel Gutmann, 'Du matériel à l'immatériel dans le droit des biens', in: *Le droit et l'immatériel, Archives de philosophie du droit*, Vol XLIII (Paris: Dalloz 1999), p 65.

creation.[31] Personality rights (*droits de la personalité*), on the other hand, don't have a passive subject: right to a name, right to honour, right to freedom, right to live ...

7. Moreover, some legal systems recognise so-called quasi-real rights.[32] This distinction covers situations where rights *in rem* and obligations tend to overlap. Some obligatory positions are protected against third persons as if they were rights *in rem*,[33] whereas some real rights also contain obligations. Precisely, this overlapping of real rights and obligations has led a number of authors to question the *summa divisio* between obligatory and proprietary rights. And this is what this contribution proposes to explore: Obligatory and Proprietary Rights: Where to draw the Dividing Line – If at All? In this respect, the paper will first analyse the *summa divisio* and the characteristics of proprietary rights and of obligations (A), before presenting the consequences and limits of these distinctions (B).

A. The *summa divisio* between obligatory and proprietary rights

I. Proprietary rights

8. Proprietary rights or rights *in rem* (*droit réel* or *jus in re*) are rights that are linked directly to a thing (*res*). They represent the power that a person has in respect to this thing. This person is the only party to this legal relationship.[34] The main example of a right *in rem* is the right of prop-

---

[31] France: Article L 111-3 *du Code de la propriété intellectuelle*: '*la propriété incorporelle (...) est indépendante de la propriété de l'objet matériel*'. – Possession of the corporeal thing that entitles to ownership under art 2279 CC does not have any effect on the ownership of the incorporeal intellectual rights. See Paris, 17 févr 1988: D 1989, somm p 50, obs Claude Colombet. – Pascal Kamina, 'L'indépendance des propriétés corporelles et intellectuelles', *Revue de la Recherche Juridique* (RRJ) 1998/3, 881.

[32] Germany: '*Quasi-dingliche*' *Rechte*: Baur and Stürner (*supra* footnote 3), § 3, n 47. – Austria: Koziol and Welser (*supra* footnote 6), p 241. – England: Roy Goode, 'Ownership and Obligation in Commercial Transactions', [1987] *Law Quarterly Review* (LQR) 433.

[33] Gerhard Dulckeit, *Die Verdinglichung obligatorischer Rechte* (Tübingen: Mohr-Siebeck) 1951, p 51.

[34] France: Atias (*supra* footnote 6), p 2, n 3. – Spain: González Pacanowska and Diez Soto (*supra* footnote 3), Part I, 1.2. – Austria: Koziol and Welser (*supra* footnote 6), p 241.

erty/ownership. The right of property is the fullest right *in rem* as it encompasses all others.[35]

9. Rights *in rem* have an active subject (the creditor), and an object (the thing).[36] This right gives the owner *direct and immediate power* over the object of the right. Rights *in rem* are recognised only for existing things.[37] Possession as such is not a right *in rem*,[38] but a simple factual situation which generates legal consequences.

10. In most jurisdictions, the sole function of rights *in rem* or proprietary rights (*jus in re*) is to distribute the uses of things between persons.[39] Austrian law[40] speaks of a *'Zuordnungsfunktion'* (function of allocation). Scandinavian jurisdictions have a different approach.[41]

11. Proprietary rights are subject to a number of general principles[42] common to all legal systems that acknowledge the distinction between property rights and obligations. One of the most important principles is the *numerus*

---

[35] France: Atias (*supra* footnote 6), p 53, n 75. – Yet see TOM Report for England and Wales by Sandra Frisby and Michael Jones, at 1.2: ownership 'consists of a bundle of various "incidents"'.

[36] France: Atias (*supra* footnote 6), p 46, n 69.

[37] France: Atias (*supra* footnote 6), p 51, n 72-73.

[38] France: See Jean-Louis Bergel, Marc Bruschi and Sylvie Cimamonti, *Traité de Droit civil, Les Biens* (Paris: Librairie Générale de Droit et Jurisprudence 2000), p 146, n 134, and p 143, n 129: «*La possession n'est pas actuellement un véritable droit subjectif. (…) On peut néanmoins avancer que la possession, si elle est à l'origine un fait, tend à se cristalliser en un droit par la volonté du possesseur. On dira qu'il s'agit d'une situation volontaire, légitime ou illégitime, juridiquement protégée qui constitue, selon les cas, l'anticipation ou la preuve d'un droit*». – The situation is similar in Belgian law, where possession is generally not considered as a property right nor as an obligatory right, but rather as a legal fact to which the law attributes legal effects. See in this respect the Belgian TOM report drafted by Cauffmann and Sagaert (*supra* footnote 5), Chapter 1, part II, footnote 29. – Germany: Baur and Stürner (*supra* footnote 3), § 7, n 1: '*tatsächliche Sachherrschaft*'. – Austria: Koziol and Welser (*supra* footnote 6), p 258: '*tatsächliche Innehabung*'. Yet see § 308 ABGB that lists 'possession' (Besitz) within the category of *'dingliche Sachenrechte'*.

[39] France: Atias (*supra* footnote 6), p 1, n 2.

[40] Austria: Koziol and Welser (*supra* footnote 6), p 241.

[41] *Supra* n 5.

[42] For a general presentation see the table at: Baur and Stürner (*supra* footnote 3), § 5, n 58.

clausus principle. Most European legal systems[43] consider that rights *in rem* are listed in a limited way by statute and that new property rights can only be created by way of statute[44] and not by parties to a contract.[45] This principle fulfills a number of functions;[46] in particular it ensures legal security through the publicity of the content of ownership rights.

12. In common law countries,[47] such as England and Wales, several judges and academics therefore support the idea of a *numerus clausus* of property rights,[48] *ie* a closed circle of rights, without however formally listing them. In a similar manner, in Germany, Italy and Scotland there are no legislative

---

[43] Except the Scandinavian jurisdictions such as Denmark, Norway and Finland (Kartio (*supra* footnote 17), p 211-244, p 216), which do not have a principle of *numerus clausus*, as they do not acknowledge the distinction between proprietary rights and obligations.

[44] See TOM Report for Slovenia by Claudia Rudolf, Vesna Rijavec and Tomaž Keresteš, 3., citing Matjaž Tratnik, *Stvarnopravni zakonik z uvodnimi pojasnili in svarnim kazalom* (Ljubljana, 2002), p 31 and also art 2 SPZ (Slovenian Code of Property law). – Austria: Koziol and Welser (*supra* footnote 6), p 238. – See also the jurisdictions cited by Bernard Rudden, 'Economic Theory v. Property Law: The *Numerus Clausus* Problem', in: John Ekelaar and John Bell (eds), *Oxford Essays in Jurisprudence*, Third Series (Oxford: Clarendon Press 1987), 239-263 (243), but also, article 175 of the Japanese civil Code, article 2536 of the Argentine civil Code, article 185 of the Korean civil Code, article 476 of the Louisiana civil Code and article 1298 of the Thai civil Code.

[45] Thomas W Merrill and Henry E Smith, 'Optimal Standardization in the Law of Property: The *Numerus Clausus* Principle', 110 Yale L J (2000), pp 1-70.

[46] Bénédict Foëx, *Le 'numerus clausus' des droits reels en matière mobilière* (Lausanne: Payot 1987), p 29 *et seqq* who lists a series of functions of the *numerus clausus* principle: publicity, clarification, protection of the freedom of ownership, ethics of ownership rights ... – See also Rudden (*supra* footnote 44), pp 239-263 (245 *et seqq*) – For economic functions, Merrill and Smith (*supra* footnote 45), pp 1-70 (24-42).

[47] For American law, see Merrill and Smith (*supra* footnote 45), pp 1-70 (9-24).

[48] For example, Millett LJ in *Re Cosslet (Contractors) Ltd* [1998] Ch 495, 508: 'There are four kinds of consensual security known to English law: ...' – Rudden (*supra* footnote 44), pp 239-263 (244) quotes five other cases: Brougham LC in *Keppel v Bailey* (1834) 2 My & K 517, 535 – Pollock CB in *Hill v Tupper* (1863) 2 Hurlst & C 121 –Wilde B and Bramwell B in *Stockport Wwks v Potter* (1864) 3 H & C 300, 314 – Holmes J in *Norcross v James* (1885) 140 Mass 188, 2 NE 946, 948 – Olney J in *Werner v Graham* 183 P 945, 947 (1919 Cal Sup Ct). – Merrill and Smith (*supra* footnote 45), pp 1-70 (3). – Yet see Frederick H Lawson, 'Structural Variations in Property Law', in: *International Encyclopedia of Comparative Law*, Vol VI/2 (Tübingen: Mohr-Siebeck 1975) p 22, p 137.

provisions or catalogues, but the *numerus clausus* principle is firmly adopted by writers[49] and court practice.[50]

On the contrary, in some continental legal systems, such as Portugal[51] and the Netherlands,[52] there is a formal *numerus clausus* catalogue.

In other countries, there is simply a catalogue of real rights which have a similar effect.[53] However, as an exception,[54] the idea of a *numerus clausus* of property rights is controversial in France[55] and in Belgium.[56] Article 543 of

---

[49] See the table at Baur and Stürner (*supra* footnote 3), § 3, n 46, and also § 1, n 7, § 49 n 4.

[50] Austria: Koziol and Welser (*supra* footnote 6), p 238. – Germany: Hanns Prütting in: Hanns Prütting, Gerhard Wegen, Gerd Weinreich, *BGB Kommentar* (Neuwied: Luchterhand, 2nd ed 2007), § 854 Einführung, n 14. – Italy: Paolo Gallo, *Istituzioni di diritto privato* (Turin: Giappichelli 1999) pp 185-187. – Scotland: *Carse v Coppen* (1951) SC 233, 242 per Lord President Cooper.

[51] The Portuguese civil Code of 1966 provides in art 1306 para 1: '*1. The creation of restrictions with a proprietary effect upon the right of ownership or of dividing up that right is only permitted in the cases provided by the law; any restriction of that right resulting from a legal transaction which does not comply with these conditions, has the character of an obligation.*'

[52] The Dutch Civil code Book 3 of 1992 states in art 3:81 para 1: '*1. He who holds an independent transferable right may create within the limits of that right the limited rights provided by law.*'

[53] Austria: § 308 ABGB; Greece: art 973 of the Civil code.

[54] But not only, see critics in Merrill and Smith (*supra* footnote 45), pp 1-70 (6-7).

[55] Jean Carbonnier, *Droit civil, Les biens* (Paris: Presses Universitaires de France, 18th ed 1998) n 44. – François Chabas, 'Biens: droit de propriété et ses démembrements', in: Léon Mazeaud and Henri Mazeaud (ed), *Leçons de droit civil*, Part 2 Vol II (Paris: Éditeur Montchrestien, 8th ed 1994), n 1287 – *Contra*: In favour of contractual rights *in rem*: Atias (*supra* footnote 6), p 47, n 71. – Philippe Malaurie and Laurent Aynès, *Les biens* (Paris: Defrénois, 2nd ed 2005), p 91, n 359. – Terré and Simler (*supra* footnote 28), p 60, n 52. – This creates specific problems when foreign property rights are to be recognised in France. See in particular, Michel Cabrillac, 'La reconnaissance des sûretés réelles sans dépossession constituées à l'étranger', (1979) *Revue de droit international et de droit comparé* (Rev crit dr int priv), p 487. – F.E. Klein, 'La reconnaissance en droit international privé helvétique des sûretés réelles sans dépossession constituées à l'étranger', (1979) Rev crit dr int priv, p 507. – Karl Kreuzer, 'La reconnaissance des sûretés mobilières conventionnelles étrangères', (1995) Rev crit dr int priv, p 465. – Frédérique Dahan, 'La floating charge, Reconnaissance en France d'une sûreté anglaise', (1996) *Journal de Droit International* (JDI), p 381. – Nevertheless, a controversial court decision decided in 1834 that rights *in rem* could also be created on a contractual basis. This would mean that parties to a contract may agree on new types of rights *in rem*. See, Cass req, 13 févr 1834 (*arrêt* Caquelard): D 1834.I.218; S 1834.I.205; *Grands Arrêts de la Jurisprudence Civile*, Paris: Dalloz 11e ed 2000), François Terré and Yves Lequette, n 60: '*ni*

the French and Belgian civil code[57] is not regarded as limitative and freedom of contract is invoked as authorising the creation of all rights that are not prohibited by the law. In a similar manner, the issue is debated in Spain; where a majority opinion pleads for the freedom to create new real rights.[58]

13. This principle of a *numerus clausus* of property rights which exists in a great number of member States,[59] contrasts with the general principle of freedom of contract in contract law. Yet even in property law, the parties remain free to agree or not to agree on the creation of an 'admitted' real

---

ces articles (C. civ., art. 544, 546 et 552), ni aucune autre loi, n'excluent les diverses modifications et décompositions dont le droit ordinaire de propriété est susceptible'. This faculty has only been used on very few occasions: Bergel, Bruschi and Cimamonti (*supra* footnote 38), p 48 n 53 and p 287, n 283. It is considered to be a factor of uncertainty because it creates a risk in respect to third parties.

[56] See on the other hand, the TOM report on Belgian Law by Cauffmann and Sagaert (*supra* footnote 5), Introduction, footnote 17: citing the Belgian *Cour de cassation* (Cass, 16 sep 1966, *Journal de tribunaux* (Journ trib) 1967, 59 and Cass, 17 oct 1996, *Rechtskundig Weekblad* (R W) 1996-97, 1395, note Matthias E Storme) that does not allow parties to create real rights that have not been recognised by law. This report cites critics by Belgian academics: Jacques Hansenne, 'La limitation du nombre des droits réels et le champ d'application du concept de service foncier' (comment under Cass 16 September 1966), (1968) *Revue critique de jurisprudence belge* (RCJB), p 181, n 13; François Laurent, *Principes de droit civil*, Vol VI (Brussels: Bruylant-Christophe & Cie 1878), n 84. But the *Cour de Cassation* ruled that parties cannot create real rights which have not been recognised by law: Cass 16 September 1966, Journ Trib 1967, 59. Also: Cass 17 October 1996, R W 1996-97, 1395, note Matthias Storme/Henri De Page, I, n 130; Walter van Gerven, 'Algemeen Deel', in: *Beginselen Belgisch Privaatrecht*, Vol 1 (Brussels: Story-Scientia 1987), n 34.

[57] Article 543 of the French and Belgian civil code: 'One may have a right of ownership, or a mere right of enjoyment, or only land services to be claimed on property.' (Translated by Georges Rouhette at www.legifrance.fr).

[58] The TOM report for Spain by González Pacanowska and Diez Soto, cites Vicente Montés-Penadés in Angel M Lopez y Lopez and Vicente Montés-Penadés (ed), *Derechos reales y Derecho inmobiliario registral* (Valencia: Tirant lo blanch 1994) 54-55 who establishes other conditions for the recognition of new property rights. – This freedom is even supported by some legislative and regulatory provisions on the registration of rights in immovables which are similar to those expressly enumerated, even if they are innominate, ie not regulated by law (Law on mortgages of 8 Feb 1946, art 2 no 2; Implementing Regulation of 14 Feb 1947, as amended, art 7).

[59] Except the Scandinavian States: See Norway and Denmark where there is no category of 'proprietary' rights, *supra* n 5. For Finland: Collan and Koivula (*supra* footnote 17), pp 209-492, p 239.

right, and they have the power to agree on those aspects of the intended property right which the law does not regulate by mandatory rules or does not regulate at all.[60] Notwithstanding these limitations in property law, German and Austrian legal practitioners have created new categories of rights *in rem* or quasi-rights *in rem* such as the various types of credit securities by transfer of ownership or equitable interests found in German law.[61] The *numerus clausus* principle has thus a number of remarkable infringements.

14. Other principles applicable to proprietary rights encompass: the principle of priority,[62] according to which, elder property rights have priority over younger ones (*prior tempore, potior iure*); the principle of publicity[63] stating both that property rights must be published either by possession or registration[64] and that the property right first published is preferred (principle of priority); the principle of speciality[65] which provides that property rights can exist only for independent assets individually identified; and the principle of transferability,[66] meaning that property rights have an economic value and can in general be transferred.

15. Most jurisdictions distinguish two types of proprietary rights: principal and accessory rights *in rem*. Principal rights *in rem* derive from the right of property (or ownership rights) and from dismemberments of this right.[67] Ownership rights encompass, in general, three characteristics: the right to use the thing (*usus*), the right to collect the fruit (*fructus*) and the right to

---

[60] Austria: Koziol and Welser (*supra* footnote 6), p 241: '*keine oder nur beschränkte inhaltliche Gestaltungsfreiheit*'. Germany: Baur and Stürner (*supra* footnote 3), § 1, n 7 – Hanns Prütting in: Hanns Prütting, Gerhard Wegen, Gerd Weinreich (supra footnote 50), § 854 Einführung, n 14.

[61] Hanns Prütting in: Hanns Prütting, Gerhard Wegen, Gerd Weinreich (*supra* footnote 50), § 854 Einführung, n 14. – Moritz Brinkmann in: Hanns Prütting, Gerhard Wegen, Gerd Weinreich (*supra* footnote 15), § 161, n 12-14. – Baur and Stürner (*supra* footnote 3), § 57, § 58.

[62] Austria: Koziol and Welser (*supra* footnote 6), p 366. – Germany: Jörg Neuner, 'Der Prioritätsgrundsatz im Privatrecht', *Archiv für die civilistische Praxis* (AcP) 203/1, p 46.

[63] Baur and Stürner (*supra* footnote 3), § 4, n 9-16 – Finland: Kartio (*supra* footnote 17), pp 211-244, (236). – Kuusinen (*supra* footnote 24), 1.1.3. – Sabine Corneloup, *La publicité des situations juridiques – Une approche franco-allemande du droit interne et du droit international privé*, préface Paul Lagarde (Paris: LGDJ 2003), pp 60-72.

[64] Von Eyben (*supra* footnote 2), pp 209-236 (220).

[65] Baur and Stürner (*supra* footnote 3), § 4, n 16-19.

[66] Baur and Stürner (*supra* footnote 3), § 4, n 20-21.

[67] France: art 543 CC.

dispose of the thing (*abusus*).[68] Ownership entitles to exclude others from the use of an asset.[69] Principal rights *in rem* use a combination of these attributes. They are rights that are autonomic and that apply directly to the use of a thing. In this respect, French law for example[70] accepts the following principal rights *in rem*: usufruct rights (*usufruit*),[71] the right of use (*droit d'usage*),[72] the right of dwelling (*droit d'habitation*),[73] the right of easement

---

[68] Stéphanie Pavageau, *Le droit de propriété dans les jurisprudences suprêmes françaises, européennes et internationales* (Paris: LGDJ 2006), pp 85-103, n 115 *et seqq*. – Yet see Baur and Stürner (*supra* footnote 3), § 3, n 23 who only distinguish two attributes: the right to use the thing and the right to dispose of it. – Comp Finland: Kartio (*supra* footnote 17), pp 211-244, p 235 who distinguishes three basic elements of ownership: the right of possession of the owner (static protection), the competence of the owner (*ie* authorisation to legally dispose of the object) and the dynamic protection enjoyed by the owner (protection in a conflict vis-à-vis third parties). Also, Kuusinen (*supra* footnote 24), 1.2. – The right to dispose of the thing is a main feature in Danish law: Berning (*supra* footnote 2), pp 177-219 (179).

[69] Finland: Kuusinen (*supra* footnote 24), 1.2. – France: Samuel Ginossar, 'Pour une meilleure définition du droit reel et du droit personnel', RTDciv 1962, pp 573, 577. – Frédéric Zenati, 'Pour une renovation de la théorie de la propriété', RTDciv 1993, pp 305, 314. – Jean-Marc Mousseron, Jacques Raynaud and Thierry Revet, 'De la propriété comme modèle', in: Mélanges offerts de André Colomer (Paris: Litec 1993), p 287, n 17: '*la propriété se caractérise donc par l'exclusivité qu'elle confère en proper à une personne sur une valeur économique*'.– contra: Jean Dabin, 'Une nouvelle définition du droit reel', RTDciv 1962, p 32. – Patrice Jourdain, *Les Biens* (Paris: Dalloz 1995), p 8, n 6. – Germany: Karl Larenz, *Lehrbuch des Schuldrechts*, Vol I (Allgemeiner Teil) (Munich: C H Beck 14th ed 1987), § 33 III, p 573: '*Rechtszuständigkeit*'. – For a general analysis, see Eleanor Cashin-Ritaine, *Les cessions contractuelles de créances de sommes d'argent dans les relations civiles et commerciales franco-allemandes* (Paris: LGDJ 2001), p 35, n 49-50 and p 39, n 53-55.

[70] Comp Austria, § 308 ABGB: '*Besitz, Eigentum, Pfandrecht, Dienstbarkeit und Erbrecht*'.

[71] Where the usufructary is entitled to the right to use the thing (*usus*) and the right to collect the fruit (*fructus*) (art 578-624 CC).

[72] Under French Law, this is a limited type of usufruct where the bearer can use a thing and collect the fruit but only to cover his own needs and those of his family (art 630-631 CC).

[73] Under French Law, this is the right for the bearer to use a building and to live there with his family only (artt 632-633 CC). A person entitled to a right of use or of dwelling cannot alienate or encumber it; nor can he allow the thing to be used or the dwelling to be inhabited by another person. This right is immovable (Cass 3e civ, 23 juin 1983: JCP 1983, II, 19928).

(*servitude*),[74] long term leases (*emphytéose*)[75] and surface rights (*droit de superficie*).[76] Most of these rights apply only to immovable property, except the right of usufruct[77] and the right of use that can be given on a movable thing.

16. Accessory rights *in rem* entitle the creditor of an obligation to a specific right on a thing owned by the debtor. This right only exists in relation to a claim. Accessory rights have a security function. Under French law, there are two main accessory rights *in rem*: the right of lien (*droit de gage* – art 2333 CC)[78] and mortgage rights (*hypothèque*).[79] In these two cases, the creditor of an obligation gets a direct right on a movable or an immovable thing owned by the debtor. This right is accessory to the obligation of the debtor and it entitles the creditor to claim the thing, regardless of in whose hands it may be (*droit de suite*).[80] It also gives him the right to be paid in preference to other creditors if the thing were to be sold (*droit de preference*). Other legal systems have developed different accessory rights *in rem*, with, however, similar preferential rights for the creditor.[81] Accessory rights aim more to give their bearer an *economic right* to the value of the thing rather than to

---

[74] This is the right for the owner of a piece of land to use some attributes of the neighbouring land, for example water rights or a right of way (art 637-710 CC). This right is immovable (Cass 3ᵉ civ, 27 oct 1993: Bulletin des arrêts de la Cour de cassation: chambres civiles (Bull Civ) III, n 132) – See also German law: *Dienstbarkeit* (§§ 1090-1093 BGB).

[75] A lease given for a period of 18 to 99 years that gives quasi-ownership rights to the tenant (Cass 3ᵉ civ, 15 mai 1991: Bull civ III, n 140, p 82: «*le bail emphytéotique de biens immeubles confère au preneur un droit réel susceptible d'hypothèque*». – Code Rural (C Rur) Art L 451-1.). See also *bail à construction*, *bail à rehabilitation* – CCH, art L 251-1 and L 252-1.

[76] That entitle the bearer to the use of the surface of an estate, but not to the underground. See for details, Jean-Louis Bergel, Marc Bruschi and Sylvie Cimamonti (*supra* footnote 38), p 290, n 285.

[77] France: art 581 CC – Example of an usufruct right on a sum of money: Cass 1ᵉ civ, 19 févr 1980: Bull civ I, n 63.

[78] Pledges were formerly ruled under art 2071 *et seqq* CC. The whole field was reformed by the Ordonnance (Ord) n° 2006-346 du 23 mars 2006. See also the right of privilege (art 2331 *et seqq* CC).

[79] France: Art 2114 CC. Yet, Emmanuel Putman, 'Sur l'origine de la règle: «meubles n'ont point de suite par hypothèque»', RTDCiv 1994/3, chr p 543. – See also the *antichrèse* (art 2085 CC), that enables the creditor to be paid with the income of an immovable thing or by preference on the price of the sale.

[80] France: With a limit concerning movables: art 2279 CC – Spanish González Pacanowska and Diez Soto, TOM Report Spain (*supra* footnote 3), Part I, 1.2.

[81] Floating charge, *Sicherungsübereignung*, *Sicherungsabtretung*.

give the bearer a direct right on the thing. In this respect, they are directly linked to the law of obligations.

2. Obligations

17. The term 'obligation' can have many meanings depending on whether one is in the field of law or in real life. Moral, social, religious or political obligations are not obligations in the legal sense.

18. It is very difficult to find a common 'European' definition of a legal obligation,[82] even though in most jurisdictions, obligations (*droit personnel* or *jus in personam* or *obligation*) represent the right given to a person (the creditor) to demand a service or a payment (a duty) from another person (the debtor).[83] The main example of an obligation is the promise to deliver a good.

19. Obligations have an active subject (the creditor), a passive subject (the debtor) and an object (the service promised). Obligations are movable[84] and incorporeal rights. Additionally, the creditor has an indirect right on the debtor's patrimony. This means that if the debtor does not fulfil his promise, the creditor can seize part of the debtor's property.[85] There are specific procedures to enforce claims.[86]

---

[82] There is no definition in the *Principles of European Contract Law*, nor in the *Gandolfi* European Contract Code, 2004. – Comp Case law under the 1968 Brussels Convention on jurisdiction showing the difficulties in localising an obligation: ECJ, 6 oct 1976 *Tessili*: D 1977, 614 note Georges A L Droz; Rev crit dr int priv 1977, 751 note Pierre Gothot et André Holleaux; Clunet 1977, 719, note Jean-Marc Bischoff. – ECJ, 6 oct 1976 *de Bloos*: D 1977, 618 note and chron 287 by Droz; Rev crit dr int priv, 1977, 751 note Gothot and Holleaux; Clunet 1977, 719 note Bischoff. – Confirmed by ECJ, 29 June 1994, *Custom Made Commercial Ltd v Stawa Metallbau GmbH* = Praxis des Internationalen Privat- und Verfahrensrechts (IPRax) 1995, 31.

[83] France: Atias (*supra* footnote 6), p 59, n 85. – Germany: § 241 BGB; – Austria: § 859 ABGB.

[84] France: art 529 CC.

[85] France: *droit de gage général des créanciers* – article 2093 CC.

[86] For example, France : Loi n 91-650 du 9 juillet 1991 (*Loi portant réforme des procédures civiles d'exécution*): reforming civil enforcement procedures.

20. Obligations can arise under contract, quasi-contract or tort[87] and in every case, they create a legal tie between two or more persons.[88] In comparative law, this legal tie has been analysed differently. German authors[89] distinguish two components to an obligation: on the one hand the debt (*Schuld/debitum*), on the other the liability (*Haftung/obligation*). The debt aspect represents the promise of a service or a payment. This promise has a monetary value. The liability aspect covers the mandatory side of an obligation: the right to request something from somebody. French law adopts another analysis. An obligation is threefold:[90] it is a promise that has legal consequences; it creates a personal relationship between two or more parties; it has a monetary value. Let us explain these criteria. First, an obligation has legal consequences because it represents a legal tie (*vinculum juris*) between a debtor and a creditor.[91] In the past, the debtor could be chained in prison and the creditor could either kill him or make him a slave. Nowadays, this legal tie only gives the creditor a legal action against the debtor who doesn't perform the obligation. Such an action does not exist for paralegal obligations such as social obligations, religious obligations, gentlemen's agreements[92] and natural obligations.[93] Second, an obligation creates a personal

---

[87] This paper will not discuss the nature nor the origin of the obligation, notably whether a *causa* or consideration is necessary for the validity of the obligation, nor the extent of the obligation.

[88] There are two other legal meanings. In some cases, the term obligation designates the written act that transcribes the legal tie. For example, in commercial law an obligation is a bond that represents the loan a person has given to a company. An obligation here is the *instrumentum*. In a broader sense, an obligation is an order, a duty imposed by the legal system the person lives in. For example: drive on the right side of the road; accomplish military service; pay taxes. In this case, an obligation is only a simple duty that does not create a legal tie between two people. There is no creditor who can request payment.

[89] Martin Schmidt-Kessel in: Hanns Prütting, Gerhard Wegen, Gerd Weinreich, *BGB Kommentar* (Neuwied: Luchterhand, 2nd ed 2007), § 241, n 25. – See also Austria: Koziol and Welser (*supra* footnote 6), p 10.

[90] François Chabas, 'Obligations: théorie générale', in: Léon Mazeaud and Henri Mazeaud (ed), *Leçons de droit civil*, Part 2 Vol II (Paris: Éditeur Montchrestien, 9th ed 1998), p 6, n 8-11.

[91] Lévy and Castaldo (*supra* footnote 9), p 644, n 436, citing the Institutes of Justinien (III, 13, pr): «*obligatio est iuris vinculum, quo necessitate adstringimur alicuius solvendae rei secundum nostrae civitatis iura*». Jean Gaudemet, Naissance d'une notion juridique. Les débuts de l'"obligation" dans le droit de la Rome antique, in: *L'obligation*, *Archives de philosophie du droit*, Vol XLIV (Paris: Dalloz 2000), p 19.

[92] Bruno Oppetit, 'L'engagement d'honneur', Dalloz 1979, chron p 107.

relationship between two or more parties. It is neither a general duty imposed by law on everybody, nor a right on a thing (*jus in re*). Third, an obligation is a right that has a monetary value and that belongs to the patrimony of both the creditor (as an asset) and the debtor (as a debt). This is one of the main differences with non-patrimonial rights such as political rights, family rights and the rights of personality (right to live, right to a name...). An obligation is the legal expression of an economic relationship between two or more people. By contrast, in Danish law, an obligation is not based on the promisor's intention to be legally bound, but what the promisee might reasonably expect in the given social, economic or commercial situation.[94]

21. Notwithstanding these three different approaches to the concept of an obligation, all European legal systems acknowledge that an obligation entitles a creditor to claim something from a debtor and that this claim arises out of a personal relationship with essentially *inter partes* effects as opposed to the *ultra partes* effects of proprietary rights. This *summa divisio* thus carries a number of legal consequences, even though a comparative law survey tends to show certain limits to this distinction.

B. Consequences and limits of this *summa divisio*

22. The distinction between rights *in rem* and obligations has a number of consequences. Obligations can be an asset in the form of claims (*créances*) or a liability in the form of debts (*dettes*), whereas rights *in rem* are always assets (*actifs*). As already specified,[95] obligations are not limited in their number whereas rights *in rem* are generally created by way of statute (*numerus clauses* principle). Proprietary rights are opposable to all,[96] and therefore have an

---

[93] Mario Rotondi, 'Quelques considérations sur le concept d'obligation naturelle et son évolution', RTDciv 1979, 1. – Cass 1e civ, 10 oct 1995: Bull civ n 352. – Nicolas Molfessis, L'obligation naturelle devant la Cour de cassation: remarques sur un arrêt rendu par la première Chambre civile, le 10 octobre 1995, Dalloz 1997, chr 85.
[94] Peter Møgelvang-Hansen, 'Contracts and Sales in Denmark', in: Dahl, Melchior and Tamm (ed) (*supra* footnote 2), pp 237-276 (239).
[95] *Supra* n 13.
[96] Austria: Koziol and Welser (*supra* footnote 6), pp 238-239. – England: Sarah Worthington, *Personal Property Law: Text, Cases and Materials* (Oxford: Hart Publishing 2000) p 18 *et seq*. – France: Bergel, Bruschi and Cimamonti (*supra* footnote 38), p 33, n 37. – Terré and Simler (*supra* footnote 28), p 54, n 47. – Germany: Baur and Stürner (*supra* footnote 3), § 4, n 3-6. – Spain: The principle is expressly laid down for mortgages in

absolute character (*caractère absolu*)⁹⁷ effective against every other person, whereas obligations can only be opposed to the debtor (*effet relatif*),⁹⁸ granting a restricted right against a certain person. In many cases, however, the universal effect of proprietary rights is subject to compliance with prescribed methods of publicity,⁹⁹ based mainly on possession and registration,¹⁰⁰ which is not, in principle, applicable to credit rights. Therefore, in the eventuality of a collision of rights, regarding proprietary rights, the preference between rights falling upon the same thing is granted to the most ancient (*prior tempore potior iure*). Regarding obligations referring to the same debtor, the general rule is that of concurrence (*par condicio creditorum*).

23. Obligations only give the creditor a general right on the patrimony of the debtor, who is entitled to manage all assets in his patrimony until the creditor makes a seizure, whereas rights *in rem* encompass the right to follow the thing in whosoever hand it might be (*droit de suite*)¹⁰¹ – unless there has been a case of acquisition in good faith – and the right to be paid in preference over other creditors if the thing were to be sold (*droit de préférence*).¹⁰²

24. Additionally, property rights – but not obligations – may be acquired by acquisitive prescription or by good faith acquisition.¹⁰³ Property rights are

---

immovables in art 1876 of the civil Code; and for mortgages in movables by the *Law on mortgages in movables and non-possessory pledges* of 1954 (art 16).

⁹⁷ Bergel, Bruschi and Cimamonti (*supra* footnote 38), p 97, n 93. – Marc Levis, *L'opposabilité du droit réel: De la sanction judicaire des droits* (Paris: Economica 1989), préface Philippe Raynaud.

⁹⁸ Belgium: Sophie Stijns, 'Les contrats et les tiers', in: Patrick Wéry (ed), *Le droit des obligations contractuelles et le bicentenaire du Code civil*, Vol I (Brussels: La Charte 2004), pp 189-239 (196 and 205). – See TOM Report for Slovenia (*supra* footnote 44), citing: Stojan Cigoj, *Teorija obligacij* (Uradni List, 2003), p 3; Matjaž Tratnik, *Stvarnopravni zakonik z uvodnimi pojasnili in svarnim kazalom* (Ljubljana 2002) p 31 *et seq*; Andrej Berden in: *SPZ commentary*, Stvarnopravni zakonik skomentarjem (Ljubljana: Založba 2004), Art 2,74.

⁹⁹ Baur and Stürner (*supra* footnote 3), § 4, n 9-16.

¹⁰⁰ Especially for real rights in immovables, but also for certain rights (especially security rights) in movables: Austria: Koziol and Welser (*supra* footnote 6), p 239.

¹⁰¹ France: Bergel, Bruschi and Cimamonti (*supra* footnote 38), p 33, n 37; Terré and Simler (*supra* footnote 28), p 55, n 47; Germany: Baur and Stürner (*supra* footnote 3), § 11, n 1 *et seqq*. – Yet see the remedy in tort under English law: Torts (Interference with Goods) Act of 1977.

¹⁰² France: Bergel, Bruschi and Cimamonti (*supra* footnote 38), p 33, n 37. – Spain: Law on mortgages in movables and non-possessory pledges of 1954 (art 10 para 2).

¹⁰³ France: Cour de cassation, Chambre des requêtes (Cass Req), 25 nov 1929: DH 1930, 3.

extinguished by the total loss or destruction of the thing upon which they are constituted, unless the so-called 'real subrogation' operates, through which the right is deemed to fall upon the asset that replaces the lost thing. Instead, the loss or destruction of the thing does not necessarily extinguish the credit right referring to that thing.

25. Finally, in Private International Law, conflict rules and those regarding the international competence of Courts are different for property rights[104] and credit rights. In particular, the 1980 Rome Convention on the law applicable to contractual obligations[105] makes a clear distinction between the law applicable to contractual rights (*lex contractus*) and the law applicable to real rights (*lex rei sitae*). In the former case, the parties can, in principle, choose the law applicable to their relationship, in the latter case, the law of the situation of the asset is applied.

26. Yet, even if the legal consequences of the distinction between proprietary rights and obligations are clearly established, a comparative survey of European jurisdictions shows that in some cases the borderline between rights *in rem* and rights *in personam* can be indeterminate. A number of exceptional legal mechanisms and theories tend, therefore, to render this distinction questionable.

27. As mentioned before, one of the major differences between property rights and contractual rights is the universal effect of property rights that are effective against the whole world (*erga omnes*). As everybody is bound to respect absolute rights, it seems a prerequisite that everybody is in a position to know the content of the right. However, in some legal systems (France, Belgium), third parties also have to respect obligations contracted by others (*opposabilité*). This means that even obligations are protected against unlawful interferences from whomsoever. As a consequence, the fact that third parties know the content of a right is not always relevant. In the case of obligations, the wilful (or through gross negligence) breach of a right gives an action in tort.[106]

---

[104] See in particular Foëx (*supra* footnote 15), p 56, n 81-84.
[105] Convention sur la loi applicable aux obligations contractuelles, ouverte à la signature à Rome le 19 juin 1980, JOCE 9. 10. 1980, n L 266/1. – Rapport concernant la convention sur la loi applicable aux obligations contractuelles, by Mario Guiliano and Paul Lagarde, JOCE 31. 10. 1980, n C 282/1.
[106] France: application of art 1382 CC.

28. Scholars have thus developed a concept that would simply lead to the disappearance of this distinction.[107] Planiol, a French legal scholar thus proposed the concept of a universal obligation (*'obligation passive universelle'*) at the beginning of the 20th century.[108] According to his view, a legal relationship must always involve two (legal or natural) persons. A legal relationship can never be established between a legal subject and a legal object since the subject-object relationship can only be a factual one. Therefore, both real rights and personal rights are created between persons, so that no difference between those categories remains in the internal structure.[109] The difference, however, remains in the external structure: a personal right is vested between one person (the creditor) and one other person (the debtor), whereas a real right is vested between one person (the holder of the real right) and people in general. All other persons except for the holder of the right have to refrain from actions which would impede the exercise of the real right. In other words, a real right is reflected in the universal passive obligation not to hamper the prerogatives attributed to the holder of the real right.[110] In conclusion, a real right is, according to the subjective approach, enforceable *erga omnes*, whereas a personal right would only be enforceable against one person (the debtor). This subjective theory is called '*personnalisme*', because it emphasises the persons involved in all legal relationships, whatever their nature may be.[111] Such an analysis could be confirmed by the functional approach of Scandinavian jurisdictions.[112] For example, in Finland, but also in other Scandinavian countries, the fundamental question behind the concepts of obligations and rights *in rem*, is actually the protection of the right itself and especially, in which relations the right can and is protected. Rights *in rem* can thus be classified as all such rights that are rights against individual and specific corporeal objects. The category of

---

[107] For an extensive analysis of this development: Vincent Sagaert, 'Les interférences entre le droit des biens et le droit des obligations. Une analyse de l'évolution depuis le Code civil', in: Patrick Wéry (ed), *Le droit des obligations contractuelles et le bicentenaire du Code civil* (Bruges: Die Keure 2004), 354-395.

[108] See also the 'obligationist doctrine' in Spain.

[109] Marcel Planiol, *Traité élémentaire de droit civil*, Vol I (Paris: Pichon, 11th ed 1928), n 2159.

[110] Henri Michas, *Le droit réel, considéré comme une obligation passivement universelle* (Thesis) (Paris: Pedone 1900). – Louis Rigaud, *Le droit réel: histoire et théories; son origine institutionnelle* (Thesis) Toulouse: Nauze 1912). See criticism at: René Dekkers, 'Du neuf sur les droit réels', Journ trib 1960, p 697, n 4.

[111] This explanation of Planiol's theory has largely been taken from the Belgian TOM Report by Cauffmann and Sagaert (*supra* footnote 5), V.

[112] See *supra* n 5.

obligations entails rights, which are rights against a *specified portion* of a person's assets.

29. For a number of years there has been a controversy on the question as to whether there can be a right of property on a claim (*notion de propriété d'une créance*), in other terms a right *in rem* on a claim. Can a creditor *own* his claim against a debtor? A famous theory developed by Samuel Ginossar, and largely discussed in France, extended the scope of the concept of property to incorporeal assets such as rights.[113] Yet, even if the terminology used in the present day by the legislator[114] and by judges[115] is not always precise, legal scholars[116] generally consider that there can be no right of property to a claim.[117]

30. Additionally, certain rights have dual characteristics: belonging both to those of rights *in rem* and to those of obligations. This is the case for long-term leases[118] and for certain rights *in rem* accessory to an obligation.[119] For instance, in all legal systems, contracts for the use of a movable asset generate obligations. By contrast, the qualification of contracts for the use of immovables is not uniform. While in most continental jurisdictions, short term leases only create obligations, English, Scottish and Irish law regard

---

[113] Samuel Ginossar, *Droit réel, propriété et créance, élaboration d'un système rationnel des droits patrimoniaux* (Paris: LGDJ 1960). – Samuel Ginossar, 'Pour une meilleure définition du droit réel et du droit personnel', RTDciv 1962, p 573. – Jean Dabin, 'Une nouvelle définition du droit réel', RTDciv 1962, p 20. – Frédéric Zenati, 'Pour une rénovation de la théorie de la propriété', RTDciv 1993, p 305. – Also: Bergel, Bruschi and Cimamonti (*supra* footnote 38), p 106, n 101 *et seqq*. – See also Christoph Krampe, *L'obligation comme bien, droit français et allemand*, in: *L'obligation, Archives de philosophie du droit*, Vol XLIV (Paris: Dalloz 2000), p 205.

[114] France: See L 511-7 C com which refers to the «property of the claim» (*propriété de la provision*).

[115] CEDH, 26 juin 1986, *Van Marle/The Netherlands*: serie A, n 101 – CEDH, 9 déc 1994, *Raffineries Grécques*: série A n 301-B.

[116] Jacques Ghestin et alii, *Traité de Droit Civil: Introduction générale* (Paris: LGDG, 4th ed 1994), n 232, p 185 *et seqq*. – Dabin (*supra* footnote 113), p 20.

[117] Nevertheless, see Michel Storck, 'La propriété d'un portefeuille de valeurs mobilières', in: Christian Atias, *Le droit privé français à la fin du XXe siècle, Études offertes à Pierre Catala* (Paris: Litec 2001), p 695. – Yet, Cashin-Ritaine (*supra* footnote 69), p 32, n 43 *et seqq*. – See also in Finnish law: Kuusinen (*supra* footnote 24), 1.2.: 'one cannot 'own' rights'.

[118] France: *Contrat de bail de longue durée* or *emphytéose*.

[119] Comp also usufruct rights on securities: Anne Rabreau, *L'usufruit des droits sociaux* (Paris: Litec [Bibl dr de l'entreprise] 2006).

them as founding a proprietary right.[120] Exceptionally, in Austria[121] and Spain[122] such contracts may, under certain conditions, be entered in the land register and thus produce proprietary effects *erga omnes*.[123] Under Slovenian law,[124] some obligatory rights in relation to an immovable,[125] such as leases, the right of preemption and the right of repurchase, can be entered in the land register and thus attain a limited absolute effect[126] (*obligatio in rem scripta*).[127] This registration, however, does not change their basic nature as obligatory rights,[128] but only renders the right opposable to third parties. However, if a third party has knowledge of the right or should have known it, this right is also effective against him/her although it was not entered in the land register.[129] Additionally, possession of the rented or leased asset, by the leaseholder or tenant also renders his/her right of lease or tenancy effective against the acquirer of the rented or leased asset.

31. Finally, the Spanish 'TOM report'[130] lists certain property rights endowed with an obligatory content. 'Situations in which different property rights fall upon the same thing, thereby arising credit rights and obligations

---

[120] In England they are considered for historical reasons as 'personal property', *ie* movables, but due to their relation to land as 'chattels real': Robert Megarry and Henry William Rawson Wade, *The Law of Real Property* (London: Sweet & Maxwell, 6th ed 2000) no 1-010. – Scotland: Paul Coughlan, *Property Law* (Dublin: Gill & Macmillan 1995) 34 *et seqq*.

[121] According to article 1095 of the Austrian civil code, the user's right is then regarded as a 'real right which for the remaining time the succeeding possessor has to tolerate'.

[122] Spanish law, art 1549 of the civil Code: González Pacanowska and Diez Soto (*supra* footnote 3), Part 1, I. 2.

[123] Comp Germany: § 566 BGB which allows similar registration, without the same 'real' consequences.

[124] See TOM Report for Slovenia (*supra* footnote 44) to be published in 2008 by Sellier.

[125] Art 13/II Land Registration Act.

[126] TOM Report for Slovenia (*supra* footnote 44), citing Vesna Rijavek, 'Sachenrechtsreform in Slowenien', in: *Freiheit, Sicherheit, Recht: Notariat und Gesellschaft; Festschrift für Georg Weissmann* (Vienna: Manz 2003), 821 (830). – See also Spanish law.

[127] TOM Report for Slovenia by Rudolf, Rijavec and Kersteš (*supra* footnote 44), citing Matjaž Tratnik, *Stvarnopravni zakonik in obligacijsko pravo* (Ljubljana) Podjetje in delo 2002/6-7, p 1392 (1396 *et seqq*).

[128] TOM Report for Slovenia by Rudolf, Rijavec and Kersteš (*supra* footnote 44), citing Andrej Berden in: *Zemljiškoknjižno pravo* (Ljubljana 2002), pp 15, 22.

[129] TOM Report for Slovenia by Rudolf, Rijavec and Kersteš (*supra* footnote 44), citing Renato Vrenčur in: *Zemljiškoknjižno pravo* (Ljubljana 2002), p 84 *et seq*.

[130] Spanish law: González Pacanowska and Diez Soto, TOM Report Spain (*supra* footnote 3), Part I, 1.2.

between the different title-holders: e.g., between owner and usufructuary, or between the co-owners of a thing (e.g., arts. 395 CC and regulation provided for by the Horizontal Property Act of 1960). Situations in which the title-holder of a property right can demand from the owner or possessor of a thing a certain behaviour in order to render possible the exercise of the property right: e.g., the title-holder of an easement to support rafters on the neighbouring wall can demand from the owner of the latter the reparations needed to keep the wall in good condition. Situations in which the owner of a thing encumbered by another's property right is obliged to pay the title-holder of the latter a certain price charging the yields of the thing, the thing itself operating as a security of the performance of such obligation: it's the case of the so-called "ground annuities" ("*censos*": arts. 1.604 *et seq.* CC).'

32. All these examples show that the dividing line between obligatory and proprietary rights is not clearly cut. Although legal doctrine prefers simple categories, that do not overlap, comparative law teaches us that a legal issue can be observed in many different ways and thus fall under different legal categories. The separation between contractual and real rights is justified historically, looking back to Roman times, yet must to be revised in modern European law, where new mechanisms appear regularly in legal practice to fulfil the needs of citizens. Many jurisdictions have thus admitted new mechanisms, such as the German *Anwartschaftsrecht*, the Luxemburg fiduciary relationships and even the recent Swiss recognition of trust relationships[131] under the Hague Convention, which belong neither to real nor personal rights[132] but create a completely new legal category *sui generis* that needs to be categorised in the light of comparative law.

---

[131] Diane Le Grand de Belleroche, 'L'intégration du concept de trust à l'échelle régionale et mondiale', in: Mireille Delmas-Marty, *Critique de l'intégration normative, L'apport du droit comparé à l'harmonisation des droits*, sous la direction de Mireille Delmas-Marty (Paris: Presses Universitaires de France 2004), p 139. *Le Trust en droit international privé, Perspectives suisses et étrangères*, Publications Institut Suisse de droit comparé Vol 52 (Zürich: Schulthess 2005), 120 pages.

[132] Jean-Paul Béraudo, *Les trusts anglo-saxons et le droit français* (Paris: LGDJ [Droit des affaires] 1992). – Alain Levasseur, *Droit des États-Unis* (Paris: Dalloz, 2nd ed 1994), n 603 *et seq* – John Anthony Jolowicz (ed), *Droit anglais* (Paris: Dalloz, 2nd ed 1992), n 362 *et seq*. – René David and Xavier Blanc-Jouvan, *Le droit anglais* (Paris: Presses Universitaires de France [Que sais-je?], 7th ed 1994), p 100 *et seq*. – Patrick Glenn, 'Le trust et le ius commune', in: Pierre Legrand (ed), *Common Law, d'un siècle à l'autre* (Québec: Vyon Blais 1992), p 87.

The German Property Law and its Principles – Some Lessons for a European Property Law

*Jens Thomas Füller**

A. Introduction

The harmonisation of European Civil Law systems towards a uniform European Civil Law changes from a mere vision to a more and more concrete project since the European Council, in *Tampere*, forced a study on the necessity of a harmonised European Civil Law. At the moment, European Civil law is partially harmonised. This harmonisation is embedded in consumer protection and is focussed on the control of preset conditions, consumer credits, unit pricing, distance selling, sale of consumer goods and injunctions.[1] In the near term, the idea of a European Civil Law will require a fundamental refinement and other perspectives have to be taken into account. The increasing pressure of the global markets stresses the necessity of establishing not only simple but also effective rules for the entities in the Single European Market. It is not to be discussed here whether this is forced by primary European Law.[2] Institutional economics attests that a harmo-

---

* Privatdozent, *Dr iur*, Free University of Berlin.
[1] On the 8th February 2007, the European Commission published a Green Paper on the review of the consumer *acquis*; Doc COM (2006), 744 final. For more details see: http://ec.europa.eu/consumers/cons_int/safe_shop/acquis/green-paper_cons_acquis_en.pdf.
[2] Especially in Germany some argue that a European civil code or a European property law are the consequences of Art 3 (1) *lit* (c); Art 28 *et seqq* EC: Dieter Krimphove, *Das europäische Sachenrecht* (Lohmar: Eul 2006), p 2. A popular opinion deduces the necessity of harmonising the law of encumbrances, as is the case for mortgages, from the Freedom of Goods (Art 28 EC: Eva-Maria Kieninger, *Mobiliarsicherheiten im europäischen Binnenmarkt* (Baden-Baden: Nomos 1996), pp 122 *et seqq*; Peter von Wilmowsky, *Europäisches Kreditsicherungsrecht* (Tübingen: Mohr 1996), pp 32-42). This is wishful thinking, however. The European Court of Justice does not apply Art 28 EC to 'selling arrangements', which do not force a change of the product. Property law does not force a change of the products, see: Jens Thomas Füller, *Grundlagen und inhaltliche Reichweite der Warenverkehrsfreiheiten nach dem EG-Vertrag* (Baden-Baden: Nomos 2000), pp 190 et seqq.

nised Civil Law will reduce transaction costs and, therefore, will lead to competitive advantages.

The German experiences in the late 19th century are, so to speak, a hatcher for a uniform civil code. After the tariff-union and the common market were established, the necessity of establishing a common Civil Law arose.[3] It took more than 30 years to complete this. One of the most emphasised accomplishments are the rules referring to property. German law, as provided in the BGB (*Bürgerliches Gesetzbuch* – *Civil Code*), knows a distinct property law regulated in the 3rd Book of the BGB (§§ 854 – 1296). This distinction and the resulting genuine property law was a result of preliminary dogmatic work in the early 19th Century. According to the thesis of *Savigny*, the first draft's preamble (*Motive*) states: 'Property law has an autonomous position within the draft's system... Its autonomy is substantially based on the antagonism between a right *in personam* and a right *in rem*'.[4] As a consequence, certain principles were allocated to genuine property law. These principles were even derived from the right *in rem*. Thus, German property law is based on the (1) *Trennungs- und Abstraktionsprinzip* (principles of separation and abstraction), (2) *Typenzwang* (*numerus clausus* of rights *in rem*) and (3) *Publizitätsprinzip* (principle of publicity).[5] As newer studies

---

[3] This discussion was initiated by the famous dispute between Anton Friedrich Justus Thibaut, *Über die Notwendigkeit eines allgemeinen Bürgerlichen Rechts für Deutschland* (Heidelberg: Mohr und Zimmer 1814) – 'about the necessity of a civil law for Germany' – and Friedrich Carl von Savigny, *Vom Beruf unserer Zeit für Gesetzgebung und Wissenschaft* (Freiburg: Mohr, 3rd ed 1840, Newprint 1892) – 'about the need of our times for legislation and science'. It is remarkable that Thibaut argued quite modernly for a German civil code, pointing out the economic necessity: 'Our German states can only obtain prosperity by intensive mutual trade'.

[4] *Motive zu dem Entwurfe eines bürgerlichen Gesetzbuches für das Deutsche Reich* (Amtliche Ausgabe), Vol III (Berlin: Guttentag, 1888), p 1: 'Das Sachenrecht nimmt in dem System des Entwurf eine selbständige Stellung ein ... Seine Selbständigkeit beruht im wesentlichen in dem Gegensatz zwischen dinglichem und persönlichen Rechte'. See also: Wolfgang Wiegand, *Funktion und systematische Stellung des Sachenrechts im BGB* in: 100 Jahre BGB – 100 Jahre Staudinger, Beiträge zum Symposion vom 18.-20. Juni 1998 in München (Berlin: Sellier – de Gruyter, 13th ed 1999), p 107.

[5] It is disputed whether a principle of certainty (*Bestimmtheitsgrundsatz*) also characterises property law. In the affirmative: Astrid Stadler in Soergel, *Bürgerliches Gesetzbuch mit Einführungsgesetzen und Nebengesetzen*, Vol XIV (Stuttgart: Kohlhammer, 13th ed 2002), Einleitung (introduction) n 43. From my point of view, this principle only affects the interpretation of laws but not the legal systems. On this point: Hans H Seiler in Julius von Staudinger, *Kommentar zum Bürgerlichen Gesetzbuch mit Einführungsgesetz und Nebengesetzen* (Berlin: Sellier – de Gruyter, 14th ed 2000), Einleitung zum Sachenrecht n 54; Jan Wilhelm, *Sachenrecht* (Berlin: de Gruyter, 3rd ed 2007), paras 15-17.

proved, a right *in rem* is just a fiction and cannot be clearly distinguished from a right *in personam* (obligation).[6] The thesis of a genuine property law perishes, when regarded from this point of view. Moreover, the practice of German courts watered down the principles, which leads to the question whether the assumption of a genuine property law is justified. This analysis, of course, is important for the discussion on the European Civil Code. It should be shown how the principles influence German property law and, on the other hand, what the similarities and differences to the various European property laws are.

B. The so-called *Trennungs- und Abstraktionsprinzip* (principles of separation and abstraction)

Most significant for German property law are the *Trennungs- und Abstraktionsprinzip*. The historic legislator justified these principles by the role of a genuine property law itself.[7] Very early, these principles were identified as an obstacle to the European unification of the various civil law systems.[8] This thesis, however, has to be verified by comparing the legal consequences of the German system with other systems. Even though these principles apply both to the transfer of movables and immovables, only the transfer of movable goods should be examined.

---

[6] Jens Thomas Füller, *Eigenständiges Sachenrecht ?* (Tübingen: Mohr Siebeck 2006), pp 27 *et seqq*, who argues for redissolving the system of rights *in rem* and rights *in personam* to a system of a bundle of rights existing between the parties to a legal relationship. See also: Wesley N Hohfeld, 'Some Fundamental Legal Conceptions as Applied in Judicial Reasoning', *Yale Law Journal* (Yale Law J) 23 (1913), 16 *et seqq*; James E Penner, 'The "Bundle of Rights" Picture of Property', *UCLA Law Review* (UCLA L Rev) 34 (1996), 711 *et seqq*

[7] *Motive*, *supra* note 4 at p 6 *et seqq*

[8] Hans Brandt, *Eigentumserwerb und Austauschgeschäft* (Leipzig: Weicher 1940), pp 116 *et seqq*; Ernst von Caemmerer, 'Rechtsvergleichung und Reform der Fahrnisübereignung', *Rabels Zeitschrift* (RabelsZ) 12 (1938/39), pp 697 *et seqq*; Philipp Heck, *Das abstrakte dingliche Rechts*geschäft (Tübingen: Mohr 1937), pp 48 *et seqq*. It is to be emphasised that Heck proposed to replace the German system of the transfer of goods by the French system. This is a *drôle d'histoire*, reflecting that Germany suffered, in those times, from the 3rd Reich.

1. Legal separation

Even in Germany, the correct meaning of these principles is often described inaccurately. The core of the *Trennungsprinzip* (Principle of separation) is the separation of the obligation from the performance of the obligation (*Verpflichtung* and *Erfüllung*). Thus, property is only acquired by a (literally translated) agreement *in rem* (*dingliche Einigung*), which is to be separated from the selling arrangement. § 929 BGB rules the transfer of movables and requires, among other things, that the proprietor and the acquirer agree that the property should pass. The Greek civil code follows this system, Art 1034. Contrary to this, especially the French *Code Civil* provides that the transfer of goods is effective with the contract of sale (principle of consensus).[9]

From the German viewpoint, both contracts are autonomous and a legal unification of obligation and performance is impossible. This differs from the other European legal systems, which are based on a principle of consensus but allow the parties to separate the performance from the obligation. The most significant example is the Italian *Codice Civile*. Normally, the property is transferred by the contract of sale (*vendita ad effeti reali* – Artt 1470, 1476 Nr 2 *Codice Civile*).[10] Nevertheless, the parties can agree on separation, which is, of course, not the rule but the exception. These contracts are so-called *vendita obligatoria*, mere obligations.[11] This technique was inspired by

---

[9] **Art 1138 (1):** «L'obligation de livrer la chose est parfaite par le seul consentement des parties contractantes. (2) Elle rend le créancier propriétaire et met la chose à ses risques dès l'instant où elle a dû être livrée, encore que la tradition n'en ait point été faite, à moins que le débiteur ne soit en demeure de la livrer; auquel cas la chose reste aux risques de ce dernier». This is completed by **Art** 1583: »Elle est parfaite entre les parties, et la propriété est acquise de droit à l'acheteur à l'égard du vendeur, dès qu'on est convenu de la chose et du prix, quoique la chose n'ait pas encore été livrée ni le prix payé«. Belgium and Luxembourg follow this model.

[10] **Art 922:** »La proprietà si acquista per occupazione (923 e seguenti), per invenzione (927 e seguenti), per accessione (934 e seguenti), per specificazione (940), per unione o commistione (939), per usucapione (1158 e seguenti), per effetto di contratti (1376 e seguenti), per successione a causa di morte (456 e seguenti) e negli altri modi stabiliti dalla legge «.

Art 1470: »La vendita è il contratto che ha per oggetto il trasferimento della proprietà di una cosa o il trasferimento di un altro diritto (1376 e seguenti, 1476) verso il corrispettivo di un prezzo (1448, 1473 e seguente, 1498)«.

[11] From a German viewpoint, see: Erik Jayme, 'Konsensprinzip und obligatorischer Kaufvertrag im italienischen Recht', *Festschrift für Otto Mühl* (Stuttgart: Kohlhammer 1981), p 339. This important difference between French and Italian law is neglected by Krimphove (*supra* note 2), p 109.

German Law but aligns some advantages of separation with the simple and efficient construction of the principle of consensus.

2. Abstraction

The *Abstraktionsprinzip* implies the *Trennungsprinzip*. It is the legal core of the *Abstraktionsprinzip*, that defects in the obligation do not influence the performance. The purpose of this principle is to guarantee a *bona fide* transaction. Some examples should clarify this:

> *(1) The vendor (A) sells a certain good to the acquirer (B) but the contract of sale is void. This doesn't affect their consensus in rem. Thus, the purchaser (B) is the covenantee. If B sells the acquired good to a third (C), this third will acquire from the legal proprietor. The former vendor has no claims against C. The principle of abstraction protects C and supplements the possibility of a bona fide acquisition.*
> *(2) As example 1, but C knew the fact that the contract of sale between A and B was void. From the viewpoint of other legal systems, the result may seem embarrassing. Even in this case, C acquires from the covenantee. The knowledge of C is irrelevant.*
> *(3) As example 1, but B transferred the good gratuitously to C. In this case, A can demand the good from C, § 822 BGB. The abstraction principle doesn't protect a gratuitous acquisition.*

To sum it up, there is no difference between the different European legal systems and German law if a relationship between two parties is envisaged. Thus, the choice of the transaction mode only influences the rescinded transaction. The rescinded transaction in German law is managed by the rules on unjustified enrichment (§§ 812-822 BGB), while the opposite model – causality – may provide claims to a proprietor.

The differences become evident when the good is sold several times. Causality has the effect that the second purchaser can only acquire *bona fide*. If the national laws envision a *bona fide* acquisition, such acquisition depends on the good faith of the third. Regarding example 2, C cannot acquire the property because he has actual notice that the seller is not the proprietor of the sold good. The decision under the abstraction principle is simply the opposite to this. In other words: It is irrelevant whether the second acquirer knows about the nullity of the first contract of sale. This doesn't affect the separate consensus *in rem*. As a consequence, the third acquires from the covenantee. The proponents of the principle of abstraction try to justify this by the protection of the third. The customer does not have the obligation to inquire whether the seller is the proprietor.[12] This consequence was often criticised by German doctrine.[13] The proponents of the abstraction principle are not able to justify this consequence but retort that otherwise the purchaser would have to comprehensively research into the seller's legal position.[14] It will later be shown that this is an unsubstantiated misgiving: Legal systems, which are based on causality and know a *bona fide* acquisition, do not impose comprehensive obligations to inquire into the seller's legitimation either.[15]

Finally, some problems of the rescinded transaction in German law should be discussed. In case the purchaser acquired *bona fide* from the (second) seller, the former proprietor can claim against the first purchaser for restoring the profit he earned from the second contract of sale, § 816 (1) BGB. In fact, this implies that the abstraction principle does not apply, otherwise the legal framework for a claim against the second seller would be § 812 (1) BGB. In this case, the second seller is not able to restore the property because the third is now the proprietor of the sold good. As a consequence, the first seller has to restore the value of the good (§ 818 (2) BGB), which is normally lower than the profit.[16] This unequal treatment of the first seller is also a consequence of the principle of abstraction and of the fact that the legislator did not harmonise §§ 812 (1), 818 (2) BGB with § 816 (1) BGB. The legal aim of the principle of abstraction does not justify this contradiction. In other words: Abstraction privileges the second buyer but penalises the former proprietor.

---

[12] See for example: Hans Christoph Grigoleit, 'Abstraktion und Willensmängel', *Archiv für die civillistische Praxis* (AcP) 199 (1999), 379, 383; Astrid Stadler, *Gestaltungsfreiheit und Verkehrsschutz durch Abstraktion* (Tübingen: Mohr 1996), pp 78, 372 *et seqq*.

[13] Franco Ferrari, 'Vom Abstraktionsprinzip und Konsensualprinzip zum Traditionsprinzip', *Zeitschrift für Europäisches Privatrecht* (ZEuP) 1993, 52, 66; Heck (*supra* note 8), p 22; Gerhard Kegel, 'Verpflichtung und Verfügung – Sollen Verfügungen abstrakt oder kausal sein ?', *Festschrift für F A Mann* (München: Beck 1977), pp 57 et seqq; Erich May, *Die Möglichkeit der Beseitigung des Abstraktionsprinzips bei den Verfügungen des Fahrnisrechts* (Mainz: Akademische Buchhandlung 1952), p 73; Karl Heinz Schindler, 'Kausale oder Abstrakte Übereignung', *Festschrift für Karl Kroeschell* (München: C H Beck 1997), pp 1033, 1039.

[14] See note 12.

[15] See *infra*, D.3.

[16] This is, of course, explained in a nutshell. The German dispute about this is widespread. See, for example: BGH (German Supreme Court) BGHZ 29, 157, 159. Doctrine: Karl Larenz and Claus-Wilhelm Canaris, *Lehrbuch des Schuldrechts*, Vol II/2 (München: Beck, 13th ed 1994), § 72 I 2a; Manfred Lieb in *Münchener Kommentar zum Bürgerlichen Gesetzbuch*, Vol V (München: C H Beck, 4th ed 2004), § 816 n 29, 30; Dieter Reuter and Michael Martinek, *Ungerechtfertigte Bereicherung* (Tübingen: Mohr 1983), § 8 I 4d.

3. Practice of the German Supreme Court

On the other side, the principle of abstraction was modified by the German Supreme Court rulings. As proved above, the principle was breached in numerous cases.[17] An example for this are immoral contracts which are void, § 138 BGB. The German Supreme Court emphasises that such contracts do not affect the agreement *in rem* unless the perfection of the contract is to be disapproved of, or the parties have immoral aims in respect of the agreement *in rem*.[18] Taken literally, every contract *in rem* must be affected by the obligation because the result of every contract of sale is its perfection.[19] However, this is not the intention of the Supreme Court, otherwise the principle of abstraction would be obsolete. The Supreme Court tends to correct the results of abstraction in particular cases. As a consequence, case law seems to replace this legal construction. A lucid example for this is the judicature about immoral chattel mortgages, known in German law as *Sicherungsübereignung*. If the value of the transferred goods represents more than 150% of the secured claim, the trustee is obliged to release some of the transferred goods. If the deed of trust doesn't provide for such a claim, the transfer of goods is invalid.[20] The Supreme Court did not even address the principles of abstraction and separation but took for granted that the consensus *in rem* could be void.[21] From the viewpoint of the judicature, this may be an acceptable way. Indeed, from a dogmatic viewpoint, this practice questions the principle of abstraction itself. As legal theory shows, a principle is not an axiom and can know exceptions.[22] But the more exceptions are accepted and the less these exceptions are based on a closed theoretic frame, abstrac-

---

[17] Füller (*supra* note 6), pp 129 *et seqq*.

[18] BGHZ 19, 12, 18; BGHZ 27, 111, 114 f; BGH *Neue Juristische Wochenschrift* (NJW) 1973, 613, 615; BGH *NJW-Rechtsprechungs-Report Zivilrecht* (NJW-RR) 1992, 3006, 3007; BGH NJW 2005, 1490.

[19] See Füller (*supra* note 6), pp 155 – 157; Stadler (*supra* note 12), p 145; Reinhard Zimmermann, 'Sittenwidrigkeit und Abstraktion', *Juristische Rundschau* (JR) 1985, 48, 51.

[20] BGHZ 137, 212, 219 *et seqq*; see also: BGHZ 117, 374, 377; Gerhard Ganter, 'Die ursprüngliche Übersicherung', *Zeitschrift für Wirtschafts- und Bankrecht* (WM) 2001, 1; Martin Schwab, 'Die Auswirkungen des Freigabe-Beschlusses auf den einfachen Eigentumsvorbehalt an Sachgesamtheiten', *Zeitschrift für Wirtschaftsrecht und Insolvenzpraxis* (ZiP) 2000, 609 *et seqq*; Friedemar Weber, 'Sicherheitenfreigabe und Regressbehinderung', WM 2001, 1299 *et seqq*.

[21] On this point, clearly: Wolfgang Wiegand in Julius von Staudinger, *Kommentar zum Bürgerlichen Gesetzbuch mit Einführungsgesetz und Nebengesetzen*, Vol III (Berlin: Sellier – de Gruyter, 14th ed 2004), Anhang zu §§ 929 *et seqq*, n 177; Füller (*supra* note 6), p 148.

[22] Ronald Dworkin, 'The Model of Rules I' in *Taking Rights Seriously* (Cambridge, MA: Harvard University Press 1997), pp 24 *et seqq*.

tion looses validity. A return to pure abstraction appears unrealistic. But, evidently, a (so-called) principle is to be doubted if it is rendered debatable by the judicature. This overview does not recommend abstraction for a European law. Some argue that abstraction reduces the information costs of the acquirer.[23] However, this is no reason to prefer this construction. A buyer who is not in good faith must not be protected. If the buyer is in good faith, it is more appropriate to solve the problems by *bona fide* acquisition. Summing up, the initial question can be answered partially: Abstraction does not justify a genuine property law due to the fact that this principle is abandoned in certain cases.

4. Separation versus unity

As mentioned above, the separation of the agreement *in rem* from the obligation is the most significant expression of a genuine property law. Even critics of abstraction think of this separation as a useful construction.[24] As advantages of separation over a consensus principle, the better legal explanation of a reservation of title and the sale of unspecified goods are often stressed. In German terms, a reservation of title (*Eigentumsvorbehalt*) consists of the obligation and the dilatory agreement *in rem*, which is completed when the purchasing price is paid completely. A consensus principle is not able to explain this and can be maintained only if the suspended transfer of goods is declared as an exception. Nevertheless, French law – as a paradigm of a consensus principle – acknowledges a reservation of title (*reserve de propriété*), which is adopted in the French Insolvency Act.[25] The *Cour de Cassation* simply justifies the conflict with the consensus principle with private autonomy.[26] As a consequence, the parties can abandon the *effet translativ* of the contract of sale.

English and Italian law know a much more elegant approach based on the consensus principle. The English law, as provided in the Sale of Goods Act,

---

[23] Krimphove (*supra* note 2), p 477 who recommends the German system for a European Law. However, the above-mentioned disadvantages of abstraction could not be avoided. Above all, this author confuses abstraction with separation.

[24] See Detlev Joost, 'Trennungsprinzip und Konsensprinzip', in *Festschrift für Wolfgang Zöllner* (Köln: Heymann 1998), 1161 *et seqq*.

[25] Loi no 80-335 of March 12th 1980; Art 121 loi no 85-98 = Loi du 25 janvier relative au redressment et á la liquidation des entreprises, *Journal official* 1985, p 1097. See, for more details: Demoures, 'La vente avec reserve de propriété et la loi du 12 mai 1980', *Revue trimestrielle du droit commercial* 1982, 33; F Pérochon, *Le reserve de propriété dans la vente de meubles corporels* (Paris: Litec 1988).

[26] Cour de Cassation, Octrobre 19, 1982, Bull 1982 No 321 «Néochome Bayer/Mécarex».

basically depends on the consensus principle but allows the parties an agreement to the contrary. Sec 19 (1) Sale of Goods Act[27] allows the seller to reserve some rights of disposal. Referring to this provision, the House of Lords judged that a reservation of title consist of two contracts. After the condition is fulfilled the mere contract alters into a sale of the good.[28] Italian Law delivers a comparable solution. The consensus principle is not obligatory and, thus, the parties can agree at which time the movables should be transferred. Besides that, the construction of a reservation of title is quite similar to the English and German law. A reservation of title (riserva di proprietà) is based on an obligation (vendita obligatoria) and the property is transferred when the purchaser pays the last rate (*condizione sospensiva*).[29]

The consensus principle fails in describing the legal consequences if an unspecified good is sold. In this case, the transfer of the property is impossible. The French courts revert to Art 1585 *Code Civil*, so the parties can agree that the property is transferred when the movable is delivered, but that is an unsatisfying method.[30] A modified consensus principle is able to handle this problem. Italian law provides that the property is transferred when the good is specified.[31] A more elegant solution is provided by the Sale of Goods Act. The property in specific or ascertained goods is transferred to the buyer at such time as the parties to the contract intend it to be transferred (Sec 17

---

[27] 'Where there is a contract for the sale of specific goods or where goods are subsequently appropriated to the contract, the seller may, by the terms of the contract or appropriation, reserve the right of disposal of the goods until certain conditions are fulfilled; and in such a case, notwithstanding the delivery of the goods to the buyer, or to the carrier or other bailee or custodier for the purpose of transmission to the buyer, the property in the goods does not pass to the buyer until the conditions imposed by the seller are fulfilled.'

[28] *Armour v Thyssen Edelstahlwerke AG* [1990] 3 All England Law Reports (All ER), 481; Len Sealy in: *Benjamin's Sale of Goods* (London: Sweet & Maxwell, 7th ed 2006), para 1-028.

[29] **Art 1523 Codice Civile:** Nella vendita a rate con riserva della proprietà, il compratore acquista la proprietà della cosa col pagamento dell'ultima rata di prezzo, ma assume i rischi dal momento della consegna. See also: Cass 3 aprile 1980, n 2167 Foro Italiano, Rep 1980; Lelio Barbiera, *Garanzia des credito e autonomia private* (Napoli: Jovene 1971), p 228; Tului, 'Osservationi sulla natura giuridica della vendita con riserva die proprietà', *Rivista di diritto commerciale* 1980 I, 335 et seqq.

[30] Cass Ci 30. 6. 1925, D 1927 I 29: Dalloz, Rép Dr Civ, Vente (Généralités), No 59. The French practice is at least inconsistent. See, for more details: Joost (*supra* note 24), pp 1161 *et seqq*; Stadler (*supra* note 12), pp 278 *et seqq*.

[31] **Art 1378 Codice Civile:** Nei contratti che hanno per oggetto il trasferimento di cose determinate solo nel genere, la proprietà si trasmette con l'individuazione fatta d'accordo tra le parti o nei modi da esse stability.

(1)). Sec 18 Sale of Goods Act establishes some rules for ascertaining intention. Rule No 5 (1) is to be emphasised: The property is transferred if the good is specified and the parties agree that the good corresponds to the agreement (*appropriation*).[32]

This overview shows that the disadvantages of the consensus principle can be avoided. The solution that English and Italian law provide is quite similar to the German separation into obligation and agreement *in rem*. But this is no reason to magnify the significance of a *separation principle*. Thinking in terms of legal separation can be useful but is not a legal principle. Most cases can be handled by a consensus principle, which is not only simple but also efficient. As long as the necessary exceptions are provided, the consensus principle is also suited to face different situations. It should be up to the parties to choose a certain system of transfer. To sum it up, the English and especially the Italian approach recommend themselves as a paradigm for European Law.

C. *Numerus clausus*

I. Legal aim

A *numerus clausus* limits the parties' freedom to design the content of certain rights. This is inconsistent with fundamental principles of Civil Law and, therefore, recquires justification. German law justifies this principle by the nature of property law and the right *in rem*. To cite it literally: 'Der Grundsatz der Vertragsfreiheit, welcher das Obligationenrecht beherrscht, hat für das Sachenrecht keine Geltung. Hier gilt der umgekehrte Grundsatz: Die Zahl der dinglichen Rechte ist notwendig eine geschlossene'.[33] Like separation, this principle should protect the contractants and other thirds. Thirds who are not involved should not be burdened with the effects of a contract. The historic background clarifies the motive behind this principle. In former times, the Old Prussian law, as provided in the *Allgemeines Landrecht*, acknowledged an *ius ad rem*. As a consequence, the parties could

---

[32] S 18 Rule 5: 'Where there is a contract for the sale of unascertained or future goods by description, and goods of that description and in a deliverable state are unconditionally appropriated to the contract, either by the seller with the assent of the buyer or by the buyer with the assent of the seller, the property in the goods then passes to the buyer; and the assent may be express or implied, and may be given either before or after the appropriation is made.'

[33] *Motive* (*supra* note 4), p 4. Literally translated: The axiom of the freedom of contract, which regulates the law of obligations, has no significance for property law. Therefore, the opposite axiom is valid: The number of rights *in rem* is listed compulsorily.

oblige persons who were not involved in the contract.³⁴ It cannot be doubted that such effects are incompatible with an efficient contract law. Thus, all European legal systems refuse contracts obliging thirds. This is based on fundamental principles of contract law. Obligations only constitute legal effects between the parties. *Prima facie*, it seems that the *numerus clausus* is not a term of property law but has its roots in the freedom of contract. From this point of view, the *numerus clausus* is just a mirror image: Only persons who consented can be affected by a contract – *volenti non fit iniuria*. Especially consumer protection law knows obligatory provisions,which try to contain the market power over the consumer. In other words, the question whether some provisions are obligatory is the decision of the legislator. This suggests a distinction between the sources of a legal position. Absolute rights, which may be claimed against anyone, have their roots in the law itself. Their existence is not the issue of a *numerus clausus*. Contractual rights can only bind the parties and a *numerus clausus* is not necessary in order to explain this.

A *numerus clausus* is known in the different systems of European civil law to diverging extents. The French *Code Civil* expressly provides a *numerus clausus* for mortgages.³⁵ On the other side, it is not clear whether this applies to servitudes as well.³⁶ The common law restricts the *numerus clausus* to mortgages, charges, pledges and liens.³⁷ Finally, German law extends the *numerus clausus* to a right *in rem*. A more detailed analysis will show that the problems arising can be solved by a different legal technique.

2. *Bona fide* rights protection

The legal point of origin is quite similar to abstraction: As long as thirds are not affected, the parties may contract within the limits of the law. To stress it again: This is a question of whether the law may be departed from by agreement between the parties. The situation becomes intrinsic if an en-

---

[34] More detailed: Wolfgang Wiegand, 'Numerus clausus der dinglichen Rechte. Zur Entstehung und Bedeutung eines zentralen zivilrechtlichen Dogmas', *Festschrift für Karl Kroeschell* (Frankfurt: Lang 1987), pp 623, 633.

[35] **Art 2115:** « L'hypothèque n'a lieu que das les cas et suivant les formes autorisés par la loi ».

[36] Art 686 *Code Civil* allows the parties, to determine the legal content of servitudes. Nevertheless, French practice reverts to the *ordre public interne* and, thus, establishes a *numerus clausus*. See: Gabriel Marty, Pierre Raynaud and Patrice Jourdain, Droit Civil - Les Biens (Paris: Dalloz, 2ⁿᵈ ed 1980), No 8.

[37] Michael Bridge, 'The English Law of Real Security', *European Review of Private Law* (ERPL), Vol IV (2002), 483, 486.

cumbered good is sold, which is illustrated by the law of trusts. American and English law allow an agreement between the beneficiary and the trustee not to dispose of the trust property. It is a breach of contract if the trustee sells the trust property none the less. However, the transferee is protected if he had neither actual nor constructive notice of the breach of contract.[38] This solution seems to be a fair balance between the interests of the beneficiary and the transferee. However, due to the *numerus clausus*, German law rejects such a balance. The trustee is considered as the proprietor, whose freedom to sell the trust property cannot be restricted, § 137 BGB.[39] Even if the transferee has actual notice, he is not obliged to the surrender of the property. The beneficiary just has claims for damages against the trustee.[40] The prevailing opinion in Germany substantiates this by means of the *numerus clausus*. Property cannot be divided in superior and inferior property.[41] But that is not the point. The German BGB does not define 'property'. It would be a more modern approach to define property as a bundle of rights emerging from a bipolar legal relationship. The exclusive right and the right of disposal are not necessarily linked.[42] Accepting this, there is no impediment to solving the conflicts in the Anglo-American way. Contractual restrictions or charges should only affect the transferee if he has actual or constructive notice of these facts.

3. Especially: Expectant rights

Some characterised § 137 BGB and the above-shown consequences as an over-reaction of the German Legislator.[43] Remembering this, it is astonishing – to put it mildly – how the dogmatic frame of expectant rights was developed. The German Supreme Court describes this right by a famous oxymoron: The expectant right is a consubstantial minus to property.[44] It is

---

[38] See: John Mowbray and Lynton Tucker, *Lewin on Trusts* (London: Sweet & Maxwell, 17th ed 2000), § 41 paras 102-126. S 1012 of the American Uniform Trust Code provides a quite similar solution. See also: Füller (*supra* note 6), pp 389 *et seqq*.

[39] BGHZ 11, 37, 43; BGH NJW 1968, 1471; Michael Gruber, 'Der Treuhandmissbrauch', AcP 202 (2002), 435, 438; Christian Armbrüster in *Münchener Kommentar zum Bürgerlichen Gesetzbuch*, Vol I (München: C H Beck, 5th ed 2006), § 137 n 18.

[40] BGH ZiP 1998, 830 = NJW-RR 1998, 1057.

[41] See, for example: Christian Berger, *Rechtsgeschäftliche Verfügungsbeschränkungen* (Tübingen: Mohr Siebeck 1998), p 156 *et seqq*.

[42] Füller (*supra* note 6), p 381, 390 *et seqq*.

[43] Wiegand (*supra* note 34), p 633 *et seqq*.

[44] 'Das Anwartschaftsrecht ein dem Eigentum wesensgleiches Minus', BGHZ 28, 16, 21; BGHZ 30, 374; BGHZ 35, 85, 89.

the secret of this judicature what would constitute something consubstantial or equivalent to the 'minus', which the property is subject to. Expectant rights arise in numerous cases and their common base is a transaction consisting of several phases,[45] the most popular example for an expectant right being the buyer's position in case of a reservation of title. The expectant right shall characterise a position of the future acquirer that cannot be destroyed by the seller. This right is to be transferred like property (§§ 929 – 931 BGB), it is protected like property (§ 823 BGB) and, finally, it allows its owner some remedies in cases of judicial execution and insolvency. Summing this up, this unwritten right grants property rights, which conflicts with the purpose of a *numerus clausus*. This contradiction was, on the one hand, realised and, on the other hand, concealed by the legislator.[46] Acknowledging such an expectant right, conflicts may arise as to how to balance this right with the rights of the proprietor. This question becomes obvious when a third damages a good which is sold under a reservation of title. Partially, the German doctrine gives the owner of the expectant right access to all claims.[47] But this solution creates a superior and an inferior property right and, as a consequence, gives rise to the condition that the legislator wanted to avoid.[48] The German Supreme Court solves the problem intrinsically and unsatisfyingly: Seller and buyer are classified as partial creditors (*Teilgläubiger*) whose claims for damages are limited respectively by the share of the good's asset value.[49] This solution privileges the seller who has a claim for damages against the third, whereas the buyer is still obliged to pay by instalments.[50] To avoid these consequences, the prevailing German doctrine classifies the seller and the buyer as co-creditors.[51] However,

---

[45] A suspended acquisition *in rem* normally creates expectant rights. For instance: reserve of title, chattel mortgage, certain cases of a register of a caution.
[46] *Protokolle der Kommission für die zweite Lesung des Entwurfs des Bürgerlichen Gesetzbuchs*, Vol I (Berlin: Guttentag 1897), p 181.
[47] Hans-Martin Müller-Laube, 'Die Konkurrenz zwischen Eigentümer und Anwartschaftsberechtigten um die Drittschutzansprüche', *Juristische Schulung* (JuS) 1993, 529, 534 *et seqq*.
[48] More detailed: Gerhard Wagner in *Münchener Kommentar zum Bürgerlichen Gesetzbuch*, Vol V (München: C H Beck, 4th ed 2004), § 823 n 146; Johannes Hager in Julius von Staudinger, *Kommentar zum Bürgerlichen Gesetzbuch mit Einführungsgesetz und Nebengesetzen*, Vol II (Berlin: Sellier - de Gruyter, 13th ed 1999), § 823 n B 155.
[49] BGHZ 55, 20, 32.
[50] Müller-Laube (*supra* note 47), p 532; Wagner in *Münchener Kommentar zum Bürgerlichen Gesetzbuch* (2004), § 823 n 146; Hager in Staudinger (*supra* note 48), § 823 n B 155.
[51] Wagner in *Münchener Kommentar zum Bürgerlichen Gesetzbuch* (2004), § 823 n 146; Hager in Staudinger (*supra* note 48), § 823 n B 155.

this is just as little convincing. Only the solution that grants the proprietor an exclusive claim for damages is consistent with the *numerus clausus*.[52]

This short survey shows that the *numerus clausus* ignores economic needs – a 'dishonest' method, if one simultaneously emphasises the significance of the *numerus clausus* as a leading principle for German property law. Indeed, the German development is not a good archetype for a European law. Even in Germany, some propose to give up the concept of expectant rights.[53] This seems to be an appropriate approach, since the other European systems of civil law do not know such a concept.

D. Publicity

I. Legal aim

Although publicity is a leading principle of (German) property law, its legal essence is often not clear. Generally speaking, publicity should visualise a legal state or relationship. German legislators consider publicity as a leading principle of property law. It is realised merely in the real property law: Every legal act, which constitutes, alters or cancels a right *in rem* has to adhere to the principle of publicity (§ 873 (1) BGB). The German Land Register has to document every transfer of property or charge on real estate. Thus, registration in the Land Register has constitutive effect. Such a system grants widespread publicity in respect of real estates, due to the fact that every contract referring to real estate has to be registered compulsorily.[54] It is mainly the Roman law family that does not provide for a comparable registration of land. It would go too far to describe all these models.

---

[52] Füller (*supra* note 6), p 96; Jens Thomas Füller in *Münchener Kommentar zum Bürgerlichen Gesetzbuch*, Vol VI (München: C H Beck, 4th ed 2004), § 951 n 6; Werner Flume, 'Die Rechtsstellung des Vorbehaltskäufers', AcP 161 (1962), p 385 (399).

[53] Eberhard Eichenhofer, 'Anwartschaftsrecht und Pendenztheorie – Zwei Deutungen von Vorbehaltseigentum', AcP 185 (1985), pp 162 *et seqq*; Matthias Armgardt, 'Die Pendenztheorie im Vergleich mit dem Anwartschaftsrecht, der Lehre von der Vorausverfügung und der Lehre vom besitzlosen Pfandrecht', AcP 206 (2006), 654.

[54] A compulsory registration of real estate is also provided for in Austrian (§ 4 Grundbuchsgesetz); Estonian; Hungarian, Latvian; Slovakian, Slovenian and the Czech Civil Law. English law seems to be more intricate. Traditionally, the Common law does not require registration. Real estate was transferred by conveyance ('signed, sealed and delivered deed'). However, the Land Registration Act 2002 provides for a 'title by registration'. It is the intention of the Law of Property Act 1925 to avoid unregistered property; see: Füller (*supra* note 6), p 258 *et seqq*.

Possession should be the vehicle of publicity in the law of movables. But a more detailed analysis shows that the position of the German legislator was hybrid. On the one hand, § 1006 (1) BGB provides a presumption in such way that possession *prima facie* indicates ownership. On the other hand, creditors may not rely on the presumption, that a possessor is always the proprietor.[55] Thus, the common opinion restricts the scope of § 1006 (1) BGB. First, this rule only encompasses the so-called *Eigenbesitzer* (proprietory possessor).[56] Second, § 1006 (1) BGB is only supposed to presume that the proprietory possessor has obtained possession and ownership simultaneously.[57] Other examples could be found to illustrate the diminishing role of possession to achieve publicity. At this point, the deliberations should be summed up:[58] One would ask too much from possession if it was supposed to grant publicity. As long as movables are not to be registered, the role of publicity in the law of chattels is small.

2. Tradition of goods

It is one of the common phrases in German law that possession of a movable should grant publicity. As a consequence, not only German law but also other European legal systems require the tradition of the sold good to accomplish the transfer of property. Such tradition can be effected in different ways. In German and Greek law, tradition is part of the separate agreement *in rem*.[59] Other legal systems have a similar approach but the distinction between obligation and agreement *in rem* is blurred. In fact, these legal systems have to supplement tradition with an intentional element, which has the function of assigning the delivered good to the contract. Only a few legal systems based on the consensus principle do not normally require tradition. Which system should be preferred? An adequate answer can be obtained by analysing the German development. The German BGB knows 4 different modes of tradition. The basic rule is provided in § 929 (1) – the tradition between the seller and the purchaser. If the purchaser already possesses the good, it is transferred by an agreement *in rem* (*brevi manu traditio* § 929 (2)). Even if the alienator should retain possession, he can transfer the good. In this case, the tradition can be replaced by an agreement between the parties that the acquirer is to be the 'indirect possessor' (*constitutum possessorium* – § 930 BGB). Finally, the proprietor may also sell a good if

---

[55] *Protokolle* (*supra* note 46), Vol III, p 3689 *et seq*.
[56] BGH NJW 1994, 939, 940; BGH NJW 1961, 777, 778; BGH WM 1964, 788.
[57] BGHZ 54, 319, 324; BGH NJW-RR 1989, 651; BGH NJW 1994, 939, 940.
[58] Detailed: Füller (*supra* note 6), p 272 *et seq*.
[59] §§ 929 – 931 BGB; Artt 1034, 1035, 976, 977 Greek Civil Code.

a third is the possessor of it. § 931 BGB rules that tradition can be replaced by the former proprietor assigning his title to the acquirer. These modes of tradition are extended and thus, withdrawn from law. It is sufficient if (1) the proprietor loses possession, (2) the acquirer obtains possession and (3) the former proprietor has initiated this change in possession. This wide definition allows the proprietor to transfer goods to a third, which neither the former proprietor possessed nor the acquirer will possess. In Germany, these constellations are summed up as *Geheißerwerb*, which can be translated as 'acquisition of ownership at someone's behest'. This short survey shows that tradition, in German law, lost its contours. It is obvious that economic exigencies induced this development in order to provide a tradition in the legal sense for various constellations in commerce. For example, a wholsaler-to-client sale at the retailer's request can hardly be subsumed under the terms of tradition, but is commonly used in the trade with mineral oil.

Examining the declining significance of tradition, the questions arises whether this development should be accepted from a dogmatic point of view. The common opinion in Germany sees tradition as an expression of publicity. Tradition is, so to speak, the visible characteristic of a transfer of goods. One the other hand, most authors admit that publicity is undermined in numerous cases, just to comply with economic needs. However, a more detailed analysis reveals that tradition does not have the function of ensuring the publicity of the transfer. The second commission for a German Civil Code described the function of tradition as indication: It has to ascertain the seriousness of the will of the parties that an agreement *in rem* is intended by them.[60] The historical background of this is to avoid simulated transactions. In respect of this, the function of tradition is not to ensure publicity but to manifest the will to transfer. If this can be established beyond doubt, tradition has no function.[61] Thus, tradition seems to be obsolete in this case. To return to the initial question: Publicity cannot be accepted as a leading principle of property law, since tradition does not express this principle. Besides that, in modern trade possession has a declining significance for alienating the property.

To sum it up, the simple consensus between the parties is sufficient for transferring goods.

3. Bona fide acquisition

Reflecting on the fact that possession has lost its function as a sign of publicity, the question arises how *bona fide* acquisition could be justified. The

---

[60] *Protokolle* (*supra* note 55), Vol III, p 147.
[61] Füller (*supra* note 6), pp 297-304.

German Supreme Court stresses that possession is the semblance for *bona fide* acquisition.[62] However, this is not convincing since possession has various meanings and lost its clear legal contours. In respect of this, German doctrine tries to justify *bona fide* acquisition by the power to provide possession (*Besitzverschaffungsmacht*).[63] But this is a *trompe de l'oeuil*: The alienator's promise to provide possession is, from this point of view, the basis of *bona fide* acquisition. The acquirer relies on the alienator's promise but not on the fact that the alienator is the possessor.

A legal rule concerning *bona fide* acquisition has to balance the transaction costs borne by the alienator, on the one hand, with the costs borne by the acquirer on the other hand. As a consequence, most European legal systems refuse *bona fide* acquisition when the good has been lost. Otherwise, the proprietor has to incur unbearable costs to avoid such an acquisition. Especially Italian and Swedish law do not go through the test of ascertaining the proportionality of transaction costs since they allow *bona fide* acquisition even if the good has been lost.[64] This seems to be too extensive. On the other hand, *bona fide* acquisition reduces the acquirer's/buyer's information costs. It is a question of law which costs should be reasonable. Generally refusing *bona fide* acquisition would be an enormous impediment to trade and would cause a macroeconomic deadweight loss.[65]

The wide definition of 'tradition' in German law delineated the requirements for *bona fide* acquisition. Not tradition is decisive, but the fact that the acquirer acquired possession disposed of by the former proprietor. This is the essence of the German practice, which acknowledges *bona fide* acquisition of ownership at someone's behest.[66] This judicature departs from the

---

[62] BGHZ 10, 81, 86; BGHZ 34, 153, 158; BGHZ 56, 123, 128.

[63] See, for example: Johannes Hager, *Verkehrsschutz durch redlichen Erwerb* (München: Beck 1990), 245 *et seqq*; Wiegand in Staudinger (*supra* note 21), § 932 n 20.

[64] These laws allow *bona fide* acquisition and do not envisage the fact that a good may be lost. **Art 1153 (1) Codice Civile:** Colui al quale sono alienati beni mobili da parte di chi non ne è proprietario, ne acquista la proprietà mediante il possesso, purché sia in buona fede al momento della consegna e sussista un titolo idoneo al trasferimento della proprietà. **LOV 1978-06-02 nr 37: Lov om godtroerverv av løsøre § 1.** 1.: Blir en løsøreting solgt av den som sitter med tingen og får mottakeren den overlevert til seg i god tro, hindrer det ikke rettsvinning etter avtalen at avhenderen mangler rett til å rå over tingen. Det samme gjelder ved annen avhending mot vederlag, hva enten det er til eie, bruk eller pant. (If a movable is sold by the possessor and transferred to a *bona fide* recipient, the fact that the alienator has no right to dispose does not hinder the acquisition. The same applies in other cases of alienation for remuneration.).

[65] The Portugese and the Czech law do not know a *bona fide* acquisition and, thus, are not an appropriate model for a European law.

[66] BGH NJW 1973, 141, 142; BGH NJW 1974, 1132.

legal point of origin, but is consistent due to the fact that tradition lost its contours. Newer German doctrine tries to establish § 934 BGB as the basis of *bona fide* acquisition.[67] But this seems to be a makeshift since § 934 BGB only covers certain cases of tradition. From the author's point of view, the development of the judicature forces one to rethink the legal framework of *bona fide* acquisition. The decisive point is that the *bona fide* acquirer obtained the possession, as was agreed. This model defines *bona fide* acquisition as immediate acquisitive prescription induced by contract. A similar approach can be found in Austrian and French law.[68]

E. Some recommendations

Some sceptics could have been irritated by the title of this article. As shown, a European property law should mainly learn from the mistakes made in German law. First, the thesis of a 'genuine property law' is unsubstantiated and its principles have been obliterated by the German courts. The most significant characteristic of German law – abstraction – cannot be recommended as a European model. It protects an acquirer who must not be protected. On the other hand, separation is a useful illustration to describe the transfer of goods under a reservation of title. Especially Italian law was influenced by this approach and was right in not emphasising separation as a leading principle and, of course, not as a justification for a 'genuine property law'. This study is not the place for extensively describing the fading significance of the *numerus clausus*.[69] The deliberations should be presented in a nutshell: *Inter partes*, the decisive point is not a *numerus clausus* but the question whether the law is mandatory. However, this is the legislator's decision and not a consequence of a right *in rem*. Thirds must not be bound by the contract's effects. This is also not a question of the *numerus clausus* but follows the axiom of private autonomy. Publicity lost its function in the German law of movables. Even the legislators recognized this over 100 years ago but were unable to break with partial traditions. The tradition of possession has no adequate function in modern economies. It should be sufficient if the buyer obtains possession or a third, as agreed. *Bone fide* acquisition should be understood as immediate acquisitive prescription. Especially the German experience could be useful, although the German practice departed from the legal framework.

---

[67] Hager (*supra* note 63). § 934 BGB: Gehört eine nach § 931 veräußerte Sache nicht dem Veräußerer, so wird der Erwerber … dann Eigentümer, wenn er den Besitz der Sache von dem Dritten erlangt …

[68] See for Austria: § 367 ABGB; for France: Art 2279 (1) *Code Civil*.

[69] The author did this elsewhere: Füller (*supra* note 6), pp 370-523.

It was the study's intention to show that a European law regulating the transfer of movables can learn from the other national legal systems. The national parties should not consider their law as legal dominion or culture. It is the collective wisdom of the national legal systems which ensures an efficient and reasonable European law. To put it in the first European *lingua franca*: *Fiat lex europaea traditionis!*

Intellectual Property Rights: 'Property' or 'Right'? The Application of the Transfer Rules to Intellectual Property

Mary-Rose McGuire

A. Introduction: Three questions

One of the issues this conference is dedicated to is, whether we should adhere to the traditional distinction between obligatory and property rights in the context of an emerging European private law. If I plead that we should, I will, of course, be obliged to provide an answer also to the second question: where should we draw the dividing line? Or with regard to intellectual property: on which side of the line does it stand? I would like to add a third question, namely: why should we deal with intellectual property rights in the present context at all? I will first provide a preliminary answer to all three questions and then explain in more detail, how I arrived at these conclusions.

The first question is, whether we need the traditional categories of '*property*' as opposed to '*rights*' in the context of transfer of movables. I believe the answer is that we do need these two categories, for two reasons. First, we need them, because the rules on transfer of title have to make allowance for the factual differences between the transfer modes. Second, we do need the distinction, because the rules on conflict of laws do rely on this traditional distinction. The classification is therefore necessary to determine the applicable law.

The second question is, where to draw the dividing line. As far as intellectual property is concerned, I believe that we may not just follow the traditional approach and simply determine the legal nature of intellectual property rights and then treat them accordingly, meaning either to apply the rules on assignment of rights or on transfer of movables. Rather, we should compare the mode of transfer of intellectual property rights to the mode of transfer for both '*property*' and '*rights*'.

The third question I would like to address is, why the issue of intellectual property rights is at all relevant for the present project of European rules on transfer of movables. The perhaps surprising answer is: although art 1:201 of the Draft Rules on Transfer of Movables (TOM)[1] explicitly excludes intellectual property rights, yet a quite important part of intellectual property rights is already within the scope of the *Draft Common Frame of Reference* (CFR),[2] namely by virtue of art 11:101 Principles of European Contract Law (PECL).[3] As this basic decision has already been taken, I believe, we should also find a convincing solution for the remaining categories of intellectual property rights.

B. The distinction between 'property' and 'right' in the context of intellectual property rights

I. What is the legal nature of intellectual property rights?

To determine the legal nature of intellectual property rights poses severe difficulties. Whether intellectual property should be categorised as *'property'* or as a *'right'* is the object of a long-standing controversy,[4] which – at least in Germany – can be traced back to the 1880s and is reflected by the discussion on the correct German term for intellectual property rights, which are either referred to as *'Geistiges Eigentum'* or as *'Immaterialgüterrechte'*;[5] the former putting the emphasis on *'property'*, the latter on *'right'*.

---

[1] As the relevant provisions are yet under discussion, this contribution is based on the draft of May 2005, available on http://sgecc.net/pages/en/texts/index.draft_articles.htm. For a more recent, but not yet final draft, cf http://www.uni-graz.at/bre1www/tom/. See also footnote 54, below, for the most relevant parts of the draft text.

[2] Cf European Commission, 'Communication – European Contract Law and the Revision of the *acquis*: the Way Forward' of 11 October 2004, COM(2004) 651 final; Christian von Bar, 'Working Together towards a Common Frame of Reference', *Juridica International* 2005, 17 *et seq*; Martin Schmidt-Kessel, 'Auf dem Weg zum gemeinsamen Referenzrahmen: Anmerkungen zur Mitteilung der Kommission vom 11. Oktober 2004', *European Community Private Law Review* (GPR) 2005, 2-8.

[3] Ole Lando and Hugh Beale (eds), *Principles of European Contract Law: Parts I & II* (The Hague: Kluwer Law International 1998); Ole Lando, Eric Clive, Andre Prum and Reinhard Zimmermann, *Principles of European Contract Law: Part III* (The Hague: Kluwer Law International 2001). The PECL will be adopted by the *Draft CFR* with minor modifications. However, the chapter on assignment of rights has in general remained unaltered and will form part of book 3 of the draft of the *Draft CFR*.

[4] Cf Ansgar Ohly, 'Geistiges Eigentum', *Juristenzeitung* (JZ) 2003, 545 *et seq*.

[5] Heinrich Hubmann and Horst-Peter Götting, *Gewerblicher Rechtsschutz*[7] (Munich: C H Beck, 7th ed 2002), 1. For a detailed analysis of this dispute see Volker Jänich, *Geistiges Eigentum – eine Komplementärerscheinung zum Sacheigentum?* (Tübingen: Mohr Siebeck 2002), 3, 169 *et seq*.

The discussion on this problem may – very briefly – be summarised as follows: The concept of proprietary rights in corporeal property is commonly described by two distinctive features: first, they confer an absolute right against any third party, and second, this absolute right can be exercised by means of factual control due to the corporeal nature of the goods. Obligatory rights are defined by the exact opposite: first, they grant a power only vis-à-vis a certain person and second, they are intangible and, therefore, the control of such rights poses significant difficulties. The distinction made between proprietary and obligatory rights by German doctrine is often summarised by the description that a proprietary right is a power of a person over a thing, whereas an obligatory right is a *vinculum iuris*, ie a legal relation between two persons.[6]

If we use these categories in order to classify intellectual property rights, the difficulty becomes quite obvious.[7] Intellectual property shares one distinctive feature with each of the traditional categories: Both proprietary rights and intellectual property rights confer an absolute power over a good. The common notion of intellectual property rights and obligatory rights is their intangible character. As both the absolute power and the incorporeal nature are held to be decisive for intellectual property rights, the comparison between intellectual property rights and the traditional categories shows a balance of similarities.

As this discussion on the true legal nature of intellectual property rights seems to lead to a dead end, we could instead resort to the black letter rules, containing the definition of '*property*' of the respective civil codes. For this purpose, we can, as an example, compare the Austrian and the German approach to intellectual property rights.

2. A short comparison between two different approaches: Austria and Germany

(a) Austria: Intellectual property rights as property in the meaning of § 285 ABGB

§ 285 Austrian Civil Code (ABGB) reads: '*Everything that differs from the person and serves for the use of men is called property in the legal sense.*' That this definition of property also covers '*rights*' is explicitly confirmed by § 298 ABGB, which states: '*Rights are considered as movable property* [...].' Accord-

---

[6] Karl Larenz and Manfred Wolf, *Bürgerliches Recht AT⁹* (Munich: C H Beck, 9th ed 2004), § 15 note 2, 38 *et seq*.
[7] See Fritz Schönherr, *Gewerblicher Rechtsschutz* (Wien: Manz 1982), p 10.

ingly, it is beyond doubt that intellectual property rights under the Austrian system qualify as 'property'.[8]

The consequence, of course, is that the transfer of intellectual property rights is subject to the provisions of § 380 ABGB. The valid transfer requires a title and a legal mode of acquisition. The first requirement of a valid title is a general requirement under the Austrian transfer system and, therefore, does not have to be further dealt with in the present context. The interesting part rather is the second requirement: the mode of acquisition.

The mode of acquisition under Austrian law generally requires factual delivery. As it is naturally impossible to physically deliver a right, § 427 ABGB provides that physical delivery may be replaced by symbolic delivery. Symbolic delivery with regard to intellectual property rights naturally is the entry into a register. From a systematic perspective the consistent treatment of the transfer of intellectual property under Austrian law would accordingly require mandatory registration as the transfer mode.

To validate this approach we may take a closer look at Austrian intellectual property law. The Austrian Patent Act may serve as an example. § 43 s 1 Austrian Patent Act obviously confirms the systematic approach. According to this provision a patent right may be acquired by legal transaction and the registration of the new owner into the patent registry.[9] It is acknowledged by doctrine that the registration under § 43 Patent Act is the mode of acquisition required by § 427 ABGB.[10]

However, if we look at the Austrian Trade Mark Protection Act, we clearly see that this systematic approach cannot be upheld. Its § 11 s 3 provides that as long as a change of ownership is not registered, it may not be pleaded before the Patent Office and all official notices may be served on the person still registered.[11] § 11 Trade Mark Protection Act thus provides for the situation that a transfer of ownership has already taken place, but is not yet reflected by the entry into the register. From this rule we can derive

---

[8] Thomas Klicka, in: Michael Schwimann (ed), *ABGB-Praxiskommentar*, Vol II³ (Vienna: LexisNexis ARD Orac, 3rd ed 2005), § 285 note 1; Bernhard Eccher, in: Helmut Koziol, Peter Bydlinski and Christian Bollenberger (eds), *Kurzkommentar zum ABGB* (Vienna: Springer 2005), § 285 note 1; Guido Kucsko, *Österreichisches und europäisches Wettbewerbs-, Marken-, Muster- und Patentrecht*⁴ (Vienna: Manz, 4th ed 1995), p 15.

[9] It reads: 'The patent, a pledge and other rights in rem in a patent are obtained and take effect vis-à-vis third parties by registration.'

[10] Leopold Friebel and Otto Pulitzer, *Österreichisches Patentrecht* (Cologne: Heymann, 2nd ed 1971), § 33 PatG note D.1.; Lothar Wiltschek, *Patentrecht* (Vienna: Manz 2006), § 43, p 74; see Fritz Schönherr (*supra* footnote 7), p 22.

[11] § 11 s 3 Austrian Trade Mark Protection Act provides: 'As long as the transfer has not been entered in the register, the trade mark cannot be invoked before the patent office and all notifications concerning the trade mark may be addressed to the person registered as proprietor.'

that the entry as such cannot be the mode of acquisition required under § 427 ABGB, but that registration – mainly for reasons of public interest – takes place after the transfer has become effective.[12] No other mode is provided for by the Trade Mark Protection Act, which could represent symbolic delivery under § 427 ABGB.

The predominant doctrine solves the apparent inconsistency, which follows from the concept of a merely declaratory trade mark register, by a recourse to §§ 1392 et seqq ABGB and applies the rules on assignment of rights.[13] These rules mainly address the problems, which arise in the course of the assignment of obligatory rights, the most prominent problem of course being the protection of the debtor of the obligation assigned.[14] It comes as no surprise that §§ 1392 et seqq ABGB do not provide for any specific concept for the transfer of absolute rights. The purpose of the recourse to §§ 1392 et seqq ABGB rather is to justify the consensual transfer of rights, an interpretation that may be exposed to criticism,[15] as § 1393 ABGB does clearly state that all transferable rights can be assigned, but it does not dispense from a mode of acquisition under § 427 ABGB.

Of course, this inconsistency may be attributed to the influence of European harmonisation as the recent version of § 11 Austrian Trade Mark Protection Act is the result of the implementation of the European Trade Mark Directive.[16] In fact, with regard to the transfer of trade marks almost the same wording may be found throughout Europe. But even if we attribute the inconsistency to European harmonisation a glance at copyright law displays a similar problem. According to the legal tradition of continental Europe, copyright as a matter of principle accrues independent of any regis-

---

[12] Egon Engin-Deniz, *Markenschutzgesetz* (Vienna: Verlag Österreich 2005), § 11 p 170.

[13] See Fritz Schönherr (*supra* footnote 7), p 22 *et seq*; see Egon Engin-Deniz (*supra* footnote 12), § 11 p 168 *et seq*; Hans-Georg Koppensteiner, *Österreichisches und Europäisches Wettbewerbsrecht*³ (Vienna: Orac, 3ʳᵈ ed 1997), § 42 note 4; Reinhard Schanda, 'Die Wirkung der Markenlizenz gegenüber Dritten', *Gewerblicher Rechtsschutz und Urheberrecht, Internationaler Teil* (GRUR Int) 1994, 283, 287; but see for a contrary opinion Peter Madl, 'Pfandrecht an Marken', *ecolex* 1991, 329 *et seq*.

[14] Cf § 1395 ABGB.

[15] Cf Brigitta Lurger, 'Die Zession im sachenrechtlichen Übertragungssystem des ABGB', in: Constanze Fischer-Czermak and Martin Schauer (eds), *Festschrift für Rudolf Welser zum 65. Geburtstag* (Vienna: Manz 2004), 639, 652 *et seq*.

[16] The First Directive 89/104/EEC of the Council, of 21 December 1988, to Approximate the Laws of the Member States Relating to Trade Marks (OJ EC 1989, L 40, p 1) was implemented into Austrian law by enactment of the new Austrian Trade Mark Protection Act 1999, BGBl I n 111/1999.

tration.[17] Accordingly, Austrian copyright law does not provide for a general copyright register.[18] Apart from practical problems, a registration requirement would also be contrary to the international standard laid down in art 5 s 2 Revised Berne Convention.[19] And it would be similarly contrary to this policy to require registration as a transfer mode for copyrights.

What can we learn from this short glance at Austrian IP-law? The determination of the legal nature of intellectual property rights according to the dichotomy '*property*' or '*right*' does not solve the problem of determining the proper transfer rules. The national legislator is no longer free to subject the transfer of intellectual property rights to the concepts of national private law. But even if he were free, a consistent approach may lead to results, which would hardly live up to economic realities. The mere idea of a mandatory register for copyrights is manifestly ill-suited. Quite obviously it is impossible to provide for a consistent transfer system based on constitutive registration for *all* types of intellectual property rights.

Naturally, it would be premature to take these inconsistencies of the current Austrian system as a sufficient proof that the same problems would arise on a European level. I therefore want to test my original assumption – that the recourse to the respective definition of '*property*' does not provide for a satisfactory solution – against the background of German law.

(b) Germany: A narrow concept of property – an absolute right in the meaning of § 413 BGB

A well-known characteristic of the German Civil Code (BGB) is its restrictive concept of property. According to § 90 BGB only corporeal things are considered property in the meaning of the Civil Code. The consequence this narrow concept has on the treatment of IP-rights is quite obvious. Intellectual property does not qualify as property under § 90 BGB and accordingly remains outside the scope of German property law and its rules on transfer of movables.[20] Instead § 413 BGB declares the rules on the assignment of obligatory rights provided for in §§ 398 *et seqq* BGB applicable to all

---

[17] See Haimo Schack, *Urheber- und Urhebervertragsrecht* (Tübingen: Mohr Siebeck, 3rd ed 2005), note 223 with further references.

[18] Cf § 14 Austrian Copyright Act.

[19] Berne Convention for the Protection of Literary and Artistic Works of September 9, 1886, as revised and amended in Paris on 24 July 1971.

[20] Cf §§ 903, 929 BGB; See Heinrich Hubmann and Horst-Peter Götting (*supra* footnote 5), p 86 *et seq*; Fritz Baur and Rolf Stürner, *Sachenrecht*[17] (Munich: C H Beck, 17th ed 1999), § 3.2.

other kinds of transferable rights.²¹ Similar to §§ 1392 et seqq of the Austrian ABGB, §§ 398 et seqq German Civil Code are designed to govern problems arising from the assignment of obligatory rights. With regard to other transferable rights its input is restricted to the declaration that transfer takes place by mere consensus.²²

The application of this concept to intellectual property leads to the imperative consequence that intellectual property rights are transferred by consensus alone and that a registration, if provided for at all, can only serve the purpose to publicise a transaction already validly concluded. We have already seen that regarding copyright this system is the only solution in line with international requirements. What about patent and trade mark law?

The German Patent Act does not even contain a general rule on the effect of the entry into the register, but merely states in § 30 that a change of the person, the name or the address of the applicant or proprietor of a patent will be registered on request and that the registered proprietor is deemed to be the recent proprietor for administrative purposes.²³ Even more explicit, § 27 German Trade Mark Act provides that the right vested in the transferee *may*, on application of a person concerned, be registered. It is therefore beyond doubt that the registration of a transfer has merely declaratory effect under German patent and trade mark law.²⁴

The rules appear to be consistent. Nothing seems to hinder the integration of intellectual property into the generally applicable rules of German private law. According to this approach, intellectual property rights are transferred by mere consensus of the parties, no act of publicity being required. As far as registration of intellectual property rights is provided for, it is of a merely declaratory character. Consequently, the register is afforded neither negative nor positive publicity. No third party may rely on the register and thus no room is left for a *bona fide* acquisition of intellectual property rights.²⁵ If the same right is assigned to different transferees, priority in time

---

[21] For details see Herbert Roth, in: *Münchener Kommentar zum BGB*, Vol IIa⁴ (Munich: C H Beck, 4ᵗʰ ed 2002), § 398 BGB note 2.

[22] Herbert Roth, in: *Münchener Kommentar zum BGB* (*supra* footnote 21), § 413 BGB note 1.

[23] Klaus Schwendy, in: Rudolf Busse (ed), *Patentgesetz*⁶ (Berlin: de Gruyter, 6ᵗʰ ed 2004), § 30 PatG note 32 *et seq*; Louis Pahlow, in: Friedrich Ekey and Diethelm Klippel, *Heidelberger Kommentar zum Markengesetz* (Heidelberg: C F Müller 2003), § 27 MarkenG note 5.

[24] Louis Pahlow, in: Friedrich Ekey and Diethelm Klippel (eds), *Heidelberger Kommentar zum Markengesetz* (*supra* footnote 23), § 27 MarkenG note 23; Alfred Keukenschrijver, in: Rudolf Busse (ed), *Patentgesetz*⁶ (*supra* footnote 23), § 15 PatG note 29.

[25] See Herbert Roth, in: *Münchener Kommentar zum BGB*, Vol IIa⁴ (Munich: C H Beck, 4ᵗʰ ed 2003), § 398 BGB note 27; Alfred Keukenschrijver, in: Rudolf Busse (ed), *Patentge-*

will be decisive,[26] whereas an entry into the register has relevance only as a means of evidence.

What is the main difference in comparison to the Austrian approach? First, German law applies the same rules to all categories of intellectual property rights. Intellectual property rights are consistently qualified as 'other transferable rights' under § 413 BGB and, accordingly, are transferred by mere consensus, an act of publicity not being required. As far as registration of intellectual property rights is provided for, it is of a merely declaratory character. The system is consistent and, at first glance, appears to be preferable as a model for European unification.

3. IP-rights in private international law

But before we recommend this approach for European harmonisation we have to take a look at a serious problem of the German approach. A problem, which is of growing importance: the present approach only works smoothly as long as we ignore the level of both international private law and European Community law.

German law does not provide for any rules in case intellectual property rights originate under a foreign legal system or under European Community law and the respective (foreign) system does require mandatory registration. Let us assume an Austrian patent is transferred according to German private law: According to §§ 398, 413 BGB the assignment would take effect immediately with the consensus of the parties, the validity would be independent of any registration. But what effect would contradicting acts of the transferor between agreement and registration have? May a third party rely on the publicity of the Austrian register? Is there room for *bona fide* acquisition?

Of course, all such problems arising from different concepts of foreign IP-laws may be solved by time-tested rules of conflict of laws. Yet, being honest, we know that conflict rules often do not actually solve the problem, but rather shift it to a different level. In fact, the same problem of categorisation reappears on the level of conflict of laws. It has led to the development of

---

setz⁶ (*supra* footnote 24), § 15 PatG note 37; see Klaus Schwendy, in: Rudolf Busse (ed), *Patentgesetz*⁶ (*supra* footnote 23), § 30 PatG note 32 *et seq*; Louis Pahlow, in: Friedrich Ekey and Diethelm Klippel (eds), *Heidelberger Kommentar zum Markengesetz* (*supra* footnote 23), § 27 MarkenG note 8.

[26] Louis Pahlow, in: Friedrich Ekey and Diethelm Klippel (eds), *Heidelberger Kommentar zum Markengesetz* (*supra* footnote 23), § 27 MarkenG note 8.

two dominant – but irreconcilable – approaches, how the law applicable to intellectual property rights should be determined.[27]

The starting point for the determination of the law applicable to intellectual property is the principle of territoriality, which is widely acknowledged.[28] It is based on the idea that intellectual property rights are not universal rights, but rather a bundle of national rights, because the protection is afforded by the individual states if and only if the requirements of the respective national statutes are met.[29] These diverse national laws accordingly govern the formation, content and limitation of the separate national intellectual property rights including whether or not the protection depends on any formalities such as application or registration. However, the width of the principle of territoriality in the context of *transfer* of intellectual property rights is a matter of controversy. Whereas some restrict its application to the question of transferability as such, others extend it also to govern requirements and effect of the transfer itself.

According to the so-called '*uniform approach*', the law applicable to the contract, the *lex contractus*, also governs the transfer of ownership, with the obvious consequence that the parties are free to choose such applicable law. The '*state of protection approach*', by contrast, holds that a distinction must be drawn between the obligation to transfer – which according to general rules is governed by the *lex contractus* – and the transfer, which according to the general rules would come within the scope of the *lex rei sitae*. As intellectual property rights are intangible the *lex rei sitae* has to be replaced by its equiva-

---

[27] For a detailed analysis of this controversy see Josef Drexl, in: *Münchener Kommentar zum BGB*, Vol X^4 (Munich: C H Beck, 4th ed 2006), Int ImmGR note 10 *et seq*.

[28] Karl-Heinz Fezer and Stefan Koos, in: *J von Staudingers Kommentar zum Bürgerlichen Gesetzbuch: IntWirtschR* (Berlin: Sellier – de Gruyter 2006), note 843 *et seq*; Dieter Martiny, in: *Münchener Kommentar zum BGB*, Vol XI^4 (Munich: C H Beck, 4th ed 2006), art 28 EGBGB note 386.

[29] German doctrine further distinguishes between the '*country of origin approach*' and the '*country of protection*' approach. The country of origin is the country where the protection was first afforded, whereas the country of protection is the state where protection is sought. However, this further distinction is only relevant in the context of copyright law, as the universalistic theory claims that copyright is a unitary right and not a bundle of national rights and thus at the moment the copyright comes into existence it will be protected throughout the world. Consequently, the state of origin is the country where the work of art was first published and may differ from the country where protection is afforded, see Marcus von Welser, in: Artur-Axel Wandtke and Winfried Bullinger (eds), *Praxiskommentar zum Urheberrecht*^{2} (Munich: C H Beck, 2nd ed 2006), Vor § 120 UrhG note 22 and Haimo Schack, *Urheber und Urhebervertragsrecht*^{2} (*supra* footnote 17), n 1147. This approach, however, has been criticised *inter alia* by Josef Drexl, in: *Münchener Kommentar zum BGB* (*supra* footnote 27), Int ImmGR note 684.

lent, the *lex loci protectionis*. The latter, of course, is the law of the country that the copyright originates from or the respective country of protection with regard to industrial property. The most important consequence of this approach is its mandatory nature. Unsurprisingly, the *'uniform approach'* – although not undisputed[30] – is the predominant view in Germany,[31] whereas the *'country of protection approach'* appears to be favoured in Austria.[32] The respective statutes on international private law mirror these different approaches.

In fact, German international private law – as the overwhelming majority of European conflict of laws statutes[33] – does not provide for any explicit rule on intellectual property rights. As intellectual property is not considered to be *'property'*, the application of art 46 EGBGB (*lex rei sitae*) is not even discussed. The predominant doctrine applies art 27 and art 30 s 1 of the Introductory Code to the BGB (EGBGB)[34] and thus the *lex contractus* both to the contract and the transfer.

By contrast, the Austrian International Private Law Act (IPRG) originally contained two separate provisions dealing with intellectual property rights. § 34 IPRG is based on the principle of territoriality and determines

---

[30] Cf Karl-Heinz Fezer and Stefan Koos, in: *J von Staudingers Kommentar zum Bürgerlichen Gesetzbuch: IntWirtschR* (*supra* footnote 28), note 905 with further references; Dieter Martiny, in: *Münchener Kommentar zum BGB* (*supra* footnote 28).

[31] Herbert Roth, in: *Münchener Kommentar zum BGB* (*supra* footnote 21), § 398 BGB note 16; Josef Drexl, in: *Münchener Kommentar zum BGB* (*supra* footnote 27), Int ImmGR note 14 *et seq*; Rainer Hausmann, in: *J von Staudingers Kommentar zum Bürgerlichen Gesetzbuch: Artt 27 et seqq EGBGB*, Vol VII (Berlin: Sellier-de Gruyter, 13th ed 2002), art 33 EGBGB note 33, 38; Axel Metzger, 'Transfer of Rights, License Agreements, and Conflict of Laws – Remarks on the Applicable Law on Transfer of IP Rights and License Agreements under the Rome Convention of 1980 and the Current ALI Draft' in: Jürgen Basedow *et al* (eds), *Intellectual Property in the Conflict of Laws* (Tübingen: Mohr-Siebeck 2005), p 61, 63 with further references. Paul Katzenberger, 'Urheberrechtsverträge im internationalen Privatrecht und Konventionsrecht', in: Friedrich-Karl Beier *et al* (eds), *Urhebervertragsrecht: Festgabe für Gerhard Schricker zum 60. Geburtstag* (Munich: C H Beck 1995), p 225, 248 *et seq*; OLG Frankfurt, *Gewerblicher Rechtsschutz und Urheberrecht* (GRUR) 1998, 141, 142 – Mackintosh Entwürfe; BGH GRUR Int 2003, 71, 71 – FROMMIA.

[32] See Michael Schwimann, in: Peter Rummel (ed), *Kommentar zum ABGB²*, Vol II (Vienna: Manz, 2nd ed 1992), § 34 IPRG note 1.

[33] Apparently apart from the Austrian IPRG (see below) only the Swiss Statute on International Private Law contains general rules on intellectual property rights (cf art 110 Swiss IPRG).

[34] Art 27 transforms art 3, art 33 s 1 transforms art 12 Rome Convention into German law.

that the statutes on intellectual property under which protection is sought are to be applied. In addition § 43 IPRG did provide a separate conflict of laws rule for *contracts* regarding intellectual property rights. Only § 43 IPRG has been repealed in the context of the implementation of the Rome Convention into Austrian law,[35] whereas § 34 IPRG has remained in place. The distinction drawn between the law governing formation, content and limitation of intellectual property rights on the one hand, and contracts regarding intellectual property rights on the other, already suggests that the rule on contracts is restricted to purely obligatory issues and does not cover the transfer requirements. The concept that the transfer requirements follow the *lex loci protectionis* and accordingly are mandatory[36] appears as the logical consequence of a system relying on a public register as a means of publicity. This can be easily demonstrated by resuming the example mentioned above: An Austrian patent is transferred on the basis of a contract for which German law has validly been chosen. If the choice of law extended to the transfer requirements this would result in the application of §§ 398, 413 BGB and the transfer would be effective prior to any (declaratory?) subsequent registration in the Austrian patent register. This consequence of course would be contrary to the concept of a register vested with publicity. It can only be prevented if § 34 IPRG – in line with the predominant legal doctrine[37] – is held to be decisive not only for the transferability, but also for the transfer requirements.

A closer look thus reveals that – although hardly ever made explicit – the underlying reason for this controversy again can be found in the difference of opinion concerning the legal nature of intellectual property rights. The uniform approach is based on the concept that intellectual property rights are *'rights'* and therefore applies the well-established conflict of laws rule for assignment of rights. The country of protection approach is based on the concept that intellectual property rights are *'property'* and considers the recourse to the *lex rei protectionis* as the equivalent to the *lex rei sitae* the most natural solution.

---

[35] Austria has implemented the Rome Convention in its original wording as a separate set of rules and repealed the rules with identical scope of application in the former IPRG 1979. The latter, therefore, now contains the rules on other than contractual issues and, with regard to contractual issues not covered by the Rome Convention, simply makes a reference to the Rome Convention, see the amendment Act of the IPRG, BGBl I 1998/119.

[36] Cf OGH ÖBl 1986, 73.

[37] See Hans-Georg Koppensteiner (*supra* footnote 13), § 37 note 4, 6; see Egon Engin-Deniz (*supra* footnote 12), § 11, p 167; OGH ÖBl 1979, 94 – Guhl; OGH ÖBl 1995, 230 – Wirobit.

4. The necessity of categorisation

Before moving on to the specific problem of Community IP-rights, I would like to summarise my preliminary conclusions on the first question regarding the necessity of the traditional categories. The statutes on intellectual property do, in general, not contain any detailed provisions on the private law aspects of intellectual property rights such as transfer of ownership. These questions must instead be solved by application of general private law rules. Many national codifications do draw a distinction between corporeal property and intangible rights; and so do the PECL and the *Draft CFR*. A similar approach may be found in international private law, both on a national and a European level.[38] As far as we have to rely on general private law to govern intellectual property rights we therefore have to fall back on the traditional categories in order to determine the applicable law and – similarly important – to allow for its application.

That intellectual property rights pose manifold difficult and unresolved questions with regard to the conflict of laws is a well-known issue and as such does not necessarily call for attention in the context of unification of substantive law. But why is this problem an issue for the present project? Or, to put it differently: where is the relevance of intellectual property rights for European private law?

C. The relevance of IP-rights for European private law

I. Reasons for the integration of IP-rights into the emerging European private law

The European Union has been very active in the field of intellectual property law within the last 10 to 15 years.[39] It has made great efforts to harmonise national intellectual property law,[40] for instance by the Trade Mark

---

[38] The Rome Convention is similarly based on this distinction as the scope of application is restricted to *contractual* issues and leaves the determination of the law applicable to rights *in rem* to the respective national international private law rules. The Draft Rome Regulation, in its recent proposal of the European Parliament Legal Affairs Committee (2005/0261[COD]), in general is similarly restricted to contractual issues, although it is supposed to introduce a new explicit provision on 'real property rights' (art 4a).

[39] For an overview see http://europa.eu/scadplus/leg/en/lvb/l26021.htm.

[40] In addition to the harmonisation efforts with regard to trade marks (see next note), models (Directive 98/71/EC of 13 October 1998 on the legal protection of designs; OJ 1998, L 298) and semiconductors (Directive 87/54/EEC of 16 December 1987, OJ 1987, L 24) the European Union has been particularly active with regard to copyright law is-

Directive[41] already mentioned, and – even more important in the present context – it has created genuine Community IP-rights. Today, Community trade marks[42] and Community designs[43] are already reality, a Community Patent Regulation is being drafted[44] – and even though it is yet unclear when the Community Patent Regulation will enter into force, due to the dispute on the language regime, the substantive rules have remained unchanged for years, providing a reliable basis for a closer examination.

These Community acts are a material and, from an economic perspective, important part of the private law *acquis communautaire*. If the purpose of the project of the *Draft CFR* is to provide a '*toolbox*' or infrastructure for the internal market,[45] it would – to say the least – be surprising to blind out an entire field of private law, an area, which is of major importance for the internal market and in fact has contributed substantially to the harmonisation of European private law. Its importance is reflected both by the number of transactions and the volume of the gross domestic product they account for.[46]

---

sues: Cf Directive 91/250/EEC of 14 May 1991 on the legal protection of computer programs, OJ 1991, L 122; Directive 92/100/EEC of 19 November 1992 on rental right and lending right and on certain rights related to copyright in the field of intellectual property, OJ EC 1992, L 346; Directive 96/9/EC of 11 March 1996 on the legal protection of databases, OJ EC 1996, L 77; Directive 93/98/EEC of 29 October 1993, harmonising the term of protection of copyright and certain related rights, OJ EC 1993, L 290; Directive 2001/29/EC of 22 May 2001 on the harmonisation of certain aspects of copyright and related rights in the information society, OJ EC 2001, L 167, 1.

[41] Council Directive 89/104/EEC of 21 December 1988 to approximate the laws of the Member States relating to trade marks, OJ EC 1989, L 40, 1.

[42] Council Regulation (EC) 40/94 of 20 December 1993 on the Community Trade Mark, OJ EC 1994, L 11, 1.

[43] Council Regulation (EC) 6/2002 of 12 December 2001 on Community designs, OJ EC 2002, L 3, 1.

[44] Proposal for a Council Regulation on the Community Patent of 15 May 2004, DOC 7119/04.

[45] Cf Hugh Beale, 'The Development of a European Private Law and the European Commission's Action Plan on Contract Law', *Juridica International* 10 (2005), 4, 14.

[46] According to recent statistics, the copyright industry contributed more than 1,200 billion Euro to the economy of the European Union, produced value added of 450 billion Euro, and employed 5.2 million persons in 2000. The total gross value added represented more than 5.3 % of the total value added for the 15 EU Member States (http://ec.europa.eu/internal_market/copyright/index_en.htm). Also see 'Study on evaluating the knowledge economy: what are patents actually worth? The value of patents for today's economy and society', Tender n° MARKT/2004/09/E, Lot 1 Final Report of

Taking a closer look at Community intellectual property rights, their distinctive feature is the grant of uniform and indivisible intellectual property rights for the entire Community. The current statistics of the Office for the Harmonisation of the Internal Market tell us that, although a relatively new development, already approximately 400.000 Community trade marks and 200.000 Community designs have been registered.[47]

The respective Community regulations are in their main parts mandatory and within their scope of application they therefore claim priority over any national IP-statutes. They provide for a comprehensive regime concerning formation, content and limitations of Community intellectual property rights. The regulations do also contain a number of specific rules on transfer, such as a distinction between obligatory and real agreement, a mandatory writing requirement and rules concerning the register.[48] Yet, they have not developed a complete system for legal transactions.[49] Again we have to take recourse to the provisions of general private law. The critical question of course is: recourse to which private law?

The most obvious solution for genuine Community intellectual property rights would be to apply genuine European private law. For obvious reasons, at present the only workable solution is to fall back on national private law. Accordingly, the Community regulations contain specific conflict of laws rules determining that Community IP-rights should be treated the same as national intellectual property rights of the respective Member State in which the registered proprietor has his seat.[50] And as a fall-back line they provide for the application of Spanish law as the law of the seat of the Office of Harmonisation for the Internal Market in Alicante.

For manifold reasons this conflict of laws rule is only a second-best solution: first, the rule does not determine the applicable law, but makes a reference to conflict of laws rules of the respective Member State, where the registered owner has his seat. This opens the possibility of a frequent change of the applicable law, which bears many disadvantages. Second, there is not even a uniform conflict of laws rule throughout Europe. Whether or not the transfer of IP-rights is within the ambit of art 12 Rome Convention on the

---

9 May 2005 and Lot 2 Final Report of 23 July 2006, both available on http://ec.europa.eu/internal_market/indprop/patent/index_en.htm#studies.

[47] The statistics on the Community IP-rights are available on http://oami.europa.eu/de/office/stats.htm.

[48] See artt 17-23 Community Trade Mark Regulation; artt 28-33 Community Design Regulation; artt 15-24 Draft Community Patent Regulation.

[49] Cf Mary-Rose McGuire, 'Die Funktion des Registers für die rechtsgeschäftliche Übertragung von Gemeinschaftsmarken', GRUR 2008 (in print).

[50] Art 16 Community Trade Mark Directive; art 27 Community Design Regulation; art 14 Draft Community Patent Regulation.

Law Applicable to *Contractual* Obligations is a matter of dispute,[51] and again depends on the preliminary categorisation as '*property*' or '*right*'. Third, a closer look at the Community IP-regulations shows that they do establish a whole bundle of criteria for the transfer of such IP-rights. As the German example displays, Member States' law may not be adequately adapted to these rules. The current legal situation thus is hardly satisfactory.

2. Possible solutions to react to the need for private law rules governing the transfer of IP-rights

There are three obvious solutions to remedy this lack of private law rules regarding intellectual property rights. The first possibility would be to set up a comprehensive set of rules for transactions of intellectual property rights. But this approach is hardly convincing. The transfer of intellectual property rights, in general, causes the same problems that may arise at the transfer of any other asset, such as a lack of authority of the transferor. There is no apparent justification to treat such problems any differently from the general private law concepts. A glance at the current national laws shows that no Member State provides for a comprehensive code on IP-law, but all apply their general private law. As, generally speaking, the Member States experience appears to be satisfactory, there is no indication that we should follow a different approach on a Community level. In fact, it seems that the current tendency rather is the opposite, namely to strengthen the coherence between special rules on intellectual property rights and the general private law rules. The recent Enforcement Directive containing rules on damages, unjustified enrichment and disclosure duties[52] may serve as an example.

A second possibility would be to determine the legal nature of intellectual property rights on a Community level and leave the rest to national laws. It may sound inviting to solve the problem of categorisation by a simple definition, without further interfering with the Member States' law. The British Trade Marks Act[53] could serve as an example for this approach: its art 22 explicitly defines that trade marks are '*personal property*' or with regard to Scotland '*moveable property*' and this definition, clearly, predetermines the

---

[51] Whereas Mario Giuliano and Paul Lagarde, *Report on the Rome Convention*, OJ EC 1980, C 282, 1 art 1 note 2, explicitly state that property rights and IP-rights are not covered by the provisions, the majority of German doctrine seems to apply art 12 Rome convention to the transfer of IP-rights, see Axel Metzger in: Jürgen Basedow *et al* (eds), *Intellectual Property in the Conflict of Laws* (*supra* footnote 31), 61, 63 with further references.

[52] Directive 2004/48/EC of the European Parliament and of the Council of 29 April 2004 on the enforcement of intellectual property rights, OJ EC 2004, L 195.

[53] Trade Marks Act 1994 as amended 5th May 2004, S I 2004/946.

application of general private law. However, it must be questioned, whether such an approach would be workable. It may solve the problem of categorisation on a primary level, but does not address the problem that the laws of some Member States may not provide for adequate private law rules for the respective category. Yet, it must be admitted that in comparison to the current situation even a mere definition may be helpful, as it would at least on the level of international private law trigger a uniform categorisation throughout the European Union.

The third possibility is to return to the well-tested and generally accepted principle of territoriality on a Community level. With respect to intellectual property rights it naturally would be the most promising solution to apply the same legal order to both genuine IP-related questions such as formation, content and limitation of intellectual property rights and to all other private law issues, including transfer. On a European level this could render the problematic conflict of laws rule for Community IP-rights superfluous. Of course, this solution relies heavily on the existence of a genuine European private law applicable to intellectual property rights. I will therefore now turn to examine whether the present drafts provide for a possible solution.

3. The application of the Principles of European Law (PEL) as a possible solution

The present version of the *Draft CFR* does not contain any rules explicitly addressing intellectual property rights. The transfer of intellectual property rights accordingly may only fall within the ambit of the project, if they either come within the scope of the rules on assignment of rights or if the general rules on transfer of movables are applicable.

Turning first to chapter 11 PECL on assignment of rights we find that art 11:101, according to its subsection 1, is applicable to obligatory rights. Subsection 2 then widens the scope of application to other transferable claims. As intellectual property rights qualify as transferable there is no apparent reason why they should not come within the scope of art 11:101 (2) PECL. The rule actually bears strong resemblance to the German model. This already indicates that PECL are not primarily designed to govern the transfer of absolute rights. However, PECL do provide rules on the time when such an assignment takes effect (art 11:103 (1)) and which of two successive assignments may claim priority (art 11:104).

The main concern regarding the application of chapter 11 PECL to intellectual property rights is art 11:101 (3). It excludes such rights '*where, under the law otherwise applicable, a transfer must be by entry in a register*'. No further explanation is given for this exception, but it may be assumed that the PECL did not want to interfere with any rules on registration and evade resulting conflicts. This underlying *ratio* would also apply to intellectual property rights as far as validity of transfer is dependent on registration. Applying this rule to Community IP-rights, thus PECL suggest to distinguish between intellectual property rights where a transfer must be by entry into the register and such that – if at all – provide for a merely declaratory registration.

The well-established dichotomy between property rights and obligatory rights further suggests that as far as intellectual property rights are excluded from the application of PECL they would be governed by the rules on the transfer of movables. A glance at art 1:201 TOM,[54] however, displays that intellectual property rights are explicitly excluded from the scope of application. Thus, even if Community IP-regulations followed the British example and explicitly defined the legal nature, they would yet remain outside the scope of TOM.

What do we gain from this analysis? Based on the two previous assumptions, namely, that first, the present conflict of laws rule is inadequate and that it would be preferable to apply genuine European private law to the transfer of Community IP-rights and that second, it is in the interest of a consistent development of European private law to integrate IP-rights, the – admittedly provocative – question would be: which of the two provisions is at fault – art 11:101 (3) PECL or art 1:201 TOM? This of course again is a question of the proper category.

D. Criteria for the categorisation of IP-rights

The comparison of the Austrian and German transfer system – although very brief – has demonstrated that it is unwise to allocate intellectual property rights, as a matter of principle, to one of the two categories, for mandatory European and international rules may either lead to inconsistencies or leave the rule fragmentary. Applying general private law to IP-rights rather requires that there is a high degree of similarity between the respective IP-rights and the assets for which the rules were originally designed. This similarity assures that the application can solve the problems arising in practice.

The most important difference in practice between the transfer system on movables and the assignment of rights is that assignment merely requires consensus of the parties and in general takes place immediately, whereas the transfer of movables generally consists of two steps, namely real agreement and delivery, which may be, but not necessarily are, performed simultaneously.

---

[54] It reads: '(1) 'Movables' in the sense of this book are corporeal movable assets, including animals, liquids and gases. […]. (2) In particular, this book does not apply to […] (c) intellectual or industrial property rights or other intangible assets; […].'

Whether transfer consists of one or two steps has two important consequences: first, a transfer of movables consisting of two distinct steps offers the possibility that there is a time span between those two steps. The transferor, in the meantime, can make contrary dispositions, the most prominent example being the double sale. Therefore, the applicable rules have to decide which disposition shall take priority. Second, the common requirement of delivery for transfer of movables is an act of publicity, which fosters legal certainty, but also has the potential to evoke reliance of third parties. The protection of this reliance is a necessary requirement of any kind of *bona fide* acquisition.

This analysis leads to the following conclusion: The application of the rules on transfer of movables does not necessarily require that the assets transferred are corporeal, but only that they provide for similar publicity. The application of the rules on assignment of rights, by contrast, requires that the transfer consist of merely one step and lacks publicity.

Applying this criterion to Community IP-rights we have to look at the function of the respective register. Only mandatory registration can qualify as a second step and vest the register with a form of publicity that may evoke third party reliance.

Taking a closer look at the Community regulations, we may find that none of them explicitly states whether or not the registration is constitutive or declaratory. However, there are two types of rules that do give us a strong indication on the function of the register. Taking the Community Trade Mark Regulation (CTMR) as an example we see that art 17 s 6 provides that '*as long as the transfer has not been entered in the Register, the successor in title may not invoke the rights arising from the registration of the Community trade mark.*' As all rights in a Community trade mark, according to art 6 CTMR Regulation, stem from registration, legal doctrine holds that the acquirer cannot exercise *any* rights before registration.[55] With regard to third party effect art 23 s 1 CTMR in addition clarifies that a transfer, grant of a right *in rem* or of a license concerning a Community trade mark '*shall only have effects vis-à-vis third parties in all the Member States after entry in the Register.*'

If we thus compare the transfer system of the Community trade mark with the above mentioned models of assignment of rights on the one hand, and transfer of movables on the other, it becomes quite obvious that the transfer system more closely resembles the second model: The registration is a necessary requirement for the full enjoyment of the rights conferred and third party reliance is protected. Similar rules are contained in the Draft Community Patent Regulation. Even though many details are still a matter of dis-

---

[55] Günther Eisenführ and Detlef Schennen, *Gemeinschaftsmarkenverordnung* (Cologne: Heymann 2003), art 17 note 29; Karl-Heinz Fezer, *Markenrecht*[3] (Munich: C H Beck, 3rd ed 2001) Introduction note 117 *et seq.*

cussion, it therefore can be stated that the registration of Community trade marks and Community patents is constitutive:[56] Third parties may rely on the status of the register, a *bona fide* acquisition with freedom from encumbrances is provided for. Things are more complicated with regard to Community designs, as the Community Design Regulation provides for two different types of Community designs, registered and unregistered designs. The rules on registered designs closely follow the model of the CTMR and it may well be argued that the registration of registered Community designs is similarly constitutive. With regard to unregistered Community designs the Community Design Regulation, apart from the general rule on transferability, hardly contains any rules on transfer. Consequently, the transfer takes place independent of any registration. As there is no act of publicity, third party reliance will not be protected.

The logical conclusion would be to transfer unregistered Community designs according to chapter 11 PECL. The same could be said for copyrights if the European Union ever decides to provide for a genuine European copyright. By contrast, all registrable Community IP-rights, *ie* Community trade mark, Community patent and registered Community designs, should be transferred according to the rules on transfer of movables.[57] This distinction is in line with the exclusion of registrable rights we find in art 11:101 (3) PECL.

---

[56] Legal doctrine on this issue is less clear as the predominant view claims that the registration is not constitutive, but due to the overwhelming importance of the registration it would be similarly misleading to call it declaratory. One of the leading German commentaries on the Community Trade Mark, Günther Eisenführ and Detlef Schennen, *Gemeinschaftsmarkenverordnung* (*supra* footnote 55), literally states: 'Der Zwischenzeitraum bis zur Eintragung schafft [...] eine Grauzone, in der weder der alte noch der neue Inhaber angemessen vom Schutz der Gemeinschaftsmarke profitieren können' (art 17 note 30). This concept of a 'grey area' – supposed to provide a rule for the time between the agreement to transfer and registration – is hardly convincing and poses many difficulties. As registration is of major importance and the register is vested with publicity it is obvious that the transfer system consists of two distinct steps and can be consistently explained with a constitutive registration requirement. For details see Mary-Rose McGuire (*supra* footnote 49).

[57] The same test of course can be applied to national intellectual property rights, and with respect to Austrian and German law mentioned above would lead to the conclusion that all German intellectual property rights should be transferred according to Chapter 11 PECL. The same holds true for Austrian copyrights and trade marks, as no constitutive registration is provided for the transfer of such rights. By contrast, Austrian patents should be transferred according to the rules on the transfer of movables to allow for the effects of the transfer to be dependent on the registration provided for in § 43 Patent Act.

Of course, a closer look at the draft rules on Transfer of Movables may prove that not all the provisions are apt for the transfer of intellectual property rights. However, we could also think of a solution similar to the caveat in art 11:101 (2) PECL, which calls for application *'except where otherwise stated or the context otherwise requires'*. The integration of Community IP-rights into the *Draft CFR* would only require minor changes: a clarification in chapter 11 PECL that it covers intellectual property rights, unless registration is mandatory, and a slight amendment of the scope of application of art 1:201 TOM.

E. Conclusions

The starting point was whether we need the traditional distinction between property rights and obligatory rights. I believe the traditional categories are necessary: First, to allow for factual differences between the transfer modes, and second, to determine the applicable conflict of laws rules and the applicable private law rules both on a European and a national level.

With regard to the second question, the analysis of intellectual property law, of course, cannot provide an answer to the question, where we should draw the dividing line with respect to general private law. But the analysis does show that we should not rely on the determination of the legal nature of intellectual property rights, but instead should focus on the criterion whether the validity of a transfer depends on an entry into the respective register and provides for a degree of publicity comparable to actual delivery, as provided for by the rules on transfer of title. We should therefore determine the rules best suitable according to the degree of similarity of the transfer mode for intellectual property rights with the traditional categories.

This approach at the same time enables us to distinguish between different kinds of intellectual property rights and to integrate them into the emerging European private law, for it clearly indicates that we do not need a separate regime for the transfer of intellectual property rights.

With regard to the third question, I believe that there are three valid arguments, why the emerging European private law should include transfer rules for intellectual property rights: The first is the imminent importance of intellectual property rights for the internal market; the second, the obvious need to supplement the present Community IP-rights by an adequate and uniform set of private law rules governing their transfer throughout the European Union. The third argument is that the current *Draft CFR*, by its adoption of chapter 11 PECL, literally only contains a half-and-half solution including copyrights and unregistered Community designs, but excluding registered Community designs, Community trade marks and Community patents.

Finally, I may add that the integration of intellectual property rights into the present draft would only require minor amendments to the scope of application and perhaps a proviso that the rules shall only apply '*as far as not stated otherwise or the context so requires*'. All rules necessary to deal with the specific features of intellectual property rights, by contrast, are to be left to the regulations on IP-law, which according to the rule of *lex specialis* claim priority over the general European private law. The examples of the Community trade mark and the draft Community patent show that the European legislator is aware of the necessity to regulate all specific questions within the IP-regulations and as far as Community trade mark, patent and design are concerned has already done so.

Unification in the Field of Property Law from the Perspective of European Law

José Caramelo-Gomes

A. European integration and private law, background

The European Commission and the European Parliament, back in 1998, called for reports about the 'European Civil Code'. The European Community Council stressed its interest in this project in 1999 at the European Council of Tampere. This concern was not at all new, as in 1989 the European Parliament adopted a Resolution[1] aiming that a start be made on the necessary preparatory work for the drawing up of a Common European Code of Private Law. Later, in 1994, it adopted a new resolution, asking the Lando Commission to draft a set of Principles of European Contract Law (hereinafter PECL).[2] This commission embodied the first effort aiming to harmonise civil law within the EC and had been created in 1982 by Ole Lando. It was a non-governmental body of lawyers and academics and it started by drafting a set of Principles of European Contract Law (PECL).

The beliefs of the European Community institutions are also clear from official documents other than the above-mentioned ones. The European Commission has consistently, but carefully, included in some of its official documents the statement that the differences, in private law, property law and contract law included, in the member states are an obstacle to the European integration and some sort of harmonisation is desirable.[3]

Moreover, the EC Commission has, in a way, included these views in the proposals for the First Council Directive to approximate the laws of the

---

[1] Resolution of 26 May 1989 on action to bring into line the private law of the Memberstates, OJ C 158, 28-6-1989, p 400.

[2] OJ C 205, 25-7-1994, p 518.

[3] See, for instance, the European Commission's 1996 commissioned 'Study on the application of Value Added Tax to the property sector', N XXI/96/CB-3021, p 3, available at http://ec.europa.eu/taxation_customs/resources/documents/report_vat_immovable_prop erty.pdf and the Commission Communications about Private Law in the EC: Communication of 12 February 2003, A more coherent European contract law. An Action Plan, COM(2003) 68 final; Communication of 11 October 2004, European Contract Law and the revision of the *acquis*: the way forward, COM(2004) 651 final.

Member states relating to trade marks (89/104/EEC),[4] Regulation (EC) No 40/94 on the Community trade mark,[5] Regulation (EEC) No 2081/92 on the protection of geographical indications and designations of origin for agricultural products and foodstuffs,[6] Directives 85/374/EEC (product liability),[7] 85/577/EEC (contracts negotiated away from business premises),[8] 87/102/EEC (consumer credit),[9] 93/13/EEC (unfair terms in consumer contracts),[10] 99/44/EC of the European Parliament and of the Council of 25 May 1999 on certain aspects of the sale of consumer goods and associated guarantees,[11] Council Directive 90/314/EEC of 13 June 1990 on package travel, package holidays and package tours,[12] Directive 97/7/EC of the European Parliament and of the Council of 20 May 1997 on the protection of consumers in respect of distance contracts,[13] Council Directive 86/653/EEC of 18 December 1986 on the co-ordination of the laws of the Member-states relating to self-employed commercial agents,[14] Directive 2000/31/EC of the European Parliament and of the Council of 8 June 2000 on certain legal aspects of information society services, in particular electronic commerce, in the Internal Market,[15] Directive 2000/35/EC of the European Parliament and of the Council of 29 June 2000 on combating late payment in commercial transactions,[16] Directive 97/5/EC of the European Parliament and the Council of 27 January 1997 on cross-border credit transfers[17] and 94/47/EEC (time-sharing).[18]

The European Parliament and the European Council appear to adopt the EC Commission's view, as all of those proposals were adopted and became secondary legislation. The European Parliament in particular is keen on promoting harmonisation in Private Law in the EC. Its Resolution of 16 March 2000 concerning the Commission's work programme 2000[19] confirms

---

[4] COM/80/635 FINAL – SYN 17, OJ C 351, 31-12-1980, p 1.
[5] COM/84/470 FINAL, OJ C 230, 31-8-1984, p 1.
[6] COM/92/32 FINAL, OJ C 69, 18-3-1992.
[7] COM/76/372 FINAL, OJ C 241, 14-10-1976, p 9.
[8] COM/76/544 FINAL, OJ C 22, 29-1-1977, p 6.
[9] COM/79/69 FINAL, OJ C 80, 27-3-1979, p 4.
[10] COM/90/322 FINAL – SYN 285, OJ C 243, 28-9-1990, p 2.
[11] COM/95/0520 FINAL – COD 96/0161, OJ C 307, 16-10-1996, p 8.
[12] COM/88/41 FINAL – SYN 122, OJ C 96, 12-4-1988, p 5.
[13] COM/92/11 FINAL – SYN 411, OJ C 156, 23-6-1992, p 14.
[14] COM/76/670 FINAL, OJ C 13, 18-1-1977, p 2.
[15] COM/98/0586 FINAL – COD 98/0325, OJ C 30, 5-2-1999, p 4.
[16] COM/98/0126 FINAL – COD 98/0099, OJ C 168, 3-6-1998, p 13.
[17] COM/94.436 FINAL – COD 94/0242, OJ C 360, 17-12-1994, p 13.
[18] COM/92/220 FINAL – SYN 419, OJ C 222, 29-8-1992, p 5.
[19] OJ C 377, of 29-12-2000, p 323.

that greater harmonisation of civil law has become essential in the internal market. The resolution of 15 November 2001 on the approximation of the civil and commercial law of the Member states[20] proclaimed that the approximation of private law is a political goal connected to the establishment of a European area of freedom, security and justice, that the internal market will only be genuinely complete when consumers can also take full advantage of the benefits it offers and regrets the fact that the Commission has restricted its communication to private contract law, although under the terms of the mandate of the European Council of Tampere it could have broadened its scope. This resolution also takes the view that directives which are not aimed at complete harmonisation but pursue specific objectives such as consumer protection, product safety or product liability, should continue to be drafted not on the basis of any particular legal system, so that they can readily be incorporated into the various national legal systems. Last, but not least, the resolution proposes the creation of a 'European Legal Institute'.

The First Council Directive to approximate the laws of the Member-states relating to trade marks (89/104/EEC), the Regulation (EC) No 40/94 on the Community trade mark, the Regulation (EEC) No 2081/92 on the protection of geographical indications and designations of origin for agricultural products and foodstuffs and Directive 94/47/EC of The European Parliament and The Council of 26 October 1994 are particularly important for this subject, as all of them are somehow related to the property legal framework – the latter directly with a right over immovable property and the others with incorporeal property. The fact is that the exclusion in article 295 EC[21] does not specify whether it concerns particular species of property, so one must assume that it includes property in general and thus incorporeal property must be considered to fall within its scope.

The Timeshare Directive is probably the best example of the EC's beliefs. Its objective is to harmonise national legislation concerning the acquisition of immovable property on a timeshare basis. Recital 1 includes the following statement:

'*1. Whereas the disparities between national legislations on contracts relating to the purchase of the right to use one or more immovable properties on a timeshare basis are likely to create barriers to the proper operation of the internal market and distortions of competition and lead to the compartmentalization of national markets;*'

Recital 3 is as follows: '*3. Whereas the legal nature of the rights which are the subject of the contracts covered by this Directive varies considerably from one*

---

[20] OJ C 140E of 13-6-2002, p 538.
[21] Article 295 EC: This Treaty shall in no way prejudice the rules in Member States governing the system of property ownership.

Member-state to another; whereas reference should therefore be made in summary form to those variations, giving a sufficiently broad definition of such contracts, without thereby implying harmonization within the Community of the legal nature of the rights in question;'

Article 1 establishes: *'The purpose of this Directive shall be to approximate the laws, regulations and administrative provisions of the Member-states on the protection of purchasers in respect of certain aspects of contracts relating directly or indirectly to the purchase of the right to use one or more immovable properties on a timeshare basis.'*

This Directive deals only with some aspects of contracts but the significant aspect of it is that those contracts relate to what is obviously a right over an immovable thing and therefore relate to the national property law excluded from the EC competence in article 295 EC.

The Brussels European Council in 2004[22] adopted the Hague Programme towards a Common Frame of Reference (CFR) in line with European Commission's 2003 Communication,[23] which states *'(…) obstacles and disincentives to cross-border transactions deriving directly or indirectly from divergent national contract laws or from the legal complexity of these divergences, which are liable to prohibit, impede or otherwise render less advantageous such transactions.'* The proposed solution is the adoption of the CFR as legislative toolkit, waiving, for now, the idea of a European Civil Code:[24] *'Although it is premature to speculate about the possible outcome of the reflection, it is important to explain that it is neither the Commission's intention to propose a "European civil code" which would harmonise contract laws of Member States (…).'*

This, however, is not a unified point of view, as the European Parliament seems to maintain its original goal. In fact, in its resolution on *European contract law and the revision of the acquis: the way forward*[25] it *'Reiterates its conviction, expressed in its resolutions of 26 May 1989, 6 May 1994, 15 November 2001 and 2 September 2003, that a uniform internal market cannot be fully functional without further steps towards the harmonisation of civil law'*.

The latest document from the European Commission, the 'Green paper on the review of the consumer acquis',[26] is not conclusive in this matter, but,

---

[22] Presidency conclusions, Annex, available at http://consilium.eu.int/uedocs/cmsUpload/EU_4.5-11.pdf

[23] Communication of 12 February 2003 (*supra* note 3), at § 25.

[24] See the 2004 Communication of the European Commission (*supra* note 3), at p 8. Instead, this Communication promotes a less far-reaching European contract law initiative, such as a Common Frame of Reference (CFR), Standard Terms and Conditions (STC), or other non-sector specific instruments like an optional instrument.

[25] 2005/2022(INI).

[26] Green paper on the review of the consumer acquis, COM(2006) 744 final of 8 February 2007

in our view, there are no signs of a major shift in the European Commission's understanding of the way to develop European Private Law. In fact, the Green paper, although limiting its scope to the consumer acquis, acknowledging the need for some deeper and better intergration of consumer law in the EU, implictly shows the EC's preference for a horizontal rather than specific instrument. This, in our view, implies a greater European integration in the field of private law, namely, consumer law and fits, quite nicely, into the European Union's fifty year old successive approach technique: to attain, as profoundly as possible, integration by successive small steps (the first example of which was the creation of ECSC – European Community of Steel and Coal, then the European Economic Community and so on). In fact, this technique has, in recent developments, lead the European Commission to drop vertical regulations adopted under Regulation 17 and to execute the EU competition policy in return for a horizontal and wider Regulation.[27]

B. The European Court of Justice and property law

Article 295 of the EC Treaty excludes the property legal framework from the EC competence. This means that such matters are the exclusive competence of the member states. There are, however, signs that the EC desires to change this situation and most probably will do so using the successive approach technique, starting by regulating other aspects of civil law rather than property law, as shown above.

Even so, property law has not completely escaped from the EC law's influence and jurisdiction. As Advocate-General Thesauro pointed out in his Opinion delivered on 28 November 1995:[28] *'What is required by Community law for present purposes is that, in any event, the necessary instruments be made available in order for individuals to be able to seek, and possibly obtain, compensation for loss or damage sustained as a result of infringements of Community law. In this connection, moreover, it should be made very clear that the problem of determining a judicial remedy which is not already known to or permitted by the judicial systems of the Member States is not insuperable or a new problem: this is so on account of the specific factors under consideration in these proceedings, and*

---

[27] Commission Regulations (EEC) No 1983/83, (EEC) No 1984/83(5) and (EEC) No 4087/88 were somehow replaced by Regulation (EC) No 2790/1999 of 22 December 1999 on the application of Article 81(3) of the Treaty to categories of vertical agreements and concerted practices.

[28] Opinion Tesauro, Joined cases C-46/93 and C-48/93, Brasserie du Pêcheur SA v Bundesrepublik Deutschland and The Queen v Secretary of State for Transport, ex parte: Factortame Ltd and others, ECR 1996 Page I-01029.

also because the problem has already been dealt with by the Court in a number of historic, uncontested passages in its case-law.' (Emphasis added by us).

The ECJ has ruled in several cases that there are some aspects of the national property law that may conflict with the European integration and thus may be incompatible with EC law. That was found to be true in Case C-302/97 (Konle)[29] and in Case C-423/98 (Alfredo Albore),[30] amongst others. These cases are related to what we may call national constraints on real estate ownership on the grounds of nationality. Member states known to apply, or that have applied, such constraints are Austria, Denmark and Italy.

The Austrian situation is reported in several cases before the ECJ, the first of which was the Konle case C-302/97. In the context of a procedure for compulsory sale by auction, the *Bezirksgericht Lienz* (Lienz District Court) allocated, on 11 August 1994, a plot of land in Tyrol to Mr Konle, a German national, on condition that he obtained an administrative authorisation required under the TGVG 1993.[31] According to Sections 9(1)(a) and 12(1)(a) of the TGVG 1993, the acquisition of the ownership of building land was subject to authorisation by the authority responsible for land transactions. Section 14(1) of the TGVG 1993 provided that the authorisation should be refused, in particular where the acquirer failed to show that the planned acquisition would not be used to establish a secondary residence. Section 10(2) of the TGVG 1993 stated that the authorisation was not required where the right acquired related to land that was built on and the acquirer had Austrian nationality. Under Section 13(1) of the TGVG 1993, the foreigner could only be granted the authorisation if the intended purchase did not conflict with the policy interests of the State and there was an economic, cultural or social interest in the acquisition.

The Danish situation is quite clear, as there is a protocol, annexed to the EC Treaty, dealing with it. Danish legislation precludes persons who are not resident in Denmark, and who have not previously been resident in Denmark for a minimum of 5 years, from acquiring real estate there without permission from the Ministry of Justice. This situation, though contrary to EC law, benefits from an exception included in the EC Treaty.

The Italian situation was reported in the case Albore (case C-423/98). Article 1 of the Italian Law No 1095 of 3 June 1935,[32] as amended by Law

---

[29] Judgment of the Court of 1 June 1999, Case C-302/97 Konle / Austria, ECR 1999, Page I-03099.

[30] Judgment of the Court (Sixth Chamber) of 13 July 2000, Case C-423/98, Alfredo Albore, ECR 2000, Page I-05965.

[31] Tyrolian Law on the Transfer of Land (*Tiroler Grundverkehrsgesetz*), *Tiroler Landesgesetzblatt* (LGBl-Tirol) 82/1993.

[32] *Gazzetta Ufficiale della Repubblica Italiana* (GURI) No 154 of 4 July 1935.

No 2207 of 22 December 1939,[33] provided that all instruments transferring wholly or in part ownership of immovable property situated in areas of provinces adjacent to land frontiers should be subject to approval by the Prefect of the province. Article 2 of the same Law prevented public registers from entering the transfer, unless evidence was produced that the Prefect had given his approval. Article 18 of Law No 898 of 24 of December 1976,[34] as amended by Law No 104 of 2 May 1990,[35] provided that those provisions would not apply when the purchaser was an Italian national.

Two properties at Barano d'Ischia, in an area of Italy designated as being of military importance, were purchased on 14 January 1998 by two German nationals, Uwe Rudolf Heller and Rolf Adolf Kraas, who did not apply for authorisation. In the absence of such authorisation, the Naples Registrar of Property refused to register the sale of the properties. Mr Albore, the notary before whom the transaction was concluded, appealed against that refusal to the Tribunale Civile e Penale di Napoli, claiming that the sale at issue, concluded for the benefit of nationals of a Member State of the Community, should not be subject to the national legislation which required only foreigners to obtain authorisation.

There are several EC freedoms and rights establishing the Community requirements that national legal systems must comply with in this specific matter. The most important is the principle of non-discrimination, sometimes called the principle of national treatment, in those matters related to the EC fundamental freedoms: the free movement of persons, services and capital.

The principle of non-discrimination is laid down in article 12 of the EC Treaty and outlaws any discrimination on the grounds of nationality. Some exceptions on grounds of public policy, security and health are accepted based on objective criteria determined by EC law.

The acquisition of real property is normally associated with one of two main goals: residence or investment. The first goal, residence, implies, together with the free movement of persons, articles 18 and 14 EC Treaty, especially the right of residence. The first beneficiaries of this right are the workers and their right of residence is linked to the right to take up a job and so should not be exercised simply in order to look for work. The right of residence for persons other than workers is regulated in three Council Directives. Directive 90/365[36] regulates the right of residence for employees and self-employed persons who have terminated their occupational activity

---

[33] GURI No 53 of 2 March 1939.
[34] GURI No 8 of 11 January 1977.
[35] GURI No 105 of 8 May 1990.
[36] OJ L 180, 13-7-1990, pp 28-29.

(retired persons). Directive 90/364[37] regulates the right of residence embracing all persons who do not already enjoy a right of residence under Community law and Directive 90/366[38] on the right of residence for students exercising the right to vocational training. These directives require Member states to grant the right of residence to those persons and to certain of their family members, if they have adequate resources so as not to become a burden on the social assistance schemes of the Member states, and also require that all be covered by sickness insurance.

The second goal of real property acquisition, investment, may be related to at least one of the two following fundamental freedoms: the right of establishment, article 43 EC Treaty and the freedom of movement of capital, article 56 of the EC Treaty. The right of establishment ensures that the self-employed, whether working in commercial, industrial or craft occupations or the liberal professions, are free to exercise their profession throughout the Community, either in a liberal profession form or in a corporate one. The free movement of capital aimed to remove all restrictions on capital movements between Member-states, thus encouraging the other freedoms (the movement of persons, goods and services) and allowing the investment, by all EC nationals, in other EC Member State under the same conditions as their nationals.

Moving from immovable to movable property, we choose three ECJ's Judgments: Case C-463/00,[39] Case C-491/01,[40] and as early as 1966, the Joined cases 56 and 58/64.[41]

The situation arising in Case C-463/00 related to the Spanish law on the legal arrangements for the disposal of public shareholdings in certain undertakings and the implementation of royal decrees enacted under Article 4 of Law 5/1995,[42] in so far as they implemented a system of prior administrative approval unjustified by any overriding requirements of general interest, not laying down objective and stable criteria that had been made public, and not complying with the principle of proportionality, thus violating Articles 43[43]

---

[37] OJ L 180, 13-7-1990, pp 26-27.

[38] OJ L 180, 13-7-1990, pp 30-31.

[39] Judgment of the Court of 13 May 2003, Case C-463/00, Commission of the European Communities v Kingdom of Spain, ECR 2003 Page I-04581.

[40] Judgment of the Court of 10 December 2002, Case C-491/01, British American Tobacco, ECR 2002 Page I-11453.

[41] Judgment of the Court of 13 July 1966, Joined cases 56 and 58/64, Consten & Grundig, ECR English special edition Page 00299.

[42] Concerning Repsol SA, Telefónica de España SA and Telefónica Servicios Móviles SA, Corporación Bancaria de España SA (Argentaria), Tabacalera SA and Endesa SA.

[43] Article 43 EC:

and 56[44] EC. One of the arguments the defendant relied upon was 'the principle of the neutrality of the Treaty as regards the system of property ownership, enshrined in Article 295 EC'. Dismissing the argument, the ECJ ruled that 'those concerns cannot entitle Member States to plead their own systems of property ownership, referred to in Article 295 EC, by way of justification for obstacles, resulting from privileges attaching to their position as shareholder in a privatised undertaking, to the exercise of the freedoms provided for by the Treaty. That article does not have the effect of exempting the Member States' systems of property ownership from the fundamental rules of the Treaty'.[45]

In the Case C-491/01 (British American Tobacco) the ECJ ruled that 'That provision merely recognises the power of Member States to define the rules governing the system of property ownership and does not exclude any influence whatever of Community law on the exercise of national property rights',[46] returning to a forty year old statement in the Joined cases 56 and 58/64 (Consten & Grundig): 'Articles 36, 222 and 234 of the EEC treaty do not exclude any influence whatever of community law on the exercise of national industrial property rights.'[47]

These situations show that, from the ECJ's perspective, there is an impact of EC law in the national property legal framework, even if for no other reason, at least because of the principle of the national treatment.

Within the framework of the provisions set out below, restrictions on the freedom of establishment of nationals of a Member State in the territory of another Member State shall be prohibited. Such prohibition shall also apply to restrictions on the setting-up of agencies, branches or subsidiaries by nationals of any Member State established in the territory of any Member State.

Freedom of establishment shall include the right to take up and pursue activities as self-employed persons and to set up and manage undertakings, in particular companies or firms within the meaning of the second paragraph of Article 48, under the conditions laid down for its own nationals by the law of the country where such establishment is effected, subject to the provisions of the chapter relating to capital.

[44] Article 56 EC:

1. Within the framework of the provisions set out in this chapter, all restrictions on the movement of capital between Member States and between Member States and third countries shall be prohibited.

2. Within the framework of the provisions set out in this chapter, all restrictions on payments between Member States and between Member States and third countries shall be prohibited.

[45] Judgment § 67.
[46] Judgment § 147.
[47] See n 41, above.

C. Roadmap to a European private law

At this point, we must address the available ways forward in the quest for a European Private Law system: National reforms? Harmonisation? Unification?

In our view, the first solution is no solution at all. National reforms, with little or no coordination will only lead to maintaining the present status with detail changes.

The Harmonisation route started long ago trough Directives regulating detailed aspects within specific regimes or legal institutions. The envisaged CFR will, in this matter, be an important achievement, especially because it will integrate into EC law concepts that will be subject to the ECJ's competence, allowing this jurisdiction to perform its usual legal integration function.

We think, however, that the ultimate way forward will be trough EC Regulations, which, in fact, are already being enacted. See, for instance, the Council Regulation (EC) No 1346/2000 on insolvency proceedings,[48] the Council Regulation (EC) No 1347/2000 on jurisdiction and the recognition and enforcement of judgments in matrimonial matters and in matters of parental responsibility for children of both spouses,[49] the Council regulation (EC) No 1348/2000 on the service in the Member States of judicial and extrajudicial documents in civil or commercial matters,[50] the Council Regulation (EC) 44/2001 on jurisdiction and the recognition and enforcement of judgments in civil and commercial matters,[51] the Council Regulation (EC) No 1206/2001 on cooperation between the courts of the Member States in the taking of evidence in civil or commercial matters,[52] the Council Regulation (EC) No 40/94 of 20 December 1993 on the Community trade mark[53] and the Council Regulation (EC) No 1435/2003 on the Statute for a European Cooperative Society (SCE).[54]

The facts show that European Private Law is growing and will, in future, become a consistent body of unified (?) rules.

---

[48] OJ L 160, 30-6-2000, pp 1-18.
[49] OJ L 160, 30-6-2000, pp 19-36.
[50] OJ L 160, 30-6-2000, pp 37-52.
[51] OJ L 307, 24-11-2001, p 28.
[52] OJ L 174, 27-6-2001, pp 1-24.
[53] OJ L 11, 14-1-1994, pp 1-36.
[54] OJ L 207, 18-8-2003, pp 1-24.

Transfer of Ownership in Recent Reform Projects: Estonia

Kai Kullerkupp

A. Introduction and background

I. Brief historical remarks

The roots of Estonian civil law lie in Roman law. In 1864, the Code of Livonian, Estonian and Curonian Private Law[1] entered into force, covering the areas of today's Republics of Estonia and Latvia. It was a comprehensive compilation of the various particular laws and usage applied in the area, largely based on Roman law. Regarding the transfer of movable ownership, the Code was based on the doctrine of *titulus* and *modus* known from Roman law, *titulus* being understood as the underlying contract for the transfer of ownership, *modus* as the delivery itself.

After the proclamation of the Republic of Estonia in 1918, efforts to elaborate a new civil code for Estonia started. A draft was completed by 1939, yet never entered into legal force due to the outbreak of World War II. According to the draft, the transfer of movable ownership was to be contingent upon two conditions: the transferor should deliver possession of the movable to the transferee and both should have reached an agreement that ownership shall pass to the transferee. The wording resembles the text of § 929 BGB. The introduction of the concept of a separate real agreement was thus contemplated.

From 1940 to the early 1990's, Soviet civil law was applied in the territory of Estonia. The law of property was almost non-existent under that system, due to the heavy restrictions on commerce and entrepreneurship, which was altogether banned. However, the few provisions on property law set forth a causal system for the transfer of ownership in movables, requiring a valid legal cause.

---

[1] See: 'Liv-, Est- und Curländisches Privatrecht; Nach der Ausgabe von 1864 und der Fortsetzung von 1890', in: Heinrich von Broecker, *Provinzialrecht der Ostsee-Gouvernements*, Vol III (Jurjew/Dorpat: J G Krüger 1902).

2. New private law system from 1993 onwards

The current Estonian civil code follows the pandectic system,[2] consisting of five 'books' which have been enacted at different times as separate laws. Of interest, with regard to the regime of ownership transfer, are the General Part of the Civil Code Act[3] and the Property Law Act.[4] When the reforms of the civil law system were commenced, a guideline decision[5] to pay attention to the continuity of legislation was taken, going back to the period preceding World War II. Thus, the Soviet-time 'heritage' was altogether discarded (with the exception of family law and, to some degree, inheritance law) and the laws and drafts from before 1940 were used as the main models in drafting new legislation. However, due to the need to take into account more recent developments in the private law thinking, the laws of modern European countries with similar legal tradition (above all, Germany and Switzerland) were also analysed.

B. The Property Law Act of 1993: From causal to abstract transfer system

As already pointed out, the 1965 Civil Code of the Estonian SSR which remained in force until replaced by a Property Act in 1990,[6] set forth a causal system of transfer. According to the Code, a transfer based on a transaction (contract) took effect from the moment of the delivery of the asset, unless otherwise provided by law or contract. Delivery was understood as handing the assets over to the acquirer, but also delivery to a carrier (transport organisation or postal handler) to be forwarded to the acquirer, or handing over the documents of title. The notion of possession as such was unknown.

The 1993 Property Law Act introduced the German system of transfer, based on a real agreement and delivery of possession. Following the German

---

[2] Paul Varul, 'Legal Policy Decisions and Choices in the Creation of New Private Law in Estonia', *Juridica International* 2000/I, pp 108-110.
[3] First version 1994, second version 2002.
[4] Enacted and entered into force in 1993.
[5] On December 1" 1992 the *Riigikogu* (the Estonian parliament) passed a decision concerning the continuity of legislation, pursuant to which laws in force in Estonia before June 16, 1940, were to be considered in elaborating bills for new legislation. This decision became an essential guideline for the legislator in selecting sources and models for new laws. See also Priidu Pärna, 'The Law of Property Act – Cornerstone of the Civil Law Reform', *Juridica International* 2001/I, p 89.
[6] An interim piece of legislation abolished by the Property Law Act in 1993.

model, whose influence was already clearly present in the 1939 Draft, the system was at the same time changed from causal to abstract.

C. Main characteristics of the new system

First, there is a 'unititular'/'unitary'/'uniform' concept of ownership. Resulting therefrom, the various entitlements arising from the right of ownership (such as the right to possess, to use and to dispose of the thing) pass to the transferee at one moment in time, rather than at separate moments depending on the 'stage' of the transfer process.

The system is delivery-based: the object of the transfer must be delivered to the acquirer in any of the recognised forms. According to the main rule, movables should be handed over directly from the transferor to the transferee.[7] However, several alternatives are provided for, in case direct delivery does not correspond to the interests of the parties. Delivery equivalents expressly recognised are: the *brevi manu traditio*,[8] assignment of the claim to recover the movable[9] and *constitutum possessorium*.[10] The forms of delivery are not to be viewed as subsidiary to one another – ie, the parties are free to choose any of the forms they find convenient.

Possession is acquired by gaining actual power over the thing or means that enable the exercise of actual power thereover. However, where the acquirer is already in a position to exercise actual power, a mere agreement between the former possessor and the possessor-to-be is sufficient.[11]

A real agreement separate from the underlying obligation is required to transfer ownership. The necessity of a separate agreement to transfer ownership is expressly set forth in the General Part of Civil Code (§ 6). The requirement of a real agreement underlines the bilateral nature of a transfer transaction, calling for declarations of intention both on the side of the transferor and the transferee. A real agreement is generally subject to all general provisions governing transactions and contracts, including the requirements on legal capacity, the making and the interpretation of declarations of intention, as well as the termination thereof as a result of defects in the decision-making; representation, conditions and the emergence of a contract as a result of offer and acceptance. A real-right agreement to trans-

---

[7] According to § 92 (1) PropLA, movable ownership is transferred by way of transfer (disposal) if the transferor delivers possession of the thing to the acquirer and they have agreed that ownership will pass to the acquirer

[8] § 92 (2) PropLA.

[9] § 93 PropLA.

[10] § 94 PropLA.

[11] § 36 PropLA.

fer movable ownership can be concluded and terminated either by explicit or implicit declarations of intention.

The transfer is abstract: the validity of the transfer is not contingent upon the existence or validity of a valid *causa* from which the obligation to transfer ownership arises. It is perhaps noteworthy that even the principle of abstraction is expressly provided for by the General Part since 2002.[12] Resulting therefrom, an obligation to transfer ownership is not considered an element of the transfer system. In essence, a transfer of ownership can be based on any type of obligation – contractual as well as non-contractual relationships. The validity of the real agreement is to be verified independently from the validity (existence) of the underlying obligation. Grounds of voidness and voidability may generally affect the validity of a real agreement similarly to that of an obligation.

As a result, a transfer will, in principle, remain valid even in case the underlying obligation proves to be without effect; the transferor cannot regain the thing by way of revindication but must rather have recourse to a claim ex unjustified enrichment. Where a transferor has transferred ownership of an asset with the purpose of performing an (existing or future) obligation, ownership may be reclaimed from the recipient if such obligation did not exist, does not arise or it ceases to exist subsequently.[13] The retransfer is to take place in accordance with the general rules – a real right agreement and delivery or a delivery equivalent, as the case may be.

There has been very little discussion on the concept of 'real agreement' in the Estonian legal literature. On one occasion, the 'artificial' nature of the real agreement with regard to movables has been pointed out.[14] The introduction of the concept of a real agreement has only rudimentarily been justified in literature, as corresponding to the idea of the separation of property law and the law of obligations, and, consequently, promoting clarity in proprietary relations.

---

[12] § 6 (4) General Part states that the validity of a disposition (*ie* the transfer transaction) is not contingent upon the validity of the obligation to transfer. Although the express provision only appeared in 2002, the Supreme Court has repeatedly confirmed that the principle was already applicable from 1993 onwards.

[13] § 1028 Law of Obligations Act.

[14] Pärna has questioned the usefulness (expediency) of distinguishing a real agreement in the case of movables with the reasoning that, as a rule, the real agreement and the underlying contract are concluded simultaneously, and, resulting therefrom, a real agreement will rarely remain in force where the underlying obligation is invalidated. However, he acknowledges the role of the real agreement in case of the sale under the reservation of title. Priidu Pärna, *Asjaõigusseadus: Kommenteeritud väljaanne* (Property Law Act: Commented Edition; Tallinn: Juura 2004), § 92 n 4, pp 181-192 (in Estonian).

D. Conclusions

Switching from a causal to an abstract, delivery-based system of transfer has not caused any noteworthy confusion or difficulties in applying the new provisions. However, it should be mentioned that due to heavy restrictions on commerce under Soviet law, the provisions concerning the transfer of ownership had a barely marginal significance in practice and no scholarly research known to the author had been carried out to analyse their fitness for purpose. Thus, the reform of the transfer system cannot really be described as replacing a well-rooted system by something completely new. It would be more accurate to view the situation as building up a new property law system from scratch.

Although the new system has by now been in use for over 13 years, scholarly positions have not yet been fully filtered out. A tendency of a more liberal approach to the provisions, compared to the views expressed in some of Germany's legal literature, is to be expected. I would explain this with the rather recent experience of extensive reforms which have been necessary to build up an efficient and workable legal and economic system and to align the whole legal framework with the *acquis* of the European Union. Against such a background, flexibility and modernity are always good arguments.

Protection and Transfer of Possession

Luboš Tichý

A. Definition of the problem

As we are to demonstrate below, the majority of laws distinguish not only between possession and ownership but they also know detention. This is alright, as this regime reflects the actual situation and is also well-founded by experience. There are other phenomenona deserving more attention. First of all, it is the distinction between the kinds of legal protection offered in all these institutions, and this distinction is not to be made only on the basis of the level of the intensity of protection, but also on the basis of the way of the realisation and even the procedural regulation of protection.

Other issues are represented by the transfer of possession in the case of derivative acquisition. Here, the regulations substantially differ from the regulations on the transfer of ownership, which is a noteworthy phenomenon.

This paper has a dual purpose:

Above all, it is important to examine the justifiability of the concept of a different protection of possession, *ie* the specific protection of possession, or more precisely, the necessity of existence of special methods of protection. Does possession require special protection? What are the reasons speaking in favour of this solution? What is it that makes it different in its essence from ownership protection? Is a special procedural regulation on the protection of possession necessary?

As has been suggested, the second problem consists in the derivative acquisition of possession. This issue is also outside the main focus of theory and practice. Therefore, it is necessary to ascertain which legal rules apply to the transfer of possession and to what extent the concept is justified in the cases where the legal regulation on the transfer of possession differs from the legal regulation on ownership. The focus is put on Central Europe, mainly the Czech Republic.

B. Essence of possession

The fact is that even though possession is one of the oldest institutions of civil law, it belongs to the most disputable ones. Randa[1] considered possession as a factual state that is protected by law. Thus, in fact, possession includes three cases:
1. The case where the law protects a certain behavior of the person having the thing in detention and disposing of the thing as his own.[2]
2. The case where a person has a legal title to dispose of the thing as if it was his own, yet he does not have the thing, even only for limited time, in his sphere.[3]
3. Another case differs from the two above and consists in the fact that there is a person factually controlling the thing, *ie* disposing of it as his own, without having any legal title, *ie* the right of possession or right to possession, yet he has a right to the protection of a peaceful state.[4]

Thus, possession is a real execution of power over a certain thing.

C. Legal regulation of possession and its development

Ius commune distinguished between possession and detention.[5] An *animus* and a *corpus* were required for possession. The *polie* action served as protection. By this action it was possible either to achieve removal of the violation, the prohibition of a further violation and the compensation for damage, or to claim surrender if the possession had been withdrawn violently. This action was also available to a detentor.[6]

Pandectistics continued in distinguishing possession and detention. Absolute and relative theories used to be distinguished, while the distinguishing criterion consisted in the question whether possession was protected by virtue of possession itself (absolute theory) and/or for legal-political reasons.

---

[1] Anton Randa, *Der Besitz nach österreichischem Rechte* (Leipzig: Breitkopf & Härtel, 4th ed 1895), 14.

[2] See various legal definitions of possession, eg Czech Civil Code (*Občanský zákoník* – CC), § 129 para 1; § 309 ABGB; § 872 BGB (*Eigenbesitzer*); Art 3:107 NBW.

[3] This is the situation which is not covered by most legal definitions of possession not presupposing *animus* (like in this case) but *corpus* (literally, the Swiss ZGB).

[4] This is the case of detention or indirect possession, which is expressly provided, for instance, in BGB § 868 (*mittelbarer Besitz*).

[5] See ia Helmut Coing, *Europäisches Privatrecht*, Vol II (Munich: C H Beck 1989), 374; Valentin Urfus, *Soukromé právo v Evropě* (Private law in Europe) (Praha: C H Beck, 1994), n 86-88, 186.

[6] See Coing (*supra* note 5) at 374.

Savigny[7] defended the relative theory and saw the reason for protection in a general prohibition of violence. In his opinion, the withdrawal of possession or its violation were violent acts against the possessor. Based on this, according to him, the entitlement to protection then is an entitlement based on a tort and therefore it is necessary to consider it as an obligatory entitlement. Ihering[8] subjected this doctrine to a severe criticism, on the basis of which the essence of possession consisted in one's relation to the thing. Possession is the reality of ownership. The protection of possession supplements the protection of ownership. Puchta belonged to the advocates of the absolute theories and he saw the subordination of a thing to the human will in possession; similarly, as in the case of ownership, he saw the 'main relation' worthy of protection in possession.

The prevailing opinion saw the most important aspect in the possessor's will to possess the thing as an owner.[9] However, this thesis was hardly compatible with the fact that Roman law[10] also provided protection of possession to the pledge creditor, indirect possessor (prekarist) and sequestrator. In these cases, pandectists speak of derived possession.

D. Development of the legal protection of possession

I. Development

(a) Austria

It is known that the ABGB made a distinction from the protection of possession by means of self-help under § 344; this unlawful interference included both necessary defence and distress, and thus it protected possession against violations, both in the form of defensive self-help and offensive self-help which involves the use of violence to recover possession if the violator failed to restore a peaceful state. Moreover, a distinction was made between the protection from the violation of possession and the protection from the deprivation of possession – in the first case (§ 339), the possessor was entitled to negatory protection (negatory legal action) and damages; in the case of the deprivation of possession, the possessor was entitled to file an action, *ie* an action for revendication. In addition to these provisions of substantive

---

[7] Friedrich Carl von Savigny, *Das Recht des Besitzes. Eine civilistische Abhandlung* (Giessen: Meyer 1803 = Goldbach: Keip 1997), § 50.
[8] Rudolf von Ihering, 'Beiträge zur Lehre vom Besitz', *Iherings Jahrbücher* 9 (1868), 44.
[9] See Coing (*supra* note 5), 376.
[10] See von Savigny (*supra* note 7), 110.

law, procedural protection of possession was and still is provided for in § 454 et seq of the ZPO.[11]

(b) Czech Republic (Czechoslovakia)

The 1950 Civil Code ('1950 CC') did not contain any specific provisions for the protection of possession, merely implying that an authorised possessor has the same rights as an owner, including adequate self-help (§ 344 ABGB and § 150 of the 1950 CC). § 151 of the 1950 CC, in a way, summarised the provisions of § 344 of the ABGB and § 454 of the Austrian ZPO and, according to the predominant opinion,[12] it constituted the protection of peace under which the possessor, whose possession was violated or who was deprived of his possession, may, within 30 days of becoming aware of the violation and the violator, request the local National Committee to prohibit the violation or demand restitution. In addition, it provided for possible damages.

The 1964 Civil Code ('1964 CC' – together with the DDR ZGB 1975, the 'most socialist' Civil Code)[13] protected peace ('socialist co-existence' in the terminology of this Code) in a peculiar way, providing for the opportunity to file a negatory action or a restitution claim.[14]

The Czech law has undergone a significant development during last 50 years (after the ABGB was replaced – 1951). After possession had been reinstated (under the 1982 amendment to the 1964 CC), the possessor enjoyed rights of protection similar (!)[15] to those available to owners (§ 132(a)(1)).

---

[11] See, inter alia, Georg Kodek, Die Besitzstörung (Wien: Manz 2002), 30 et seq, 36 et seq, 1032, 1053.

[12] See, inter alia, Gert Iro, 'Sachenrecht' in: Peter Apathy (ed), Bürgerliches Recht, Vol IV (Vienna: Springer, 2nd ed 2002), 31 et seq.

[13] These two codes are the most extreme examples of the overruling or suppressing of the Roman tradition in private law. Yet, the 1964 Czech CC followed the Austrian roots of quieta non movere, even if transformed into the term 'socialist co-existence'. One can notice that within the ambit of private law the law of property (patrimony) remained, for the most part, intact despite the 'revolutionary time' of the communist regime.

[14] See the § 5 of 1964 CC: Where an obvious breach of the principles of socialist co-existence (peace – as amended 1991) occurs, protection may be sought from the competent administrative authority. As an interim solution, the administrative authority may prohibit the breach or order restoration to the previous condition. Thereby, the right to seek protection from a court is not affected.

[15] Similar in the sense of mutatis mutandis. However, neither case law nor doctrine commented on what this provision actually meant.

The 1991 amendment introduced an express provision for the protection of peace by means of both negatory and restitutory legal actions. Under § 130(2), an authorised possessor has the same rights as an owner.[16]

(c) Other European countries

In the French Civil Code, possession is regulated in connection with prescription; though no protection of possession is provided for, the Civil Procedure Code (*code de procedure civile*) contains, in its artt 23-27, the rules on possessory claims. French law distinguishes between possession and detention with respect to the question whether the power over the thing is exercised with the will of an owner or with the will of a holder of a right *in rem*. A person who has a thing in his power as a holder of an obligatory right does not have a possession deserving protection. The protection of possession is granted by the *action possessoire* to the possession of real estate only. This concerns *compleinte*, ie the claim for a quiet and limited enjoyment; *denonciation de nouvelle oeuvre* is a possessory claim for the discontinuation of work. Both these claims presume possession for a period of one year. *Reintegrande* is the French form of the *actio spolii*.

The Italian *Codice Civile* basically sticks to the French form. It also knows the possessory claims (*azione di reintegrazione*, art 1168; *azione di manutenzione*, art 1170) or, as the case may be, the *actio spolii* (art 1169).

The Spanish *Código civil* of 1889 distinguishes between possession and detention (see art 432), while both forms are provided with protection.

The German BGB has adopted the doctrine of pandectists, yet with several novelties. Possession does not presume the will to possess; it is built on the so-called objective theory. Thus, possession is defined in the way that the possessor intends to possess as an owner. Possession is graded. If the owner surrenders the control over a thing for someone else's benefit, based on a right *in rem* or an obligational right, then they both are possessors – a direct possessor and an indirect possessor. In the case of proper possession, ownership is presumed. Both the direct and the indirect possessor, ie the detentor, are protected against unlawful interference and dispossession. Also, the BGB knows the possession of rights.

The Swiss ZGB (artt 919-941) knows a graded possession and provides protection to each possessor and also each detentor against interference and dispossession. The prerequisite of ownership is limited to real estate.

---

[16] As compared to the previous wording, the position of the *bona fide* possessor is now equal to that of the owner.

2. Institutional and procedural safeguards

Probably caused by the influence of Austrian law (see § 344 ABGB), Czech law also contains institutional safeguards of a dual nature: they apply to both civil court proceedings and to administrative proceedings brought before the administrative authorities. It is clear that, save for some exceptions (see above), this is the only case where civil-law claims enjoy a twofold procedural protection. However, in contrast to Austrian law, Czech legislation does not know any procedural regulation according to which the courts or municipal authorities may handle cases of violation of possession and grant protection.

3. Efficiency of protection

Efficiency is a particular point that simply must be commented on. The frequency and quantity of infringements of the rights to possession is remarkable. The same frequency may be observed as far as threats to the peaceful state are concerned. However, the results are hardly satisfactory.[17] As indicated by reports and critical voices, administrative authorities that are not obliged to make a decision in a case refer the case to the courts anyway, as the majority of these authorities lack professional skill. The argument that they are 'near' to the cases suffers substantially due to the insufficient professional expertise. Nevertheless, the results of court proceedings are hardly better. Instead of offering immediate protection, court proceedings are lengthy and efficient protection is not provided.[18] More importantly, in many situations the protection of possession is not enforceable due to legal regulations. For instance, if the lessee's possession rights are violated by a third person, he may not claim for protection directly against the wrongdoer, but only through the lessor (see § 664 CC).

---

[17] This is the indubitable fact. For a long time, the clear general opinion has regarded this type of protection as a clear failure. See, in the most recent time, Jiří Nykodým, 'Ochrana pokojného stavu' (Protection of the peaceful state), in: Jiří Švestka et al (eds), *Sborník statí z diskusních fór o rekodifikaci občanského práva* (Collection of Papers on the Recodification of Civil Law) (Prague: ASPI Wolters Kluwer 2007), 124 et seq. See also the critical approach in Austria: Wilhelm Bukovics, 'Diskussionsbeitrag', in: *Verhandlungen des 2. Österreichischen Juristentages Wien 1964*, Vol II part 1 (Wien: Manz 1964) 61 at p 63; Josef Pichler, 'Das Klagebegehren im Besitzstörungsverfahren', *Österreichische Richterzeitung* (RZ) 1962, 123.

[18] See also the comments with a critical tone on the protection of possession in the 1964 CC from Viktor Knapp, *Quieta non movere*, § 5 obč zák, Právní praxe (Legal practice), 1993, No 5, 270.

E. Transfer of possession

This phenomenon is provided for *ia* in the ABGB and NBW (see mainly § 315 and Artt 114, 115 of Book 3, title 5 respectively). The principal aim of this section is to provide for transfers of possession of ownership rights and transfers of possession of other rights. *Animus* and *corpus* are, in principle, required for transfers of possession. The quantitative difference compared to original acquisition rests in the fact that not only *animus possidendi*, ie the will to dispose of a thing as if it were one's own, but also an expression of will that one does not wish to possess the thing anymore is required from the existing possessor. This expression need not be explicit. The qualitative difference compared to original acquisition, in terms of the *corpus*, rests in the fact that the thing does not have to be delivered physically – it may be delivered by signs or agreement or in any other manner (see §§ 426, 427, 452 or 428). Delivery by signs (§§ 427 through 452) is deemed, in particular, to be delivery by means of documents or by sign (*traditio symbolica*).

It is clear that the most important transfer method is the transfer by agreement. However, this fact is reflected insufficiently, if at all, in the draft of the study group or elsewhere, but not so in NBW of Netherlands.[19]

It is clear that possession is transferred in the same manner as ownership rights. This fact should also be appropriately expressed in the legal provisions.

F. Critical comments, conclusions and resolution

I. Critical analysis

The described provisions, inspired mainly by the Austrian tradition, undoubtedly conform to the 'relative theory', which places a special meaning on the institution of possession and provides for possession differently than for ownership; hence, there are different provisions for the passing and protection of possession, and the passing of ownership rights. These provisions actually intend to reflect (and this applies mainly to the draft of the Study Group on the European Civil Code)[20] the differing and less important position of possession as compared to ownership. Nevertheless, the truth is that this factor cannot be reflected in practice and it is basically irrelevant. An honest possessor acting in good faith should enjoy the same position as an owner in terms of transfer and protection. Distinct and special provisions on

---

[19] See the transfer of possession by a bilateral declaration of the parties pursuant to art 115.

[20] See the Artt 6:201-6:203 of Book VIII of the Draft (edition May 2007).

institutional safeguards and procedural rules may address the situation where the mere possessor (who enjoys, as a rule, also obligatory protection) has more rights than appropriate. The mere possessor should enjoy special (*eg* procedural) protection only if such protection is appropriate in the light of the nature of the affected right and is also available to others whose rights are similarly important and, therefore, also deserve such protection.

2. Conclusions

(a) Definition of possession

Possession is a particular relation of a person to a thing.

It is deemed to involve a factual state of affairs (see below). This relation means that certain rights and certain obligations of such a person arise therefrom. Because this is a right *in rem*, these obligations and rights, on the one hand, relate to the thing itself, in regard to which certain realisations are being carried out, but primarily, and from the conceptual perspective, to third persons. The 'relation' in regard to the thing is a certain type of reflex action of those authorisations that exist in regard to third persons. The same applies as regards obligations.

Possession is a category which has two meanings (forms).

On the one hand, it forms part of ownership, or, as the case be, of a collection of other rights *in rem*, and, on the other hand, it may exist in relative isolation. Nonetheless, even in this latter form it has a certain subsidiary character. That is why – as we state below – in its existence it is conceived to be transformed into an ownership right or some other right *in rem*. Longterm, it therefore has a certain contingent, transient or relative character.

Possession is a reflection of certain entitlements of imminent ownership.

As a part of an ownership right, the content of possession is part of the content of ownership: primarily, the entitlement to possess and hold a thing for oneself in one's own name. As a part of ownership, it forms a certain segment and organic component of the content of an ownership right as a whole.

Possession requires the accordance with law, good morals and good faith. Wrongful possession is not possession.

The foregoing applies to both forms of possession. The conflict with law, good morals or a lack of good faith means either the abuse of ownership in the second form of possession, or the abuse of possession, or the absence thereof (in the case of the absence of good faith) in the first form of possession.

In the first form, possession cannot eliminate ownership. Abuse of a right of possession may entail only the violation thereof. In systems for transferring ownership rights based on tradition, however, if ownership is not assumed sufficiently this means that the 'acquirer' never became owner. Ownership was not transferred.

In the form of possession as an independent state of affairs, a lack of good faith jeopardises the existence of possession as such.

(b) Purpose of possession

Possession consists in allowing the exercise of certain 'possession entitlements', including the protection thereof and the protection of possession as such. As a part of an ownership right, possession has a more restricted function, since it relates to possession itself. Possession in itself allows the exercise of certain entitlements that exceed the right of possession itself. Its scope is closer to an ownership right and sometimes is equivalent to it. This implies that, in this form, possession also encompasses those entitlements which form the content of an ownership right; it also encompasses rights of disposal, including processing a thing and the right to transfer the possession of a thing.

In the form where possession is not a component of ownership, its purpose is also to transform possession into an ownership right.

(c) Development of possession and its current state

It is notable that Roman Law already made a relatively sharp distinction between possession and ownership. It made possession an independent institution which was subject to both examination and undoubtedly also adjudication.[21]

The further development of possession was very varied. Von Savigny achieved a relatively clear definition.[22] He, like others,[23] although for the most part authors in the German sphere, considers possession a factual state of affairs, possession is a fact for him. A further feature is the absolute distinction made between possession and ownership. This is even given an 'individual' treatment in textbooks.[24]

---

[21] See *possessio civilis* and *naturalis, possessio iusta*. Even Roman law distinguished between *possessio* as a fact and *possessio* as a right – see Helmut Coing, *Europäisches Privatrecht*, Vol I (München: C H Beck 1985), 279, 280 and *dominium* or *proprietas* (again Helmut Coing, *op cit*, 291 *et seq*).

[22] See von Savigny (*supra* note 7), 110.

[23] See Randa (*supra* note 1), 14 *et seq*.

[24] See Iro (*supra* note 12), 15 *et seq* and 53 *et seq*.

The reason for this – from our perspective bizarre – qualification we do not know.

(d) Relationship to ownership

In terms of its content, possession is a part of ownership: conceptually it cannot be anything else. A possessor cannot have a wider range of authorisations than an owner. It can therefore be stated that what applies for the content of ownership must necessarily also apply for the content of possession as regards the substance and limits of rights and obligations. Even a possessor as the sole beneficiary of possession has more entitlements, as well as more obligations, than can be derived from the content of possession as a part of ownership; according to its substance, however, he may neither be more entitled nor more encumbered than an owner.

However, from the construction of possession as a state of facts certain institutions have been developed which are typical for possession, even though, in their substance, they can hardly exceed the ones relating to ownership. This includes, in particular, the protection of possession, which in various legal codes is provided for specifically, in a manner differing from the protection of ownership. It can, however, be deduced that even these institutions – since they have a common basis with those derived from ownership – can also be used by an owner. Their substance may therefore serve to protect ownership. There is, however, the fact that in these cases it is possible to rate possession somewhat differently to ownership, if the case so deserves.

These differences, as has been indicated, may primarily exist in the form of protection, and they can be considered also in the case of acquiring ownership.

(e) Summary

1. Possession is a legal category, involving a legal relation. The fact that it is sanctioned by law, regardless of whether it is provided for by law, proves the fact that this is a legal category. The issue that possession must be proved by means of certain facts is an evidential, not an existential, issue.
2. Possession may have two forms: being a part of an ownership right or being a relatively independent category.
3. The substance of possession may not exceed ownership and it is therefore a part of an ownership right.

4. A possessor, as the enjoyer of possession as a relatively independent institution, has certain entitlements which are pertinent to an ownership right and which substantially exceed a right of possession.
5. Transfer and protection of possession are in their substance the same as possession as a part of ownership, and they may sometimes have a special form.[25]

3. Suggested resolution

(a) Transfer of possession

Some forms of transfer that exist in Austria are outdated.[26] Transfer of possession should be expressed, but other aspects thereof should be emphasised. Similar to transfers of ownership, transfers of possession are mostly effected by agreement. In the broad context, transfers of possession are implemented similarly to transfers of ownership; this applies to the moment of transfer, the method of passing, and the passing of risks associated with the relevant thing.

(b) Protection of possession

Special provisions on possession, different from those governing ownership, are not worth the effort. Therefore, the procedure should be the same to that applicable to ownership, with special provisions for injunctions to protect ownership and possession against infringements. Without adequate procedural tools (see the situation in the Czech Republic), the protection is inefficient.

---

[25] See Ludwig Eneccerus, Martin Wolf and Ludwig Raiser, *Lehrbuch des Bürgerlichen Rechts* (Tübingen: Mohr-Siebeck, 10th ed 1957), §17 and Winfried Kralik, *Besitz und Besitzschutz – Gutachten zum 2. Österreichischen Juristentag*, Vol I part 1 (Vienna: Manz 1964), 27.

[26] See the critical voices like Kralik (*supra* note 25).

List of Contributors

Steven Bartels
Professor of civil law at Utrecht University;
Professor of civil law at Radboud University Nijmegen as of February 2008

José Caramelo-Gomes
Professor of European Law at the Universidade Lusíada

Eleanor Cashin-Ritaine
Director of the Swiss Institute of Comparative Law, Lausanne

Caroline Cauffman
Attorney at law and scientific collaborator at the K U Leuven and
University of Antwerp

Wolfgang Faber
Assistant professor at the University of Salzburg,
Department of Private Law

Jens Thomas Füller
Privatdozent at the Free University of Berlin

Selma de Groot
Researcher at the University of Amsterdam,
Centre for the Study of European Contract Law of the
Amsterdam Institute for Private Law (CSECL)

Kai Kullerkupp
Lecturer of private law, Faculty of Law of the University of Tartu

Brigitta Lurger
Professor of Private Law at the University of Graz

Claes Martinson
Adjunct professor at the Department of law, School of Business,
Economics and Law, Gothenburg University

Mary-Rose McGuire
Research and Teaching Assistant at the Department of
Private Law, Commercial Law and International Civil Procedure,
University of Osnabrück

Vincent Sagaert
Professor at the University of Leuven, Department of Private Law,
Professor of Property Law at the University of Antwerp and
Catholic University of Brussels, Attorney at the Brussels Bar

Arthur F. Salomons
Professor of Private Law at the Universiteit van Amsterdam,
Centre for the Study of European Contract Law (CSECL)

Luboš Tichý
Chair of the Department of European Law, Charles University,
Prague